Introduction to Propriety Economics

T0294929

Introduction to Propriety Economics

Zhaohui HONG

香港城市大學出版社
City University of Hong Kong Press

ISBN: 978-962-937-689-5

Published by
City University of Hong Kong Press
Tat Chee Avenue
Kowloon, Hong Kong
Website: www.cityu.edu.hk/upress
E-mail: upress@cityu.edu.hk

Printed in Hong Kong

For Professor Lan Shen, my beloved wife

Table of Contents

Preface

After spending many years deeply immersed in the world of "critical thinking," the author has achieved proficiency in critiquing various schools of thought and perspectives but had somewhat neglected the aspect of "critical creating." Critical thinking, which is distinct from critical creating, often involves passive and negative analysis. As a result, the author developed a strong desire to make a positive and constructive contribution to economic research, specifically by writing a comprehensive monograph on propriety economics—a subject that has been overlooked for far too long. This decision was spurred by the challenging times of the COVID-19 pandemic, motivating the author to turn this long-held aspiration into reality and leave an original mark in the academic arena.

Recognizing the interdisciplinary nature of propriety economics, this book employs historical research methods to examine the differences and similarities between Eastern and Western cultures. It explores how the concepts of moderation and propriety in the East and the West have interacted and transformed over time, drawing insights from philosophy to trace the development of propriety economic ideas within Western economic thought. Additionally, it incorporates knowledge from the natural and social sciences, including physics, biology, computing, logic, psychology, political science, and sociology, to enhance our understanding of propriety economics.

The narrative embarks on a comprehensive literature review on economics, starting from the era of Adam Smith and documenting the interdisciplinary evolution that has shaped this field. It delves into the idea of balance in classical economics, the equilibrium of neoclassical economics, the impartiality of institutional economics, the subjective aspects of behavioral economics, the shared values of cultural economics, and the integration of humanistic and complexity economics. The book introduces readers to the triangular model of propriety economics and supplements it with propriety diagrams and curves as a tool for synthesizing ideas. The book also embarks on the journey of policy design and clarifies the criteria for implementing policies inspired by propriety economics. Additionally, it examines macroeconomic case studies, shedding light on the historical processes of modernization in both the United States and China. Drawing from 2,500 years of economic thought, it advocates for economics to progress towards relative, partial, limited, and rational propriety, fostering evolutionary consolidation, innovative synthesis, and inclusive integration.

Consequently, this book emerges as a multidisciplinary, interdisciplinary, and cross-disciplinary exploration at the intersection of history, philosophy, and economics. It represents a dedicated effort to harmonize these fields to shed light on the concept of propriety economics and bridge the perspectives of East and West.

It is important to note that propriety economics is a subject that cannot be easily quantified or mathematically modeled. Therefore, this book can only propose a framework of thought, provide theoretical approaches, discuss research methods, and outline policy principles from the perspective of economic philosophy. Its aim is to encourage collaboration among scholars to establish a new school and discipline of propriety economics.

The concept of propriety economics aligns with the views of many Western economists, even if they have not explicitly articulated it. The book's chapters are outlined as follows:

Chapter 1 (Introduction): Analyzes the contemporary need to develop the concept of propriety economics, highlighting the challenges of understanding and practicing moderation. It delves into the academic foundations for the creation of propriety economics and explores links to evolutionary economics, the Goldilocks economy, and the economics of good and evil.

Chapter 2: Summarizes the ideas of Chinese moderation and Western propriety, drawing comparisons to discern their roles in guiding economics. It introduces the six elements of propriety philosophy proposed by the author, including middle range, ordinariness, subjectivity, historicity, neutrality, and relativity, which provide guidance and regulation for the composition and development of propriety economics.

Chapter 3: Provides a literature review focusing on classical and neoclassical economic thought in order to discover, collect, and evaluate hidden points related to propriety economics. In particular, the chapter discusses the role of balance in classical theory and equilibrium in neoclassical theory in inspiring the idea of economic appropriateness.

Chapter 4: Discusses the contributions of institutional economics and behavioral economics to propriety economics, including the functional neutrality, value relativity, and historical evolution revealed by old and new institutional economics. Chapter 4 also addresses the bounded rationality, subjectivity, and psychological effects studied in behavioral economics.

Chapter 5: Examines the relevance of cultural economics to propriety economics, discussing shared values, regulatory diversity, and multifaceted distributions. This chapter integrates the six elements of propriety philosophy and draws insights from the five major economic schools, defining propriety economics based on five key characteristics: balance, equilibrium, evolution, rationality, and sharing.

Chapter 6: Proposes the triad theory as the core theory of propriety economics. It validates the interdisciplinary applicability of propriety economics across the humanities, social sciences, and natural sciences and introduces the triangle paradigm as an analytical framework for understanding propriety economics.

Chapter 7: Analyzes various mainstream economic research methods and their alignment with propriety economics' fundamental requirements. It discusses suitable methods for propriety economics research and presents several propriety diagrams and curves for analyzing economic issues.

Chapter 8: Discusses policy making principles for propriety economics, emphasizing the moderation and rationality expected of policymakers. The chapter introduces principles for evaluating propriety economic policies, designing fundamental policy measures, establishing quantitative indicators for propriety economic performance, and creating mechanisms to prevent and penalize excessive or deficient economic behavior.

Chapter 9: Utilizes four case studies of economic development (colonial economic growth, early industrialization, government intervention in the economy, and the war on poverty) to illustrate the experiential lessons of success and failure in the context of propriety economics in the United States. It also offers a concise analysis of four notable cases in China during the economic reforms of the last two decades of the 20th century (land ownership, township and village enterprises, state-owned enterprises, and urbanization) to evaluate whether China's economic system aligns with the objectives, principles, and essence of propriety economics.

Chapter 10: Summarizes the novel perspectives, frameworks, methods, and policy making principles of propriety economics. It situates the historical significance of propriety economics within the context of Western economic thought, outlining potential directions for the future development of economics. The chapter calls for an expansion of economic research toward relative propriety, fostering coordination among methods, disciplines, and ideas in an era marked by impermanence.

In contrast to similar monographs, this book exhibits several distinct writing features. One is its structural integration. The chapters are intricately linked and form a cohesive narrative, differentiating it from monographs structured around disparate individual articles, such as W. Brian Arthur's *Complexity and the Economy*.[1] The second is its sources. The book, comprising approximately 100,000 words, is rich in resources, drawing from both English and Chinese sources. It is supplemented by nearly 700 notes to substantiate its content. Notably, it references specific page numbers for most citations and provides the original source for important quotations, as well as key academic terms, facilitating reader verification. Third, the content is easy to read and understand. Given the nature of propriety economics, the book relies on qualitative research without complex mathematical models. It employs straightforward language and examples, ensuring accessibility for readers without specialized training in economics or history. Finally, the book maintains a moderate, rational, and neutral tone. It avoids radicalism, extremism, and sensitivity, aligning with the theme of propriety philosophy while upholding scholarly objectivity and balance.

This book originated from the author's experience teaching a doctoral student graduate course, History of Economic Thought, since 2017. This course was primarily offered to students in a doctoral program in finance and management, jointly sponsored by the Gabelli School of Business at Fordham University in the United States and the National School of Development at Peking University in China. Over the past six years, the author's interactions with students have provided invaluable academic nourishment, profoundly influencing the genesis and development of this book. Four doctoral students—Dr. Xiangguo Zhang, Dr. Yan Han, Dr. Yuanqu Xu, and Dr. Xinxin Kong—played instrumental roles by actively contributing to discussions and offering constructive comments. The author also drew inspiration from discussions with doctoral students, including Xinyu Yang, Chen Wei,

Guangshu Hu, Shencong Ma, Hanbing Dong, and Lili Pan from the class of 2019; Kaiyu Ji and Xiaodong Jin from the class of 2018; Qiyan Li from the class of 2017; and Yan Zhao from the class of 2016, during our book club sessions.

This book's ideas were further enriched through interactions with professors and experts, such as Qiren Zhou, Zhuang Yang, Miaojie Yu, and Jinjie Wang from Peking University. Throughout the writing process, the author received invaluable assistance from specialists across various disciplines, including Professors Jin Lu and Xing Lu in the humanities; Professors Qin Gao, Guoqiang Tian, and Meiping Sun in economics; and Mr. Weiping Tian, the former editor-in-chief of the University of Macau's journal, *South China Quarterly*, who provided editorial guidance for my article titled "Interdisciplinary Evolution of Propriety Economic Thought." I extend my special thanks to Ms. Sydney Stonner, editor at the City University of Hong Kong Press, for her exceptional assistance and outstanding editorship. She truly deserves my sincere acknowledgment.

Lastly, the author extends heartfelt gratitude to his family. My wife, Professor Lan Shen, served as the first examiner of my pivotal ideas, engaging in spirited debates and resonant discussions that significantly contributed to the book's completion. My daughters, Nicole Hong and Emma Hong, offered their insights, further shaping some of the book's concepts. My father, Chuanhao Hong, and my mother, Huiyu Sun, both profoundly influenced my passion for economic history. Naturally, I willingly embrace full responsibility for any shortcomings found within its contents.

Zhaohui Hong

Chapter 1

Introduction

As the world enters the extraordinary 2020s, it is becoming increasingly important to understand and study a concept called "propriety economics." The evolving global circumstances and shifts in human perspectives and behaviors underscore the importance of focusing on this concept. As scholars, our task is to explore the academic possibilities and prepare the theoretical groundwork for the field known as propriety economics. We want to have a better understanding of what propriety economics is and how it works. This chapter serves as an introduction to the book, focusing on the basic utility, academic background, and intellectual elements of propriety economics.

1.1 What is Propriety Economics?

Over the past 250 years or so, some Western economists have consciously and unconsciously constructed five bridges to propriety economics under the influence of Aristotle's virtue of propriety. They include balanced supply and demand in classical economics, equilibrium price in neoclassical economics, evolutionary development in institutional economics, bounded rationality in behavioral economics, and shared value in cultural economics. These ideas demonstrate balance, equilibrium, evolution, limitation, and sharing, which together form the five basic elements and philosophical concepts of propriety economics.

1.1.1 Definition

To expedite readers' comprehension of propriety economics, the author provides a concise definition, to be further elaborated upon in Section 3, Chapter 5 of this book. Generally speaking, propriety economics by definition aims to study the moderate factors affecting economic development. This includes the economic theories, methods, policies, and cases that seek the balance of supply and demand, market price equilibrium, institutional evolution, bounded rational behavior, and cultural value sharing. Propriety economics comprises the different effects of three dimensions on economic development: deficiency, excess, and moderation. These three variables are reflected in economic subjects, market objects, and the third parties between the subjects and objects, such as governments, institutions, collectives, corporates, communities, cultures, morals, technology, and international aspects. Propriety economics is crafted to rectify the excessively conservative or overly liberal conduct of economic agents, adjust very interventionist or too permissive government policies, and coordinate the highly unpredictable or extremely stagnant market. In essence, propriety economics aims to establish a framework that incorporates middle-ground, neutral, and mutually beneficial economic resources and mechanisms concerning individuals' rights, government power, and market capital. The goal is to cultivate a balanced, evolving, limited, and collectively shared economic system, contributing to the development of a propriety society.

1.1.2 Ideological Essentials

In addition to the definition of propriety economics, discussing its ideological essentials and thoughts is crucial. Generally speaking, an economic school consists of five major components—philosophies, theories, methods, case studies, and policies—but its thoughts and ideological essentials are the most critical. Only by understanding the true meaning of economic thought can we understand and analyze the characteristics of each economic school more effectively. By drawing on core elements from Eastern and Western philosophy, the author proposes four major concepts—awakening, comprehension, reason, and Dao—as the foundation for the philosophical thought of propriety economics.

All crucial ideas and thoughts begin with an awakening, and this is also one of the essential elements of philosophical thought in general. The ancient Greek philosopher Socrates (470–399 BCE) made a great contribution to the awakening of human consciousness which, according to Socrates, requires at least three key practices—the first of which is questioning. For example, when discussing the concept of happiness with his student Aeschines of Sphettus (425–350 BCE), Socrates asked him 22 times what it meant to be happy.[1] In the process of endless questioning, Socrates was teaching his students that any knowledge could be challenged. Doing so allowed Socrates to nurture students such as Plato (427–347 BCE) who, using a similar methodology, in turn mentored Aristotle (384–322 BCE), who coined the legendary phrase "I love my teacher, I love the truth more." This approach awakened the spirit of critical thinking among students and encouraged them not to follow their superiors, books, and teachers; instead, they were expected to challenge any mainstream theories and through curious probing, searching, and questioning to continuously innovate philosophies and research methods.

The second practice that can enhance awakening is engaging in constant debates. One of Socrates' outstanding abilities was to continually clarify and deliver his views through persistent dialogue and debate, highlighting the contradictions of the other side and encouraging opponents to revise their original views and accept his own arguments, thus producing an awakening effect. In particular, he had a habit of inspiring students to reflect through the presentation of paradoxes, such as the famous Meno paradox.[2] Similar paradoxes appear widely in economic research, which stimulate economists to think, explain, and deal with the confusion and dilemmas they cause.

Enlightening the human mind or exposure to new ideas is the third practice to inspire awakening. Socrates insisted that philosophers represent the light due to their ability to awaken the ignorant and open people's minds. The allegory of the cave, proposed by his student Plato in his *Republic*, asks people to turn around in a dark cave, be brave enough to get out of the cave instead of settling for the status quo and clinging to the comforts of tradition, and welcome the choice of light and freedom.[3] But the more profound meaning of this cave metaphor is that human beings need to constantly turn around, shift directions, change perspectives, and improve their minds. Moreover, this change, physical or intellectual, does not necessarily follow a linear direction; it does not go from darkness to light and then to greater light. Instead, it may move in a circular motion from darkness to light and then back to darkness. Obviously, this repetition is not a simple recurrence but a dialectical selection that involves negating the negation. This is precisely the triangular paradigm and cyclical thinking that is emphasized in propriety economics (see Section 2, Chapter 6 of this book).

Beyond awakening, comprehension stands as the second significant element in philosophical thought and serves as a key indicator of the transition from awakening to the next level of understanding. The Socratic awakening is the starting point of human thinking, while the Eastern way of thinking helps to inspire comprehension and enhance enlightenment. Primarily, the enlightenment of the mind and heart constitutes the initial facet of comprehension. Confucianism suggests following one's heart to enlighten one's mind, while Zen Buddhism promotes enlightenment through heightened awareness of the environment. Thus, the idea of enlightenment is important in traditional Chinese culture. The second part of comprehension is consciousness designed to discover the directions and fundamentals of thought by understanding phenomena thoroughly. Only through consciousness can we enhance awareness, observe the world, and reach thought. In addition, comprehension requires understanding which refers to the breadth and depth of knowledge. It also requires analyzing profound principles and complex phenomena to grasp the mysteries of life and solve puzzles effectively. Certainly, comprehension and penetration form the bedrock of enlightenment, capable of elevating human understanding from the superficial to the profound, from the external to the internal, and from the imaginary to the tangible.

Therefore, in the realm of cognitive processes, awakening without comprehension signifies a deficiency in both awareness and understanding. Similarly, merely grasping a concept without integrating it into one's broader understanding results in partial or incomplete comprehension. Consequently, understanding the features of major economic schools becomes imperative for developing one's distinctive perspectives and methodologies.

The third portion of philosophical thought is the reason aimed at integrating the various elements of awareness and comprehension to arrive at a rational conclusion, which in turn requires the ability to deduce and generalize from the abstract. Reasoning, encompassing both induction and deduction, prioritizes rationality. The classical school of economics emphasizes full rationality and is good at using empirical and experimental methods to clarify and rationalize the causes and consequences of economic behaviors while rejecting prejudice and extremes. Yet, in practice, achieving rationality has proven challenging for humanity, as irrational, extreme, and absurd rhetoric and actions often stem from a deficiency in reason. Thus, the ideas of propriety and moderation are important concepts to support reason, which also favors logic. Western logic advocates the absolute nature of regular patterns, which opposes speciousness. It also embraces the law of non-contradiction, in other words, nothing contradictory can be in simultaneous coexistence. Moreover, Western logic is more inclined to exclude the middle. If A is true, then non-A is false. There is no possibility of half-truths and half-falsities, and everything must be clear-cut without a hazy middle between black and white. Logic is a way of thinking to make a clear, precise judgment, focusing on organized certainty to oppose the specious, ambiguous, and self-contradictory. Science is another key driving force for promoting reason. The essence of science is discovery, not invention, and one of the major purposes of science is to discover the laws of existing phenomena.[4] As such, scientific exploration and technological innovation exhibit distinct characteristics. Needham's Grand Question probed into the reasons behind the predominant development of modern sciences in Europe rather than in China. It is noteworthy that the achievements of ancient China, commonly referred to as the four great inventions, were not scientific revelations but rather advancements in technology.[5] Although it is inventions that are responsible for changing the world, the real driving force for understanding the world comes from discovery. Thus, discovery is the prerequisite for invention, and science is the foundation of technology. Notably, rationality, logic, and science are the foundations of established economics, but the lack of rationality, logic, and science in economic reality thrives. This contradiction between theory and reality has allowed for the emergence and development of propriety economic thought, which is designed to balance empirical science and experimental science, economic theory and objective reality, conservative thinking and radical behavior, and government intervention and the free market.

Furthermore, the Dao is the fourth critical ingredient of philosophical thought in addition to awakening, comprehension, and reason. One must establish reason before attaining the Dao, and to attain the Dao, one must first grasp reason.[6] Although reason is important relative to the Dao, reason is simpler, more straightforward, and clear-cut. The concept of the Dao contains human wisdom and thought other than knowledge and theory. Moreover, the reasons for different things vary, but the Dao applies to all things with its shared universality.[7] Generally speaking, the Dao can initially be comprehended through its metaphysical nature. English speakers are unable to find a suitable word to translate the Chinese word "Dao" and can only use pinyin (*Dao* or *Tao*) as a substitute. After evolving from a philosophy into a religion, Daoism has been developed with metaphysics, thus rendering it even more difficult to explain. For instance, the concept of good fortune emerging from adversity or that of the latter existing within the former signifies a theory of dialectical transformation and metaphysics, lending support to the equation "A is B and B is A."[8]

In fact, the Dao is rooted in the philosophical wisdom which shaped Chinese economic development. All axioms, principles, theories, and philosophies may obey the Dao. In particular, the Dao in part means nature. The *Dao De Jing* (*Tao Te Ching*) persuades us that the Dao is the ultimate way. The Dao mainly refers to the laws of nature and the origin of the universe, and seeks to be calm and harmonious because life is short but nature is eternal. The author believes that economic principles are fundamentally derived from or connected to the inherent laws that govern how markets function. In other words, economic practices should align with the natural laws of the market economy while avoiding extremes or imbalances.

Therefore, economists need to know and understand the Dao and apply it to economic thought and theory to guide economic practice and policy. The philosophy of propriety benefits not only from Confucius' moderation but also aligns with the Daoist principles of harmony, dialectics, and non-interference. These ideas encompass economic concepts like laissez-faire, governing through non-action, and the government not competing with the people for profit.[9]

In short, the function of awakening in Western philosophy is conducive to innovation; the emphasis on comprehension and enlightenment in Eastern philosophy facilitates learning. At the same time, while reason in Western philosophy promotes scientific approaches, logic, and science, the Dao in Eastern philosophy prefers dialectical thinking and returning to nature. The mission of propriety economics is to integrate and intersect the four elements of thought, combining the role of completed awakening, thorough comprehension, scientific reason, and the natural Dao in a creative synthesis that maximizes the appeal of economics. Although the various schools of economics are vast, in fact, economic philosophy, ideology, and thought often determine economic theories, methods, models, and policies. Many legendary economists were thinkers first and economists second, and indeed, they were economists with innovative thoughts.

1.2 Why Study Propriety Economics?

It is imperative to clarify the objectives, significance, and necessity of delving into propriety economics when constructing a research framework for this field. This approach aids scholars in shedding light on the discipline's contextual background, its relevance to human needs, and the academic groundwork required for its development.

1.2.1 The Contemporary Imperative

In the 21st century, our world has transitioned into an era characterized by volatility, uncertainty, complexity, and ambiguity, often referred to as the VUCA era.[10] Especially after the global financial crisis in 2008 and the COVID-19 pandemic, human beings have experienced unwanted unrest, improbability, complexity, and chaos. In such adverse situations, the human mind is prone to polarization, changing from one viewpoint to another, and becoming either helplessly panicked or having "thrown up its hands and backed away."[11] Consequently, unscrupulous politicians may sow discord, incite confrontations, and escalate conflicts for personal and partisan gains. The public may sometimes blindly follow such radical, misleading actions by politicians and the media. This will lead to upward and downward, left and right, and internal and external forces pushing, fueling, and increasing the speed and extent of negative feedback effects. Nationalism, populism, racism, authoritarianism, and other fundamentalist ideologies have started to gain prominence, leading to societal polarization and extreme behaviors. This has resulted in a collective loss of reason and sanity. Recurring occurrences of such phenomena have been witnessed both pre- and post-World War I and II. Cold wars, economic crises, as well as natural and man-made disasters have gradually become commonplace throughout history.[12]

In facing such difficult, uncertain, and high-risk situations, economists need to take care to prevent an overheated economy (bubble) or an overly cold market (depression) and to explore propriety economic philosophy, theories, methods, and policies to explain and deal with the issues at hand. All these dilemmas of the times show the necessity and urgency of supporting rational, moderate, and appropriate minds and behavior.

1.2.2 The Demand for Humanity

Starting with Confucius (551–479 BCE) in China and Aristotle (384–322 BCE) in Greece, human society has been pursuing moderate and propriety ideas systematically for more than 2,500 years. Since then, numerous sages and scholars have tried to go beyond the masters of the Axial Age,[13] and many state policymakers have continued to practice the philosophy of the middle way and moderation in the hope of preventing economic crises. Beginning with Adam Smith (1723–1790), the idea of propriety was gradually presented and interpreted in a piecemeal but unsystematic manner in Western economics. Meanwhile, propriety economic concepts were validated and expanded by various theories in the humanities, social sciences, and natural sciences.

However, recognizing moderation is difficult, and acting on it is even more challenging because going to extremes and capitalizing on polarization often make the process of human choice simple, easy, and efficient, without the need to struggle for middle choices, repositioning, and self-correction. Furthermore, the voice of polarization tends to be more distinct, explicit, and fervent, thereby enabling the creation of potent rallying power and collective impact. In addition, for most people it is hard to avoid left and right bias, conservative and liberal extremes, selfishness, and narrow-mindedness, which makes it even more difficult to maintain long-term cooperation and continuous moderation in reality. As a result, inflation or depression caused by human greed and supply-demand imbalances have been a common issue for the world economy for more than 200 years. During the 2020–2023 global pandemic, some leaders were slow to react and missed the best window for the prevention and treatment of the new virus. Others panicked and overreacted, locking down cities, roads, and buildings, and completely shutting down the economy. Moreover, as the pandemic waned, certain individuals promptly returned to their work and school routines, inadvertently triggering a fresh surge in infections. Conversely, there were those who found a selfish satisfaction in the crisis affecting others, observing the turmoil from a distance. This group often evaded their responsibilities, resisted wearing masks, and opposed the practice of social distancing. All of these reflect the lack of humanity in the face of disaster either taking the form of deficiency or excess. While discussing moderation during a catastrophe might be perceived as somewhat insensitive by some, it is undeniably advantageous to contemplate this aspect. Such reflection can significantly enhance our ability to respond effectively to future crises.

Both theory and reality confirm that a substantial number of individuals are open to embracing middle-ground and moderate policies. However, it is infrequent for moderation to emerge as the unanimous choice for everyone, turning it into a challenging aspiration. Perhaps, many individuals pursuing moderation lack the fervor of Don Quixote and demonstrate less passion and persistence compared to religious preachers. Many individuals of ordinary nature favor the use of rational discourse and moderate actions to uphold the concept of propriety. However, they often find themselves sidelined and disregarded amidst the impassioned appeals of both left and right ideologies, at times yielding to irrationality and excess driven by minority influences. Consequently, the pursuit of answers should delve deeper into the realms of human nature, transcending the boundaries of diverse cultures, races, nationalities, social strata, systems, and political affiliations.

Today, the study of the interpretations and interactions surrounding the concept of propriety within economics holds profound significance. It serves as a means to rectify the extremes inherent in economic policies, mitigate imbalances in supply and demand markets, and foster the betterment of human behavior. As long as the inherent weaknesses of human nature persist, the notion of moderation remains relevant. As the human psyche tends toward prejudice and paranoia, an economic framework guided by the principles of moderation becomes not just necessary but crucial. Even though irrationality and extremism may temporarily dominate certain times, places, and populations, policies possess the capacity to self-correct through confrontation, friction, and mutual complementarity. Over time, they can naturally redirect towards a more moderate trajectory.

It is vital to emphasize that while the pursuit of propriety is a commendable endeavor, it, like equilibrium and rationality, is an ideal concept with a low probability of realization in the real world. Nonetheless, this should not deter us from striving for propriety. We acknowledge that imperfections and excesses are commonplace, and the process of rectifying human errors may sometimes overshoot the mark. Yet, recognizing the challenge of achieving moderation is an essential step.

Immanuel Kant (1724–1804) openly admitted to not personally subscribing to a belief in God, yet he did not actively reject the concept of God. Despite the unverifiable nature of the hypothesis concerning the existence of God, Kant argues that it is crucial in offering guidance and purpose to individuals. Positing that the termination of physical life is not the ultimate end, he contends that without an ideal God, adhering to and observing moral laws becomes challenging.[14]

When considering economic philosophy, skepticism may arise regarding the attainability of moderation. However, the absence of the ideal of moderation in economic development can lead to a loss of fundamental criteria, potentially resulting in a state of chaos, confusion, and uncertainty. The most pragmatic realization of this moderate ideal in economics is the ability to balance and harmonize supply and demand, equity and efficiency, employment and inflation, and free market dynamics and government intervention in a timely, appropriate, and rational manner. These manifestations of propriety economics are not lofty utopian concepts; they do occur from time to time, and sometimes persist for extended periods, often accompanied by positive economic advancements and significantly reduced social tensions.

1.2.3 Relevant Academic Perspectives

The 21st century has seen the emergence of academic ideas in propriety economics, as the established discipline of economics arrives at a period of upheaval.[15] Although the classical and neoclassical schools of economics have dominated Western economics for 250 years, since the 1970s, emerging schools of thought such as new institutional economics, behavioral economics, cultural economics, and complexity economics have been questioning, challenging, and revising the traditional economic ideals. They have systematically doubted and thoroughly criticized the fundamental hypotheses and cornerstones of the "economic man": full rationality, profit maximization, perfect competition, complete information, and market clearing. Similarly, they have extensively questioned conventional theories and methods, such as general equilibrium, positive feedback, diminishing returns, and mathematical modeling. Neoclassical economics faces challenges in explaining the universal nature of all human beings due to factors such as human irrationality or bounded rationality, utility maximization, monopolistic competition, information asymmetry, and instances of market failure. It is also problematic to explicate the presence of disequilibrium, negative feedback, increasing returns, and dynamic evolution. For the time being, it is not appropriate to exclude the validity and practicality of non-mathematical research methods such as experimental, computer, qualitative, and inductive methods.

It has become increasingly evident that the dawn of a new era necessitates the cultivation of fresh ideas. However, economists have yet to embark on a comprehensive, systematic discussion of the philosophy, theory, methodology, and policies underpinning propriety economics. Though some existing schools of economic thought have illuminated aspects of propriety economics, a holistic exploration remains lacking.

One notable perspective is that of evolutionary economics, which emphasizes the dynamic and historical nature inherent in economic propriety. This approach shifts the focus towards examining the totality, diversity, and complexity of economic development. Notably, the principle of satisfaction and the pursuit of improved outcomes championed by evolutionary economics, as opposed to the pursuit of optimal outcomes in traditional economics, align with the relative nature of propriety economics.[16]

However, it is important to note that the core views of evolutionary economics are not essentially tied to moderation or the middle way. Instead, it emerged as a challenge to the other extreme of neoclassical economics, without addressing the imperative of balancing and reconciling traditional and modern economic thought within the context of a moderate approach.[17] The analytical framework found at the opposite end of the spectrum, often presented as opposition research, is precisely what propriety economics stands against. Such perspectives hinder economic research from breaking free from the ceaseless fluctuation between extremes, impeding significant advancements in the field.

In addition, the Goldilocks economy[18] aims to depict a brief golden period of economic development, the so-called Great Moderation, which symbolizes a period of economic growth between two major economic crises, indicating a moderate state in economic development.[19] Although the Goldilocks experience is somewhat similar to the ideal of propriety economics, these "golden beauties" may be false, short-lived, and unsustainable, and may feed the conditions for the next, more serious economic crisis because any situation caused by excessively low interest rates (less than 0%) and high unemployment (more than 15%) is not moderate. Instead, it may set the stage for an imminent real estate bubble, an accelerated stock market rise, and monetary inflation. At the same time, these "golden" times are sometimes a good opportunity for bankers to get rich and speculate, while those in the middle or lower-middle classes are burdened by rising mortgages or inflation. And if the mortgage bubble bursts, as it did in 2008, there is a risk that people will lose money again.[20]

Moreover, the Czech economist Tomáš Sedláček published *The Economics of Good and Evil* in 2011, explaining the problem of good and evil in economics in terms of Greek mythology, and then looking at mythology and philosophy in the context of economics.[21] The central point of view is inherited from Aristotle's idea of moderation: moderation is good, and insufficiency or excess is evil. Sedláček criticizes human greed and desire from a fundamental good vs. evil standpoint. He deems the excessive promotion of human self-interest in classical economics as a contributor to human evil induced by irrationality. He also questions the dominant influence of mathematics on the study of economics for overlooking the exceptions and specific conditions that are often found in economic phenomena. Therefore, the economics of good and evil emphasizes the principles of humanity, ethics, morality, and value that economics must uphold. However, the economics of good and evil, as refreshing as it is, still falls within the realm of moral and ethical theories and is hardly an independent, unique new discipline of economics.

In short, none of the three prominent theories mentioned above directly or explicitly introduces the concept of propriety economics. Likewise, they do not engage in a systematic, comprehensive, and in-depth exploration of the definition, philosophy, theories, methods, and policies associated with propriety economics, which constitutes the central subject and aspiration of this book.

1.3 How to Study Propriety Economics

To effectively promote the study of propriety economics, scholars need to systematically research at least Eastern moderate philosophy, Western propriety ideas, and the history of Western economic thought. These efforts will be required to find the philosophical basis and economic ideas, discover the main theories and research themes, identify research methods, and propose policy principles for implementing a propriety economy. In particular, propriety economics will offer guidelines and measurable criteria on how to achieve moderation in the process of economic operations.

1.3.1 Eastern Moderation and Western Propriety

To study propriety economics, it is essential to understand the origin and core of its philosophical thought. The roots of moderate philosophy should be attributed to Chinese philosophy. Although Confucius was the master of the philosophy of moderation, the idea of moderation was already found and discussed in the classical literature of all the pre-Qin thinkers before Confucius, including the *I Ching, The Books of Shang, Rites of Zhou,* and *Zuo Tradition.* By the Spring and Autumn Period (770–481 BCE), the philosophy of moderation was maturing and was enriched and developed by many scholars during the Han dynasty (206 BCE to 220) and Cheng Zhu in the Song dynasty (960–1279).

Generally speaking, Eastern moderate philosophy advocates nonpartisanship, impartiality, neutrality, and adherence to the middle, and also emphasizes that the middle is a kind of correctness, which is constantly changing. The value orientation of the middle is positive and active.

The concept of propriety in the Western tradition has its roots in the work of Aristotle in ancient Greece. It was further developed and expanded upon by Adam Smith, who introduced it into the field of moral sentiments. In Western philosophy, propriety is regarded as a virtue characterized by impartiality and underscores the objective of moderation. Perhaps most significantly, it champions the primacy of rationality, which is a fundamental distinction between Eastern and Western perspectives on moderation and propriety.

In a broader context, Western propriety philosophy emphasizes centrality, normalcy, subjectivity, historicity, neutrality, rationality, and relativity. These principles form the foundational framework and guiding tenets of propriety economics, as expounded in Chapter 2 of this book.

1.3.2 Propriety in the History of Economic Thought

Different ideas that inform the basis of propriety economics can be found in the literature throughout the history of economics. While the explicit concept of propriety economics has not been put forth by economists since the time of Adam Smith, a careful examination of their ideas, theories, methods, and policies reveals several distinct aspects that align with the principles of propriety economics.

First and foremost, classical economics introduced the notion of propriety through concepts like the "invisible hand" and the theory of supply and demand within market economies. These ideas form the bedrock of propriety economics. Furthermore, neoclassical economics has enriched propriety economics by providing valuable insights through the general equilibrium theory, offering micro-level guidance as detailed in Chapter 3.

Institutional economics has enriched propriety economics by emphasizing the significance of neutralization. Furthermore, the relative value theory and the importance of consciousness in economics, as emphasized by both old and new institutional economics, provide a foundation for propriety economics to evolve in a softer, less mathematical direction. In particular, the theory of institutional change, championed by institutional economics, imparts historical background and methodological inspiration to propriety economics (see Chapter 4).

Behavioral economics, characterized by its theory of bounded rationality, challenges the concept of full rationality. It introduces key notions such as prospect theory, assumptions of bounded self-interest and willpower, and mental accounting, all of which establish a theoretical basis for propriety economics. Notably, behavioral economics distinguishes itself through its inherent psychological nature, disrupting traditional neoclassical assumptions of stationarity and generality. Instead, it underscores contrasting effects, historical evolution, and special exceptions. This psychological dimension constitutes a foundational aspect of propriety economics (refer to Chapter 4).

Lastly, cultural economics, rooted in shared ideologies, values, benefits, cohesion, and efficiency, serves as a fundamental pillar of propriety economics. It offers theoretical and practical insights into moderate regulation, such as moral regulation, and moderate distribution, as exemplified by the concept of the third distribution, both of which are advocated by propriety economics (see Chapter 5).

The philosophies, theories, and methodologies of these five economic schools collectively provide the groundwork and foundational concepts for propriety economics. Through analysis, synthesis, and innovation, they contribute to the emergence and development of propriety economics.[22]

1.3.3 Theories and Research Themes of Propriety Economics

The study of propriety economics involves understanding its fundamental theories and research themes. At the heart of propriety economic theory is a concept of dividing one thing into three parts instead of just two. The key idea is to find a balanced middle ground between two extremes, avoiding both excess and insufficiency. This core concept is known as trichotomism.

In the context of economic research, this triad theory aims to break down economic phenomena into three distinct variables. It takes into account a multitude of factors, including time, space, diverse groups of people, and varying values. This evaluation encompasses positions such as left, center, and right; top, center, and bottom; inside, middle, and outside, among others. These variables are then analyzed and discussed within a unified framework, promoting a more rational, comprehensive understanding. This approach helps avoid biases, ignorance, and hasty judgments.

When it comes to designing economic policies, the triad theory suggests considering three options: the best, second best, and worst. Each option is evaluated in terms of its cost, risk, and benefit. This approach allows for a balanced consideration of the interests of various groups, whether they lean to the left, center, or right. It seeks to find common ground and maximize shared interests. Additionally, the triad theory of propriety economics encourages a shift from linear thinking to a triangle paradigm. It advocates for unbiased judgments and inclusivity, promoting the study of interdependence and compatibility among three key economic actors. This approach helps in dealing with the uncertainty and complexity of the real economic world, reinforcing the circular and relative value perspective advocated by propriety economics.

Furthermore, the triad theory of propriety economics can help identify unique research themes. One fundamental principle of propriety economics is that research should involve three comparable variables. By introducing a third variable between two existing ones, which necessitates comparative research, economists can explore alternative options and identify the second-best choice. Propriety economics enables scholars to explore three perspectives within a single variable, such as inadequacy, excess, and moderation. It also accommodates three choices, akin to yin, yang, and harmony, wherein the combination of yin and yang results in a balanced state. This can inspire economists to offer three explanations under the same concept, breaking down government intervention or market mechanisms into good, neutral, and bad evaluations, thus opening up new avenues for economic research. For more details, please refer to Chapter 6 of this book.

1.3.4 Propriety Economics Research Methodology

In propriety economics, the key to effective research methods lies in an evolutionary approach that leverages the richness of complexity economics. Rather than striving to invent entirely new research methods, the emphasis is on skillfully combining existing methods in a manner that aligns with the specific objectives and themes of propriety economics research.

The first approach involves integrating qualitative and quantitative research methods, employing a sophisticated blend of methodologies such as grounded theory, mixed methods, experiments, and value index research. This fusion enables a comprehensive exploration of research questions within the context of propriety economics.

The second approach centers on the strategic combination of inductive, deductive, and abductive methods. This amalgamation is designed to address the limitations inherent in each method and capitalize on their individual research strengths through a unified approach.

The third approach centers on refining and adapting classical economic curves. This involves creating distinctive propriety economic diagrams and curves, strategically applying them to specific subjects. For a more in-depth understanding of these methodologies, please consult Chapter 7 of this book.

1.3.5 Governmental Policies in Propriety Economics

The success of propriety economic policy relies on the attributes of policymakers. These characteristics include impartiality, openness to public opinions, the courage to reject inappropriate public demands, and the competence to rectify errors.

While the concept of moderation is challenging to quantify precisely, centuries of economic practice have led human societies to develop widely accepted criteria, evaluation standards, and quantitative benchmarks. These benchmarks are generally agreed upon by most countries and encompass facets such as full employment, stable operations, significant benefits, and the maximization of human welfare. In this context, metrics like the unemployment rate, inflation rate, Gini coefficient, interest rate, fiscal deficit, and gross domestic product (GDP) growth rate play pivotal roles.

Furthermore, achieving a rational and moderate economic growth rate necessitates the consideration of a delicate balance between needs and possibilities, production and quality of life, equality and efficiency, and short- and long-term goals. These considerations aid policymakers in addressing three fundamental questions regarding intervention policies: Is government intervention justified? If so, in which areas and at what junctures should intervention take place, and to what extent in a measured, reasonable capacity? Lastly, what is the suitable and sustainable duration for the intervention?

Consequently, propriety economic policy aims to establish boundaries for economic growth. These boundaries represent the flexibility of economic factors, indicating the optimal limits they can reach, and the point of moderate equilibrium based on their inherent tensions. For a comprehensive exploration of this topic, please refer to Chapter 8 of this book.

1.3.6 Case Studies of Propriety Economics

In addition to policy principles, case studies can help to address the questions of how to achieve moderation, manage a propriety economy, and attain moderate objectives. Using more than three centuries of case studies as a foundation, the author primarily delves into the essence of moderation in U.S. economic development and applies propriety economic research methods to clarify the trajectories of U.S. economic history.

For instance, employing the lens of evolutionary rationality, an examination of the economic structure and function of the British colonies in North America unveils their interdependent economic relationship with Britain. Faced with the task of preserving individual freedoms while addressing social unrest arising from early industrialization, a propriety economic perspective underscores the importance of implementing gradual social reforms (1800–1860) to achieve a balance between risks and benefits. Furthermore, an analysis of U.S. poverty alleviation policies in the 20th century offers valuable insights into the American experience, lessons learned, and the pursuit of a more moderate direction.

Beyond the United States, the experiences and lessons drawn from China's economic reforms in the 1980s and 1990s contribute significantly to the discussion of propriety economics. The resulting uniquely Chinese economic framework can be viewed as a product of propriety economic reform, avoiding both stagnation within a conservative planned economy and the abrupt shift toward a free-market economy via "shock therapy." This deliberate evolution of the economic system is illustrated through four pivotal cases: China's rural land system, property rights within township and village enterprises (TVEs), state-owned enterprise (SOE) reform, and the townization approach to urbanization. Each of these cases followed distinctive, indirect paths toward achieving moderation. For a detailed exploration, please refer to Chapter 9 of this book.

In essence, propriety is primarily a philosophical concept, but when applied to economic theories, methodologies, and policies, it assumes a distinctive significance and effectiveness. In the face of profound conflicts between government and the market, efficiency and equity, and intervention and freedom, the concept of propriety economics becomes even more deserving of thorough scrutiny and analysis.

The author's aspiration for this book is to contribute to the clarification of common misconceptions and biases surrounding moderation and propriety. It aims to encourage critical examination of mainstream economists' perspectives on propriety economics and provide academic groundwork for the future of propriety economics, encompassing its ideas, theories, methodologies, policies, and case studies.

Chapter 2

The Origin and Definition of Propriety Philosophy

Tracing the origins of ideas and delving into influential works is a crucial academic endeavor. When interpreting the concepts of propriety economics, it is essential to review the related theories and foundational literature.

The theory of hermeneutics acknowledges that scholars' interpretations of historical texts are inherently influenced by their existing knowledge and ideological perspectives. These factors, in turn, shape their selection and comprehension of the texts they examine. It emphasizes the fact that each researcher's present interpretation of literature is shaped by their prior knowledge, cultural influences, and biases. These factors inevitably exert a subconscious influence on their preconceptions.[1]

The author's objective is to scrutinize the historical literature surrounding moderation and propriety philosophy. This involves proposing new interpretations by reconstructing concepts and revising perspectives, thus contributing to a fresh understanding of these ideas.

2.1 Moderate Philosophy Before and After Confucius

The idea of moderation in economics is closely related to the philosophical ideas of the Axial Age in the East and the West, so it is helpful to investigate Eastern moderate philosophy to understand and define Western propriety philosophy and economics.

2.1.1 Moderate Philosophy in the Pre-Confucian Period

In the East, although Confucius was the master of moderate philosophy, many pre-Qin literary texts (before 221 BCE) mentioned the idea of the middle ground and moderation before him. While the exact period when he lived remains a subject of debate in academia, during the 11th century BCE, Ji Chang, known as King Wen of the Zhou dynasty (1046–256 BCE), asserted in the *I Ching* that a lawsuit successfully resolved in accordance with the principles of moderation and justice is deemed a success. This ancient text claims that staying in the middle position is superior. The *I Ching* also highlights the importance of maintaining and practicing the middle position.[2]

The Books of Shang discusses the idea of moderation at great length and asks rulers to learn about the middle virtue and middle position advocated by the Duke of Zhou, who was a member of the royal family of the early Zhou dynasty and played a major role in consolidating the kingdom. The first requirement outlined in the book is to prioritize moderation in one's mind. The second is to act in the middle, requiring the ruler to realize the importance of the middle because the one who gets the middle gets the world. The third is that the execution of laws by leaders should cautiously follow the middle and punishment should be neither overly light nor excessively heavy.[3]

Rites of Zhou also proposes that the middle should be associated with education and virtue which are critical to promoting harmony, friendship, peace, and filial piety.[4] In particular, *Zuo Tradition* connects the middle to both heaven and earth because human beings are born between the two.[5]

2.1.2 Moderate Philosophy from the Time of Confucius Onwards

By the Spring and Autumn period, the idea of moderation was taking shape. The main text in which Confucius discusses moderation is the *Analects*, which was elaborated on by his grandson Zi Si (483–402

BCE) in the book *Moderation* (*Zhong Yong*), or Doctrine of the Mean, and also developed by pre-Qin scholars and the Cheng-Zhu school in the Song dynasty.

The middle is in harmony with the principles of nonpartisanship, neutrality, and adherence to the center. In the first chapter of *Moderation*, it is said that moderation is the fundamental base of the world.[6] A passage from *The Books of Shang* quoted in the *Analects* of Confucius assumes that it is the will of heaven for leaders to adhere to a neutral strategy of governance.[7] Confucius also underlines that politics should be righteous and just, noting that only when a ruler's mind and body are sound can their words and actions be moderate and neutral.[8] However, Confucius admits that it is difficult to find a moderate politician or scholar, but it is acceptable to have an aggressive reformer and a conservative maintainer.[9]

The *Analects* also maintains that excessive actions are similar to insufficient actions.[10] But in reality, Confucius found that moderation cannot be attained because wise people fully understand it but are unwilling to practice it. By contrast, small-minded people do not understand moderation and are therefore unable to practice it. One implication seems to be that it is better to be excessive than insufficient because the public respects wise people rather than their less intelligent counterparts.[11]

Since then, most scholars have regarded moderation as a kind of "political correctness" and vied with each other in praising it. The aforementioned *I Ching* was further interpreted during the Warring States period, and the phrase "the dragon is the one who is virtuous and righteous" promoted the dragon, a totem of the Chinese nation, as a symbol of virtue. The *I Ching* also remarked that a great ruler should be in the middle which makes a close connection between moderation and virtue. It seems that not being moderate is viewed as evil without intention.[12]

Subsequently, the pre-Qin schools of thought (before 221 BCE) followed suit, praising and expounding on moderation. For example, Zhuangzi (369–286 BCE) proposed that people should neither be too low profile nor shown off too much, but should be moderate, embodying the common ground between Daoism and Confucianism in the principle of moderation.[13] Mencius (Mengzi) (372–289 BCE) also held a similar view[14] that rulers should be neutral in selecting moderate officials without bias.[15] In addition, Han Feizi (280–233 BCE) said, if you go to the middle, your body will be unharmed, emphasizing that you should not go too far.[16] Guanzi (719–645 BCE) also believed that harmony between extremes can result in moderation, which in turn can protect the peace.[17] The above-mentioned literature seems to indicate that most of the Confucian and Daoist cultures in China attached importance to the realm of moderation and righteousness.

In the Song dynasty, Cheng Yi (1033–1107) further illuminated that moderation is the right way and a key principle for the world.[18] Xi Zhu (1130–1200) also noted that the middle—no excess and no deficiency—means no bias, with a balance of the two poles.[19]

It must be pointed out that the middle or moderation is impartial, covering and connecting the middle between the top and bottom, left and right, front and back, and inside and outside.[20] That is to say, the middle is not only the middle of time or location[21] but also refers to appropriate behavior and speech, as well as a higher level of inner balance and harmony.[22]

In short, impartiality and neutrality are the fundamental ideas of moderation. "One" in Chinese philosophy advocates unanimity and common ground and discourages opposition or conflict. And "two" underlines difference and duality and opposes unity and uniformity. While moderation or the middle recognizes that one should be divided into two, it supports the transition from "two" to "three." The term "three" has many philosophical implications, stressing the examination of the two opposing sides and the formulation of appropriate suggestions and methods, including advising, penetration, and observation. The utility of such reference is to approach and select moderation.[23]

As mentioned, moderation aims at searching for a middle position. Mencius underscores that insisting on one principle means being stubborn while holding the middle is to make judgments and choices properly.[24] Therefore, the essence of the middle lies in "searching." However, the act of searching involves subjective judgment, without specific, clear, and quantitative measurements, focusing on an ideal reference and state. Searching is different from "balance" because the standard of judgment emphasized by the search is constantly changing, while balance is unchanging. And the criteria when searching for the middle will always adapt according to the changing situation and people's preferences at a certain time and place. Thus, the middle ground becomes a dynamic, subjective goal of searching, which is beyond what ordinary people can reach. According to Confucius, the middle way is more difficult than governing a state, resigning from a high office and giving up a decent salary, or enduring attacks by knives and blades.[25] The difficulty in approaching the middle is that ordinary people are happy to do easy things and generally cannot resist the temptation of desire.

Furthermore, moderation has a profound implication for harmony. Wang Fuzhi (1619–1692) during the late Ming and early Qing dynasties first assumed that the character "middle" (中) in Chinese has vertical coherence, which displays the functions of reconciliation and neutralization. Wang Fuzhi also asserted that the principle of the middle way is embodied through the tool of harmony. According to Wang, moderation, when attaining the middle ground, serves as a means to achieve peace.[26]

People who are seeking moderation need to reach a state of equidistance and peace. In traditional China, a scholar (*shi*) advocating for the middle course typically belonged to the middle class. Faced with the extreme encroachment of the upper class and the defense of their rights by the lower class, scholars often opposed both while striving to serve as an intermediary between the two by emphasizing the role of reconciliation, neutralization, and compromise to maintain social stability, harmony, and progress. Therefore, the functions of the middle and peace can have an organic interaction, as upholding and practicing the middle will help to achieve peace, and the attainment of peace is also conducive to the return to the middle. It can be said that approaching the middle will lead to harmony, while going against the middle will lead to chaos.[27]

Actually, moderation and harmony refer not only to reconciling the conflicts between specific interest groups but also to neutralizing and balancing one's inner world and spirituality. *The Book of Rites* states that only a person with a harmonious, righteous inner mind can achieve long-term harmony in interpersonal relationships.[28] Moreover, the *I Ching* elevates neutral harmony to the realm of aesthetics and believes that a moderate person is the most beautiful.[29]

Additionally, moderation holds a positive value judgment. The middle contains righteousness without compromise. The *Analects* specifies that moderation should be the highest level of morality, but people have lacked this kind of morality for a long time.[30] Therefore, moderation is a value that exercises a positive driving force to lead people toward goodness and upward mobility.

Confucius also argues that the middle is the division between the gentleman, a morally upright or noble individual, and the small-minded person (*xiao ren*), typically someone of lesser moral character or lower ethical standing, noting that the gentleman not only cultivates his inner heart but also abides in the right way. In contrast, the small-minded person who does not have high standards does not have a sense of reverence, is willing to speculate, and is accustomed to opportunism.[31] Therefore, moderation represents nature which is purely neutral and fundamental to human morality, so acting with nature is the right way, and acting against nature is the evil way.[32]

2.2 Ideas on Propriety During and After Aristotle's Age

About 50 years before Aristotle, the ancient Greek Isocrates (436–338 BCE) mentioned the word appropriateness (πρέπον, *kairos*).[33] However, the Western concept of propriety was largely outlined by Aristotle, who used alternatively "appropriate,"[34] "intermediate,"[35] and "mean."[36] Aristotle's discussion of propriety is reflected mainly in his book *Nicomachean Ethics*, while David Hume (1711–1776) developed the idea of propriety, and Adam Smith (1723–1790) applied propriety to economic theory in his *An Inquiry into the Nature and Causes of the Wealth of Nations* published in 1776. Although Western philosophers after Smith, such as Immanuel Kant, Friedrich Nietzsche, and Jean-Jacques Rousseau, have enriched and developed the philosophy of propriety, this chapter will focus on its origins, thus omitting the discussion of Western propriety philosophy after Smith.

2.2.1 Virtue

Aristotle's ideas have been developed by Smith and others to shape the Western concept of propriety. Generally speaking, it is consistent with the Eastern idea of moderation, though with its own distinctive features.

According to Aristotle, virtue refers to an intermediate (mean), and the goal of virtue is to reach an intermediary between the two vices of excess and deficiency.[37] Such vices are not intentional, nor criminal in nature; rather, they are habitual and caused by a lack of virtue, mediocrity, and evil without intension. By contrast, the intermediate between these two vices is the "moral virtue" that Aristotle esteems the most.[38] Thus, although Aristotle's value judgment on the mean is similar to Confucius' moderation, it seems to be stronger and more explicit in support of the mean than Confucianism. Confucius at most lists the middle way as a criterion for distinguishing the gentleman from the small-minded person, while Aristotle makes intermediate the ideal choice over good and evil.

In Adam Smith's view, without propriety, there is no virtue.[39] Smith's *The Theory of Moral Sentiments* advocates that moral sentiments must encompass the six central values of sympathy, justice, conscience, prudence, benevolence, and self-command, but the main principle that constrains them all is propriety. Propriety is the central concept that runs through Smith's entire book. For instance, Part I of Smith's book is entitled "Of the Propriety of Action," and Part II and Part III are both on the subject of propriety. The word "propriety" is used 327 times and appears in each chapter, and it also appears in *The Wealth of Nations* 13 times. In contrast, his famous "invisible hand" reference appears only once in each book.

2.2.2 The Intermediate

Similar to moderate philosophy, the core of propriety is intermediateness which is the opposite of excess and insufficiency, though the boundary between the latter two is marked by relativity.[40] Aristotle lists 12 important values of human virtue, including courage, temperance, liberality, magnificence, magnanimity, proper ambition, patience, truthfulness, wittiness, friendliness, modesty, and righteous indignation. The essence of these values is the intermediate, designed to provide a reference for comparing the different concepts of insufficiency, excess, and appropriateness. For example, in Aristotle's view, insufficient modesty is shamelessness and excessive modesty is shyness, and the midpoint is to be natural. Similarly, lack of courage is cowardice and excessive courage is rashness, thus the intermediate option is bravery. He also mentions the standard of appropriate jokes in that excessive joking equates to teasing while the absence of joking results in dullness. Therefore, jokes need to be proportionate, witty, and popular, which requires the tellers' ability to adapt to the situation and act on it.[41] He reveals a simple quantitative concept of the intermediate: if 10 is too much and two is too little, then six is the center.[42]

The economic significance of propriety may necessitate a quantitative approach with measurable outcomes,[43] though this measure is not necessarily the absolute half of the middle point but refers to a middle range or interval. For example, ancient Greek aesthetics proposed a golden ratio of aesthetic beauty, not 0.5, but 0.618. The Parthenon in Athens was designed in strict accordance with the requirements of the golden ratio regarding its width and height, thus resulting in symmetry, harmony, and beauty. This also shows that an absolute, too-perfect midpoint is inappropriate and that the proper intermediate is more realistic, flexible, and feasible in giving certain mean boundaries and intervals.

Smith also stressed the need to constantly search for propriety. For example, to achieve proper and meaningful sympathy, a person needs to practice and experience a succession of errors, thereby developing a capacity to summarize and generalize their experiences.[44] According to Smith, as a basic ethical principle, it is common sense to seek benefits for oneself while avoiding doing harm to others, but it is not just to benefit oneself and harm others.[45] Therefore, in Smith's view, there is nothing wrong with the self-interest of businesspeople, but their self-interest must be within the appropriate middle range. In *The Wealth of Nations*, he argues that self-interested individuals should engage in fair exchanges of benefits and resources with competitors rather than resorting to unjust plunder.

2.2.3 Level of Difficulty

The achievement of propriety is simultaneously difficult and easy. Aristotle argues that it is not easy to find the middle because it requires the right person, acting in the right sphere, at the right time, in the right way, and with the right motivation.[46] Aristotle associates the intermediate with human character, emphasizing that the mean is the highest virtue and the ultimate right, thus making it more difficult for mortals to achieve.[47]

But Marcus Tullius Cicero (106–43 BCE), in his famous work *De Officiis* (*On Duties or On Obligations*), argues that appropriateness can be divided into two categories. One is universal propriety which exists in all noble activities, that is, propriety is noble for everything, and everything noble is propriety.[48] The other is subsidiary to universal propriety and involves specific, individual examples of noble action. Cicero's definition of universal propriety is a characteristic consistent with the excellence (*excellentiae*) that distinguishes man from other animals. Another propriety can be defined as moderation that is consistent with nature, in which moderation and self-restraint are expressed with a certain dignity in keeping with family status.[49] In other words, Cicero intends to divide propriety into two levels: the noble principle of excellence and specific acts of moderation, the first of which is difficult for ordinary people to attain, while the second is feasible and attainable with effort.

When it comes to Adam Smith, he did not agree with Confucius' or Aristotle's standard of nobility but borrowed from Cicero's idea of subsidiary propriety. In *The Theory of Moral Sentiments*, Smith proposes that one of the major meanings of propriety is "mediocrity," arguing that one's objective evaluation of propriety should also emphasize its ordinary nature. Like compassion, propriety is something that everyone can achieve because they are both natural traits innate in human existence.[50]

Smith's view is consistent with the interpretation of *yong* (庸) in the first Chinese classical text, *Erya*: "*yong* is also common," specifically referring to its ordinary nature.[51] Xi Zhu (1130–1200) adopted this interpretation, arguing that "*yong* is simply common."[52] During the Song dynasty, Chen Xiang (1017–1080) even emphasized that *zhong* (中) is a natural virtue, and *yong* is its common application.[53] Fuguan Xu (1904–1982) also believed that the so-called *yong* refers to ordinary behavior that everybody should practice and can achieve anytime and anywhere.[54] In this regard, Yuechuan Wang (1955–) outlined the interconnected meanings of *yong*: using the middle after identifying the two sides and achieving peace through common, consistent practice. These are all the essential meanings of moderation provided in Confucian texts.[55] Perhaps scholars after the Axial Age have lowered the standard of moderation and propriety, thus encouraging more ordinary people to learn and practice propriety.

Of course, others have offered alternative interpretations of the relationship between the common people and *yong*. Xun Zi (c. 313–238 BCE) mentioned that the hardened criminal requires immediate execution without the need for rehabilitation, while ordinary citizens should be educated without facing persecution from the government.[56] This means that wise people will succeed without education, unintelligent people will not benefit from education, and common people will need education before they understand.[57] Lu Xun (1881–1936), on the other hand, directly classifies moderation as laziness, the most common form of which is submission to destiny and the second form of which is mediocrity.[58]

2.2.4 Rationality

One of the major fundamentals of propriety is rationality. Unlike Confucius, Aristotle underscores that the virtue of the intermediate lies in reason, which in turn determines human wisdom. Since it is possible for many poor and rich people to lose their rationality, Aristotle closely links the intermediate with virtue, value, and reason.[59]

To attain the middle ground, Cicero proposes three fundamental principles: firstly, to subordinate desire to reason; secondly, to allocate greater efforts to tasks of utmost priority in accordance with their sequential importance; and thirdly, to be mindful of all matters influencing one's appearance and identity. But he underlines the first of these three principles as the most important. Obviously, the obstacle of reaching modest goals is greed and desire, but reason is a necessary or a sufficient condition for realizing propriety.[60]

However, Cicero opposes the "rational" sacrifice of propriety and moral standards in the name of national interest for which there can be no justification. Due to the ugly or despicable nature of some events, in his view, intelligent people would feel inclined to reject propriety for national salvation or other noble goals but such a sentiment is not based on sound moral principles.[61] As long as there is evil and ugliness, according to Cicero, there can be no efficiency.[62] Ugliness and vice are contrary to nature, which desires all things proper, moderate, and stable. Therefore, benefit and baseness cannot coexist. The typical manifestation of this inappropriateness is unlimited greed for wealth and power with its destructive consequences.[63] In this regard, David Hume (1711–1776) applies the standard of propriety to human self-interest in his *A Treatise of Human Nature,* emphasizing that most people, in reality, must love themselves more than others, but are not so selfish as to completely disregard the feelings and interests of others.[64]

Adam Smith also highlights that propriety lies in reason and self-command,[65] which is less stringent than self-control. While the latter is similar to religious precepts, the former is more rational, an essential element in propriety. The virtue of self-command comes from understanding and respecting others' emotions, a prerequisite to consciously restraining excessive passion, selfish actions, and irresponsible violence. Rationality is the natural enemy of arrogance, lack of control, and self-indulgence. Fear of the negative consequences of one's actions is only a superficial driving force, as it is phony, temporary, and incomplete, and will lead to more dangerous, frenzied outcomes over time. Only an impartial spectator with self-command can truly harness and control their passions and maintain stable, long-lasting rationality. Smith, in the sixth edition of *The Theory of Moral Sentiments* in 1790, begins to criticize the corruption of moral sentiments caused by admiration of the rich and contempt for the poor, which is precisely a manifestation of a lack of self-command and humanity.[66]

2.3 Definition of Propriety Philosophy

The synthetization of the above information from Eastern and Western literature makes it possible to give a definition of propriety that reflects both Chinese and Western philosophies, offering the guiding principles for economic thought. Philosophically, propriety can be defined as an impartial middle range of speech and action recognized by ordinary people under certain spatial and temporal conditions. This middle range comes from the subjective, evolutionary, rational, and relative assessment of normal people and has a positive, harmonious function with a moral, virtuous orientation. This definition reveals the six main principles of propriety philosophy.

2.3.1 Six Principles of Propriety Philosophy

The middle range represents the first aspect of propriety philosophy. Propriety requires that observation, analysis, and decision-making should follow a triadic perspective—insufficiency, excess, and moderation—because without the existence of the two ends, there is no middle; without the comparison of good and bad, it is impossible to find the appropriate boundary. Hence, the foundation of propriety is the concept of one divided into three.[67] However, this middle range is not the midpoint because the middle is not the absolute half, but a kind of moderate interval. In different situations, the propriety interval can be adjusted appropriately, and the range can be large or small. In contrast, the midpoint must be precise, fixed, and difficult to change.

Ordinariness is the second property of propriety following the common sense, knowledge, habits, and customs that are recognized by common people. The propriety standard must be subject to the constraints of common people's perceptions and public opinion, and can only be adjusted and changed in a timely, continuous manner. It is challenging to sustain any moderate words, actions, and standards that go against the majority of the people. More importantly, the author agrees with Xi Zhu and Adam Smith's views that moderation and propriety are not a dream that is unattainable for ordinary people, but realistic goals that can be achieved through proper efforts.

As the third fundamental aspect of propriety, subjectivity plays a pivotal role. In navigating the middle ground, it is essential to engage in the counterexample training advocated by Immanuel Kant (1724–1804), a process inherently subjective. First, it is crucial to define the boundary between inadequacy and excess and subsequently discern the midpoint between these extremes.[68] According to behavioral science's ideas of motivation and difference, the subject distinguishes diverse elements by identifying variations.[69] Recognizing the positive and negative poles aids in comprehending the world through distinct subjective judgments. By acknowledging these opposites, we can subjectively identify middle, appropriate, and neutral options. Collaborative efforts are necessary for a collective definition of "propriety." It is worth noting that subjectivity aligns with objectivity, and sensibility corresponds to rationality, drawing parallels between subjectivity and sensibility. However, subjectivity does not inherently imply irrationality. Different rational decision-makers may adopt diverse subjective choices to rectify deficiencies or excesses, giving rise to the possibility of subjective rationality or rational subjectivity.

The fourth critical feature of propriety is its historicity because the identification of propriety has a historical context, characterized by evolutionary development. Needless to say, what was deemed as propriety yesterday may not be applicable to the contemporary situation, hence it is problematic to build mathematical models of propriety economics, most of which are based on the stationary state of variables. However, propriety derives from evolutionary rationality that, although difficult to quantify, can still reduce emotional and impulsive short-term behavior.

The fifth attribute of propriety is its emphasis on neutrality, middle ground, and harmony which play a role in reducing polarized conflicts by facilitating a compromise between radical and conservative sides. Obviously, peace comes from compromise, which results from seeking the middle ground. Therefore, the middle is not only the essence of propriety but also a critical factor in promoting social and economic coordination, balance, and development.

The last aspect is relativity. Although propriety generally has a positive moral orientation, such a positive value is not absolute and unchanging. If propriety is pursued with excessive zeal, it would lead to excess. Extreme pursuit of propriety for a long period may lead to a lack of motivation and vitality for progress and provide an excuse for stagnation, laziness, conformism, and inertia.

In a nutshell, the philosophy of propriety is composed of six basic ideas—middle range, ordinariness, subjectivity, historicity, neutrality, and relativity—and they are the six keys to discovering, understanding, and explaining the concept of propriety economics.

2.3.2 Comparison of Eastern Moderation and Western Propriety

According to the above discussion of Chinese moderate philosophy and Western ideas of propriety, they are highly compatible in terms of intermediacy, subjectivity, relativity, and morality. However, the greatest difference between Confucius' middle ground and Aristotle's intermediate lies in rationality. Ancient Greek philosophy is based on reason and logic, emphasizing wisdom and knowledge, as well as legal balance and justice, thus providing the unique DNA for today's Western culture and science. In contrast, Confucius' Doctrine of the Mean is less entrenched in Western formal logical thought, and it is challenging to find direct literature addressing reason and science. Confucius places greater emphasis on moral evaluation, emotional states, human benevolence, and spiritual harmony, particularly advocating "respecting those worthy of respect," "keeping family matters private," and "keeping the secrets of the wise."[70] He introduces the perspective of "mutual concealment among family members," stating, "A father conceals for his son, and a son conceals for his father; it is straight within this."[71] Proposing that family faults should not be publicized, this approach appears to be driven not by a rational assessment of right and wrong or legal considerations but rather by a sentimental emphasis on family bonds and benevolence. However, Confucian benevolence does not necessarily oppose rationality; it might encompass an aspect that transcends rationality. Confucius' assertion, "At seventy, I could follow my heart's desire without overstepping the bounds,"[72] suggests that even when acting according to personal desires, one should not exceed established norms and regulations, reflecting a high degree of alignment between desire and reason.

Meanwhile, Confucius' moderation emphasizes a cycle of obedience— individual to family, family to state, and state to ruler. It supports the ethical observance of a hierarchical system and the pursuit of realistic compromise and harmony. Aristotle's and Adam Smith's propriety, on the other hand, respects individual freedom and satisfies self-interest, although it also underlines the pursuit of metaphysical virtue.[73]

Additionally, Adam Smith's view of the impartial spectator, developed from Aristotle's philosophy of the intermediate, does not mention Confucius' ideas of neutrality and harmony. However, the function of the impartial spectator is to mediate the confrontation and conflict between the two extreme sides and provide arbitration among reality, rationality, and spirituality from a moderate, moral perspective, so that the two opposing sides can reflect on themselves and resolve conflicts. Therefore, there is a certain intersection between the impartial spectator and the ideas of neutrality and harmony.

Actually, Smith's moral philosophy, which incorporated Aristotle's idea of the mean, also has many intrinsic similarities with Confucian thought. The Confucian concepts of benevolence, righteousness, courtesy, and wisdom have essential compatibilities with Smith's ideas on sympathy, justice, respect, and self-command. Moreover, the relationship between Confucian authority and Smith's views on judges and politicians also requires attention.[74]

After establishing a clear definition of propriety philosophy, the following chapters will proceed to scrutinize the theories and methodologies of significant Western schools of economics. This entails an in-depth analysis of the implicit notions of propriety within these theories and methods, concluding in the formulation of a comprehensive definition and research framework for propriety economics.

Chapter 3

Balance and Equilibrium in Classical and Neoclassical Economics

Aristotle's concept of propriety has exerted a profound influence not only on Western philosophy but also on the underpinnings of Western economic thought. This influence is discernible within the frameworks of five major economic schools: classical, neoclassical, institutional, behavioral, and cultural economics. This chapter seeks to furnish a comprehensive literature review that serves as a foundation for a systematic exploration of the propriety concepts embedded within classical and neoclassical economics.

3.1 The Idea of Balance in Classical Economics

In 1733, 26 years before Adam Smith published *The Theory of Moral Sentiments*, the English poet Alexander Pope (1688–1744) published *An Essay on Man*, in which he wisely proposed that:

> All Nature is but Art unknown to Thee
> All Chance, Direction, which thou canst not see
> All Discord, Harmony, not understood
> All partial Evil, universal Good:
> And, spite of Pride, in erring Reason's spite
> One truth is clear, "Whatever is, is right."[1]

When exploring the idea of propriety in classical and neoclassical economics, we need to comprehend it in art, discover it in coincidence, understand it in chaos, and recognize short-term, fragmented, and partial evil as a kind of overall balance, harmony, and goodness. This would help scholars approach the ideal, overcome arrogance, discover existing truths, and know reason. The origin of propriety economic ideas probably began with Adam Smith after Aristotle devised the philosophy of propriety. As a founder of classical economics, Smith was the first person to bring together moral philosophy and economic theory. Through two important works, *The Theory of Moral Sentiments* (1759) and *The Wealth of Nations* (1776), Smith synthesized, articulated, and developed the philosophy of propriety and provided an important starting point for the creation of propriety economics.

3.1.1 Propriety Ideas in *The Theory of Moral Sentiments*

Smith's *The Theory of Moral Sentiments* serves as a philosophical foundation for propriety economics, mainly in ethical and intellectual perspectives, while *The Wealth of Nations* proposes an economic theory. His first book, *The Theory of Moral Sentiments*, suggests that moral sentiments must include the core values, such as sympathy, justice, conscience, prudence, benevolence, and self-command, but the main principle guiding these core values is the philosophy of propriety, which provides the philosophical foundation for the balance of market supply and demand. Although *The Wealth of Nations* became a classic in economics, Smith believed *The Theory of Moral Sentiments* to be "superior to *The Wealth of Nations*,"[2] and the philosophy of propriety became an axiomatic foundation for Smith's moral philosophy and a major guide for other disciplines, including economics.[3] Given the fact that the emphasis on the importance and necessity of propriety philosophy is not original to Smith, it is a major ethical innovation for Smith to identify and determine what constitutes propriety, and his works provide an important resource for propriety economics.

For one thing, Smith promotes the view of the impartial spectator, emphasizing that the judgment of propriety cannot be rendered by two subjective parties, but by a neutral third party thereby promoting the principles of objectivity and neutrality. Moreover, this spectator gradually evolves from a real spectator to an ideal spectator, and finally to an invisible spectator with a spiritual perspective.

This spiritual spectator is the individual within, residing in the conscience or the heart. As highlighted by Weidong Luo and others, Adam Smith's concept of the "invisible hand" represents self-interest within the bounds of propriety. Yet, adhering to the principle of propriety, individuals may naturally cultivate a measure of concern for others, inadvertently shaping society[4] and fostering a balanced social environment.

Conceiving the spectator as having three possible levels of relationships with the person in question—stranger, acquaintance, and friend— Smith describes the differences in the behavior of the same individual in different situations.[5] According to Smith, a major condition for the proper use of moral sentiments is to know the other person and to be in agreement with the other person's passions. Smith makes two points in this regard: first, to be well-informed about the other person; second, to be unbiased and neutral. In Smith's view, precision or clarity of feeling can only be found in the sympathetic, impartial, and well-informed spectator.[6] Therefore, Smith suggests that there is often a difference in the degree of sympathy generated by the geographical proximity of the sympathizer and the sympathized.

In addition, Smith underscores prudence and benevolence. For the sake of our happiness, people's motives and goals are enshrined in self-interest, which in turn may produce negative social effects. Thus, we are required to be prudent in self-interest: in assessing our motives, taking actions, and predicting their consequences. Smith argues that our happiness requires the virtue of prudence, while caring about others' happiness requires the virtues of benevolence, righteousness, and charity,[7] which serve to enhance their happiness rather than harm them. While good intentions, in general, do not give rise to negative results, rendering good deeds in a particular fashion, such as giving alms in a high-profile public manner and expecting gratitude from the beneficiaries may, in fact, constitute secondary harm. In the summary of Part VI of *The Theory of Moral Sentiments*, Smith states that there are five principal virtues beneficial to the well-being of oneself and others: prudence, justice, benevolence, self-command, and propriety.[8]

Finally, many of the core values articulated in *The Theory of Moral Sentiments* can be demonstrated by experiments in neuroscience. For example, Tania Singer has shown that the neuronal circuit of empathy exists in every human brain, concentrated in about eight regions.[9] In addition, Paul Zak's experiments provide physiological and psychological neuroscientific support for Smith's *The Theory of Moral Sentiments*. There is a widely held belief in the existence of a hormonal triangle in humans: oxytocin, responsible for compassion; serotonin, involved in punishment; and dopamine, regulating generosity. Moreover, these three hormones play a dominant role in three categories of moral behavior: sympathy, retribution, and altruism. In particular, sympathy controls sentiments regarding generosity and punishment. In contrast, compassion is inversely proportional to punishment and revenge—the stronger the desire for revenge, the less the feeling of compassion. In this regard, Zak provides an "Empathy-Generosity-Punishment" model for Smith's *The Theory of Moral Sentiments*.[10]

Therefore, Smith provides the means of understanding, observing, and practicing propriety from the perspective of human beings' moral sentiments. In this way, Smith elevates the moral level of propriety and offers a basis for the regulation and development of propriety in economics. More importantly, Smith puts forward a criterion: the key to making propriety policy is to have a decision-maker with a due measure of moderation as well as a moral sense of propriety.

3.1.2 Propriety Economic Function of an "Invisible Hand"

It must be clarified that Adam Smith's metaphor of an "invisible hand" is not directly related to the market, but to the idea of balance and propriety. It is necessary to point out that Smith mentions an invisible hand only once in one article and once in his two famous books.

For example, Smith first mentions an invisible hand not in his *The Theory of Moral Sentiments* (1759), nor in *The Wealth of Nations* (1776), but in his earlier "History of Astronomy" written before 1758. Although it was not published during his lifetime, it was the only manuscript that he did not want to destroy when burning all his papers before his death, clearly demonstrating how much he cherished this work.[11] In 1980, it was included in a collection of Smith's writings from the archives of Glasgow University in Scotland where he had served as chancellor, edited and published by Oxford University Press.

> For it may be observed, that in all polytheistic religions, among savages, as well as in the early ages of Heathen antiquity, it is the irregular events of nature only that are ascribed to the agency and power of their gods. Fire burns, and water refreshes; heavy bodies descend, and lighter substances fly upwards, by the necessity of their own nature; nor was the invisible hand of Jupiter ever apprehended to be employed in those matters.[12]

This is Smith's attempt to explain the limitations of the invisible hand from the perspective of the universe, Jupiter, or God, because earlier societies had not discovered or could not explain the phenomena of water, fire, or geocentric attraction that occurs on Earth.

The second time the phrase an "invisible hand" appears was in Smith's *The Theory of Moral Sentiments*, published in 1759. He describes a selfish landowner who is led by an invisible hand to distribute his harvest to those working for him.

> The proud and unfeeling landlord views his extensive fields, and without a thought for the wants of his brethren, in imagination consumes himself the whole harvest ... [Yet] the capacity of his stomach bears no proportion to the immensity of his desires ... the rest he will be obliged to distribute among those ... all of whom thus derive from his

> luxury and caprice ... The rich ... are led by an invisible
> hand to make nearly the same distribution of the necessaries
> of life ... and thus without intending it, without knowing it,
> advance the interest of the society.[13]

This example indicates that while the selfish desire of the rich is
unlimited, their ability to consume is limited. Without the desire
and imagination of the rich to create wealth, they will not have the
motivation to invest in the land and employ farmers. However, once
a rich man succeeds in becoming wealthy, he can only consume
the excess resources, thus, as self-interested as he is, the landowner
unknowingly provides benefits to society as a whole.

The third and last reference to an invisible hand is found in Smith's
The Wealth of Nations published in 1776.[14]

> He generally, indeed, neither intends to promote the
> public interest, nor knows how much he is promoting it.
> By preferring the support of domestic to that of foreign
> industry, he intends only his own security; and by directing
> that industry in such a manner as its produce may be of
> the greatest value, he intends only his own gain, and he is
> in this, as in many other cases, led by an invisible hand to
> promote an end which was no part of his intention. Nor is
> it always the worse for the society that it was not part of it.
> By pursuing his own interest, he frequently promotes that of
> the society more effectually than when he really intends to
> promote it.

The meaning here is that the primary purpose of investors in
domestic industries over foreign industries is security rather than the
maximization of direct profits, although the security of such domestic
investments helps to promote the interests of society in an objective,
long-term sense.[15] This rational consideration of investment security

satisfies two assumptions of classical economics: full rationality and the pursuit of profit maximization.[16]

Although the meanings of the three aforementioned "invisible hands" differ, they all reflect an invisible function of balance and moderation: the subjective will of the individual is often the opposite of the objective, and self-interested subjective desire often leads to consequences that benefit society and others. This divine function of balance and moderation is omnipresent, especially in the economic sphere where supply and demand are out of balance.

3.1.3 *The Wealth of Nations* and the Idea of Propriety Economics

If *The Theory of Moral Sentiments* provides guidance and prescriptions for the ideas, morals, and concepts of propriety, Smith's *The Wealth of Nations* reveals a theory of the market that directly reflects the essence of propriety economics. Smith mentions the market as many as 623 times in *The Wealth of Nations*, although he does not define it. Smith believes in "an open and free market,"[17] where buyers and sellers make exchanges voluntarily. Buying and selling, supply and demand, or producers and consumers determine the results of market transactions and competition. The most important factor in determining the market mechanism is price, which is the "third party" of the game between supply and demand, both objective and measurable. The price is capable of forcing both sides of the transaction to be rational, appropriate, and balanced. Moreover, the price of free competition is the lowest, while the price of monopoly is the highest.[18]

For example, if a producer is too greedy and the price is too high, then consumers are bound to choose other products, thus creating a chain reaction—generating extra supply over demand, forcing producers to reduce prices, leading to economic depression, and ultimately harming their interests. Similarly, if manufacturers offer too low prices and expect to profit through massive dumping, it will probably destroy the market price mechanism, which will lead to higher production costs, lower wages for employees, and reduced employee retention. This may also lead to insufficient production capacity, unsustainable costs of low-priced products, and corporate bankruptcy.

Therefore, in the game of consumers seeking maximum satisfaction and producers chasing maximum profit, both sides can only compromise and follow the principle of propriety. On the one hand, enterprises must be fine-tuned and effectively use human capital and material resources to reduce costs, control prices, and ensure quality, while satisfying the need for profit and maximizing resource allocation, ultimately leading to a balance between corporate profits and societal interests. On the other hand, consumers should not be too greedy by seeking excessively cheap products while insisting on good quality because doing so will result in lower consumer demand and less purchasing power. Consequently, this may lead to market supply surpassing demand, forcing enterprises to close, and finally, demand exceeds supply, sending prices soaring and engendering an inflationary crisis. In a fair, free market system, price is a major signal. In a time of poor harvest, the price of food must rise, which will encourage landlords to invest in agriculture and produce more food, and the food crisis will be alleviated, so that individual and societal interests may be rationally and appropriately balanced.[19]

Smith devotes Chapter 5 of Book I of *The Wealth of Nations* to the relationship between the actual price and the natural price of commodities.[20] In commercial trade, Smith believes that there are two prices: the natural price of a commodity, measured by money; and the actual price of a commodity, which comprises labor and risk, including non-economic risks. In other words, the actual price of a commodity is the amount of labor, not the amount of money, required. Additionally, Smith analyzes the difference between the market price and the natural price in Chapter 7, Book I of *The Wealth of Nations*. The natural price consists of the rent, wages, and profits paid at the natural rate for the production, manufacture, and transportation of goods to the market.

Although the natural price is the one floor that every investor wants to accept in a market where supply and demand are equal, due to the invariable fluctuation of market supply and demand, price changes due to these variations are the actual market price.[21]

For example, a natural or human disaster in a certain place at a certain time that results in an increased demand for food will lead to a higher market price than the natural price. Similarly, if the number of people involved in investment and production has increased extraordinarily, resulting in a greater supply than demand, then the market price will be infinitely close to or even lower than the cost. Smith's view is that, when the market price is high, there will be a large number of investors and a labor influx, thus creating a greater supply than demand and a gradual shift of market price closer to the natural price. On the other hand, when the market price is low, the lack of profit will lead to the withdrawal of a large number of investors and labor, which will in turn gradually rebalance supply and demand and approximate the market price and the natural price. Propriety philosophy has a positive effect on society, similar to the balancing effect of the price mechanism on economic operations and market supply and demand.[22] Therefore, price, market, impartial spectator, and propriety are like valves that can restrain excessive human greed from getting out of control. Admittedly, people need passion and an "accelerator" to pursue wealth, but they must use the "brake" of rationality and moderation, which is also the ideological basis of *The Wealth of Nations*.[23]

Smith pays particular attention to the balance of the market and the propriety achieved through such balance. The question of supply and demand, in Smith's view, is the essence of a balanced market. *The Wealth of Nations* mentions "demand" 319 times and "supply" 178 times while emphasizing that the market price of each particular commodity is regulated by the relationship between the actual commodity quantity in the market and the demand of those willing to pay its natural price or, rather, the full value of the rent, labor, and profit that must be paid in order to bring the commodity to the market.[24] This statement reflects Smith's unique understanding of the market, where the market price is determined by the number of goods supplied and the consumers' willingness to demand them. In addition, the determination of this ratio of supply to demand is a regulated market.

It is worth noting that Smith mentions the word "balance" 90 times in *The Wealth of Nations*, which clearly reveals his idea of propriety economics. Broadly speaking, Smith's concept of balance is expressed in six main themes. The first is to balance the supply and demand equation, expressed in the supply and demand of products,[25] production, and consumption.[26] The second is to balance the labor issue, demonstrated by wages and commodity prices,[27] wages and profits,[28] and the free movement of labor.[29] The third is to balance financial calculations, including profit and loss,[30] income and expenditure,[31] borrowing and loans,[32] and income tax and customs duties.[33] The fourth is to balance the trade ledger, including imports and exports[34] and free trade and monopoly trade.[35] The fifth is to balance the connection between religion and politics, seen in the relationship between the British King's autocracy and colonial self-government,[36] monarchical power and divine power,[37] and the royal authority and the landed aristocracy.[38] Finally, it is imperative to strike a balance in the conundrum of freedom and security.[39] For example, Smith focuses on the balance of trade, mentioning this issue 29 times, but he opposes both the unfavorable balance of trade[40] and the over-balance[41] in other areas, embodying the principle of propriety. At the same time, he believes that all government "statutory regulations" must demonstrate great propriety;[42] in addition, banks can pay advances to traders, but must pay "propriety advance."[43]

In particular, Smith addresses the principle of "equal propriety,"[44] reminding both parties involved in the transaction of the need for reason, compassion, and mutual respect. According to Smith, both government regulations and market mechanisms need to be guided by propriety. *The Theory of Moral Sentiments* is of a higher or more advanced level than *The Wealth of Nations*,[45] where propriety moral sentiments constitute the philosophical guidelines and basic criteria for propriety market regulation.

However, Smith's *The Wealth of Nations*, published 17 years later, developed the notion of propriety that had been articulated in *The Theory of Moral Sentiments* and put forward the idea of "equal propriety" subtly and wisely.[46] For example, when referring to citizens' obligations, he argues that all members of the public must contribute generally to the maintenance of good roads and communications and the promotion of the societal good as a whole and that such contributions are not unjust, but natural.[47] Smith's concept of free government[48] provides a new way to interpret his ideas: the market can be free and monopolistic; similarly, the government can be autocratic and free. In other words, freedom is not reserved for the market only and autocracy is not the sole purview of government. Moreover, in *The Theory of Moral Sentiments*, Smith repeatedly emphasizes the idea of propriety government[49] and encourages people to think deeply about the positive relationship between "good government" and wisdom, order, reason, sensibility, divinity, life, and happiness.[50] According to Smith, commerce and manufacturing may by degrees introduce order and good government, and with them, the liberty and safety of individuals,[51] thus demonstrating that commerce can first introduce order and then liberty, and that the interaction of government stability and market liberty can achieve positive effects. At the same time, Smith is by no means opposed to law and government regulation, pointing out that those laws and customs that are very favorable to small farmers may have contributed more to the prosperity of England than all the commercial regulations advocated by merchants put together.[52]

The concept of equal propriety is crucial because it advocates the idea of a balance between market and intervention, and promotes the establishment of a two-way responsibility between the market and the government, so as to eliminate the exclusive, extreme choice of market monopoly or government monopoly. Yining Li has also proposed that moral regulation can serve as a lever for propriety economic development and a middle way to bridge bipolar choices,[53] aiming to promote moral market and moral government, as well as the controllability of the market and the limitation of government.

As Maria Paganelli adds, "For the classical Greeks and Romans, extremes are dangerous because they are too far away to be seen and known. A middle position is therefore preferred to an 'extreme' position." Furthermore, Paganelli asserts that, in contrast to modern economics, which assumes unbiased information and error-free behavior, Smith's economics scrutinizes and dissects systematically biased information that gives rise to consistent errors. Recognizing this systematic bias and endorsing a middle-ground stance allow us to grasp Smith's perspective on usury, where he champions a balanced, middle-of-the-road approach. He contends that "the free market and legally controlled interest rates are both ways to follow the general moral rule, 'in medio stat virtus,' (virtue stands in the middle) and to maintain an orderly good society."[54]

Hence, the market theory of supply and demand, which is based on the philosophy of propriety, can guide the linkage and balance between the theory of individual behavior and that of social order. It can also provide a feasible, logically self-consistent path for later economists to combine empirical evidence and mathematical models, ultimately incorporating the three dimensions of philosophy, ethics, and circumstance into the framework of economic analysis.[55] It will provide great possibilities and opportunities for developing propriety economics.

3.2 Equilibrium in Neoclassical Economics

If Smith's theory of balance between supply and demand, which is embedded in the theory of prices and markets, laid the foundation for the concept of propriety in economics, then the general equilibrium theory of neoclassical doctrine has further enriched it. Alfred Marshall

(1842–1924), a representative of the Cambridge School, proposed the general equilibrium theory in 1890, which exemplified propriety economic thought to some extent.

3.2.1 General Equilibrium Theory

Marshall published *Principles of Economics* in 1890 and proposed the three aspects of equilibrium price, which were similar to Smith's principles of balance and propriety.[56] Marshall uses the idea of marginal utility to show that the demanded quantity increases as prices fall and decreases as prices rise; at the same time, he applies the concept of the marginal cost of production to indicate that high prices lead to more supply and low prices result in less supply. More importantly, he combines the principles of demand and supply to form the law of equilibrium price, wisely proposing that when the price of supply and the price of demand are consistent, the demanded quantity and the supplied quantity will also be consistent, creating the equilibrium price.[57]

The general equilibrium price system proposed by Marshall's neoclassical theory reveals that for consumers, equilibrium prices can help determine the inputs they need at a given price to maximize their consumption ability without being wasteful or extravagant. As for producers, firms also need to be bound by a given price to decide on inputs and outputs to maximize their production profits by neither overestimating nor underestimating their capacities or wasting valuable resources. Given this price system is shaped by both supply and demand, each product market and input market will reach an equilibrium of total supply and total demand. Therefore, to ensure that a unique, predictable equilibrium is obtained, neoclassical economic theory assumes diminishing returns. If a firm is far ahead in the market, it will experience higher costs or other forms of negative feedback, and as a result, market share will stabilize at a predictable unique equilibrium level.[58]

Correspondingly, classical game theory studies the idea that, given the possible choices when dealing with one's opponents, the economic subject needs to choose the correct strategies, actions, and resource allocations based on a certain criterion that aims at the optimal choice. For example, the rational expectations theory is the study of what expectations are consistent with the outcomes created when combining all the potentials together. This convenient "equilibrium shortcut" is a natural approach to the study of economic models and it also leaves room for mathematical analysis.[59]

Marshall combines the traditional supply determination (Smith's labor theory of value) with demand determination. He believes that the market price of commodities determines the balance of power between supply and demand, like the two edges of a pair of scissors, which act and interact together, thus establishing the theory of equilibrium price.[60] Marshall also trusts that there seem to be two opposing forces in human progress. On the one hand, the pursuit of satisfaction, like a car's throttle, motivates human beings to constantly pursue the maximum benefit; on the other hand, the avoidance of sacrifice inhibits impulsiveness or excess, like a car's brake, and compels the driver to act cautiously. There is no value judgment on the functions of the throttle or brake. They adequately reflect the ideas of propriety and equilibrium,[61] which are in line with the third principle of the aforementioned philosophy of propriety—the principle of historicity.

3.2.2 Benchmark and Assumptions

Neoclassical economic theory proposes an ideal benchmark for economic functions and performance though in reality such near-perfect assumptions and ideals are difficult to achieve. However, for the sake of mathematical modeling, such pure benchmarks become necessary, and in the design of goals for economic development, the establishment of high standards helps to motivate the degree and direction of efforts.

Based on the two major assumptions of classical economics, rationality and profit maximization, Léon Walras (1834–1910) proposed three other major assumptions. One is that of full or perfect information, which supposes that economic subjects know the price, quality, utility, and production methods well when they sign contracts and conduct transactions, and that they will invariably make decisions based on sufficient information. Thus, it is useless to cheat each other because the other party will surely find out the truth sooner or later.

The second is the market-clearing assumption, that is, prices have complete flexibility and can be automatically adjusted; various markets can always achieve complete balance between demand and supply, and there will be neither a continuous surplus nor a persistent shortage. That is to say, all the market products will be sold out or clear, maintaining perfect balance, equilibrium, and constancy, thus the price is called the market-clearing or equilibrium price.

The third is the assumption of perfect competition, that is, all enterprises in the industry practice perfect competition, but each small enterprise cannot create any significant impact on the industry as a whole or become a monopoly. In particular, each firm uses the same technology and the same cost to produce the same product, the product is sold at the same price, and the firm does not have any pricing power. Only when these conditions are met, the market is the best and the result will be Pareto optimal. Once there are deviations from this model of perfect competition, a monopoly is formed.[62] These assumptions represent the benchmark of neoclassical economic theory, demonstrating an ideal goal.[63]

But in reality, people need to choose between their behavior and the outcome of such behavior under given constraints to achieve the optimal equilibrium, which may combine individual, collective, and societal benefits. Thus, producers and consumers through tangible or intangible competition with each other will eventually obtain market equilibrium. The theoretical and philosophical support behind this equilibrium is propriety.

3.2.3 The Propriety of General Equilibrium Theory

The general equilibrium theory promoted by the neoclassical school of economics embodies some of the ideas of propriety economics. First of all, it demonstrates the aim to balance the contradiction between infinite desire and limited resources, and between equity and efficiency. The infinite desire for self-interest vs. limited economic resources is an eternal dilemma.[64] Neoclassical economics adds a fourth element to Smith's three factors of production (labor, land, and capital): the owner of a business organization.[65] In this regard, Ronald Coase (1910–2013) argues that not only did Marshall mention the organization, but John Bates Clark (1847–1938) also discusses the existence of the organization as a coordinating function for entrepreneurs.[66] Of course, there are also economic entities that are subject to the constraints of time, knowledge, technology, management, data, and resources. Due to infinite desire and limited resources, human beings must search for assessments, choices, and balance, as advocated by the third principle of propriety philosophy, to minimize resource consumption, increase output, and maximize the satisfaction of social needs.[67] As a result, Pareto improvement (an idea derived from neoclassical economics which refers to a situation where it is possible to make one party better off without negatively affecting another party),[68] marginal utility, and the Lausanne School have led to the creation and development of welfare economics.

Welfare economics believes that the main motive of economic research is to "help social improvement."[69] The first fundamental theorem of welfare economics proves the optimality of the competitive market system in allocating resources because competitive equilibrium leads to perfect compatibility between the rational profit-seeking behavior of individuals and the optimal allocation of social resources.[70] In view of the fact that markets are not omnipotent and market failures are inevitable, economists need to design the boundaries of market applicability. For example, once any of the three neoclassical assumptions fail to materialize, including incomplete information, imperfect competition in the market, and the economic externalities or the spillover effect, etc., the mathematical models of Pareto improvement and welfare economics may need to propose a series of mechanisms to correct the market failure and prevent inefficient allocation in the market.[71] As another example, the competitive equilibrium with transfers promoted by welfare economics aims to redistribute the wealth of individuals, so as to take the middle path and act appropriately in dealing with the dilemma of efficiency vs. equity, and finally reach economic equilibrium.[72] At the same time, according to the second theorem of welfare economics, any Pareto optimality can be successfully realized through the redistribution of individual wealth appropriately and then promote the competitive market mechanism. The essential meaning is that in reality, the market may lead to unfair distribution, uneven allocation of resources, and serious polarization between the rich and the poor. As a result, it may be useful for the government to impose progressive tax policies, such as income tax, real estate tax, etc., to compensate the poor. It is also possible to increase various kinds of subsidies and concessions, introduce support for industrial policies, increase tariffs, and subsidize compulsory education and other policies.[73]

The above discussion demonstrates the most basic function of propriety economics: if the market mechanism is overused, resulting in excessive efficiency and deficient equity, then it is highly necessary to use the government's function to correct it, especially in public services, including public health, public education, public security, etc. Similarly, if government intervention is excessive, resulting in an inefficient market, it is essential to rely on the market mechanism. However, the vital point of propriety economics is that once the market is overly competitive, it is clearly not acceptable to abandon the market. Correspondingly, low efficiency does not mean that the government should be abolished. Rather, the market and the government need to coordinate and operate appropriately, through the reallocation of initial endowment, redistribution of wealth, and reoperation of the competitive market. In particular, the government should not interfere with prices and confuse the market[74] because these initiatives are not in line with the six fundamentals of propriety philosophy. In fact, propriety is also an ideal state, similar to the five assumptions of classical and neoclassical economics that are difficult, if not impossible, to achieve, but without this lofty goal toward propriety, human conduct tends to be more prone to the two extremes, thus creating either insufficiency or excess.

Incorporating the principle of propriety, competitive equilibrium shares a close relationship with general equilibrium. Competitive equilibrium denotes a state where the total demand for all goods does not surpass the aggregate supply, all while maximizing consumer satisfaction and producer profits. The idea of propriety, as reflected in the concept of competitive equilibrium, is mainly inherent in the welfare nature of neoclassical economics. On the one hand, competitive equilibrium needs to consider the most efficient allocation of resources; on the other hand, it needs to reflect the equality and fair utility of such resource allocation.[75]

For example, although dealing with the COVID-19 pandemic gave governments significant power to deploy resources rapidly and reduced friction during a particular period, speedy action may lead to an unfair skewing of resources and the reality that disadvantaged groups have less access to treatments and high mortality rates. Hence, economists need to strengthen the study of the external phenomena of consumption and production to explore the balance between efficiency and equity, which is also a problem of propriety faced by welfare economics.[76]

Further, the general equilibrium theory was initially completed with mathematical modeling. In 1874, Walras used a mathematical model of a competitive economy to explain how many small economic entities interact with each other to achieve equilibrium. Later, the Italian economist Vilfredo Pareto (1848–1923) refined the mathematical model. Both of them, similar to Marshall, wanted to study the efficiency of equilibrium and the optimal social development, stressing the link between demand and consumer preferences, and the relationship between manufacturers and profit maximization. In this regard, Walras argues that equilibrium should exist as long as the number of price variables is equal to the number of equations.[77]

However, the biggest problem of neoclassical equilibrium theory is that it is too idealistic and, as Herbert Simon points out, it is a kind of "economics of static equilibrium,"[78] which lacks a historical evolutionary perspective on economic phenomena. It also places too much emphasis on the optimal, while in reality, economic entities often get only temporary satisfaction or barely acceptable results.

In essence, the concept of balancing supply and demand, as evident in classical economics, and the pursuit of price equilibrium in neoclassical economics continue to be the central tenets of Western economics. It is essential to note that "balance" and "equilibrium" carry distinct meanings. "Balance" primarily refers to the interaction of two forces (such as demand and supply) within a medium (such as the market), even if these forces offset each other. In this context, the market remains in a state of ongoing motion, and external interventions (such as government actions) can be introduced to continually monitor and stabilize the market, aiming for a measure of equilibrium. Conversely, "equilibrium" signifies that opposing elements (e.g., efficiency and equity, price and cost) are in equal measure, proportion, and strength. When two forces reach equilibrium, they not only share equal magnitude but also maintain an opposite relationship. For instance, higher efficiency may come at the expense of equity, and higher prices might entail lower costs.

While it is true that many economists have challenged or even rejected classical and neoclassical notions of balance and equilibrium since the 1970s, the principle of the "middle way" or propriety economic thought prompts us to reevaluate the contributions of our predecessors. This reevaluation should focus on their ideological and historical significance. Importantly, the concepts of balance and equilibrium serve as the initial reference points for propriety economics and form the essential foundation for its ongoing development and refinement.

Chapter 4

The Neutrality of Institutional Economics and the Subjectivity of Behavioral Economics

Beyond the concepts of balance and equilibrium found in classical and neoclassical economics, both institutional and behavioral economics offer valuable insights for propriety economics. A concise literature review will serve as a valuable tool to unearth key concepts and further enrich the academic study of propriety economics.

4.1 The Neutrality of Institutional Economics

Institutional economics, encompassing both old and new institutional economics, harbors numerous elements that comprise the core tenets of propriety philosophy, namely, neutrality, historicity, and relativity.

4.1.1 Neutralization Efforts of Old Institutional Economics

Emerging in the 1920s as a response to critiques of neoclassical economics, old institutional economics represented a distinctively American perspective on economic theory. Notably, John Commons (1862–1945), a prominent economist, played a pivotal role in shaping the neutral, moderate stance of the old institutional economics school. His ideological alignment leaned toward moderation and neutrality.

Commons promotes the neutralizing function of institutions and laws designed to resolve conflicts and reconcile different interests. The law, in his view, can play the most effective neutralizing role by helping to resolve disputes peacefully, reasonably, and legally. The two sides of the transaction will not fall into a zero-sum game because they have a mutual need for interdependence, which will help a capitalist society to respect the legal system, dilute class confrontation, avoid war and conflict, and promote sustainable economic development.[1]

While stressing the role of law, Commons particularly praises the position of the courts. He proposes a concept of "reasonable value"— not any individual's opinion of what is reasonable, but a reasonable decision made by the court in light of the different claims of the plaintiff and the defendant. It is objective, measurable in monetary terms, and mandatory,[2] showing that through the court system, it is possible to reconcile the interests of different individuals and to obtain an obligatory arrangement acceptable to the contending parties, thereby alleviating social conflicts. In a sense, the function of the judge regarding the plaintiff and the defendant is similar to that of the impartial spectator, who represents an objective, institutional, and compulsory law.[3]

In this regard, Commons emphasizes the significance of the Supreme Court, which represents an "unwritten constitution."[4] He argues that the Supreme Court played a critical role in the 1930s in setting the United States on a different path from that of the German and Italian fascist states because it inhibited the development of monopolistic capitalism in the U.S., a likely bridge to fascism.[5] Through the Court's efforts, its decisions could either punish bad behaviors or evolve good social customs into law. As a result, "a local practice becomes common law for the nation."[6] But Commons overlooks the role of culture as a constraint on institutions although "bad" culture can be destructive to "good" institutions. For instance, in a culture where power and wealth hold sway, lawlessness may proliferate, regardless of court rulings. Consequently, we cannot separate the discourse on the system from the prevailing culture.

In addition, old institutional economics supports collectives and organizations that are capable of transcending the individual-led market and state-led government by proposing a moderately regulated collective between the individual and the state. Commons' theory of the collective proposes an institutional hypothesis in the sense that it is the "collective action in control of individual action."[7] Moreover, according to Commons, the constraints on individual "working rules" by firms, companies, unions, employers' associations, or trade organizations are more powerful than the collective action of national politics.[8] That is, individuals are subject not only to general social and national rules but also to the rules of particular organizations. This coincides with the role of corporations, as later emphasized by Ronald Coase, as an important collective between the individual and the state.

According to Commons, ostensibly, collective actions control individual actions to the detriment of individual liberty and interests, but the purpose and outcome of such control are always beneficial to the individual. Indeed, collective actions establish the boundaries between people in terms of their rights and obligations, as well as social relations in terms of the absence of rights and obligations. For example, collective action can effectively require individuals to implement a specific goal and refrain from certain behavior and can produce a sense of security, compliance, and freedom for individuals. Collective operating rules also become common principles that guide individuals' economic behavior and can help compel, prevent, and determine what a person can or cannot, must or need not, do. In particular, Commons argues that the creation of such collective organizations and their rules are based on historical experiences of conflict, negotiation, compromise, and the contract between individuals. Thus, the decisions of some organizational leaders provide the conventions to be followed in the future.[9] In this way, the collective institutional identity, through collective actions, can help to reconcile conflicting interests among individuals, constrain their irrational behaviors, and ultimately determine rational institutional arrangements that promote individual conduct in the interests of society.

Rational trading is another principle supported by old institutional economics. Commons argues that traditional economics, such as classical and neoclassical schools, has been the study of material goods.

However, the subject of economics, in his view, should be expanded from the old concepts of commodities, labor, and desires to the most basic formula of economic activity, namely, transaction. In this way, a transaction evolves from a simple transfer of goods or labor to a relationship between people, which gives a human significance to transactions. Thus, traditional trading activities, managers' supervision of workers, and the state's taxation of individuals can all be linked and grouped together through transactions for in-depth study and comparison.[10]

The transactions of economic activity can be divided into bargaining transactions, managerial transactions, and rationing transactions, but, according to Commons, all of these are units of social activity between people of equal status or between superiors and subordinates. The units of the transaction can more effectively explain and resolve the relationship between "conflict, dependence, and order," overturning the traditional concepts of "commodity, labor, desire, individual, and exchange." As a result, the nature of people's transactions is closely linked to ethics, law, and economics, and legal economics and ethical economics may become two new disciplines.[11]

Moreover, Commons elevates the transaction to an institutional level, that is, the transaction of ownership, which must involve the social habits, traditions, and customs of both parties to the transaction. Their different or similar cultures, values, and concepts determine to a large extent the quantity, quality, and results of their transactions. Thus, the transaction is embedded in a particular culture and values, and the nature of economics may be transformed from material to institutional economics, and even open up a world for the emergence of cultural economics in the future.

Old institutional economics proposes to reconcile class conflicts. Commons was not only a scholar but also a practitioner who helped the governor of Wisconsin to plan and implement policies during the Progressive movement in the late 19th and early 20th centuries. He rejected both conservative conciliation and radical revolution. On the one hand, he accepted the reality of conflicting interests, but on the other hand, he strongly advocated negotiation and compromise amid conflict. He put forth intensive efforts to promote the need to support a conflict mitigation model of mutual understanding, concession, negotiation, and win-win situations in solving real problems. Commons' advocacy and actions demonstrated that he was neither a radical individualist nor a fully conservative collectivist.[12]

In practice, Commons advocates an active institution-building and mediating role for the government. Such institution building is also a kind of middle way that is neither overly accommodating to individual self-interest nor subservient to the government's authority. In this way, he transforms the role of government from a passive "night watchman" to a moderate mediator, neutralizing the confrontation between different interest groups, and balancing and coordinating the tensions between individual freedom, government power, and legal coercion.[13]

It is essential to note that Commons' book uses his own experience as a case study to examine the process of collective bargaining between employers and employees in Wisconsin and reflect on the process of drafting an unemployment insurance bill. Faced with serious disagreements between business and labor, the Wisconsin state government established the Wisconsin Industrial Commission in 1911 and invited an advisory group of representatives from both employers and employees to participate in the process. As a result, the government passed the law successfully. The Commission was elevated to the "fourth branch" of government and became a major vehicle for easing labor conflicts. This proves that the spirit of cooperation, propriety, and collective bargaining is an effective way to resolve conflicts.[14]

Finally, in terms of methodology, old institutional economics supports synthesis and cross-sectional research. Commons' neutral proposition was an effort to synthesize research with a propriety function. He and his school organically integrated and intersected with law, economics, and ethics, and enhanced transactions to have the institutional position of law and the moral status of ethics, which made transactions have many non-material, institutional, and human elements. Their efforts greatly expanded the connotation of transactions out of the narrow confines of traditional economics.[15]

4.1.2 Neutralizing Contributions of New Institutional Economics

In addition to the neutralization efforts of old institutional economics contributed by Commons, the representative of new institutional economics, Coase, also created a new concept of collectives—the firm. Coase's first famous academic study in 1937 was intended to play a propriety role by building a bridge between two gaps: the hypothetical use of prices and the hypothetical use of entrepreneurial cooperation to control resources. The bridge to fill the major gap between prices and entrepreneurs was the business organization.[16]

While Coase may not entirely align with Commons' ideas, which do not fully adhere to the study of economic theory, there exist significant connections between Coase's new institutional economics, legal economics, transaction cost theory, and Commons' transaction theory. This connection is mainly attributed to Commons' extension of the transaction concept to the interpretation of proprietary economics.[17] Commons provides a realistic potential for the application of Coase's concept of transaction cost, determined through negotiation.[18] Another important representative of new institutional economics, Douglass North (1920–2015), also believed that "the costs of transacting are the key to the performance of economies."[19]

In his paper on social costs published in 1960, Coase outlined in detail several functions and reasons why firms are different from markets. First of all, market transactions are characterized by the notion of everyone for themselves, with each individual searching for how to maximize their interests. In contrast, when considering the internal transactions of enterprises, the interests of both sides of the transaction should be coordinated and consistent because if both sides engage in mutual sabotage or selfish opportunism, it is not beneficial to anyone. Coase explains the concept of reciprocal harm—when A is hurting B, A is also hurting A itself. For instance, if a cow eats some wheat nearby, the result is a profit for the owner of the cow and an increase in the supply of beef, but a decrease in the supply of wheat and an increase in its price. So, a choice must be made: meat or wheat? Coase argues that this needs to be determined by the value of cattle and wheat on the market, and the need to assess who is likely to sacrifice more to obtain their respective value. Similarly, Steven Cheung's "The Fable of the Bees" published in 1973 suggested that the market and transaction contract should determine the relationship between beekeepers and fruit farmers in terms of mutual benefits or harms and that the government should not intervene.[20]

In response to this issue, Zhaofeng Xue referred to Richard Epstein's view that the problem can be solved by assuming that both parties in conflict are the same person. For example, if one person owns both the cow and the wheat, then whether the cow is allowed to eat the wheat depends on the local market at the time. If the price of wheat is higher than that of beef, then the owner must not allow the cow to eat wheat; but if the price of beef is higher, then the owner not only allows the cow to eat wheat but also provides music and massage in order to comfort the cow.[21] This notion of harmful effects[22] is a development of Adam Smith's impartial spectator theory. If Smith's impartial spectator aims to design an objective third party, then Coase's property right dispute combines two opposing parties into one and designs a subjective third party. In other words, Smith is in favor of an objective observer while Coase supports a subjective transposition, and the symbiotic organism embodied in it reveals a truth: if we love and accommodate each other, both sides will gain; if we hurt and harm each other, both sides will lose together. The symbiotic relationship developed from Smith and Coase's theories also provides a new perspective for the enrichment and improvement of propriety economics.

Further, market transactions are equal, but the parties involved in an enterprise transaction have complex connections with an administrative, hierarchical entity. In a single enterprise, resource allocation is not solved by negotiation, but by administrative order, and entrepreneurs have the power of command. This centralized feature leads to enterprises being able to reduce the administrative cost of transactions and condense the uncertainty of transactions more than the market.[23] It means that markets need to be free, but enterprises need to be centralized and efficient. Democratic elections stipulate one person, one vote, with poor people, rich people, men, and women being treated equally; but enterprises generally implement one share, one vote and more shares, more votes. Workers without shares cannot enjoy the same voting and decision-making status as the CEO of an enterprise; otherwise, modern capitalist enterprises would lose their essence and follow socialist principles in favor of egalitarianism.

It should be pointed out that market transactions are characterized by external trades where each party is completely independent, while enterprise transactions are internal. Within an enterprise, the individual bargaining between various factors of production is eliminated, so there is no need "for bargains between the owners of the factors of production,"[24] which saves transaction costs. Moreover, the professionalization of decision-making and the effective communication of internal information will result in an increase of rational decision-making because professionalism lends itself to rationality and calmness, while amateurism leads to emotion and impulsiveness. In addition, internal communication can also reduce opportunistic behavior and enhance response within an organization.

Finally, although the market can control production costs more effectively, enterprises can be more flexible in response to economic crises because they have an alternative form of economic organization. The enterprise can offer lower costs than those generated by the market, and "could achieve the same result at less cost," thereby increasing the value of production. Thus, "the firm represents such an alternative to organising production through market transactions."[25] Coase points out that the firm emerged to solve a problem that the market could not because if firms could enter into long-term rather than short-term contracts with each other, it would create another way of allocating resources. Moreover, once the market fails, firms can generate some value from existence and substitution.[26] In particular, Coase emphasizes that the price mechanism of the market alone is not sufficient and requires "the co-ordinating function of the 'entrepreneur'."[27] This suggests that the reduction of transaction costs cannot rely solely on prices and markets, but also requires firms or entrepreneurs to supplement and regulate them.

4.1.3 Neutralizing Perspectives of Other Institutional Economists

In addition to Coase's emphasis on the moderating and neutralizing role of firms, other economists and theories attribute various distinct functions to firms.

Economists such as Paul Zak argue that firms can reduce uncertainty. Good institutions can diminish ambiguity, and trust between firms can reduce transaction costs. Uncertainty is the natural enemy of profitability, and bounded rationality and opportunism are the main causes of uncertainty. Therefore, economic development should not rely too much on the capricious market and instead seek non-market organizational arrangements such as enterprises. Given the fact that internal actions in enterprises as a whole are the result of collective decision-making, the results obtained by any individual within the firm depend on how others make their choices, and no individual can maximize their own self-benefit. The Pareto optimization of the enterprise as a whole should be the ultimate goal of common efforts.

Specifically, in an effort to reduce uncertainty, institutional economics proposes the first condition that is psychological understanding. The economics of communication believes that, through long-term communication in a familiar environment, people can produce a tacit understanding because common work experience can generate an unspoken resonance of words and actions.[28] As a result, they may produce a collective unconscious or subconscious momentum, which can finally reduce the cost of communication, alleviate uncertainty, and stabilize expectations.[29]

The second condition is to reach a focal point for decision-making based on the theory proposed by Thomas Schelling (1921–2016), a Nobel laureate in economics, in 1960. He argues that in the absence of effective communication, people can usually coordinate their intentions or expectations with others with whom they are in cooperation, but the success or failure of this coordination depends on the existence of a focal point, the discovery of which is contingent upon the time, space, and personalities of each side.[30] The focus of decision-making sometimes comes from the intuition and tacit agreement of both sides, rather than reason, logic, and science. The emergence of such a focus indicates the availability of opportunities for cooperation by helping both parties find expectations, make judgments, and reduce uncertainty. As seasoned poker players or chess players know, the focus of decision-making must be found at the right place and time. Of course, it is difficult for professionals to work with amateur poker or chess players because the latter often do not play with high standards of professionalism, and thus it is difficult for both sides to find the focal points. A homogeneous corporate culture can help to create psychological understanding, a meeting of the minds, and a focus for decision-making.

The third condition to reduce uncertainty is to manage personal preferences. People's subjective preferences can be entirely different, but corporate culture has the ability and mechanism to reshape employees' ideas and modify their perceptions. Employees may have to quit or be fired if they do not follow or are not accustomed to a particular corporate culture. By contrast, in a democratic society outside of a business environment, citizens may not support the president, but the president cannot remove them from the country for this reason. Thus, corporations may create a culture of unity, a degree of loyalty and trust, and a suppression of individual preferences with a collective system. For example, many large corporations are happy to provide corporate uniforms, a symbol for regulating employees' personal preferences and unifying their collective identity. For this, there is a major paradox in the United States today: on the one hand, society is becoming more and more individual and free; on the other hand, Americans have a high level of trust in each other, second only to people in Germany and Japan. Addressing this paradox, Francis Fukuyama believes that the United States relies on the community tradition. That is to say, as an "eagle," which always flies alone instead of in flocks, the United States nonetheless operates on shared group principles and values. Americans cooperate through churches, enterprises, associations, and non-governmental organizations, resulting in the prevalence of community groups.[31] This reveals the propriety effects of communities in the face of conflicting personal and social interests.

Another propriety function of enterprises discussed in institutional economics is that enterprises can compensate for incomplete contracts. Due to bounded rationality, opportunism, uncertainty, and information asymmetry, people are often troubled by contract failure in the process of signing and implementing contracts. In other words, people are too calculating to be governed by a written contract, but many social relationships do not have legal enforcement, especially in countries that lack a tradition of the rule of law. In China, for instance, the word for trust, *xin* (信), is composed of two linguistic elements—*person* (人) and *word* (言)—indicating that trust in Chinese culture is premised on an individual's verbal promise rather than a written legal stipulation.

Thus, enterprises have the potential to play a unique role because corporate culture, with its ethical implications and social norms, can compensate for the incompleteness of formal contracts. Haocai Luo proposes a concept of "soft law," which is between law and lawlessness, similar to between natural law and social customs, and its main manifestation is the rules and regulations between law and morality.[32]

Karl Polanyi also articulates the concept of "active society," which refers to a society based on habits, rules, and customs, and it may be the intermediate between the two poles of market and government.[33] Similarly, during Emperor Kang Xi's reign in Qing China, Jiashu (Longqi) Lu (1630–1693), a native of Pinghu city in Zhejiang Province, served as the leader of Jiading and Lingshou counties. When disputes arose, Mr. Lu was able to convince with passion, persuade with reason, and clarify the law, thus effectively easing the ruthlessness of laws and regulations and ending with the retraction of lawsuits and reconciliation between the people of the two counties.[34] These "soft law," "active society," and "lawsuit-free" approaches, when applied to corporate culture, can generate a kind of social capital, spiritual capital, and virtuous customs that compensate for and even supersede laws and contracts.

Enterprises can also convey effective information to reduce certain contractual risks. Excellent corporate culture can transmit the right "signal" to the market, aiding enterprises in receiving feedback, selecting consumers, and establishing trust between enterprises and customers effectively and in a timely manner. As a result, enterprises can receive recognition and endorsements from their customers who "vote" with their pocketbooks.[35] Consequently, the enterprise can build a credit economy, a concept created by Bruno Hildebrand (1812–1878), a representative of the old German school of historical economics. Hildebrand proposed that human society has evolved from a barter economy to a monetary economy through currency transactions, and then to a credit economy with credit transactions as the core. On the surface, the credit economy mainly takes place in the financial world or monetary field, but the core behind it is credit, that is, compliance with agreements to fend off risk.[36] If a credit economy is implemented in a country that lacks a credit culture, even the strictest legal system will not be able to overcome the local culture and habits. In other words, culture, in reality, is much more powerful than institutions and the legal system when it comes to credit, and legal codes are no match for lawless people who refuse to abide by them. Paul Zak suggests designing systems and organizations to promote trust and happiness because there is a virtuous cause-and-effect relationship between institutions, trust, and moral sentiment. Accordingly, some of the main causes of a lower index of trust are social, political, and economic instability. In terms of physiology, good expectations and interpersonal trust can reduce tension.[37]

Correspondingly, Coase compared the different functions of markets, government, and firms, and discussed the unique advantages of firms.[38] He reviews the propriety of government intervention, arguing that government interference may be effective and even help in reducing costs. Government intervention is not necessarily unwise, but the real danger lies in "extensive government intervention in the economy."[39] He emphasizes that the government's role in resource allocation should not be considered necessarily worse than that through the pricing mechanism because "the operation of a market is not itself costless."[40] However, government-like interventions and allocations must be "curtailed" and have a "boundary line."[41] This sense of boundary is the basic requirement of propriety philosophy because "the middle range" is an important means of reducing the effects of mutual harm.

Therefore, if the market is invisible and the government is tangible, enterprises are somewhere in the middle. Given the innate shortcomings of the invisible market in terms of its instability and unpredictability, as well as the inherent subjectivity of government policy, enterprises, collectives, and organizations can fulfill their unique functions of neutrality, balance, and propriety in mitigating the opposites of the market and the government.

4.2 Value Relativity in the Institutional Economics School

As mentioned in Chapter 2 of this book, one of the six elements of propriety philosophy is relativity, which has been influenced by the institutional economics school.

4.2.1 The Relative Value Theory

In his book *Institutional Economics* published in 1934, John Commons offers the relative value theory, which applies the idea of propriety and the principle of the middle way against absolutism. First of all, Commons' believes that value is closely related to culture, which in turn determines the merit and orientations of different values. A value judgment, in his view, is similar to cultural evaluation without any measurable, universal standard. Although in a particular time and space, there may be some special criteria, value judgment cannot be used as a singular standard to evaluate various economic operations or behaviors.[42]

Since Commons introduces interpersonal relationships into the study of institutions, he has addressed that different people have different traditions, customs, values, and rules; hence, subjective customs will have an impact on the control of property rights.[43] At the same time, Commons distinguishes between habits, common practices, and common law, emphasizing that customs often appear as common law[44] because they are derived from past experiences that guide people's plans and their future behaviors. Subsequently, customs provide the expected security and serve as an enduring part of human tradition and heritage. However, cultural customs are different among different economic groups, which can lead to interpersonal conflicts during business transactions, so it is important to make appropriate choices among various customs.[45] Moreover, given that customs can be both good and bad—some are endorsed and others are condemned—they have a compulsory force: those who observe them are protected while those who violate them are shunned.

In this regard, Commons proposes the concept of "citizens of an institution" because people have established various institutional customs and values that are connected to different elements of society, such as families, businesses, and collectives. Thus, a "collective human will" and an "institutionalized mind" emerge.[46] Institutions cannot be separated from people; people cannot be separated from customs, and customs are by nature relative in value. In fact, the essence of relativism is to advocate that there is no absolute in reality. Relativism seeks concrete experience, thought, and value. This also reflects one of the principal ideas of propriety economics: more relative, less absolute; more specific, less universal.

Meanwhile, there is no scientific standard that justifies the choice between pure laissez-faire policies and absolute government intervention in economic activities. In grasping and searching for the standard of moderation, it is essential to understand the relativity of propriety. Following John Locke (1632–1704) who proposed the complete separation of internal concepts from the external world, Commons divides institutions into internal and external mechanisms. According to Commons, the internal mechanism includes traditions, moral rules, customs, and non-official rules, which highlight that truth cannot be certain but can be approached through trial and error.[47] Subsequently, institutions can also be divided into formal and informal ones. Formal institutions refer to tangible laws, rules, and contracts, as well as the hierarchical structures created by laws and rules, which establish coercive power. However, Commons emphasizes the need for the selective use of power, the main point of which is the "limit of coercion."[48] The informal system, by contrast, is shaped unconsciously by people during long-term interactions and consists of values, ethical norms, moral concepts, customs, and ideologies, among which ideologies are the core. Together they constitute the theoretical basis and ideological criteria for formal institutional arrangements. When the informal system and the formal system coexist harmoniously and the direction of institutional change is consistent, society may reduce the costs of institutional operation, innovation, and change.

4.2.2 The Role of Ideology

In the new institutional economics school, Douglass North places greater emphasis on the mental models of customary behavior and belief systems, stressing that understanding institutions is related to the evolution of "ideas, ideologies, myths, dogmas, and prejudices," and that the influence of these cultural elements on today's practice provides "path dependence."[49] In particular, North notes that "mental models" come partly from culture and partly from experience, where culture results from the intergenerational transformation of knowledge, values, and rules while experience is very unique and specific. Different cultural environments must have various identities so that people's mental models also have multiple characteristics.[50]

Thus, new institutional economics treats culture as the carrier of institutions, and formal or external institutions can only work if they are compatible with informal or internal institutions.[51] An effective propriety institutional arrangement must be an optimal combination of formal and informal institutions. However, since informal institutions are characterized by relativity, subjectivity, and evolution, it is difficult for society to deal with their uncertainty in an appropriate way. Thereafter, North argues that the economic subject needs to be constrained by formal institutions and that institutions are designed to reduce the uncertainty of interpersonal communication. At the same time, one of the major differences between new institutional economics and neoclassical economics is that the former is able to insert the concepts and ideology of economic theory into the process and mechanism of analysis. Having provided a model of the key role of political processes in economic performance, new institutional economics successfully explains "inefficient" markets.[52]

Hence, new institutional economics offers a propriety research direction to connect subjective ideology with the more objective formal system under the framework of economics in order to implant the relative value system and mental model. Accordingly, it makes the economic system more humanized, diversified, and individualized, and thus promotes institutional transformation as more active, resilient, and sustainable.

4.3 The Historical Evolution of Institutional Economics

The old and new schools of institutional economics share the view that the object of study in economics is not static but is changing, evolving, and dynamic, with a distinct historical dimension, thus reflecting the fourth characteristic of propriety philosophy: historicity or evolution. In this regard, Paul D. Bush argues that the essence of institutional economics is "evolutionary economics."[53]

4.3.1 Veblen's Efforts

Thorstein B. Veblen (1857–1929), one of the founders of old institutional economics, systematically criticized the static theory of neoclassical economics in 1898.[54] He contended that neoclassical economics overuses static and fixed models that lack a dynamic evolutionary framework to analyze the economic activities of human society. This will inevitably lead to, in Veblen's view, the detachment of economic theories from actual reality. Similarly, Commons underscores that economists need to study economics from historical, practical, and empirical perspectives by focusing on experiential investigation and evidence over theory.[55]

In general, old institutional economics criticizes the neoclassical static model analysis, opposes the narrow use of economic variables, and declines to pay excessive attention to the non-realistic nature of price signals. In particular, the old institutional school rejects the neoclassical over-promotion of rationalism, individualism, and mutual benefits, including "instrumental values" that are centered on rationalism but ignoring "ceremonial values" that are based on tradition and custom.[56] In contrast, the old institutional school draws on pragmatist philosophy, evolutionary theory, and psychology to suggest that the factors influencing economic subjects' decisions are pluralistic. Economic subjects should aim for a propriety combination of instrumental and ceremonial values, but with particular emphasis on the decisive influence that institutional habits and rules may have on the subjects' decisions. Moreover, in discussing instrumental and ceremonial values, the institutional school promotes "the dialectical nature of behavior," accentuating that economic behavior is first instrumental, then ritual, and finally both.[57]

4.3.2 Theory of Institutional Change

To highlight the evolutionary nature of economics, new institutional economics proposes the theory of institutional change. North argues that "one of the most evident lessons from history is that political systems have an inherent tendency to produce inefficient property rights which result in stagnation or decline."[58] On the other hand, institutional changes can prompt each interest group to find a balance point and a middle ground for maximizing its interests. At the same time, in order to satisfy this interest maximization, economic subjects will make the most favorable contractual arrangement for their interests, which will promote changes in the original interest structure and the emergence of new institutional arrangements. This process of inheritance and innovation of the old system is characterized by dynamic evolution and rational adaptation.

This shows that institutional change is a continuous evolutionary process from institutional equilibrium to disequilibrium and then to equilibrium again.[59] In particular, North proposes the theory of "path dependence," which shows that in addition to the instrumental rationality emphasized by classical and neoclassical economics, there is also the more important evolutionary rationality.[60] The present generation must look for historical lessons and experiences from previous generations to avoid taking wrong, immoral paths in the future.

4.3.3 Research Methodology

In terms of economic research methodology, Commons disagrees with Veblen although they together contributed most to old institutional economics. Veblen completely rejects traditional methods and orthodox economic theory, while Commons advocates a "non-dichotomist" moderate research approach, which acknowledges the need for the critical inheritance of traditional theory. Lin Zhang cites Yngve Ramstad's argument[61] that institutional economics is, first of all, an evolutionary approach, as economic processes are constantly evolving and various outcomes are difficult to predict, so they do not necessarily tend to equilibrium. Second, the school takes a realist approach, opposing the organization of economic theory through abstraction, similar to the neoclassical assumption of perfect competition. Third, the school promotes an empirical method, underlining that economic theories need the support of experience and background, rather than determining their validity through imagination and perception. Fourth, the school adopts a holistic approach, given the complex, systemic, and comprehensive nature of human behavior, so that human motivations cannot be rigidly separated into economic, social, or political ones. The fifth contribution of the school is a cultural approach that aims to introduce cultural contexts and elements into the variables of economic research, study collectivities, explore values, and highlight relativism. In addition, the school also follows a non-mechanistic approach that combines economic concepts with real systems rather than with artificial instruments such as price mechanisms. Moreover, the equilibrium or order of the economic system does not come from the spontaneous force of the market but is created by society and ensured by institutions. Finally, the institutional school also takes a coercive approach because the assumptions of economic behavior come from coercive structures and the system of power, and power relations determine the evaluation of the results of economic behavior.[62]

The introduction of evolutionary, realistic, empirical, holistic, cultural, and non-mechanistic theories into institutional economics has helped to soften economics in its methodology, and as Frank Hahn pointed out, in a hundred years, "economics will be a much softer subject than it now is."[63] Western economics has evolved from a qualitative-oriented approach in the classical period to a quantitative-oriented approach in the neoclassical period and has gradually developed into a state where mathematics is the essence of economics, putting the cart before the horse. In order to challenge and revise the mathematical, static, and absolute mainstream economics, new institutional economics after the 1970s seems to have a propriety tendency in its methodology. First of all, its research intends to focus on dynamic history, soft institutions, and individual specificity while reducing the mathematical threshold of economics and returning economics to a soft science with propriety boundaries and relative values.[64] Institutional economics has also developed empirical fieldwork and archival data analysis, focusing on accurate definitions and self-consistent logic to discuss the real world. It has delivered a strong message that, different from the real economic world, the mathematical modeling system poses difficulties to establishing a perfect, compatible matching system. Therefore, when confronted with the dilemma of prioritizing the accuracy of analysis over truthfulness, most contemporary new institutional economic scholars, like Coase, opt for authenticity and abstain from employing mathematical formulas or models. This research methodology aims at correcting the tendency of excessive mathematization but still retains a modest mathematical modeling approach. In fact, changes in research methodology are also a propriety process of continuous adjustment.

The ideas of neutrality, relativity, and evolution from institutional economics in terms of economic theory and methodology contribute to propriety economics. Only when there is neutrality can there be harmony; only when there is a middle can the relativity between the left and the right be highlighted and the absolute be avoided; only with a sense of historicity can we consider the evolutionary path of yesterday in addition to the present. Therefore, the neutrality, relativity, and evolution embodied in institutional economics are examples of propriety. Only by following the path of propriety and practicing moderate economic thinking can we gradually achieve balance, harmony, and prosperity in our theories, methods, and practices.

4.4 The Bounded Rationality of Behavioral Economics

Generally speaking, behavioral economics is logically related to the ideas of institutional economics. Economic behavior is evolutionary, dynamic, and institutional, so it is difficult to achieve perfect, objective rationality. As Paul D. Bush defines it, an institution is "a set of socially prescribed patterns of correlated behavior."[65] Moreover, behavior is a demonstration of a person or institution's values.[66]

Herbert A. Simon (1916–2001) was the first economist to propose a theory of bounded rationality. His efforts have enriched the subjective, intermediate, and variable nature of propriety philosophy and moderate thought, and perhaps without his knowledge, led to the idea of propriety economics. Behavioral economics benefited from the emergence of behavioral science in the 1930s, including the contributions of the great B. F. Skinner (1904–1990). By the 1950s, behavioral science had evolved into a systematic discipline, and behavioral scientists started to engage in interdisciplinary research, particularly in conjunction with economics. The Nobel Prize in Economics has been awarded four times since the 1970s to seven scholars associated with behavioral economics or the theory of bounded rationality, including Simon in 1978, psychologists Daniel Kahneman and Vernon Smith in 2002, and Robert Shiller, Eugene Fama, and Lars Hansen in 2013. A behavioral economist won the Nobel Prize for the fourth time in 2017, with the award going to Richard Thaler. The fruitfulness of behavioral economics shows both the success of behavioral economics' "rebellion" in challenging mainstream economics and the effectiveness of mainstream economics' "recruitment" of behavioral economics. Unlike classical full rationality, the assumption of bounded rationality is similar to Aristotle's idea of appropriateness.

4.4.1 The Myth of Full Rationality

It must be noted that Adam Smith did not formulate the idea of *Homo economicus*, the symbol of full rationality, in his work. The first scholar to propose the axiom of maximization of individual economic interests was the British economist Nassau William Senior (1790–1864).[67] Later, the classical economist John Stuart Mill (1806–1873) offered the concept of the economic man,[68] which was formally coined by Vilfredo Pareto.[69] Some scholars have addressed analogous misunderstandings of Smith's market theory.[70]

As early as 1955, Simon directly challenged the idea of the rational "economicus," the most important cornerstone of classical economics that assumed rationality of the "economic man"—someone who has sufficiently clear, quantitative knowledge, sound and stable judgment, and first-class computational ability.[71] Challenging this myth, Thaler also trusts that many extremely "rational" and "scientific" models of economics simply cannot accurately predict economic trends. For example, no economist could have predicted the arrival of the 2008–2009 financial crisis. "Worse, many thought that both the crash and its aftermath were things that simply could not happen."[72] Thaler defines economics in an ironic tone: Optimization + Equilibrium = Economics.[73] However, in reality, the premises of economic theories are flawed, so human behavior cannot achieve optimal results, as concepts constructed by humans may be biased.[74]

In real life, bounded rational or irrational behavior abounds. For example, influenced by the psychology of conspicuous price and profligate price, some people just buy expensive, not necessarily good, products because the more expensive the item, the more consumers feel "noble and honorific," the so-called Veblen effect.[75] It is interesting to note that Veblen is the founder of old institutional economics and the innovator of the idea of consumer irrationality in behavioral economics, straddling the two schools of thought, thus illustrating the relevance of institutional economics and behavioral economics.[76] Moreover, people may not always be able to control themselves, and the most notable manifestation of this is that many people only focus on immediate interests and ignore their long-term, overall interests.

For example, people generally give in to short-term temptations, and as a result, ignore their plans to save money or lead a healthier lifestyle.[77]

Behavioral economics also argues that because human rationality is not complete, people are often too greedy, lack restraint, and engage in excessive opportunistic, speculative activities, happy to take a free ride. Thus, moderation has become an important guide for human economic behavior. According to Simon, bounded rationality is the central theme of behavioral economics.[78]

The Diderot effect, which is related to this bounded rationality, is also worth observing. Denis Diderot (1713–1784) is not only known for compiling the first encyclopedia but also for serving as the titular example of the "Diderot effect," which occurred when Diderot was given a gift—a luxurious dressing gown. In order to ensure that it matched his other possessions, Diderot behaved irrationally and successively acquired new desks, flowered carpets, chairs, statues, bookshelves, alarm clocks, and other things that it was not necessary to replace. In the end, he regretted throwing away his old clothes out of vanity and wrote an essay entitled "Regrets on Parting with My Old Dressing Gown."[79] Grant David McCracken introduced the term "Diderot effect" in 1988 based on this phenomenon.[80] Economist Juliet Schor in 1999 and 2005 conducted a detailed analysis of "the upward creep of desire," which is the result of the Diderot effect.[81] Although the Diderot effect is open to interpretation, it is impossible to deny its essence. Bounded rational or irrational consumer behavior will ultimately lead to consumer regret. As a result, this effect will increase consumption and waste resources for no reason, and of course, will stimulate demand and increase supply.

4.4.2 Bounded Rationality Constraints

Due to the frequency of bounded rationality, humans need to appropriately constrain and control their economic behavior. Simon contends that human behavior must be controlled through the following conditions: 1) alternatives available; 2) a clearly defined relationship between risk and benefit; and 3) the ability to determine the order of trade-offs and preferences between revenues and expenditures if conflicts arise between them.[82] Clearly, the limitations of human capabilities and resources will lead to limitations on human rationality. At the same time, Simon stresses that when discussing bounded rationality, five realistic elements must be considered: risk, uncertainty, incomplete information, alternatives, and complexity.[83] These five constraints make the ideal of full rationality difficult to achieve and determine the inevitability of bounded rationality.

It is important to note that Simon's famous paper from 1955 does not mention "bounded rationality" but only "approximate rationality."[84] There is a difference between the two because "bounded rationality" should be interpreted as constrained or restrained rationality, not "limited rationality." Only "constrained rationality" is a concept between "full emotionality" and "full rationality," which reflects the true meaning of propriety economics, indicating that human beings should pursue "moderate rationality" or "moderate emotionality" between excess and deficiency.

Notably, people need to maximize rationality, but in reality, this goal meets with internal and external constraints, so at most, only moderate rationality or constrained rationality can be pursued.[85] When Simon proposed the theory of "bounded rationality" in 1972, he also highlighted constraints, saying that "theories that incorporate constraints on the information-processing capacities of the actor may be called theories of bounded rationality."[86] However, Simon emphasized "the limits" of rationality in 1991, arguing that bounded rationality is "about the limits upon the ability of human beings to adapt optimally, or even satisfactorily, to complex environments."[87]

Simon defined bounded rationality more explicitly in 2000, accentuating that not only the availability of external resources but also the "inner environment" of people's minds determine the limits of rationality. The dual bounded nature of the external and the internal determines the realistic choices people make to pursue fulfillment. "Rationality is bounded because these abilities are severely limited."[88] Thaler's definition more directly and explicitly underscores the limitation and complexity of human behavior: "Behavioral Economics is the combination of psychology and economics that investigates what happens in markets in which some of the agents display human limitations and complications."[89]

W. Brian Arthur, one of the founders of complexity economics, also believes that there are two reasons why the full rationality of the classical school of economics cannot explain complex reality. One is that human thinking is unable to cope with complex reality, so the limitation of human rationality is inevitable. In addition, there is more than one subject of behavior, and in the case of many subjects interacting with one another, it is impossible to predict any behavior precisely. Thus, there can be no "objective, well-defined, shared assumptions" about their behavior, which will lead to more chaos and uncertainty, and perfect logical reasoning will only fail.[90]

4.4.3 Improving the Concept of Bounded Rationality

Simon claims that human knowledge of bounded rationality started in ancient Greece. By 1746, Voltaire proposed in the *Dictionnaire Philosophique* that "the best is the enemy of the good" and, corresponding to this, he suggested: "Optimizing is the enemy of satisficing." This profoundly reflects the essence of propriety economics, showing that human beings should not be bound by the prejudice of "optimizing" for the best; the second best or any psychologically acceptable outcome is one that fits the criterion of moderation.[91] Therefore, managing one's own rational expectations has become a major theme of bounded rationality and a realistic but effective way for human beings to cope with complex and uncertain environments.[92]

At the same time, in the face of these bounded rational behaviors, Thaler and his co-author borrowed the concept of "libertarian paternalists" from Milton Friedman (1912–2006), hoping that private employers, institutions, and the government would jointly "nudge" people to make better choices, especially in two areas where they are often less than rational: pensions and health insurance.[93] They cite diabetes and obesity in the U.S. where the percentage of obese Americans was as high as 20% in 2009, and 60% of Americans consider themselves overweight or obese. However, people simply cannot consciously and rationally control their diet, tobacco, and alcohol intake because they are not absolutely rational "econs or homo economicus," but normal human beings. For individuals lacking self-consciousness, self-control, and rationality, external nudges become necessary because they "can improve our ability to improve people's lives, and help solve many of society's major problems."[94] Of course, Thaler and his colleague repeatedly emphasize that such nudging need not be mandates or interventions, but rather provides more choices to the economic subjects.[95] They also insist that benign government promotion should not be turned into a haphazard manipulation.[96]

These ideas of "libertarian paternalism" and government nudging are similar to the system of constitutional monarchy, which retains the traditional royal infrastructure but assigns only limited power to the monarch. While it is not possible to completely abandon the government as a "parent," it is also unwise to totally rely on individual rationality and market freedom. This "parent" has to be a liberal one, not an authoritarian one. While moderate nudging is helpful, excessive nudging becomes interference, restriction, and "sludge." Therefore, the intention of Thaler and his co-author is clear: they want their proposals to be moderate, so that they "might appeal to both sides of the political divide" and believe that the policy of "libertarian paternalism" is acceptable to both conservative Republicans and liberal Democrats in the United States.[97] This is what they jointly promote as "the real third way."[98]

The idea of using government to nudge the market and individual decision-making was conceived as early as 1790 by Adam Smith in the sixth edition of *The Theory of Moral Sentiments*. With the onset of the industrial revolution in England in the 1770s, Smith made significant revisions to the first edition of *The Theory of Moral Sentiments*, published in 1759. At that time, Smith began to express his disappointment with British society's tendency to look down on the poor, believing that "this disposition to admire, and almost to worship, the rich and the powerful, and ... to neglect persons of poor and mean condition ... is the great and most universal cause of the corruption of our moral sentiments."[99] Smith underlines that "to attain to this envied situation, the candidates for fortune too frequently abandon the paths of virtue; for unhappily, the road which leads to the one, and that which leads to the other, lie sometimes in very opposite directions."[100] Especially, driven by frustration with avaricious merchants and volatile markets, Smith turned his optimism towards government officials, statesmen, magistrates, and judges. He advocated for two aspects of patriotism: a love for the government and a love for the people. According to Smith, "the love of our country seems, in ordinary cases, to involve in it two different principles; first, a certain respect of reverence for that constitution or form of government which is actually established; and secondly, an earnest desire to render the condition of our fellow-citizens as safe, respectable, and happy as we can." A citizen who is unwilling to "respect the laws and to obey the civil magistrate," in Smith's view, "is certainly not a good citizen."[101]

This idea of nudging can be easily ambiguous because if the businesspeople and individuals on the receiving end have bounded rationality, does it mean that the government officials who do the nudging are more rational? Who can prove empirically and logically that officials are less materialistic than businesspeople? After all, there are numerous corrupt, greedy officials. Moreover, there is a paradox: since behavioral economists deny the possibility of perfect, full rationality, why do they hope to help people approach perfect rationality and compensate for irrationality through government nudging? In addition, the irrational wrong decisions recognized by behavioral economists are actually a kind of evolutionary rationality because making mistakes is itself part of a process of gaining experience. People are constantly progressing through their mistakes because failure is the mother of success.

4.5 The Subjectivity of Behavioral Economics

Behavioral economics not only supports bounded rationality but also believes in the subjective, evolutionary nature of economic behavior, which is an idea it shares with propriety economics.

4.5.1 The Prospect Theory

The prospect theory of behavioral economics, which reflects the subjectivity of economic behavior, was outlined by Daniel Kahneman, a Nobel laureate in economics, and his colleagues in 1979. The prospect theory is based on a critique of the expected utility theory, which assumes that human decision-making behavior is rational, almost regardless of individual subjective pursuits and probabilities, and supposes this rational capacity to be general, common economic behavior. The expected utility theory "has dominated the analysis of decision making under risk. It has been generally accepted as a normative model of rational choice, and widely applied as a descriptive model of economic behavior." Thus, it holds that "all reasonable people would wish to obey the axioms of the theory, and that most people actually do."[102] In contrast, the prospect theory demonstrates through choice experiments with several types of people that many personal preferences often violate the axioms of the expected utility theory, finding that an individual's choice actually depends on the difference between expectations and outcomes rather than on the outcomes themselves. When making decisions, people first create a "prospect," an expectation or reference point, and then measure whether the outcome of each behavior meets their expectations. For positive prospects, people often have an aversion to risk and are happy to reap the benefits of high certainty; for negative prospects, people show a preference for risk and hope for the next instance of good fortune to compensate and recoup a current loss. In other words, people are reluctant to take risks when they are doing well and are more likely to take risks when they experience losses because "certainty increases the aversiveness of losses as well as the desirability of gains."[103]

However, losses and gains are relative to a default reference point and once the reference point changes, so does the attitude toward risk. This reference point in fact represents propriety and moderation, which require constant adjustment and modification of the target and scope of the reference point according to changes in time and space. Hence, the adjustment and reference points are relative and subjective, serving as crucial measures to accommodate and align with the bounded rationality of individuals.

According to the prospect theory, people are often very sensitive to the small probability of a black swan event due to its unusual nature, and often underestimate the large probability of a white swan event. For example, the probability of success in lotteries and gambling is very low, but many people will happily try their luck repeatedly; conversely, the probability of a car accident is also very small, but most people still buy insurance, resulting in insurance companies having a high probability of making a profit. Therefore, Kahneman believes that the profitability of casinos and insurance companies is based on the subjective psychology of the bounded rationality of a significant number of people.[104] However, many people completely ignore the large probability of developing cancer or harming the liver by smoking cigarettes or drinking alcohol. Therefore, the expected utility theory under the assumption of the rational economic man belongs to traditional and normative economics, guiding people on what they should do; while the prospect theory belongs to behavioral and empirical economics, which describe what people actually do.

In addition, there is an important "weighting function" in prospect theory,[105] which basically explains that the pleasure of 100 successes can hardly offset the pain of one failure because there is a "pleasure-pain" curve of incremental gain and loss in the human psyche. If the incremental pleasure index is about 0.5 times, and the pain index from the loss is about 2.5 times, the difference between the two is about 3 times. For example, if you invest $1,000 in stocks today and make a 10% profit of $100, you get $1,100 in total, and your happiness only increases by 50%; but if tomorrow you lose 10% of the $1,100, i.e., $110, you still have $990 left, but your misery increases by 250%. In this way, the pain caused by a loss is three times greater than the pleasure one gets from a gain. The results of this experiment challenge the rationality of economic people because economic men calculate gains and losses from a purely quantitative point of view, and a loss of $100 on $1,000 in capital is only 10%. However, this rational thinking ignores a person's concern about the increment of wealth: because you had won 10%, i.e., $1,100 in hand, and now you only have $990 left, you have lost $110 instead of $100. More importantly, psychological loss is hard to measure, similar to the psychology of a gambler, with a highly inflated desire to win.[106]

4.5.2 Bounded Selfishness and Willpower

From bounded rationality, scholars such as Thaler have derived ideas on bounded selfishness and bounded willpower, which together with bounded rationality, constitute the triple bounds of human nature. The term "bounded selfishness" describes the fact that many people are neither completely selfish nor completely selfless, but somewhere in between. Moreover, people are sometimes self-serving and other times altruistic and cannot be either all the time. Such a reality in fact embodies the idea of propriety. The idea of bounded selfishness challenges the assumption of complete self-interest of the "economic man" as advocated by classical and neoclassical economics, which assumes that if A is better than B, rational people must choose A instead of B. In reality, many people just choose B for many reasons.

One is that when they choose, they simply do not know which one is better, hence the constant regrets due to a general lag in human judgment. Second, if a businessperson tells someone that A is better than B, the rebellious nature of human beings may still lead to the selection of B because a businessperson is often considered unscrupulous and not trustworthy. Third, someone who employs dialectical thinking would think that good and bad things are relative and that B may turn out better than A after all. Such thinking often guides the decisions of university admissions offices when selecting new college students. If student A is more qualified than other students, B may indeed be accepted rather than A because of the anticipation that A would likely apply to a more prestigious school and end up going there instead, thereby declining the offer from the said school. To improve the success rate of the school's admissions, student B is often offered a place. Thaler also cites an example of the American public's charitable donations as a way of explaining "bounded selfishness." The notion of pure selfishness would mean that ordinary people are not likely to donate their limited supply of money to help others but in 1993, 73.4% of American households donated to charity, the average amount of donations accounted for 2.1% of their annual income, and 47.7% of the public contributed 4.2 hours of volunteer time per week.[107] In other words, innate human selfishness is mitigated by other factors.

The bounded willpower idea is similar to the assumptions concerning bounded resources and bounded capability. It emphasizes that human willpower, resources, capabilities, and means are always severely scarce relative to the infinite desires of human beings. The reason is simple: if there is no scarcity, then all desires can be realized, and if desires can be realized, then there is no need for cautious, propriety actions. Thaler and his colleague emphasize that it is entirely too naive to apply the assumption of the "economic man" seeking the best to ordinary people because human nature is such that most people always eat, drink, or spend more, but exercise, save, or work less.[108] Therefore, when both institutional and behavioral economics underscore that human beings are bounded rational individuals rather than perfectly rational economic men, they essentially point to the second principle of propriety philosophy: ordinariness, which does not envision ordinary people to be entirely rational, all-powerful, and perfect. In this regard, North also argues that "individuals typically act on incomplete information and with subjectively derived models that are frequently erroneous; the information feedback is typically insufficient to correct these subjective models," so that "efficient economic markets are exceptional."[109]

4.5.3 The Mental Accounting Theory

The mental accounting theory also reflects the subjective nature of human economic behavior. Articulated by Thaler in 1985, the theory was explained through various examples of mistakes that people often make due to insufficient rationality.

For instance, a couple went fishing in another state and then transported the salmon home, but the airline lost the fish and provided $300 in compensation. Theoretically, a mere increase of $150 per person with a modest income should not lead to the decision to spend the $300 immediately. However, people, in general, have different expectations when it comes to anticipated income and plans to spend because in their mind they have a "windfall gain account" and a "food account." While they may not be willing to spend money from the food account, it is not painful to spend the unexpected windfall, hence the notion of mental accounting.[110] The same principle can apply to the way that people spend their time—some are happy to spend three hours watching TV, while others go shopping for 20 minutes but feel distressed.

Such different ideas about consumption caused by subjective psychological factors directly affect the economic behavior of different people, and their effect on the real economy cannot be underestimated or predicted. In this regard, economists should not only take into consideration this bounded rational psychology and behavior but also its possible impact on society and the economy, and design corresponding economic policies to reduce the negative effects of such behavior as much as possible.

4.6 The Psychological Nature of Behavioral Economics

Behavioral economists emphasize the close relationship between economics and psychology. This psychological factor directly determines the equation between supply and demand, and it is also related to the subjectivity of propriety economics.

4.6.1 Contrast Effect

The contrast effect in psychology directly affects human economic behavior. According to Thaler, people's quality of life and happiness are directly related to interpersonal psychological contrast. Traditional economics is concerned only with materialized and measurable income, housing, and assets, based on which the quality of life is defined and the level of happiness is inferred. However, psychologists emphasize the mental accounting theory in that people's happiness mainly comes from horizontal and vertical contrasts.[111] Since ancient times, people have not necessarily suffered from scarcity but unfairness. Therefore, people's feelings of happiness and monetary possessions do not have a proportionate relationship, and quality of life has little to do with economic conditions but is mainly a subjective judgment at a psychological level.

4.6.2 Historicity

There is a history of human economic behavior. According to the fourth principle of propriety, the historicity of human behavior must be considered when judging and searching for the appropriate range of economic behavior because bounded rationality and the evolution of rationality indicate that human behavior in the present depends not only on the immediate situation but is also closely related to the historical context.

Dingding Wang argues that human rationality is evolutionary rationality with historical depth and constant change, and is severely limited by historical context and subjective imagination.[112] Of course, once bounded rationality and historicity are introduced, the universality, objectivity, and uniqueness of classical economics' full rationality will be challenged, and several cornerstones of modern economics will be questioned, including the general equilibrium theory with static logical framework.

4.6.3 Specificity

Behavioral economics also focuses on the specificity and individuality of human economic behavior. This approach has something to do with Thaler's personality, as he writes in a very accessible and humorous way, going so far as to thank the staff of a Chicago noodle shop in the acknowledgments of his co-authored book, *Nudge*, promising that he would be back the next week.[113] He laughs at himself for being so lazy that he only studies things of interest, which must be specific rather than universal, such as classical topics that have been prescribed by previous generations, and which are extremely tedious. This is very much like most people, who are more interested not in the happy stories of all people, but the tragic episodes of various unfortunate families. As the Chinese saying goes, good things often do not travel out the door, but bad stories tend to spread across a thousand miles.

However, in the realm of behavioral economics, emphasizing the specificity and subjectivity of human behavior poses challenges in crafting a unified hypothesis regarding bounded rationality. The basis for a unifying hypothesis often hinges on mathematical modeling, yet capturing the diverse spectrum of bounded rational human behaviors in a single mathematical model proves to be a challenging task. While describing perfectly rational behavior mathematically may not be overly complex, attempting to define and clarify the myriad forms of bounded rationality, irrationality, extreme rationality, and extreme irrationality exhibited by the world's seven billion individuals within a single model is a virtually impossible undertaking. Consequently, behavioral economics encounters difficulties in presenting a systematic framework capable of consolidating the entire relevant body of literature and lacks a cohesive set of core hypotheses. This challenge may be one of the significant reasons why behavioral economics has not yet achieved mainstream status.

In essence, the emphasis on bounded rationality, subjectivity, and psychology advocated by behavioral economics underscores the notion that we are all human beings rather than mere economic agents. Furthermore, behavioral economics emphasizes the primacy of subjective psychology, historical evolution, and the evolving expectations that influence economic behavior. In doing so, it intersects with propriety philosophy and propriety economics, particularly concerning reference point composition and changes, thereby enriching and reinforcing the principles of propriety economics.

Chapter 5

Shared Values in Cultural Economics and the Definition of Propriety Economics

In addition to classical economics, neoclassical economics, institutional economics, and behavioral economics, the realm of cultural economics encompasses numerous ideas, theories, and methodologies that align with the principles of propriety economics. This expansion of the moderate approach within modern economics after World War II extends both its depth and breadth.

The field of cultural economics, which centers on the examination of cultural values, emerged in the 1970s. A notable milestone in the establishment of cultural economics was the launch of the *Journal of Cultural Economics*, edited and published by William Hendon in 1973. Furthermore, the International Conference on Cultural Economics has been held regularly since 1979, and the Association for Cultural Economics International was established in 1992.

Within the domain of cultural economics, the study of cultural value, with its focus on the cultural factors that impact economic development, holds greater significance than the economics of cultural industries.[1] It is this emphasis on cultural value that resonates more closely with the principles of propriety economics.

Generally speaking, culture can be defined as consisting of four major elements: first, it is shared by a group of individuals; second, it has shared beliefs and preferences of respective groups; third, it is capable of being transmitted; and fourth, it can produce informal constraints on interpersonal interactions.[2] Related to the definition of culture, cultural economics is the study of whether the shared beliefs and preferences of relevant groups have an impact on economic development. How do they affect economic development? What is the relationship between this cultural influence and institutional effects? In general, cultural economic research focuses on the relationship between economics and religious studies, social norms, social identity, social justice, ideology, trust, and family.

For example, there are currently several concepts that are beginning to intersect heavily with economics, such as religion, happiness, equity, and trust. Two articles on "fair economics" published in 1986, by Daniel Kahneman, a behavioral science expert, and Richard Thaler, suggested that the introduction of fairness into economics, similar to the integration of morality, happiness, religion, justice, and trust with economics, could be classified as cultural economics. In addition, Tania Singer, a German neuroscientist, co-edited a collection of papers on caring economics in 2015.[3]

In short, the subject of analysis in cultural economics is how individuals' ideas and behaviors are transmitted through channels and modes of social capital, social relations, social learning, and social evolution. In this way, cultural economics is closely related to institutional and behavioral economics, since culture often acts through institutions and has a positive or negative impact on economic behavior, as well as on corporate management, production efficiency, and asset value.

5.1 Shared Concepts in Propriety Economics

The essential principle of cultural economics is the search for shared beliefs and preferences. The idea of shared values is a propriety convention between universal values and individual values, so it has the function of the middle way and is worthy of in-depth analysis.

5.1.1 Shared Values and Universal Values

First of all, universal values denote the same values that exist in two or more groups, representing a general concept that requires a high degree of commonality before cooperation between groups and communities. The initial point of cooperation is high, and both need an extraordinary, comprehensive convergence of values. For example, if culture A pursues freedom and individualism while culture B prefers stability and collectivity, it will be difficult for them to cooperate on these two major concepts. Moreover, once culture A believes its values are universal, politically correct, and cannot be challenged, then not only is it impossible for A and B to cooperate, but also their conflicts are inevitable. This unilateral positioning of one's values as universal values inevitably leads to a formal binding, non-reciprocal relationship, which violates the fourth element of the definition of culture above: informal constraints. Such a universal value often has a sense of moral superiority and political coercion. In particular, universal values imply that all countries, nations, and cultures must abide by them and that they are universally applicable, both in the past and in the present. This concept is incompatible with the subjectivity, variability, evolution, and bounded rationality emphasized by institutional economics, behavioral economics, and cultural economics.

Different from universal values, shared values are based on the principle of seeking common ground while preserving and respecting differences. In other words, shared values can be discovered, cultivated, and developed in the current or future state through effort. While common universal values are established, shared ones can be evolving. The shared increment can be built on the maximum infusion of ideas from the cooperating parties, who can continuously work, explore, enrich, and change these increments. In this regard, all parties should not only recognize, respect, and preserve established values, but also seek, cultivate, and develop shared values. They can operate in parallel or be developed appropriately with different emphases and trade-offs according to different times and spaces, but the common goal is to promote rapid, effective cooperation.

For instance, a multi-party system may not be a universally embraced value across both East and West. However, the concept of democracy is a potential shared value among certain countries in those regions, enabling diverse parties to initiate cooperation on this foundation. In the process of cooperation, they can expand their respective definitions, categories, and action plans of democracy; continuously enrich, adjust, and improve their respective understandings of democratic procedures; and search for the largest common denominator of cooperation, especially for an impartial, appropriate range of democracy. The shared values of China and the United States can be found in books that have shaped their cultures, such as the Confucian *Analects,* the Daoist *Dao De Jing,* and the Christian Bible. They all subscribe to three major shared values—love, peace, and tolerance—which form the basis for ideological cooperation between the two countries.[4]

The shared values of cultural economics are embodied in many fields, but this chapter will focus on the shared values of corporate culture in terms of propriety philosophy. In a narrower context, corporate culture refers to the specific ideological values embraced by individual enterprises, while corporate culture in the broad sense can be extended to material, institutional, behavioral, spiritual, religious cultures, etc. In short, corporate culture can be defined as the ideas, values, and behavioral standards accumulated and shared by employees, as well as their external manifestations.

To attain the objectives of reducing transaction costs, enhancing management efficiency, and optimizing economic efficiency, it is essential to focus on these factors: clear visions, government oversight, legal systems, contractual arrangements, institutional structures, and information symmetry. However, given the bounded rationality, natural self-interest, opportunism, uncertainty, and complexity of human behavior, the tangible forms of government, laws, and systems sometimes fail. Therefore, it is desirable to include or even lead with some cultural elements, such as sentiments on happiness, understanding, consensus, sharing, loyalty, caring, trust, faith, ethics, cooperation, teamwork, and other invisible and spiritual-cultural connotations. Consequently, a successful business needs to build consensus, reduce transaction costs, and enhance cohesion.

According to the American economist Michael Dietrich, people's different views of the world will result in high transaction costs because different understandings lead to different behaviors, which in turn cause friction and increase the costs of smooth communication and effective transactions. Therefore, it is essential to establish a corporate culture to promote employee consensus and enhance the consistency, coordination, centripetal force, and cohesion of corporate employees. Specifically, it is vital to enhance a propriety sense of sharing, including that of ideology, values, benefits, cohesion, and efficiency.[5]

5.1.2 The Principles of Propriety Sharing

It is important to note that sharing is a key point of corporate culture, but such sharing cannot be excessive or inappropriate. Therefore, when discussing the shared culture of enterprises, particular attention should be paid to the meaning of propriety sharing.

The first requirement of propriety sharing is shared ideology. Herbert Simon believed that loyalty is required to establish a shared ideology, while Francis Fukuyama argues that trust is essential for its creation.[6] Obviously, there is a certain point of intersection between loyalty and trust. Loyalty is a kind of corporate soft power, which can shape cohesion internally, generate resistance, and weaken negative incidences externally. In corporate culture, both loyalty and trust can build a variety of shared group ideologies and are a major condition for doing so. Loyalty and trust also derive from habits, including moral obligations and common responsibilities rather than utilitarian calculations.[7] However, shared ideology, loyalty, and trust must be moderate because insufficient loyalty and trust will make it difficult to construct a shared corporate culture, while excessive loyalty and trust will lead the company to centralization and autocracy.

In addition, propriety sharing supports shared values. Values are mostly derived from social norms, including habits, customs, beliefs, and other unorthodox constraints. Fukuyama believes that shared values create trust, which has great, measurable economic value.[8] Whether a group can maintain a shared language that denotes the concept of good and bad, in Fukuyama's view, is critical to building trust and generating economic benefits.[9] In this context, Fukuyama commends the German apprenticeship system, reminiscent of medieval guilds, characterized by rigorous training, certification, and serving as a testament to the German nation's history of craftsmanship.[10] Apprenticeship has three main functions: shared values, a sense of loyalty, and craftsmanship. However, such shared values must also be based on propriety. Some social habits may become negative factors that hinder the sustainable growth of the economy, such as the absolute obedience of apprentices towards mentors, which leads to mistakes that are difficult to correct, and the lack of an innovative environment.

The third key aspect of propriety sharing is shared benefits. Aside from shared ideology and values, it is highly necessary to promote the implementation of propriety shared benefits and distribution mechanisms in enterprises. At present, many business practices demonstrate an inappropriate benefit-sharing mechanism. Traditional exclusive ownership obviously lacks a sharing mechanism because it insists that only the owner of the enterprise is eligible to share all benefits and profits, and the strong and the rich take it all. This promotes a popular capitalist principle that gives most of the rights and benefits to those who have the most responsibility. Such a system can be interpreted as a type of shared rights and responsibilities, as the spheres of responsibility, rights, and profits seem to be clear and seamlessly dovetail with one another, which reduces the transaction costs of property rights and distribution. Another popular benefit-sharing mechanism is the shared equity for the business owner and manager. However, in China, this system may lead to the possibility of unclear property rights for state-owned enterprises because the owner and the manager of the enterprise may merge into one, resulting in the absence of an owner. In this regard, it may be compulsory to consider commission-agent relationships between society and the enterprise, i.e., society, as the owner, commissions the enterprise to act as an agent and forces the enterprise to assume social responsibility for its operation. As the third format of benefit-sharing, the shareholder model proposes that all stakeholders share the benefits and profits. Given that the aforementioned two models may lead to the marginalization of workers' interests, the shareholder model aims to advocate for the participation of workers, consumers, lenders, suppliers, and residents of the enterprise's locality to share corporate governance, with the aim of sharing corporate benefits, limiting the power of large shareholders, and preventing the disregard of small shareholders' interests. This distribution model has a long history in China. For example, it was practiced by the Jin merchants in the Qing dynasty (1644–1912), where the year-end dividend was traditionally divided into three parts: one for the owners, one for the managers and the bookkeepers, and one for the employees.[11] The problem is that, in practice, once this model of benefit-sharing is overdeveloped, there is a risk that, in the name of mixed ownership, the assets and profits of existing private enterprises will be taken away by the government. As a result, the motivation and enthusiasm of private entrepreneurs would diminish, leading to a repeat of the tragedy of public-private partnerships in China in the 1950s and the emergence of public-private cooperation 2.0 in the 21st century.

The fourth principle is the propriety of shared cohesion. Efficiency comes from cohesion, including that of workers and society; nevertheless, the degree of cohesion depends on to what extent interpersonal relationships are coordinated. In other words, the more harmonious interpersonal relationships, the stronger the cohesion of the enterprise, leading to collective prosperity. However, the key factors to determine whether the employees of an enterprise can be united and have cohesion are loyalty and commitment. In this regard, Yining Li suggests that shared hardship is a moral state, which has little to do with the benefit mechanism. Once an enterprise encounters a bankruptcy crisis, for example, rational employees who pursue the maximization of personal interests will generally choose to leave. Therefore, the ability to retain employees in a crisis mainly depends on a sense of justice, spiritual trust, and moral identity.[12] Similarly, a person's identification with a family enterprise does not depend on valuable, tangible profits, but on priceless, invisible factors such as feelings of affection and a sense of responsibility, loyalty, commitment, and morality. However, an excessive emphasis on shared cohesion can also lead to the violation of individual rights. Overemphasizing the moral dimension and shared hardships may result in moral coercion and infringe on the individual autonomy of employees. Moreover, if the employer does not compensate the employees for their support and contributions after the company has overcome its difficulties, the formed cohesion will be vulnerable and unsustainable.

The last value is the propriety of shared efficiency. It is also called extraordinary shared efficiency, which mainly refers to the efficiency achieved by morality and emotion with little to do with material stimulation, market mechanism, and government compulsion. However, the result of such extraordinary efficiency can be shared by all stakeholders, hence the term "shared efficiency." According to Yining Li's research, extraordinary shared efficiency generally occurs in times of war, such as World War II when the functions of the market and the government were severely weakened, but nationalism and patriotism were able to stimulate superb efficiency among people in various countries. Their voluntary contributions and participation during the war became the norm. This self-sacrificing behavior is not necessarily related to the assumptions of classical economics, such as rationality, self-interest, and profit maximization. Meanwhile, in recovery efforts after huge natural disasters, there are non-economic behaviors such as sacrificing oneself to save others even at the risk of drowning. Moreover, immigrants and refugees typically support each other in the absence of effective government regulations and market supports, relying instead on moral regulation within these communities.[13]

In fact, this kind of extraordinary efficiency also occurs in many family businesses that are able to cultivate a unique culture of trust. For example, three brothers in a family share the belief that their father will ultimately be fair in his investment practice even though in the short-term, market realities would compel this father to be temporarily unfair to his sons. The sons trust that once their family business becomes profitable, the father would no doubt invest the new profits in the respective divisions managed by the sons who have made sacrifices during a time of difficulty and provide more than sufficient compensation. This kind of trust based on blood relationships can give rise to a timely, effective compensation mechanism acceptable to multiple parties. Yining Li mentions two perspectives on a family business: the interest account, which focuses on visible profits, and the super interest account, which involves invisible love and care.[14] Moreover, in order to strengthen trust and enhance extraordinary efficiency, family businesses often implement two strategies: one is to seek experts among relatives, that is, not to abide by the system of inheritance based on the seniority of the sons, thus allowing more talented sons, daughters, nephews, nieces, and other relatives to inherit. The second is to seek relatives among experts, that is, turning wise people from outsiders into relatives, such as sons-in-law, daughters-in-law, godsons, and goddaughters. The son-in-law culture promoted by the Japanese aims to ensure the intergenerational transition of an enterprise by seeking relatives among the wise. Family business culture is closely related to family culture. Zeng Guofan stresses that only when the spiritual wealth of the family is passed on could the long-term inheritance and sustainable growth of its material wealth be guaranteed.[15]

Extraordinary shared efficiency, closely linked to ethical perspectives, demonstrates that for some Chinese enterprises, the moral principles of their employees, such as migrant laborers or rural workers, are embodied in the simple yet profound righteousness of Guan Gong. Guan Gong, both as an individual and as a symbol, has evolved as a deeply ingrained concept in Chinese culture and history. It is closely associated with Guan Yu, a prominent figure from ancient China renowned for his steadfast commitment to honor and justice. He stands as an enduring symbol of integrity and righteousness in Chinese folklore and literature. These migrant laborers, including those who have persevered through times of war, natural disasters, and immigration, exhibit incredible productivity in unexpected circumstances. However, this productivity does not necessarily align with the noble virtues of ancient Greece or the benevolent principles of Confucius and Mencius. While morality often focuses on the concepts of virtue and vice, righteousness places greater emphasis on kinship and affinity, often sidestepping ethical judgments.

However, morality and righteousness are often merged into one in Chinese culture. In this regard, in his *A Theory of Justice*, John Rawls proposes two major concepts: one is the definition of good, i.e., the conception of good and bad; the other is the definition of right, i.e., the conception of right or wrong.[16] Many Easterners are accustomed to asking about the value judgment of good and bad, focusing on emotion and irrationality. The *Analects* of Confucius emphasizes that fathers and sons should not expose each other for their misconduct, and similarly, relatives should refrain from doing the same.[17] Many Westerners, on the other hand, are happy to ask about right and wrong and rational judgment. Therefore, business leaders cannot completely discourage extraordinary shared efficiency which will gain corporate cultural support for business operations; at the same time, extraordinary shared efficiency cannot be overly promoted either because it may deprive self-interest, bounded rationality, and individualism of the room for existence. Propriety economics promotes a balance between good and bad, right and wrong, economics and morality, rights and responsibilities, East and West, and neutralization and integration.

There is a logical relationship between the aforementioned five principles of propriety sharing. Their common goal is to enhance the efficiency of enterprises. To enhance efficiency, it is necessary to create an appropriate shared ideology and then establish propriety shared values. This intangible sharing needs to be accompanied by tangible shared benefits in order to be sustainable. With both spiritual and material sharing, it is possible to have shared cohesion, and finally to achieve shared efficiency or even extraordinary shared efficiency.

However, all the above-mentioned types of sharing must follow the principles of propriety. If there is too much sharing, the enterprise may transform into a "gang," with excessive obligations and insufficient rights. Or, it may turn into an ideal utopia in disguise, where everyone dedicates themselves to sharing all they have. Furthermore, it may provide a breeding ground and conditions for the abuse, infringement, and centralization of power by business owners. Moreover, the measurement of business efficiency cannot be based on the cohesiveness of a time and place but needs to include the evolutionary rationality and comprehensive examination of long-term and short-term effects. In addition, the nature of the enterprise is also important, as railroad management demands a centralized model, but high-tech and internet enterprises should not follow the same model. In the short term, corporate democracy and pluralism may lead to higher transaction costs, while the costs of autocracy may be lower and more efficient at times, but not in the long run. Moreover, many examples have proved that democratic corporate governance, although not necessarily able to achieve the best outcomes, can usually avoid the worst. Whereas authoritarian governance sometimes may yield expedient results in the moment but is more likely to have the worst long-term outcomes, not to mention the fact that once bad results are observed, it lacks a corrective mechanism. Therefore, the right principle is propriety democracy, centralization, or sharing.

5.2 Moral Regulation

In the face of frequent failure of government and market regulations, cultural economics advocates a third type of regulation with moderate implications: moral regulation, which facilitates the allocation of resources. Morality is a part of culture. This kind of moral regulation reflects propriety principles beyond market regulation and government intervention. It can help to restrain the excessive greed of the market and weaken the extreme intervention of the government, thus balancing the different utility of these forces and providing human and moral support for the healthy operation and sustainable development of economic activities.

It is well known that before the emergence of markets and governments, human civilization was sustained and developed not by governments and institutions, nor by markets and technology, but by morality, including customs, traditions, beliefs, and language. When faced with a shortage crisis where demand exceeded supply, the customary norm in matrilineal societies was to give priority to women, while patrilineal societies promoted an ethical order in which male elders benefited first. The British economist John R. Hicks (1904–1989) coined the term "custom economy" to describe a component of this third regulatory system that exists alongside government and market regulations.[18]

The medieval scholar Thomas de Chobham initiated moral economics in 1215 with the publication of the *Summa Confessorum*.[19] Different from the tangible legal contract, morality is an intangible social contract, but the legal and moral rewarding and punishing functions are similar because their common goals are to maintain order. Given the significant expenses associated with comprehensive monitoring, it becomes challenging to uphold the rule of law in its entirety without any gaps. Consequently, the moral code wields considerable influence in regulating social order when the legal framework falters. Morality is also capable of regulating and mitigating economic crises after the failure of the market by playing a propriety corrective role.

5.2.1 The Third Regulation: Morality

As the third regulation, different from market and government regulations, moral regulation contributes propriety functions of the moral economy. First of all, morality helps to enhance the index of trust for both sides of the transaction. Moral self-discipline and integrity are capable of enhancing the trust and credit between people. Without ethics, there is no integrity; without integrity, there can be no long-lasting business transactions. Thus, trust and credit are critical for business behavior. Usually, there are at least factors to discourage businesspeople from committing commercial fraud. One is their fear of external legal sanctions and another is their intrinsic moral conscience. The legal system would be overwhelmed and prisons would be overcrowded if businesspeople had no moral conscience at all. Theoretically speaking, even if the crime rate is very high and so is the cost of the rule of law, society is also full of churches, non-governmental organizations, and community organizations, which may greatly reduce the cost to the legal system and of maintaining social order. As a result, to a certain extent, this increases the trust between people, especially because religion plays a crucial role in maintaining and improving the morality of society. The convergence of internal moral convictions and external legal and tax frameworks catalyzed the establishment of numerous charitable and philanthropic foundations in late 19th-century America. The prospect of generating positive social impact served as a driving force, motivated in part by concerns among the affluent about the imposition of high income taxes on their estates and apprehensions about potential divine retribution in the afterlife.

Further, morality helps enhance the index of ethics and the index of the generosity of economic activity.[20] Pure economic activities can only enhance economic value, but once ethics are involved, it is conceivable to add ethical value to economic activities, products, and investments. Correspondingly, moral dedication will increase the real value of products and services, the added value of ethics, or moral dividend. For instance, if a doctor possesses exceptional medical skills but engages in unethical behavior by accepting bribes from patients, it is bound to have a detrimental impact on both the quality of service and his or her medical reputation. On the contrary, in times of disaster relief, if enterprises make donations or reduce the price of their products, they will certainly be able to enhance their image and index of ethics. Consequently, their sacrifices will inspire psychological associations with affection, warmth, and reliability, all of which have priceless, invisible, and indefinite ethical significance.

Moreover, morality encourages public goods' consumption in an orderly fashion. Public goods are generally more in demand than in supply, including public transportation, restrooms, parks, etc. In addition to economic, legal, and policy measures to control demand, it is also necessary to preserve public morality. Public morality ensures public order which will maintain sustainable economic development. That is to say, the law only governs the lower line of our behavior, but morality oversees the upper line of our conduct. Sometimes, this moral autonomy and self-discipline exceed the effectiveness of the law. There is something to be said about the practice where the new President of the United States, upon taking the oath of office, does not hold the Constitution but the Bible in his or her hand. While the Constitution has no moral sway over the President if he or she engages in immoral or unethical conduct, the Bible may instill a sense of guilt as regulatory leverage over his or her behavior.

The question that needs to be asked is whether moral regulation continues to be effective after the emergence of a mature market and limited government in modern society. According to Yining Li, moral regulation does not fail because if the market is an invisible hand and the government is a tangible hand, then morality is a hand between the tangible and the invisible.[21] Morality here can sometimes serve as a "third hand" to balance the two hands of the government and the market. For example, some self-disciplinary morality is intangible, but some of the local, informal rules and regulations embodying morality are carved on stone monuments or placed in ancestral halls. The prestige of many sages depends not only on tangible tombstones for display but also on intangible oral traditions passed on from generation to generation.

Therefore, the three types of regulation from the market, the government, and morality should moderately complement one another. The market desires morality to enhance its integrity and improve social capital; at the same time, the government also needs morality to advance its reputation and justice. Needless to say, the market and the government would fail if morality collapsed. A market and government without morality as the foundation will not be able to win the trust of the people in the long run, and a market that loses the public trust will not be effective or efficient in the long run. Similarly, a government without the trust of the people will find it impossible to do anything, let alone be good and virtuous. However, the primary and secondary roles of these three types of regulation are determined by the specific time, space, and population, and the actual utility of the three often waxes and wanes. The concept of evolution from propriety philosophy will guide the different roles of the three regulations under different circumstances.

5.2.2 The Third Choice: Distribution

In addition to the third regulation in the form of morality, Yining Li proposes the third distribution, which also reflects the function and idea of propriety economics in cultural economics. At present, the mainstream distribution of income seems to have only two opposing categories. The first one follows market rules and mechanisms to distribute income and revenue according to the quantity, quality, and efficiency of people's output, but this income distribution is not necessarily based on work performance because many wealthy people's prosperity is not obtained through hard work, but privilege, monopoly, and fraud. Instead of market distribution, the second distribution is regulated by the government's tax policy, such as income tax and real estate tax, to narrow the gap between the rich and the poor. In contrast, under the third regulation of morality, many individuals and organizations contribute to society by making donations to public welfare and charity consciously, voluntarily, and continuously, which is the third distribution of income.[22]

The third distribution is a powerful supplement to the mainstream distribution led by the market and the government because the market often lacks relief mechanisms, while government relief usually lacks wide coverage and efficiency, leaving gaps that can be filled by moral efforts. In this way, financial donations have the unique function of filling in the gaps, serving the neutral, peaceful function advocated by propriety economics. Hence, the critical mission of cultural economics is to study the significance of the third distribution, the psychology of its participants, and its cultural, social, and propriety utility. However, the third distribution presupposes an institutional arrangement that requires the widespread existence of non-governmental organizations, including non-governmental charitable organizations, designed to establish a healthy, sound civil society. If the government were to exercise full control over individual contributions in the context of the third distribution, there is a potential risk of coercive donations within certain societies. This could occur when the government and the public impose mandatory donations, disregarding the intentions of the donors. This would not be the normal meaning of the third distribution but may be malformed into the "fourth distribution" in the name of the third distribution. The act of deceit, by exceeding the ethical boundaries of the third distribution, can be used as a distorted mimicry of the notion of wealth redistribution to aid the less fortunate. This constitutes a significant breach of the fundamental principles of propriety economics.

This also leads to the possibility of a third hypothesis. There is already the concept of the economic man in economics, which advocates rationality, self-interest, and profit maximization; there is also the assumption of the "animal man," which endorses irrationality, selfishness, and social Darwinism. The third hypothesis, in contrast, is the supposition of social men, which is between the rationality of the economic man and the irrationality of the animal man, encouraging the so-called rationality, self-interest, and altruism of propriety.[23] Different from both the rational and the irrational human assumption, this social man hypothesis is difficult to explain with the theoretical framework of classical or neoclassical economics, and must be analyzed using some cultural, moral, and psychological factors.

The third moral regulation, the third distribution, and the third hypothesis seem to be the third pole that is independent of the market and the government, but in fact, the market and the government should share these propriety values. Doing so will help to provide a moderate tool for the market and government to implement the ideas of propriety economics sustainably. In fact, the moral regulation advocated by Yining Li and the corporate regulation proposed by Coase can be combined into one under the framework of propriety economics. Given different time and space conditions, "moral regulation of corporations" or "moral corporate regulation" can be advocated. That is to say, whether enterprises can complement or even replace the role of the market or government at a certain time and place will depend on their moral power and image. A business perceived as dishonest and devoid of charitable activities will encounter challenges in achieving sustainable success.

Alan Greenspan, the godfather of the U.S. free market and former chairman of the Federal Reserve, said in 1999 that he had stubbornly believed that effectively implemented modern economic policies would produce the same results in any country, regardless of culture, because capitalism is human nature. But in the face of the catastrophic transformation of the Russian market economy in the 1990s, Greenspan revised his conclusion that it is not a question of human nature at all, but of culture. The so-called "czar" of the Western free economy agreed with the sociologist Max Weber (1864–1920), who believed that culture could change almost everything.[24]

Finally, it is worth mentioning that institutional economics, behavioral economics, and cultural economics actually share common features— challenging the basic ideas of classical and neoclassical economics, opposing full rationality, and advocating bounded rationality. They also oppose static economics, deny universality, and value the particular institutional, behavioral, and cultural factors inherent in economic subjects and governance in particular locations. Moreover, these three schools of thought mostly disapprove of advanced mathematical modeling and encourage investigative, empirical, and inductive research methods.

More importantly, these post-neoclassical schools, especially cultural economics, began to discard the methodological individualism promoted by neoclassical economics. Notably, neoclassical economics strongly advocates that the object of economic research is the individual and that the smallest, most central unit of economic analysis must be the individual and never the group, organization, society, or state.[25] Following this methodology, Armen Alchian (1914–2013) emphasized the personal worth of individuals and promoted the individuality and subjectivity of property rights.[26] The valuation of individuals, in Alchian's view, must be made by individuals, not by the collective or the state because the latter two do not think or evaluate. From the perspective of neoclassical economists, collectives and organizations that fail to manifest as distinct entities are likened to educated fools or misguided politicians. This viewpoint has played a role in shaping the Austrian school of individualistic subjectivism, emphasizing that all personal valuations derive from the subjective judgments of individuals.[27]

However, there is a paradox in economics: compared with moral ethics, economics is very materialistic, objective, universal, and scientific, but individual-centered economics is very anti-materialistic and anti-universal. Moreover, economics is very practical, but Adam Smith connects practical economics to moral sentiments and even metaphorically refers to such applied economic behavior as a metaphysical, divine "invisible hand." In particular, personal valuation is not based on one's wishes but must be expressed by actions, calculated by the number of commodities that economic subjects are willing to give up, and these actions are observable and measurable by outsiders. That may lead to another major paradox: subjective, intangible, and widely varying personal wishes need to be measurable and observable. This subjective theory of value and personal valuation directly challenges Smith's classical view and a Marxist cornerstone: the value of labor. It also provides a gateway to the application of psychology to economics since subjective values are determined primarily by human psychological behavior.

The neoclassical schools of economics, in which the individual is the sole subject of study, have been attacked by many modern economists. Mark Blaug argues that this over-reliance on methodological individualism is tantamount to abandoning almost all macroeconomics and that there must be something wrong with this destructive, absolute methodological principle.[28] Similarly, Alan Kirman emphasizes that individualistic competitive equilibrium is not necessarily stable or unique and that economists should give up the idea of studying isolated individuals.[29] Therefore, the overemphasis on methodological individualism is often at odds with methodological holism, methodological pluralism, and the research methods of institutional and cultural economics.

5.3 Definition of Propriety Economics

By exploring moderate thought and propriety philosophy in Chapter 2; reviewing classical and neoclassical economics in Chapter 3; and delving into institutional economics, behavioral economics, and cultural economics in Chapter 4 and Sections 1 and 2 of Chapter 5, the author has provided a comprehensive overview of the contextual framework of propriety economics within the five major schools of economics mentioned above.

Over the past 250 years or so, Western economists, both consciously and unconsciously, have constructed five bridges to connect with propriety economics, guided by Aristotle's philosophy of the intermediate. These bridges encompass the notions of balancing supply and demand in classical economics, establishing equilibrium prices in neoclassical economics, embracing evolutionary development in institutional economics, acknowledging bounded rationality in behavioral economics, and emphasizing shared values in cultural economics. These theories collectively embody the five fundamental principles of propriety economics: balance, equilibrium, evolution, bounded rationality, and sharing. They have the potential to inspire and progressively integrate the philosophy of moderation and the principles of propriety economics into mainstream economics in the future.

Based on the concepts of moderation and propriety philosophy, along with the review of the five major Western economic schools, it becomes evident that propriety economics aims to examine the moderate factors influencing economic development. Its essence lies in the pursuit of economic theories, methodologies, policies, and case studies that seek equilibrium between resource supply and demand, market price equilibrium, the evolution of institutions, bounded rationality of behavior, and shared cultural values. This encompasses the various roles played by the three dimensions of economic development—insufficiency, excess, and appropriateness—and is reflected in economic subjects and objects, including markets, as well as entities that bridge the gap between subjects and objects, such as government, institutions, collectives, enterprises, communities, culture, and morality.

Propriety economics endeavors to rectify excessively conservative or overly liberal consciousness and behavior among economic entities, to balance exaggeratedly interventionist or exceptionally laissez-faire government policies, and to coordinate overdevelopment or stagnation within the market. Its overarching goal is to seek a harmonious, moderate, and mutually beneficial economic mechanism, mediating the rights of individuals, the power of governments, and the capital within the market. This collaborative effort aims to construct a dynamic, sustainable economic system and a society characterized by propriety.

5.3.1 Principles of Propriety Economics

According to the above definition, propriety economics can be understood by its unique characteristics and basic connotations. First of all, balance is a vital principle for understanding propriety economics. Given the shortage of human capital, material assets, and market resources, propriety economics aims to explore the balance of supply and demand in the market. Balance is both a critical part of propriety and the essence of impartiality. Any market situation in which supply exceeds demand or demand outstrips supply is the main cause of an economic depression or economic bubble. Moreover, this balance is also reflected in that of human desires because excessive greed or frugality in consumption is not only a human weakness but also a hindrance to economic development. In order to guide the development of balanced supply and demand, propriety is an important ideological principle. The same is true of excess or insufficiency, but they are the necessary price of and channel to propriety. Human beings can only gradually approach the ideal state of propriety by constantly learning the lessons of excess and insufficiency.

The second principle of propriety economics is equilibrium. Market price equilibrium is an ideal state which is difficult to achieve, but it is the goal for the pursuit of maximum efficiency and a rational constraint to maximize satisfaction. Absolute equilibrium is not necessarily the goal because it will lead to static, sluggish economic development. It will also mislead the community into being overly optimistic and complacent about economic development, weakening the momentum for timely adjustments and improvements to the economic system. Although achieving perfect equilibrium is difficult, such a goal cannot be abandoned. As long as we maintain the integration of propriety equilibrium and propriety disequilibrium, the direction of economic development is likely to remain on a productive course without significant deviations.

Evolution is the third key principle of propriety economics. The desired system is built during the process of evolutionary development with obvious historical dependence. This evolution not only exists in the "former life" of the economic system but also points toward its "afterlife." Therefore, it is vital to examine the path dependence of the "former life" of economic development, discover the defects in its "present life," and design the "afterlife." Thinking about the past, present, and future should be guided by propriety economic philosophy. Comprehending and analyzing the past demands a balanced perspective to avoid bias, crafting present policies necessitates a middle-of-the-road approach, and shaping the future direction calls for propriety. It is obligatory to learn from the failures of the past and present and to continually adjust the relationship between the economic institution, the market, and the government. At the same time, an open mind and relative standards are needed to make propriety value judgments and learn to constantly adjust the standards of appropriateness under the guidance of evolutionary rationality. Yesterday's propriety may be today's excessiveness, which may again turn into tomorrow's propriety. Therefore, it is necessary to establish a strong sense of time and space, and avoid rigidity in mindset and conception.

The fourth principle is bounded rationality. The imperfections of ordinary people mean that they can hardly fit the classical definition of the "economic man," or become beings with perfect rationality as if designed by artificial intelligence. It must be acknowledged that pure rationality may be ingenuous or transient in nature. Likewise, absolute irrationality does not characterize human beings though it is a common feature of other animals. The loss of reason and rationality from time to time is normal for humans. Therefore, between full rationality and complete irrationality, propriety bounded rationality should be promoted. In fact, propriety rationality is more precise than bounded rationality because the former does not exclude rationality or reject sensibility but only emphasizes moderate rationality and propriety sensibility. Moreover, reason and sensibility are sometimes interdependent and entangled with each other. For example, is it rational or emotional to save the life of a dying relative at any cost? In this context, promoting propriety rationality is crucial. On one hand, our emotions urge us to do everything in our power to save the life of a loved one, while on the other, we must heed the doctor's professional guidance and make a rational decision to discontinue medical treatment when all hope of recovery is lost. Striking a balance in this dilemma embodies the essence of propriety rationality.

Finally, sharing is critical to understanding propriety economics. The frequent failure of the market shows that its plurality is not conducive to healthy stability and its inherent self-interest can hardly result in balance and equilibrium. Therefore, collectives, enterprises, and society can play a role in reducing uncertainty and complexity, through constructing shared ideology, values, interests, cohesion, and efficiency among individuals. The establishment of a shared community will curb the market's selfish desire and resist government encroachment, thus effectively overcoming the deficiencies of individuals, the market, and the government, and guiding economic development in the right direction.

5.3.2 The Intersection of Propriety Economics and Moderate Philosophy

The six principles of propriety philosophy discussed in Chapter 2 (middle range, ordinariness, subjectivity, historicity, neutrality, and relativity) have many intersections with the five principles of propriety economics deliberated in this chapter (balance, equilibrium, evolution, bounded rationality, and sharing). The philosophy of propriety serves as a guiding principle for propriety economics, while propriety economics, in turn, enriches and further evolves the concepts of propriety and moderate philosophy.

First, the middle principle of propriety philosophy directly powers the balance and equilibrium of propriety economics. Only with a clear concept of the middle can we define the two sides, poles, parties, and factions, and compare the boundaries among insufficiency, excess, and moderation. The middle, hence, provides a reference for balance and equilibrium, including the balance between supply and demand, input and output, inflation and depression, as well as the price equilibrium, incremental revenue, positive and negative feedback, etc.

In addition, the historicity of propriety philosophy is similar to the evolutionary nature of propriety economics. They share comparable emphasis on the longitudinal changes in time and promote a strong sense of historicity, opposing a static, isolated, and one-sided understanding and analysis of problems. The evolution of dynamics is one of the fundamental ideas of propriety economics.

Furthermore, the ordinariness of propriety philosophy is a kind of guide to the bounded rationality of propriety economics because perfect rationality represents a super-ideal, extraordinary perfection, which is the rational expectation of the "economic man," but most ordinary people can hardly achieve it. Therefore, propriety rationality or bounded rationality reflects the mediocrity, middle ground, and reality of ordinary human beings, which is the normal state for most of us.

Finally, the neutrality of propriety philosophy guides the sharing of propriety economics. In essence, sharing involves fostering cooperation among economic entities in the midst of their divergent ideologies, values, and interests. In particular, shared interests are more critical because many economic conflicts originate from the inequitable distribution of benefits. If benefit sharing can be realized, many conflicts and confrontations can be solved and the concept of peaceful neutrality can be realized.

In short, we need to ask: what does a propriety economy depend on? In addition to the propriety of human nature, a propriety economy requires rationality, market, production, supply, and balance as advocated by classical economics. Meanwhile, propriety economics entails demand, price, and equilibrium as promoted by neoclassical economics. Propriety economics also strongly supports the concepts of institutions, laws, values, firms, collectives, organizations, communities, psychology, culture, and bounded rationality emphasized by institutional economics, behavioral economics, and cultural economics. Actually, all components of propriety economics are based on the reality of limited resources and the constraints of human cognition, which are the basic preconditions for all economic behavior. The classical and neoclassical ideals are beautiful and rich, but limited resources and limited abilities determine the harsh reality.

Therefore, the mission of propriety economics is based on the fact that objective resources are limited; thus, subjective economic behavior must be appropriate. The excessive squandering of resources is both wasteful and unsustainable; excessively inefficient use of resources is extravagant and creates deficiency. In this way, propriety economics embodies the moderate path that has been gradually moving the world economy toward balance, neutrality, and relativity for nearly 250 years.

Chapter 6

Trichotomism and Propriety Economic Theory

Trichotomism is a concept often used to describe a division or classification into three distinct parts or categories. It implies a tripartite or threefold division. In various contexts, trichotomism can refer to the idea of dividing something into three distinct elements or principles.[1] This chapter will explore the fundamental principles of propriety economics, particularly focusing on trichotomism and triad theory—a guiding concept derived from the foundational values of moderate philosophy. While philosophical thought stands as a superior intellectual pursuit, theory serves to enhance and fortify cognitive processes. The discussion of the triad theory represents a pivotal endeavor aimed at elucidating the principal framework, structure, and themes inherent to propriety economics. This endeavor ultimately contributes to a deeper, more critical understanding of the field.

6.1 Trichotomism

Given that the two elements of excess and insufficiency often violate the principles of propriety, trichotomism is an important reference for understanding propriety economics. Finding, judging, and choosing the third path is vital for economists to identify whether economic operations and policies are excessive, adhere to the principle of moderation, and find the appropriate middle choice at the end.

6.1.1 The Core of Trichotomism

Trichotomism is also known as triad theory. The essence of trichotomism is to challenge the traditional dichotomism and monism by trying to find a third element between or in addition to the two elements.[2] For example, trichotomist ontology, in a philosophical context, typically refers to a worldview or metaphysical framework that revolves around the idea of a triad or triadic structure as fundamental to understanding the nature of reality or being. It suggests that reality can be best understood in terms of a tripartite or threefold division, where three elements or principles are interconnected and interdependent. In general, the first component represents the subjective and spiritual mind, the second part refers to the objective and material energy flow, and the third portion signifies human cognitive and intellectual reasoning.[3] Confucian philosophy also refers to heaven, earth, and human as the three poles, which symbolize the qi, form, and virtue of the universe, respectively.[4]

At the same time, trichotomist epistemology holds that the human cognitive system is constructed through thinking (a priori and rational), action (experience and sensibility), and learning (studying and enlightenment). Just as Kant goes beyond the two ends of sensibility and reason and proposes knowledge, he believes that the human mind should have three aspects—sensuality, understanding, and reason—and advocates the concept of innate comprehensive judgment.[5]

In addition to trichotomist ontology and trichotomist epistemology, there is also a need to construct a trichotomist value theory, including truth, goodness, and beauty. According to the triple elements of yin, yang, and harmony; the triple positions of the upper, middle, and lower; and the triple values of radical, conservative, and moderate, the trichotomist value theory is prevalent in things and people.[6] The fundamental mission of trichotomist ontology, trichotomist epistemology, and trichotomist value theory is how to realize the middle way and the way of propriety among the three.

In fact, in addition to the Confucian philosophy of moderation in favor of dividing one into three, Daoism also advocates the essence of three.[7] In ancient Chinese philosophy, "three" signifies wisdom with proverbial sayings such as "when three people walk alongside one another, one of them must be my teacher." "Three" also has a unique function of stability. In addition, "three" has an inherent harmonizing role that can approach coordination between the left and right, upper and lower, and internal and external poles. As Liqiang Wang points out, the core of the *I Ching* is not just yin and yang but is rooted in three elements: yin, yang, and harmony. He thus emphasizes that "three" is the core of everything, as there are invariably three "sources" that are independent of yet interacting with one another at all levels. He realizes that the world is defined by three distinct characteristics, much like how three non-collinear points determine a surface.[8]

According to Fuxiang Ye's research, human knowledge about economics covers three major principles: the cyclical changes of economic development; harmony, which is similar to Adam Smith's principle of an invisible hand; and optimization. Given that the mathematical description of optimization is the extreme value, it is the market function idealized by the classical and neoclassical schools of economics.[9]

Trichotomism enhances comprehension of propriety economics because it divides existing economic phenomena into three different elements and variables as far as possible and puts them in the same system for observation. This triangular perspective supports forming different spatial and temporal references of left, middle, and right; top, middle, and bottom; inside, middle, and outside; front, middle, and back; and morning, noon, and evening. By embracing a perspective grounded in the principle of one divided by three, trichotomism can streamline the analysis and comparison of the best, second best, and worst options for each economic policy, aiming to achieve the impartial spectator that Adam Smith esteemed. Further, while looking for solutions to economic problems and designing policies, it is wise to propose three choices, top, middle, and bottom, to respond to different possible consequences comprehensively, systematically, and sophisticatedly.

6.1.2 The Role of Trichotomism in the Humanities and Social Sciences

The idea of trichotomism has been widely applied in the humanities and social sciences, providing a richer academic basis for propriety economics. According to Christian theology influenced by trichotomism, human beings are composed of three parts, spirit, soul, and body, which in essence suggest that the spirit is a higher level of intermediary between the body and the soul. Only through the spirit can a human being live a noble spiritual life and create a relationship with God because the spirit is above the soul.[10] Trichotomist theology is evident in the New Testament of the Bible. In 1 Thessalonians 5:23, Paul speaks of the spirit, soul, and body. Matthew 22:37 indicates that we should love God with heart, soul, and mind. In Hebrews 4:12, Paul also mentions the need to gain insight into God in man, and to separate the soul from the spirit.

Proposed and developed by Robert Sternberg, the triarchic theory of intelligence is also meaningful because it believes that human beings enhance their intelligence through three channels. The first one is how the human subject adapts, chooses, and transforms the external world, while the second is how the human subject understands external information and internal psychological characteristics. Thirdly, human beings must experience the connection between the external world and the internal world in reality. The ability and experience of connecting the inside and outside are crucial to balancing and optimizing the two previous efforts.[11]

In this regard, John Holland (1929–2015) mentions in his famous book *Hidden Order* that the ancient Greek Thales of Miletus (626–548? BCE), who lived more than 2,500 years ago, contributed to the development of logic, mathematics, science, rules, and order. But these rigid disciplines have severely constrained the imagination, which involves the creative use of metaphors to enhance understanding and generate new insights, just as rhyme constrained Western poetry. The combination of the logical-mathematical approach of Western science with the metaphorical analogies of the Chinese tradition may effectively break down the limitations of these two existing but separate traditions. In human history, we have faced complex problems, and combining these two traditions may enable us to do better at solving them. For this reason, Holland describes complexity as a "hidden order," because it is not an explicit, visible order that can be modeled mathematically, but a hidden one with Eastern mystical and metaphysical genes.[12] This is similar to the metaphor of an invisible hand, as the word "hidden" and the word "invisible" are simply synonyms.

Ternary aesthetics is also desirable because, historically, Western aesthetics uses binary logic, dividing beauty into "beautiful" and "sublime." Generally speaking, beauty refers to women, while sublime may apply to men, without paying attention to the intermediate states and areas between the two. The neutral beauty of classical Chinese aesthetics is in fact a ternary aesthetics.[13] This concept is exemplified in traditional Chinese painting, which often incorporates the practice of leaving significant blank spaces on the canvas. These empty white areas create a considerable distance between heaven and earth, as well as between people and scenery. This technique forms a philosophical realm where, at times, the absence of something painted on a canvas is more profound than any actual painting. Therefore, ternary aesthetics is inspired by the fact that beauty is not limited to the two poles of yin and yang. The beauty between yin and yang should not be excluded or ignored because beauty is not necessarily expressed only by tangible, colorful, and tasteful art. Rather, this propriety beauty is transcendent and neutral.

Furthermore, Robert Sternberg not only proposes the triarchic theory of intelligence but also the triangular theory of love, which posits that human love is composed of three basic components: intimacy, passion, and commitment. This breaks with the two elements of love that people often see, intimacy and passion, and adds a rational third element: commitment. Commitment is a responsibility and a covenant, in Sternberg's view, the sense of which distinguishes human beings from animals because it transcends affection and sexual desire. In particular, his analysis of the interaction of the three components is enlightening for the study of propriety economics. Of course, people usually hope that the so-called perfect love will include intimacy, passion, and commitment, with trust as the cornerstone, sexual attraction as the catalyst, and obligation as the constraint. In reality, however, such love is both scarce and difficult to sustain.[14]

Trichotomism in the social sciences and humanities has gone beyond the binary opposition between two choices and introduced a third reference. This third aspect can often provide a higher overall advantage and a more optimal outcome than the other two, helping to minimize deficiencies and imbalances of existing theories.

6.1.3 Trichotomism and the Natural Sciences

The concept of trichotomism is not only promoted in the social sciences and humanities but also supported and evidenced by various theories and research in the natural sciences.[15] It is worth discussing the phenomenon of symmetry breaking, which was pioneered by physicists in the 1830s, as part of quantum field theory. It mainly refers to the emergence of asymmetric factors in an original system with a high degree of symmetry. However, according to this theory, the world will lose its vitality and there is a possibility for chaos without symmetry breaking.[16]

In propriety economics, this theory implies that in the polar environment of supply and demand markets, sometimes asymmetry, imbalance, incompleteness, uncertainty, simplicity, and unconventionality are required. A defect represents a kind of vitality and charm, such as the Apple logo with a missing piece and the Venus de Milo with a missing arm. The imbalance also serves as a catalyst for innovation, propelling the world forward in a cycle of equilibrium, disequilibrium, and equilibrium once more. Moreover, this is a kind of affirmation of negation, which allows inner tension to be brought into play and expressed through the breaking of deficiencies. In a bipolar confrontation, hence, the external influence as the third option is not necessarily conservative stability, but an innovative, non-homogeneous new alternative. The choice is a test of appropriateness; its tension, elasticity, and transformation are the advantages of multiple options.

In addition, the idea of three-valued logic, which was developed by Lewis Carroll (1832–1898) and Jan Łukasiewicz (1878–1956) in the late 19th and early 20th centuries, sets the first value as "true," the second as "false," and the third as "unknown."[17] Three-valued logic is also corroborated by fuzzy logic, which shows that in reality, we do not just have a binary choice between black and white, as many phenomena are in the fuzzy middle.[18] This challenges the binary Boolean logic, which provides only two states of truth and falsity, rejecting the third possibility between right and wrong.[19] Meanwhile, the existence of a large quantity of dark matter and dark energy phenomena has connections to three-valued logic. Dark energy refers to the accelerated expansion of the universe, resulting in a large amount of negative pressure, i.e., dark energy equals 68.4% of all energy. Similarly, according to the velocity-rotation relationship, which is a fundamental principle that describes how the rotational speed (velocity) of stars and other visible matter in a galaxy is related to the distance from the center of the galaxy (rotation), we know that there is a large amount of non-luminous material in the universe, i.e., dark matter equals 26.6% of all matter. The total amount of dark energy and dark matter is as high as 95%, which indicates that a large amount of cosmic matter is hidden in the space-time tunnel or inside the universe.[20] Therefore, humans may be ignorant of about 95% of all matter.[21] Dark matter and dark energy are like the driving force behind propriety, and they are both the basis of the inner tension and the origin of the elasticity of things. Weijia Wang also proposes the concept of tacit knowledge and dark knowledge for this purpose.[22] The invisible dark matter or dark knowledge is not equal to the absence of matter or nonexistent matter.

Julong Deng (1933–2013) developed the gray system theory in 1982, using black to indicate unknown information, white to denote explicit information, and gray to signal partly explicit and partly unknown information, and this gray system has the characteristics of three-valued logic.[23] Correspondingly, Zhengfei Ren has also proposed the term "grayscale," the essential meaning of which is to pursue the gray between black and white. Moreover, clarity and unclearness come from chaos and opaqueness, so we should be adept, courageous, and confident enough to be content with opacity. The compromise between positive and negative results in harmony. Moreover, the flexibility of grayscale is higher than that of black and white, hence its elasticity and changeability. In fact, grayscale implies propriety, while either black or white means too much or too little; further, grayscale represents a kind of grace and impartiality. Of course, different levels of emphasis exist. The higher the level, the more we should talk about grayness, appropriateness, and moderateness; the lower the level, the more we should talk about strict adherence to rules, black and white, and right and wrong procedures.[24]

The significance of three-valued logic, fuzzy logic, dark matter/dark energy phenomena, gray system theory, and the concept of grayscale to propriety economics is that, beyond the limit of human cognition, there is a large amount of unknown or half-knowledge, and we cannot simply conclude that anything must be right or wrong. The existence of a large number of unknowns in the world proves the ignorance of human beings, which in turn creates more unknowns. The more ignorant humankind is, the more unknown the world is. Therefore, people must take care to avoid foolhardiness and over-intelligence in their economic decision-making.

In addition, incompleteness theorems are useful for understanding propriety economics. In 1931, Kurt Gödel (1906–1978) proved the incompleteness theorem: no proposition can satisfy both completeness and consistency because the complete, consistent system is either contradictorily inconsistent or incomplete and can neither be proved nor disproved. That is, if a strong system is complete, it is impossible for it to be consistent; if the system is consistent, it cannot be complete.

Gödel argues that the ultimate form of a theoretical physical system as a standard formal system eventually leads to an incompatibility between completeness and consistency.[25]

The economic implication of this theory is that many economic theories can neither be proven true nor false, as there is always discord between completeness and consistency, and in a strong system, there must be something that cannot or will not be proven. Some premises, assumptions, and paradoxes in economics, at least in the existing system, are unprovable, such as Arrow's impossibility theorem[26] and Sen's Paretian liberal paradox,[27] etc.

Concepts in traditional Chinese medicine may support propriety economic theory. It emphasizes the triad of toxicity, depression, and deficiency, which constitute the cause, pathology, and treatment of the patient. Toxic substances (*du*) represent heat, depression (*yu*) means impassability, and weakness (*xu*) is a deficiency. The natural world is united which produces the duality of yin and yang; however, toxicity, depression, and deficiency transcend unity and duality, and exist in discriminatory opposition and balance with the united natural world and the five elements of yin and yang. Chinese medicine also follows systematic cycles and combinations among toxicity, depression, and deficiency, because toxicity itself must contain depression and weakness, and depression also includes toxicity and weakness. Weakness or deficiency is more likely to have both toxicity and depression in it, appearing in the integration and interdependence of various elements. Therefore, a disease often has one in three or two in three causes, and it is necessary to analyze and treat the disease systematically to go beyond the symptoms to tackle the root cause.[28]

Inspired by Chinese medicine, propriety economics requires that the whole society needs to carry out systematic "treatment" of economic issues and try to achieve a three-pronged approach in light of the doubtful, difficult, and stubborn "diseases" in economic operations. Meanwhile, we need to identify the main contradictions and give priority to solving the most critical problems without expecting to achieve them overnight or address them in a vacuum. Moreover, implementing economic policies cannot be too fierce and too fast, or too conservative and too slow.

Furthermore, in physics, an object that can conduct electricity is called an electrical conductor. In philosophy, dualists emphasize the existence of the subject and object of the world.[29] However, in reality, sometimes the subject does not have a direct relationship with the world of the object, but through numerous social conductors, including the media (such as print media, internet, TV, etc.) and groups (such as family, friends, schools, communities, military, churches, etc.). Conductors often cause the subject's perception of the object to be misleading and affect the subject's destructive behavior toward the object. In other words, sometimes the conductors can be so powerful that they can recreate the subject and the object. The role of such conductors is even more frightening and unpredictable in the age of the internet, artificial intelligence, and metaverse.

Introducing the conductor as the third element and transforming the conductor, subject, and object into the same system for comprehensive observation and testing is critical for propriety economic research. For example, according to the research framework of meso-history, if macro-history focuses on the objective world and grand narratives and micro-history concentrates on subjective individuals, then meso-history is mainly about the conductors, including groups (e.g., families and schools between individuals and society), media (e.g., various media between subjective judgment and the objective world), and regions (e.g., cities and industries between communities and countries).[30] The study of these meso-historical issues is similar to that of the principles of meso-economics.

In conclusion, trichotomism, which is supported by natural science, also inspires the construction of propriety economics. The balanced nature of propriety economics determines that defects and imbalances are both dangers and opportunities, providing conditions and a basis for a moderate balance. The evolutionary nature of propriety economics, further, means that temporary confusion between right and wrong or truth and falsehood is not necessarily negative. Scholars and policymakers are required to be calm and rational, to find moderate solutions from the historical evolutionary path, and to encourage decision-makers not to be impatient and arbitrary. Propriety economics also suggests that self-contradictions and paradoxical dilemmas are not terrible. Instead, they may provide an opportunity to stimulate people not to obey political leaders or follow famous scholars, and to help them think independently and make propriety decisions. Additionally, the intermediate, balanced nature of propriety economics requires that people not be afraid of introducing complex third elements, but regard them as prospects for solving problems and helping decision-makers analyze and tackle them in a systematic, holistic, and pluralistic manner. Finally, the conductivity, neutrality, coordination, and compromise of the third element are the essence of the shared nature of propriety economics, which pursues harmony with differences and seeks common ground while preserving variances.

6.1.4 Trilemma and Dilemma Enlightenment

The trilemma, like a three-way dilemma, is related to trichotomism, also known as the trilemma choice or the impossible trinity.[31] A trilemma is a situation in which there are three choices for a given condition, but any one of them is, or seems to be, unacceptable or undesirable. Thus, people are faced with two logically equivalent choices: one is to choose one of three; the other is to choose two of three.

Many trilemmas have been found in economics and economics-related disciplines, which have inspired the study of propriety economics. One of them is Mondale's triadic paradox, or the impossible trinity. This refers to the fact that in international finance, a country cannot achieve the following three policy objectives at the same time: free capital mobility, fixed exchange rate, and independent, autonomous monetary policy. According to the Mundell-Fleming model, no small open economy can achieve all three at the same time but must choose one or another.[32] This is also similar to the trilemma of globalization, that is, when faced with the three options of globalization, democratic politics, and the integrity of state sovereignty, it is difficult to practice all three.[33]

The wage policy trilemma is another example. Peter Swenson points out that in the process of fighting for higher wages, labor unions need to navigate three mutually constraining concepts of equality in wages, employment, and profits, and are thus caught in two trilemmas. If unions want to fight for the ideal wage for workers in a specific industry, it is difficult to maximize the employment opportunities in that industry because high wages will lead to unemployment, thus giving rise to the so-called "horizontal trilemma." At the same time, when the union seeks a wage increase, it faces limitations in requesting the employer to allocate a larger portion of its profits toward wages. Similarly, it is challenging for the union to demand job security for the workers, leading to what is known as the "vertical trilemma." As a result, unions can only sway from one side to the other in formulating their wage policies and political strategies.[34]

Likewise, there is a trilemma around price stability, full employment, and unrestricted wages. If the government must guarantee full employment under a given condition, there is a risk of inflation and price hikes. When the government is compelled to intervene in the economy, its policy may lead to deflation.[35] John Maynard Keynes also believed that, if we do not sacrifice labor rights and people's freedoms while forcefully stabilizing prices and employment, the consequences are serious as these three goals are incompatible.[36]

In the social trilemma, there cannot be fairness, freedom, and equality at the same time, according to Steven Pinker, because in a fair society, those who work more get more; and in a free society, those who own wealth want to pass it on to the next generation freely and autonomously. Such a fair, free society cannot be equal because some people are born with more advantages and wealth than others and it is not easy to level the playing field.[37]

The corporate management trilemma is effective in understanding propriety economics. When faced with the triple choice of completing production quickly, saving money, and ensuring high-quality products, it is possible to choose two of the three at best.[38] The project manager must choose the two highest priorities among fast, good, and cheap.

The earth trilemma is a study of the three "E" trilemma of economy, energy, and environment. Given this trilemma, we can only increase energy supply and expenditure, which will lead to environmental pollution. However, to protect the environment, we must reduce the energy supply, which will hinder the development of the economy.[39] It is almost impossible to achieve a win-win situation for all three.

Finally, it is worth mentioning a religious trilemma proposed by the Greek philosopher Epicurus (341–270 BCE) who challenged the notion that God is all-powerful and all-good.[40] This trilemma arises from three paradoxes: first, if God cannot prevent sin in the world, then God is not omnipotent; second, if God is unwilling or unable to prevent sin, then God is not omnibenevolent; third, if God is able and willing to prevent sin, then why is there still sin in the world?

The above trilemmas generate many useful thoughts on the construction of propriety economics. For example, we cannot be stuck with two choices or two variables because the dilemma of choosing one or the other will limit our options, and the either/or choice will lead to more dilemmas. Therefore, we should enlist a third party to aid in the selection of two out of three options (67%). It must be better than to choose one out of three (33%) or choose one out of two (50%), which expands the reference and allows space for more choices. Moreover, a trilemma can help people to compromise and exchange between the

Figure 6.1 Diagram of the trilemma of fast/good/cheap

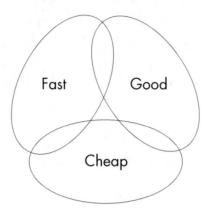

three options to get the largest common denominator among the three. It is worth noting that this paradox and difficulty of choice are also mentioned by the social choice theory.[41]

Figure 6.1 shows that, in the trilemma of choosing fast, good, and cheap, it is compulsory to hold on to the most important element (A), and then try to achieve the other two goals, B and C. Yet all three—A, B, or C—can only be part of the end result, not all of them, and it is impossible to obtain all three. Of course, there is still the worst possibility that all three are not available. Therefore, the trilemma tells economic subjects not to be greedy because, if it is difficult to pursue the first best, then the second-best or the second-worst should be seen as the acceptable result. Otherwise, there is a risk of losing all three.

Needless to say, traditional Western economic philosophy is very unaccustomed to triadic choice but obsessed with the simple confrontation of the two. A long period of entanglement in the opposites between devil and angel, hell and heaven, static and dynamic, equilibrium and disequilibrium will probably result in left and right, fast and slow, and bubble and collapse. In this way, the trichotomism and trilemma advocated by propriety economics become more essential.

6.2 Triangle Paradigm

The above trichotomism, trilemmas, and their applications in other fields help to summarize a triangle paradigm as a major component of the research methodology of propriety economics. This triangular research paradigm aims to consider one of the functions of propriety economics: Is there a third model between the two opposites? Can this third model be neither true nor false, neither good nor bad, neither complete nor incomplete? Rather, it is temporarily unknown, uncertain, unclear, asymmetrical, inconsistent, and incomplete, and is part of the unknown 95%. It is like Schrödinger's cat, in a state of superposition between life and death.[42] With a regular emphasis on three classifications, Aristotle also notes three choices and outcomes: insufficiency, excess, and intermediate.[43] Broadly speaking, the triangle paradigm and triangular thinking have the following functions to improve the understanding of propriety economic thought.[44]

6.2.1 Value-Free Judgment and Value Inclusiveness

By diluting the dichotomy between right and wrong, the triangle paradigm may avoid the linear polarities of progress and promote value-free judgment. In contrast to the triangle paradigm, the linear mindset has a strong value judgment because having applied linear thinking, it is easy to conclude that anything deficient or excessive is negative and that only the middle one is best (see Fig. 6.2, the straight line).

However, while practicing triangular paradigm thinking, it is possible to be relatively tolerant of the inadequate and excessive because the three angles can be observed from different perspectives without a static, fixed positive or negative value. The three angles themselves are not good or bad, only effective or ineffective (see Fig. 6.2, triangle section). The infinite size and infinite smallness represent a propriety degree of free movement between the two poles and various transformations.

Figure 6.2 Comparison of linear thinking and the triangle paradigm

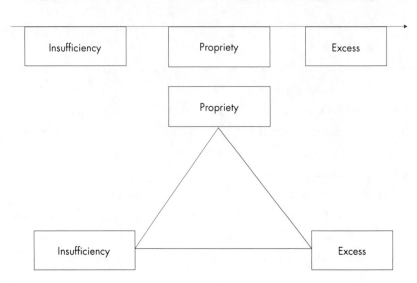

For example, using linear thinking it is easy to conclude that a planned economy is backward and wrong, and a market economy is advanced and right, thus predicting that the Chinese economic system will sooner or later move to a market economy advocated by the West (see the straight part of Fig. 6.3). However, applying the triangular model it is possible to understand China's existing economic system not simply as a market economy or a planned economy, but as a peculiar economic system with Chinese characteristics (see the triangle in Fig. 6.3). Of course, this equilateral triangle is only a hypothesis. In reality, the angles and sides of the triangle cannot be identical, and even the normal distribution has characteristics such as left-leaning, right-leaning, and fat-tailed.

6.2.2 Interdependence and Grammaticality

The triangle paradigm also helps us to understand the function of the three angles as interdependent, co-supporting, and even cyclically aggressive, without one of which there would not be a triangle resulting

Figure 6.3 Linear and triangular diagrams of the three economic systems

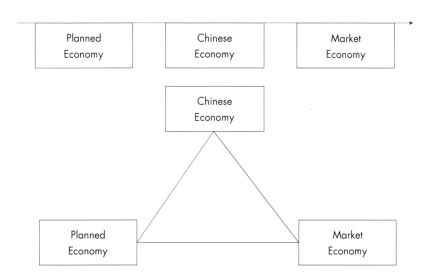

in a degeneration into linear thinking. The Spanish architect Antoni Gaudi (1852–1926) believed that straight lines belong to human beings and curved lines, including the triangular shape, to God because man thinks simply and only wants to take the straight line and seek a shortcut. Therefore, we cannot find any straight lines in his works but only curved ones that represent God and dynamic life.[45]

In this way, without the angle of "excess," the other two angles of "insufficiency" and "propriety" would not exist (see Fig. 6.2). The relationship among the three, namely, moderation, inadequateness, and excess, is like a common entity with a shared destiny. Therefore, the concepts of moderation and propriety, promoted by Confucius' view of the gentleman and Aristotle's view of virtue, are precisely the reasons for the existence of over-radicalization or over-conservatism. How can we talk about the middle and moderation without reference to radical and conservative poles? Based on this understanding, it is easy to be tolerant of the long-term existence of a planned economy, a market economy, and an economic system with Chinese characteristics. Various economic forms will show their respective status and share in different times and spaces, but they may be relatively stable in the long-term and coexist because their economic system is mostly rooted in the specific culture of a particular country.[46]

Moreover, there is a cycle of conflict between the triangles. Like the game of rock, paper, scissors, it shows the unique strengths and weaknesses of the three items, but it also demonstrates the mechanism of mutual survival and suppression, forming dynamic checks and balances. This may avoid the possibility of one angle dominating the other two angles, encouraging each angle to be cautious and fearful of one another and to therefore be self-regulatory.

6.2.3 Uncertainty and Complexity

Furthermore, the triangle paradigm can help people understand the consistency and regularity of historical development. While linear thinking can predict the direction of change and determine that historical development must be wave-like, the triangle paradigm has no direction and can hardly be regular. In light of the triadic perspective, the triangle paradigm will enhance our comprehension of uncertainty, complexity, and the unknown world, in contrast to the certainty, simplicity, and polarity of linear thinking. On the other hand, the triangle paradigm sets the boundaries and scope of the triangle, indicating restrictions and fixed intervals for future changes, unlike the chaotic, unpredictable curve. Although the three angles can become larger and smaller, the shape itself cannot become cornerless or quadrangular.

Numerous historical facts have proven that it is almost impossible to assert that a certain path or economic system of human development is universally applicable, and it is even more difficult to determine whether a country's economic development model is excessive, inadequate, or moderate. Therefore, it is necessary to advocate less for the definite and more for the possible; less for the rule and more for the exception; less for the universal and more for the shared. Obviously, there may be negative consequences to unifying some fundamentally different beliefs and systems. Instead, the right procedure for seeking cooperation in opposition to uncertainty is to identify the differences, discuss the correspondences, and set moderate shared goals in an effort to respect variances, maintain similarities, and promote the sustainability of shared values.

6.2.4 Circularity and Value Relativity

Lastly, the triangle paradigm gives people a cyclical mindset, where today's "big angle" may become tomorrow's "small angle," and yesterday's "small angle" may change to today's "medium angle." The "small angle" of yesterday may develop as the "medium angle" of today. Similarly, yesterday's moderation may be converted into today's excess, and today's excess may become tomorrow's failure. As the ancient Greek philosopher Heraclitus argued, on the circumference of the circle, the starting point and the endpoint are coincident.[47]

Correspondingly, the Western market economy in the classical sense may be the long-term unchanging choice, but perhaps in extraordinary times and places, the planned economy will have a genetic mutation or ecological variation and resurrection. As a result, an economic system with Chinese characteristics may also lead the way for a long time in China, containing elements of both the market economy and the planned economy.

The cyclical, repetitive nature of the triangle paradigm also reveals the value relativity of propriety economics. Just as fashionable apparel does not remain popular forever, undesired products would have a better market with persistence and improvement. Therefore, one should not become complacent when successful and should not give up in case of failure. Propriety economics provides hopeful expectations as well as frustrating uncertainty, showing that the triangle of A, B, and C is constantly changing without absolute certainty.[48]

The triangle paradigm demonstrates that things should be done in moderation. The essence of a coin is not its two sides but the third dimension connecting them. One could perceive the role of the third side as that of communicating and compromising with the two opposing sides of the coin. When it comes to the judgment of complex issues, there is a saying that the ordinary person often sees one side, a wise person observes two, and the brilliant person discerns all three. In other words, those who understand the two sides are considered wise at most, but those who wish to be brilliant must comprehend all three dimensions. Interestingly, in the preface to the Chinese edition of his famous book *Hidden Order*, Holland specifically dissects the hidden meaning of the characters *ming* (明) and *zhi* (智) in Chinese. *Ming* (brilliant) conveys knowledge of both the sun (日) and the moon (月); while *zhi* (wisdom) indicates knowledge (知) of the sun (日) only. With a deep understanding of the Chinese language, Holland interprets *ming* as brilliant, a profound linguistic rendering.[49]

6.3 Research Themes

Under the guidance, regulation, and inspiration of propriety philosophy as well as trichotomism, trilemma, and the triangle paradigm, the unique research themes of propriety economics have emerged.

6.3.1 Significance of the Third Variable

The concept of involving three variables merits particular attention. In view of the trilemma, it becomes crucial to introduce a third variable, positioned between the two extremes, in order to facilitate comparative research from the perspective of retaining one while discarding two, or vice versa. This underscores the rationale behind the practice of comparing the same products from three different stores before making a purchase decision. Only through this method can a customer access a more comprehensive information set, enabling them to make a more informed choice and have confidence in their ultimate decision.

Guoqiang Tian points out that it is vital to integrate the relationship between the three basic coordination mechanisms of government, market, and society because the three correspond respectively to governance, incentive, and social norms.[50] An advantage of propriety economics is that its main mission is not to study the interaction between government and the market, but the "third party" outside of government and the market—society—which is both independent from and dependent on political and economic systems. It is an informal institutional arrangement designed to save both the operational costs of the government and the transaction costs of the market.

In the confrontation between government power and civil rights, likewise, the introduction of the third element of economic capital may make it possible for the government to more vigorously infringe on the rights of the people, but it may also help people to more effectively defend their rights to counter government pressure. It is an effective criterion to identify and test "good" capital and "bad" capital. Correspondingly, on the issue of property rights, it is necessary to study the intermediary, neutral role of joint-stock, collective-cooperative, and mixed-ownership systems between the public and private sectors. When considering the role of government, going beyond the dilemma of either/or between government regulation and market regulation is encouraged. By introducing moral regulation or enterprise regulation, it is possible to study moral economics to supplement the checks and balances between the government and the market. When studying distribution, meanwhile, the third distribution through charity, donation, and public welfare plays a critical role in promoting and interacting with the first distribution by the market and the second distribution by the government.

6.3.2 Three Perspectives on a Single Variable

In addition to introducing a third variable as a research theme in propriety economics, there is also a need to apply three perspectives to each single variable for an in-depth analysis, including deficiency, excess, and appropriateness, or top-middle-bottom, left-middle-right, and yin-harmony-yang. For example, in the study of rationality, a systematic examination of the relationship between excessive rationality, no rationality, and moderate rationality should be performed. While studying government intervention, it is also essential to look at the choices and consequences of excessive, inadequate, and moderate involvement. Studying self-interest requires exploring the distinction between excessive/deficient self-interest, excessive/deficient altruism, moderate self-interest, and moderate altruism.

Specifically, scholars need to divide people into three categories— economic men, natural men, and ethical men—while examining the role of human morality in economic development. Doing so will make it possible to compare and choose one or two of them for the economic operation. Moreover, we need to investigate "benevolent government" in addition to "capable government" and "incapable government" to effectively study the role of government itself. "Benevolent" or good government may be what is referred to as "libertarian paternalism" advocated by Richard Thaler. Similarly, when considering the distinct function of markets, it is essential to scrutinize the concept of a "good market" in addition to both efficient and inefficient markets. This approach allows us to delve into the potential and alternatives presented by efficient markets alongside their inefficient counterparts. Moreover, trust, as a critical factor of economic transactions, should be divided into three perspectives—full trust, no trust, and limited trust— to deepen the understanding of the full range of issues related to trust.

At the same time, in measuring urbanization, the traditional method focuses on the ratio of the urban population to the rural population and considers urbanization complete when an urban population exceeds 50%. The U.S., thus, arrived at full urbanization when its urban population reached 51.49% for the first time in 1920.[51] However, a single standard is not enough to define full urbanization. For example, India has a very high percentage of urbanized population, but their quality of life is not necessarily high, as the conditions in slums are very poor. The measure of urbanization completion, hence, needs to take into account two other quantitative variables, including urban infrastructure[52] and technological development,[53] to avoid over-generalization. In addition, a good economic system should not emphasize only one or two factors, which would make it difficult to be comprehensive and balanced, but also should not introduce too many elements, which may lead to difficulties in calculation and blurred assessment.

A more appropriate variation of economic system elements generally requires three, information, incentive, and efficiency, because a good economic system needs to effectively collect, analyze, and utilize all kinds of information to effectually allocate all kinds of resources and prevent waste. A good system needs to formulate an incentive mechanism to promote the alignment of individual and collective rationality to reduce transaction costs.[54] The ultimate goal of optimizing resource allocation and incentive mechanisms is to improve and perfect the efficiency of economic growth and reduce information costs.[55] Therefore, these three basic elements should be combined for the goal of choosing and improving an economic system. However, sometimes an economic system is not perfect, so it is difficult to achieve a flawless combination of the three elements. Thus, economists and policymakers are required to understand the trade-offs; seek, exchange, and choose the maximum denominator among the three elements; and learn when, where, and who needs to choose which one or two elements as the priority of their particular economic system arrangement. In this way, the universal requirements of a successful economic system can be met, and such a system can be better adapted to specific national conditions so as to achieve an appropriate combination of universality and specificity.

6.3.3 Three Interpretations of the Same Concept

The changeability, relativity, and inclusiveness of propriety philosophy determine the discursive nature of propriety economics, which helps economists to interpret the same concept in three different ways according to different times and contexts, thus enhancing the opportunities for critical thinking. For example, the interpretation of the important economic concept of creative destruction is a highly inclusive proposition that reflects the essence of propriety economics. The first interpretation of this concept comes from the leftist viewpoint of Marxism, proposed by the radical German sociologist Werner Sombart (1863–1941) in 1913, whose original meaning was that capitalist society keeps creating wealth on the one hand but keeps destroying it through wars and economic crises on the other, and finally, capitalism is bound for extinction. This is similar to Marx's theory of alienation: capitalism creates the working class, and once the working class is strong enough, it must eventually overthrow capitalism through revolutionary violence and hence establish socialism.[56]

This concept, created by the left, was interpreted and developed by the right in 1942 as a powerful defense of capitalism. At that time, Joseph Schumpeter (1883–1950), representing the Austrian school of liberalism, expanded upon this Marxist concept of "creative destruction."[57] He believed that innovation by entrepreneurs leads to a wave of creative destruction, which is the driving force of economic growth. Consequently, their innovation will eliminate the old system in terms of order and structure within the firm, causing old stock, concepts, technologies, and equipment to be abandoned. In the process of dynamic competition, entrepreneurs are able to continuously transform and restructure their businesses. Of course, this creative destruction also means reducing the scale of operations, improving the efficiency and vitality of the company, and promoting the development of the market in a more efficient direction.

Meanwhile, Schumpeter disagreed with the neoclassical assumption of full or perfect competition because it means that all companies in an industry produce the same goods, sell them at the same price, and obtain the same technology, the result of which will not be conducive to innovation. Schumpeter defends monopoly, emphasizing that a certain degree of monopoly is better than perfect competition and that firms need an "ever-present threat" when they try to maintain continuous innovative competition. He cites the example of Alcoa (Aluminum Company of America), which continued to innovate while maintaining a monopoly and their product prices fell to only 8.8% of 1890 levels, but according to Schumpeter, output had soared from 30 tons to 103,400 tons. In this way, he concluded, contrary to the Marxists, that the existence of creative destruction made capitalism the best economic system for mankind.[58]

Faced with these dual interpretations of the same concept, propriety economics helps economists to find a third balanced, moderate interpretation. Obviously, the left emphasizes destruction and the right focuses on creation, but both sides ignore the interactive, balanced relationship between creation and destruction as mutual cause and effect. Given that systems and institutions cannot be overly stable, systems that refuse to change against historical trends will only be short-lived. Moderate destruction hence is the driving force for the regeneration and renewal of systems. Innovation, further, also should not be overdone. Although Western culture advocates change and creativity, over-innovation means unnecessary depletion of resources and continuous fatigue of the system, which eventually obstructs the vitality and dynamics of economic development. Innovation itself has a great deal to do with the prime conditions regarding time-space and people because innovation is a double-edged sword that can both promote economic growth and erode morality. If capitalism inevitably leads to polarization, then such "bad capitalism" is ultimately unsustainable. More importantly, the view of propriety economics is that creation and destruction are a kind of virtuous cycle, in which creation leads to destruction, but destruction promotes rebirth, forming a continuous evolutionary process of formation, damage, re-creation, and re-destruction. Obviously, risk and opportunity complement each other, and fortune and misfortune depend on each other. This is how capitalism can continue to develop in a resilient, dynamic, and sustainable manner. Therefore, the concept of creative destruction has enabled contemporary economists to integrate dynamic market mechanisms with development economics, offering a technically intrinsic viewpoint and emerging as a pivotal element within the field of endogenous growth theory in macroeconomics.[59]

It is central to note that such mechanisms of destruction can, on the one hand, produce conditions for the emergence of other newer technologies, economies, institutions, and cultures, providing market supply. On the other hand, creation can generate social demand, especially because it not only leads to one-time destruction and disruption of the equilibrium but is a constant driving force, thus becoming the creator and demander of new economies and cultures. Moreover, this process is self-reinforcing in nature, and the result is not episodic destruction, but continuous, ongoing waves of disruption. Throughout the economy, such disruptions occur in parallel, in all dimensions, and technological changes, similar to cultural, institutional, and behavioral changes, endogenously and continually create further changes, thus keeping the economy in a perpetual state of flux.[60]

For example, in addition to the three interpretations of creative destruction, the explanation of negative feedback is also similar. The neoclassical school of economics emphasizes positive feedback, equilibrium, and diminishing returns, while complexity economics advocates negative feedback, disequilibrium, and increasing returns. The two views are opposed to each other, and it is either one or the other. In this regard, under the guidance of propriety economics, economists may generate three possible ideas. First of all, positive and negative feedback are entangled with each other and difficult to distinguish. In addition, their economic value and utility, depending on the specific time, space, and population, are difficult to mechanically divide into positive and negative. Thirdly, there are various positive combinations of feedback, which may contribute to the consistency of equilibrium and earnings progression; it is also possible to see disequilibrium associated with earnings progression. In a steady-state economy characterized by equilibrium, there exists a theoretical potential for the convergence and overlap between partial increments and partial decrements.

Similar triple interpretations and discussions of the same concept are abundant in the field of economics. For example, government intervention can be bad, good, or neutral, while market failure can also be all three. Similarly, high rates of interest, economic growth, employment, inflation, and high wages can yield three distinct interpretations, understandings, and outcomes.

Hence, when we shift our perspective from viewing the left-center-right spectrum as a linear path to one resembling a flexible triangle or a continuous circle, we introduce a profound shift in the paradigm of human thought. As the left and right points on this linear spectrum converge, we begin to discern an unexpected resemblance, blurring the intrinsic differences that once seemed evident. In a dynamically rotating world characterized by circular or angular motions, distinctions between high, middle, and low, as well as left, center, and right, fade away. Each point or corner assumes its own unique value of existence, relying on one another for mutual sustenance. Skepticism directed at the extremes of left and right can paradoxically propel them further apart, pushing the pendulum to the far ends of the spectrum before it eventually swings back toward its initial position. In this context, Adam Smith's metaphor of the invisible hand becomes applicable, illustrating how subjective intentions can lead to unforeseen objective consequences, often resulting in a shared adverse outcome of impropriety.

In conclusion, embracing the concept of triangular thinking and the triangle paradigm can unlock new avenues of research aligned with propriety economics. It enables exploration of diverse research topics, enhances research methodologies, and elevates research quality, promising a richer understanding of this intricate subject.

Chapter 7

Research Methodology
of Propriety Economics

Propriety economics, in alignment with the principles of propriety philosophy, is inherently subjective, relative, and evolutionary in nature. Like institutional economics, behavioral economics, and cultural economics, it defies precise mathematical modeling to measure proper quantitative standards. However, this does not preclude the utilization of certain tools such as diagrams, curves, quantitative questionnaires, statistical methods, and skillful integration of qualitative and quantitative approaches. These resources allow for thorough, innovative research within the realm of propriety economics.

In accordance with the tenets of propriety philosophy and trichotomism, the research methodology of propriety economics must encourage the fusion and synergy of the two traditional facets of research methodology while pioneering a third approach. W. Brian Arthur introduces the concept of combinatorial evolution or evolution by a combination.[1] It is different from Darwinian evolution, which posits that today's discoveries build upon yesterday's foundations and inspirations. Evolutional combination suggests that advances in technology and methods often result from non-linear, horizontal combinations, especially within the same era and location, while historical paths and ancestral footprints guide technological progress.[2]

It is crucial to recognize that Darwinian evolution embodies incremental change and innovation, while combinatorial evolution represents a form of stock transformation and improvement. Combinatorial evolution involves utilizing existing advanced technologies and methods to create innovative approaches through recombination, with an emphasis on amalgamation rather than mere juxtaposition.

What the evolution of combinations reveals about research methods in propriety economics is twofold: firstly, innovative research methods need not always be entirely novel, as previous generations have explored nearly all avenues; secondly, new methods can emerge through the fusion, adaptation, and incorporation of existing research techniques. This concept resonates with the essence of trichotomism in propriety economics, where the combination of A and B results in C, yielding an effect greater than the sum of its parts, sometimes even surpassing C^2.

In essence, propriety economics underscores inclusivity and advocates for the coexistence of various evolutionary research approaches, including linear and non-linear, qualitative and quantitative, deductive and inductive, among others. These approaches do not exist in isolation but coexist, mutually influence, and interact with one another.

7.1 Qualitative and Quantitative Combinations

Based on this idea of evolution by combination, it is necessary to first combine the two most important research methods in economics, quantitative and qualitative, in order to provide effective tools for the study of propriety economics.

7.1.1 Grounded Theory and Mixed Methods

Grounded theory, a qualitative research method invented by Barney G. Glaser and Anselm Strauss in 1967, contains many propriety economic ideas. It is characterized by the utilization of mixed methods, offering an effective, innovative approach.

Grounded theory is in favor of inductive rather than deductive methods, although most mainstream economists believe in the deductive method because it supports designing hypotheses. It seems that there are two major risks when a hypothesis is formulated before research has begun. If the premise of the hypothesis is wrong, it will lead to all-encompassing mistakes. It has been proven that the probability of error for hypotheses without case studies and evidential support is very high. At the same time, assumptions based on inadequate samples or poor sample quality will be limited in their academic significance because, according to the law of large numbers, the larger the sample, the smaller the variance; and the smaller the variance, the higher the precision rate. Moreover, if the main premise is of little significance to begin with, then all the subsequent evidence may be too obvious, similar to the conclusion that people will die if they do not drink water. In contrast, the inductive approach works from the bottom up, in which the researcher does not have theoretical assumptions in advance, but starts with actual observations, surveys, and experiences, and then summarizes the conclusions and theories from a lot of first-hand information and data.

In addition, grounded theory is an optimized combination that introduces certain methods from quantitative research into qualitative research to solve the common problems seen from the lack of standardization and poor credibility of qualitative research procedures.[3] Grounded theory is more inclusive, advocating that the data obtained from quantitative and qualitative research are both complementary and necessary data,[4] including qualitative interviews, literature and quantitative questionnaires, experiments, economic parameters, and of course, newly emerged big data.[5]

Furthermore, grounded theory codes interview data at three levels to increase the scientific validity. The first level of coding (open coding) mainly lists all the collected concepts. The second level of coding (axial coding) aims to discover and establish organic connections between similar concepts. The third and final level of coding, referred to as selective coding, is where the core category is identified based on insights from axial coding. It is essential to ascertain the regular and recurring appearance of keywords linked to the core category. For instance, in Adam Smith's *The Theory of Moral Sentiments*, the core category is "propriety," not "sympathy." Moreover, the core category shares a spectrum of relationships, encompassing causal, correlative, semantic, similar, differential, reciprocal, and functional connections with other categories.[6]

In addition to three types of coding, grounded theory also requires scholars to record memos, similar to diaries, which contain the insights, observations, thoughts, and questions that they observe at any time during the interview process. One of the three types of memos is analytical notes and reflections on the content of the interview. There are also methodological memos reflecting the methods of collecting information. The last type is theoretical notes aimed at summarizing concepts, domains, and reflections.[7]

Many historians prefer grounded theory because they are against the approach of formulating a concept or theory before collecting evidence and data. Most historians do not believe in assumptions but value actual results and consequences. Furthermore, grounded theory does not endorse the use of mathematical modeling or other advanced quantitative research methods. As a result, this theory lowers the mathematical threshold for the study of economics.

In light of the aforementioned characteristics, when employing the grounded theory approach in research, it becomes imperative to judiciously integrate and utilize mixed methods. Mixed methods research advocates the use of semi-open interviews with qualitative meaning, aiming to design appropriate and effective questionnaires, followed by quantitative questionnaires, and finally, on the basis of the questionnaires, a certain percentage of randomly selected respondents are interviewed qualitatively.[8] This hybrid method can also be called the "sandwich" method because it is similar to the function of a sandwich—the best part is often the "intermediate" quantitative part of the questionnaire, where the qualitative interviews in the first and third steps serve to initiate and deepen the quantitative questionnaire in the second step.

In this regard, research into propriety economic thought can consider following a mixed method approach by inserting a questionnaire into the grounded theory process between the three levels of coding and the three memo types. In other words, it can treat the three levels of coding and the three types of memos as the top and bottom of the "sandwich," but add a questionnaire as the delicacy in the middle of the sandwich. For example, once the three levels of coding are completed, a questionnaire survey should be implemented to verify if the core categories and core concepts are reasonable and correct. Then, the survey will be used to confirm the validity and complementarity of the information in the three memos, so that the survey can serve the function of carrying on from the top (three levels of coding) and inspiring the bottom (three types of memos). Through this combinational evolution, a more effective quantitative and qualitative research method has evolved.[9] This approach can be called the qualitatively quantitative method with propriety, similar to "grounded theory with mixed quantitative/qualitative data."[10]

More importantly, grounded theory believes that "all is data,"[11] so all written literature or literature reviews are also data and can be used as a supplement to empirical research.[12] In other words, grounded theory is a very inclusive research method, which encompasses both qualitative and quantitative research designed to promote both empirical evidence (questionnaires, interviews, and observations) and literature. The principal advantage of incorporating documentary research into grounded theory is that the former can be easily replicated and validated. For example, Smith's *The Wealth of Nations* contains 623 uses of the keyword markets (which can be determined by the first level of coding advocated by grounded theory). After analyzing and summarizing them, the 623 references to markets can be divided into several categories (similar to secondary coding), including market and price, balance, competition, open, resource allocation, and government. Finally, based on these classifications, the three core meanings of markets (three-level coding), such as free competitive pricing, equal propriety, and labor, land, and capital allocation, are found. Using this classification, all scholars can validate and revalidate the definition of the market by studying the same literature.[13] This type of literature verification is sometimes more precise, objective, and reliable than interviews because the conclusions of interviews are difficult to replicate. In addition, the immediate views of the parties are distinctly spatial and temporal, and it is difficult for other scholars to objectively verify original data from hundreds of interviews. In short, grounded theory provides an inspiring research tool for many scholars in the humanities, which can be used to conduct both empirical and literature research, organically combining appropriate research methods according to the needs of different research themes.

Moreover, the emerging digital humanities and spatial humanities can benefit from the research methods of propriety economics. For example, in the study of spatial religious sites in China conducted by the author in 2010, we first collected the changes in religious sites for the five major religions (Buddhism, Daoism, Protestantism, Islam, and Catholicism) in China from 1911 through various quantitative research methods, and then conducted data correction, validation, synthesis, and analysis. Based on the results, the data were visualized using a geographic information system (GIS) to review the shortage of religious sites in China. This was difficult to address with traditional statistical methods because we had to precisely calculate the average time and distance required for all members of each religion to reach the nearest place of worship from their residence.[14]

However, these digital and spatial quantitative research methods suffer from serious errors because scholars are unable to find the latest additions and subtractions in a precise, timely manner. For example, most of the longitudes and latitudes of the officially registered Protestant Three-Self churches in Hangzhou, China that we obtained from a database were out of date, so we needed to visit the sites in person, using a cell phone to locate each church accurately. Meanwhile, we had to observe the actual number of participants in each Three-Self church to get a real sense of the shortage of churches on the ground;

and we had to supplement our digital and spatial research by randomly asking congregants in person about the time and distance they traveled from their homes to church.[15]

It is evident that digital, quantitative research cannot completely replace qualitative on-site interviews, participation, and observations. Therefore, in order to more accurately engage in the study of religious economics or church economics, more avant-garde digital and spatial research is important, but traditional field, qualitative and empirical research is never obsolete. Propriety economics advocates the combination of quantitative and qualitative research methods, and the complementarity of digital, spatial, and field surveys.

7.1.2 Three Experimental Methods

The empirical approach is another attempt to combine qualitative and quantitative methods. As early as 2000, when predicting the future direction needed for behavioral economics, Simon mentioned the need to explore new research tools, including tools for observing phenomena, discovering theories, validating theories, and dealing with uncertainty. In particular, he noted the contribution of experimental economics and experimental game theory to behavioral economics.[16] It is essential, thus, to explore the possibility of a propriety experimental approach characterized by evolution by combination, coordinating three experimental methods: field, computational, and physiological experiments.

At present, field experiments are recommended to support research in propriety economics. Traditionally, the study of human psychology and behavior mainly relied on observation, interviews, and questionnaires, but now it is possible to discover changes in human behavior and psychology through neuroscientific experiments and to obtain direct visual evidence of emotions, including sympathy, altruism, generosity, and compassion. Culture and morality need to be expressed through appropriate behavior, which is in turn linked to psychology that is closely related to the brain. Therefore, experimental methods in neuroscience have become an important means to support and deepen research in propriety economics.

For example, according to the findings of German neuroscientist Tania Singer, there is a neuronal network of empathy in every human brain, and through experiments similar to the Buddhist practice of mindful meditation, it is possible to effectively enhance people's feelings of sympathy and compassion. By training the human brain, self-interest can be transformed and altruism can be enhanced. This combination of Eastern meditation and Western neuroscience is revolutionizing human behavior, helping people become less isolated and indifferent, and more caring and compassionate, thus potentially changing the methods and models of economics research.[17] However, such studies also reveal three possible consequences: 1) brainwashing is not only possible but also effective; 2) experiments can turn bad people into good ones and vice versa; 3) if the meditation practice is not continued, there will be a retaliatory rebound, just as weight rebound is certain once a person's weight loss efforts are stopped.

This kind of field experiment is also commonly found in group games, for example, in the contributions of Edward Glaeser and colleagues. They asked 258 Harvard students to participate in a questionnaire and organized 196 undergraduates to play two games in order to test the index of trust among them.[18] These experimental group games serve as an important supplement to questionnaires, interviews, and neuroscience experiments. Three Nobel laureates in economics in 2019, Abhijit Banerjee, Esther Duflo, and Michael Kremer, made their greatest contribution, not through their innovations in anti-poverty theory, but with their unique, effective experimental methods.[19] They established a rigorous scientific framework and employed empirical data to pinpoint the root causes of poverty, estimate the impacts of various policies, and assess their cost-effectiveness. In particular, they pioneered the use of randomized controlled trials (RCTs) for these purposes. RCTs enabled them to observe the practical outcomes of different policies and advocate for those that demonstrated the highest effectiveness.[20]

Scholars can also use field experiments to discover the different effects of blood relationships, location, and kinship on trust. Is it easier to build trust among compatriots, clansmen, classmates, and colleagues, or is it easier to build trust between them because of similar religious beliefs and common experiences? In addition, an experiment can also help to understand the value orientation of the study subjects, including the extent to which they agree with the concepts of propriety and moderation. It can also be used to find the relationship between culture and productivity, such as testing the effect of emotional investment on productivity. If the boss, for instance, invests more in flowers for an employee's sick family member or cakes for an employee's birthday, is that more helpful than increasing wages and bonuses to boost productivity and increase output? This should fall under the aforementioned "caring economics." Of course, this type of experimental approach is costly, requiring continuous experiments on the same individual and comparative experiments on different individuals.

The second type of experimental method uses computers, and was first applied extensively by economists in the field of game theory. For example, the American political scientist Robert Axelrod, since the 1970s, has conducted a series of computer simulations, human-computer confrontations, and other scientific experiments to prove that in continuous and repeated games, the most successful factors are kindness, tolerance, and cooperation. Players may lose a short-term battle but win a long-term war. This is a defining feature of the well-known "tit-for-tat" strategy, which implies that in the initial round of a game, irrespective of the opponent, players will instinctively opt for cooperation. After that, each round of action depends on the performance of the opponent in the previous round—an act of betrayal is reciprocated with betrayal on the other side; the same holds for an act of cooperation. But after many negative interactions or confrontations, a player can also take the initiative to break the deadlock through forgiveness, and start a new round of cooperation. This is like the strategy of an honest person who chooses to trust another person when they first meet and will only retaliate if they are cheated. The person can also take the initiative to forgive their opponent and restart cooperation at any time. In terms of probability, this kind of honest person will eventually emerge as the winner of the conflict. The conclusion is that kindness is more effective than cunning, and forgiveness is more likely to win than revenge. However, such experiments do not work with rogues who do not adhere to the normal rules of conduct, prefer short-term speculative behavior, and frequently act irrationally and unscrupulously. Consequently, it is not uncommon for honorable individuals to lose to such sly players.[21]

Meanwhile, W. Brian Arthur, the founder of complexity economics, has demonstrated the feasibility and effectiveness of computer experiments in his books and articles. He practices such methods as nonlinear dynamics, nonlinear stochastic processes, agent-based computation, and, more generally, computational theory, but he rejects mathematical methods.[22] In 2005, Arthur and Wolfgang Polak designed a computer algorithm to examine combinatorial evolution by starting with a set of primitive logic circuits and letting them randomly combine to form other more complex circuits. In their experiments, they found that this sequential integration was successful over time. Their experiments convincingly demonstrate that it is promising to recombine and evolve complex technologies by creating multiple simple technologies, which coincides with one of the principles of biology. Complex technologies are built on top of simpler technologies, and the evolutionary function of simpler technologies is like a "stepping stone" according to the theory of evolution in biology. This is in fact consistent with the inductive approach promoted by propriety economics, where cases are first followed by conclusions, and micros are first followed by macros. Experiments in complexity economics have demonstrated the powerful utility of combinatorial evolution.[23]

The third type of experiment is a more complex physiological experiment, which may be able to compensate for the shortcomings of mathematical modeling, field experiments, and computer experiments. For example, Paul Zak has published a series of articles that have made significant contributions to physiology through experiments. The conclusions drawn from Zak's approach are extremely surprising. First of all, moral sentiments are real, measurable, and significant.[24] The human index of trust, in addition, can be physiologically "manipulated."[25] In Zak's research, trust was affected by injecting oxytocin into a person's nose intranasally. This resulted in the trust coefficient of the participants being more than doubled, causing them to have increased trust in strangers and a greater willingness to donate money.[26]

A common feature of the three different experimental methods practiced by Arthur, Singer, Glaeser, Zak, and Axelrod is that, although their methods are mostly quantitative, they generally do not use mathematical modeling but rather meditation, computers, and statistics. Due to the limitations of the author's knowledge of computers, physiology, and medicine, it is difficult to propose a specific combination of these three experimental methods to discover a more advanced, optimized method for the study of propriety economics, but this possible recombination gives at least some insights into methodological ideas.

Simple research methods should not be taken lightly, ignored, or even disregarded, as they may become valuable "stepping stones" for evolution by combination. Combining the inherent methods of economics from essence to phenomenon, from hypothetical conclusion to empirical verification, and from the interior to exterior, with the methods of history or biology from phenomenon to essence, from empirical evidence to conclusion, and from outside to inside, is the focus and an opportunity to discover new methodological evolutions and innovations.[27] These seemingly "small methods," similar to grounded theory, can provide the conditions for the birth of "little theory" and become a "stepping stone" for the birth of "big theory."[28]

It seems that economics is more in line with what the author views as four cornerstones of Western science—order, mathematics, equilibrium, and predictability—but biology and history mostly deviate from these four cornerstones. History is similar to biology in that it is open but lacks order, especially the history of economics, which is often creatively destructive in its disorder and chaos. In addition, the author suggests that biology and history do not rely on mathematics and are difficult to express in mathematical equations and models. Many experts in economic history, such as Douglass North and Robert Fogel, rarely use complex mathematics such as calculus, although they do use some basic statistical methods. Again, both history and biology are in favor of evolution which is generally very difficult to predict, especially since many historical events are accidental, sudden, and man-made, like the butterfly effect.[29] In addition, equilibrium is a black swan phenomenon in biology and history, which, although it exists, rarely occurs. Biological evolution is so uneven and historical development is so oscillating that it is challenging for historians and biologists to recognize the neoclassical belief in "miracles" such as supply-demand price equilibrium, and it is even more difficult to exercise precise, measured, and static control over price changes.[30]

In particular, the four cornerstones of economics mentioned above are the main principles of classical and neoclassical economics, which are also the basic manifestations of agricultural and industrial societies. But now that we are well into the 21st century information society, Newton's mechanistic model and Darwin's theory of evolution are being challenged by quantum mechanics, artificial intelligence, and the internet. The mainstream of economics today must face complexities, uncertainties, and disequilibria. As a result, new economic disciplines such as institutional economics, behavioral economics, cultural economics, complexity economics, and even propriety economics have emerged. In response to catastrophes like the COVID-19 pandemic, the paradigms, methods, and tools of mainstream economics are in need of a significant overhaul.

Furthermore, given that single-dimensional research methods are no longer sufficient, we need a combination of experimental methods and synthesis in order to find their complementary, interactive effects. For example, Arthur's team not only uses probability and computer tools but also proposes the concept of "emergent orders," which refers to the advent of some new development at the system level when the individual components within form a whole through local interactions. In other words, in an analytical framework (quantitative or qualitative, macro and micro, deductive and inductive), if they appear in random combinations, it is possible for a phenomenon to emerge along with new attributes, laws, and paradigms.[31] Some scholars have also proposed the concept of "system building blocks," which refers to the fact that complex systems are often formed by several simple elements constantly changing the way they are combined. In this way, the complexity of the system is not in the number of blocks or their size, but in who combines them, when and where the combination, or especially the recombination, takes place.[32]

Moreover, the combination of experimental methods and formats needs to be appropriate, as its effectiveness should not be measured by size. Otherwise, it may lead to confusion and disorder in the system. Hence, the careful selection of research methods, their thoughtful integration, and their skillful application form a methodological guideline that must be adhered to in order to prevent the undesirable outcome where 1 + 1 is less than 1. This means that the combined effect of two elements should not be weaker than the individual impacts of these elements. In essence, the combination should enhance the original purpose and goal, rather than diminish it.

7.1.3 Cultural Values and Indexing Research

The indexing of cultural values is also a propriety combination of qualitative and quantitative research. Cultural values (such as beliefs and trust) are very qualitative and difficult to quantify, but on the other hand, they can be indexed, which provides a new reference for study. More importantly, their creative combination is a major portion of propriety economic research methodology.

The indexing of cultural values requires a precise definition of the values in question by scholars in cultural studies and a scientific definition of their extension and connotation. Then, a series of research tools, including experiments, statistics, computers, questionnaires, interviews, observations, and literature, are required to collect, analyze, and summarize the indexes based on the definition of the values. A qualitative study of cultural values, further, is required for re-validation and filtering to achieve consistency in terms of logic, semantics, and literature, such as the hybrid or "sandwich" research approach.

For example, since 1970, the emergence of the happiness index has paved the way for the indexing of cultural values, with the concept of national happiness [Gross National Happiness (GNH)] first introduced by the King of Bhutan in 1970 and later developed into the National Happiness Index. The GNH index system consists of nine major themes: psychological well-being, health, education, time use, cultural diversity and resilience, good governance, community vitality, ecological diversity and resilience, and living standards.[33] Having compiled the National Happiness Index since 2004, American psychologist Daniel Kahneman and other scholars have been working on several projects intended to improve quality of life. They studied 1,018 respondents, including questions about demographics and overall satisfaction, by creating a short diary of the previous day, imagining the day as a series of scenes or episodes, and giving each episode a short name, including working and eating. The respondents were asked to write down the duration of each episode, the specific content and location, whom they interacted with, and how they felt. They also answered questions about their job and personal life. Finally, a weighted average was used to calculate the happiness index for each individual.[34]

The study of the happiness index has opened up a world of cultural value indexes, and economics and management are increasingly focusing on the index of trust, while studies of the indexes of faith, loyalty, tolerance, and generosity have gradually become popular by combining qualitative and quantitative research.

7.2 Integration of Deductive, Inductive, and Abductive Reasoning

Along with the appropriate combination of qualitative and quantitative research methods, propriety economics also attaches great importance to the combination of inductive, deductive, and abductive methods.

7.2.1 Deficiencies of the Deductive Approach

The deductive method has emerged as the primary research and cognitive approach in mainstream economics, owing its prominence to the contributions of both the classical and neoclassical schools of economics. But a requirement attached to the deductive method is hypotheses, which, as Arthur points out, are like "a very strong filter" that may make it difficult for us to avoid bias or preconceptions about the objective observations of real cases. These preconceptions often obstruct the researchers' analytical horizon and their ability to rectify mistakes promptly as well as disallow the possibility of any temporary conclusions, thus further limiting the prospect of exploration and creativity.[35]

At the same time, Arthur believes that economic choices are often made in unconscious, semi-conscious, or misinformed situations and that the economic subject in the vast majority of cases simply cannot estimate the "realistic probability distributions." But given this unfavorable state of incomplete information and fundamental uncertainty, people often act rashly or compulsively. Their behavior is like that of a gambler, and it is difficult to perform the so-called "optimal move." In particular, an individual is not the only participant in the economic game, as others are also widely involved, hence the magnification of uncertainty.

Thus, economic subjects need to first establish their own optimal subjective beliefs, and then form "subjective beliefs about subjective beliefs," and other actors must do the same. Consequently, "uncertainty engenders further uncertainty," and "pure deductive rationality" is not only a "bad assumption," but it cannot exist at all.[36] Therefore, the deductive method of assuming, verifying, and then concluding has a high probability of error and is more likely to be one-sided and presumptuous.

7.2.2 Advantages of the Inductive Method

The inductive method, in contrast, starts from individual designs and specific cases aiming to establish a special form by attempting induction and then conducting investigations to shape a universal pattern. The El Farol Bar problem proposed by Arthur demonstrates the importance of inductive reasoning. It assumes that 100 consumers want to go to the bar and to avoid overcrowding, the 100 people assume that it is optimal if they go to the bar when there are fewer than 60 people. As a result, most people will select weekdays, which will result in fewer people actually going to the bar on weekends, thus falsifying the model of deductive reasoning. However, if they apply inductive reasoning, they can make all behavioral subjects compete in the "ecology" they create. Through fieldwork, they can continuously adjust the time to visit the bar, gradually move from concrete to abstract choices, and finally determine the best, least crowded time to enjoy the bar. As a result, the average number of attendees will soon converge to a moderate state, i.e., an attendance rate of between 40 and 60 people. In this way, the system reverts to a rare moderate level, with 40–60% of the total customers becoming a range that emerges as a natural balance.[37]

Arthur advocates the method of inductive reasoning based on the El Farol Bar case, emphasizing the need for the subject to constantly and promptly "adapt, disregard and replace" his or her actions and strategies according to the specific time and space to proceed by induction.

This exploration, learning, and adaptation of the economic subject's behavior will lead the economy to be "permanently in disruptive motion,"[38] similar to Schumpeter's creative destruction theory. The creative destruction theory claims that there is a force in the economy that can disrupt any equilibrium that might be achieved, and this force comes from new combinations of production modes.[39]

Arthur also takes the opportunity to highlight the relationship between induction and mathematics. He believes that the inductive method embodies a process and a theory, not a mathematical one, so mathematics is not necessarily a vital tool for the study of economics. According to Arthur, in general, economics deals with the concepts of formation and change, making it inherently procedural. To illustrate his point, Arthur frequently cites biological theory in general as an example, emphasizing that biological theory is not expressed in mathematical form; instead, it is rooted in processes rather than quantities. In summary, Arthur contends that a general theory of biology is fundamentally procedural.[40]

7.2.3 Utility of the Abductive Method

Faced with the opposites of inductive and deductive methods, the abductive method provides a third alternative. It was proposed by the American philosopher Charles Peirce (1839–1914) at the end of the 19th century[41] and was endorsed by the economist Herbert Simon.[42] The abductive method is designed to search for the cause of any phenomenon. Similar to the general approach used in criminal investigation, it not only focuses on past experiences but also investigates the scene in detail. Therefore, this retrospective method entails the observation of phenomena and speculation on the cause. Compared with the deductive and inductive methods, the abductive method has various unique features.

As one of its key characteristics is retroactivity, the abductive method goes in a kind of backward and forward direction, rather than a top-down deduction or bottom-up induction. It is a historical retrogression from backward (the phenomenon that has already occurred) to forward (tracing the antecedent cause) by following the characteristics of a phenomenon. This is a research method that helps economists make "economic explanations" for economic phenomena.[43]

Creativity is another feature of the abductive method designed to discover causes and mechanisms from various phenomena, requiring speculation and imagination. It may result in a certain degree of flexibility, responsiveness, and trade-offs in the retrospective technique. While the abductive method maintains a logical foundation, it operates with less strict adherence to the rigors of formal logic, allowing economists to harness their creativity and imagination. As a result, it facilitates research that delves deeper, moves beyond surface-level analysis, and progresses from the background to the forefront. In this way, the conclusions drawn by the abductive method are more speculative.[44] Sometimes, phenomena in economic history are difficult to observe directly, such as the tobacco trade in colonial North America in the 18th century, and it is also difficult to conduct direct empirical studies and field surveys. Therefore, economists need to be bold and creative in their imaginings based on data and literature.[45] Obviously, without creative thinking, it is impossible to gain insight into the mystery and truth behind the phenomenon.

The third aspect of the abductive method is its tolerance for trial and error. Because of the complexity of economic situations, there may be various causes, a combined effect, and temporarily unknown factors. Therefore, the explanation for the phenomena must be made via several attempts, through a repeated process of failures and retrospections, until a relatively clear, comprehensive conclusion is possible. The example of a blind person touching an elephant is often seen as a simple, biased way of analyzing things. In the story, each blind person touches a different part of the elephant and thinks they understand the whole thing. This shows that relying on just one subjective perspective to evaluate complex issues can lead to misunderstandings, as it does not give the full picture, similar to how each blind person only experiences a small part of the elephant. For example, when studying the controversial fact that the life expectancy of slaves in the southern United States was longer than that of free laborers in the north, a comprehensive, in-depth, and careful review is required. It is not appropriate to conclude, as Fogel and Engerman did, that slaves were happier than free laborers, using a seemingly "scientific" but one-sided approach, let alone draw conclusions using anthropometry. Looking at people's age, sex, and other physiological characteristics, including height, weight, waist circumference, menstruation, and other data, is an accurate, comprehensive way to measure the "biological living standard," but does not apply when studying happiness.[46] Someone who lives a long life is not guaranteed to be happy, and similarly, some happy people do not necessarily live a long life. Therefore, to prevent such one-sided cause tracing, it is essential to use the pluralistic detection of the abductive method; compare the characteristics of different locations, different periods, and different groups of people; conduct continuous, sustained trial and error; and gradually approach the historical facts.

Randomness is the last feature of the abductive method. The results obtained from the abductive method do not imply the inevitability and absoluteness of the conclusion, but only a relatively correct probability, randomness, and contingency. Economics is not mathematics because human economic behavior and the economic operation of society cannot be calculated in an absolute way, nor is it a science that is universally applicable, like $1 + 1 = 2$. The principles of propriety economic thinking stipulate that economists only estimate the general, partial causes of a certain economic phenomenon, or predict the probability of a certain phenomenon. It is impossible, thus, to obtain a unique, absolute, and total conclusion. Therefore, it is worthwhile for any scholar who acknowledges the existence of uncertainty in economic operations to rely on the abductive method for their humble conclusions.[47] Furthermore, this approach advocates the use of terms like "best available" and "most likely" to convey the idea of "inference to the best explanation" and to describe findings that may be random and contingent in nature.[48]

It must be pointed out that any causal linkage has its inherent complexity, multiplicity, and variability, including the possibility of multiple causes with one result, multiple results with one cause, multiple causes with multiple results, mutual causes and results, and causal entanglement, i.e., both cause and effect. Therefore, the study of economics cannot be confined to a single research method, especially with the emergence of new technologies such as big data and artificial intelligence.[49]

7.2.4 The Possibility of Propriety Combinations

In view of the fact that no single method is a solution, economists need to combine different research methods appropriately and vary them according to different topics. It is imperative to emphasize that propriety economics is different from complexity economics and neoclassical economics in that it opposes the total rejection of deductive or inductive methods because all methods have a reason for existence. For example, the essence of inductive and deductive approaches lies in the priority and order of how to treat experience and theory, concrete and abstract, and these two ways of thinking are not completely opposed to each other, because the relationship between them is similar to a spectrum. At one end is narrow accuracy (theory and conclusion), and at the other end is wide inspiration (experience, historical cases, and practice).[50] The key is to find the connection between these two methods and to shape a new reasoning of induction with deduction, and vice versa, which becomes the third method supported by propriety economics, that is, to find the triad among the monad, the binary, and the plural.

The conventional view is that the economy should be an object, and the public can deal with it mechanically and statically. However, the economic object itself emerges from the subjective beliefs of the economic subject, which constitutes the micro-economy and becomes the DNA of the economic operation. In this way, the economic subject and object are in fact not separate binary opposites but evolve, generate, decay, change, strengthen, or negate each other. More importantly, they are often substituted for each other by blurring boundaries. Therefore, the trajectory of the economy is sometimes not orderly, but organic; at all levels, it contains uncertainty. It emerges from subjectivity and will return to subjectivity.[51]

Consequently, to combine the three ways of thinking—deductive, inductive, and abductive—it is crucial to use the triangle paradigm of propriety economics. It requires accepting the principle of non-linearity, cycling through the three methods with the same problem, and continuously generalizing from bottom to top, deducting from top to bottom, and abducting from back to front. But more importantly, scholars should try to comprehend economic behavior and economic policies from the middle up and from the middle down, in addition to from bottom to middle and from top to middle. In this way, improving the verifiability, repeatability, and credibility of economic research is feasible and deliverable so that finding the propriety interval is possible.

For example, to study the condition of the forest, we can use the inductive method: from specific trees to the whole forest; we can also use the deductive method: from the whole forest to specific trees. However, more creatively, we should take a middle-top method: divide the forest into 10 categories according to tree species, study the characteristics of each tree group first, and then look for the overall forest overview. Likewise, we can adopt a middle-down approach by gathering characteristics of individual trees within comparable tree groups. Ultimately, this method helps in understanding the collective appearance of the tree groups and the entire forest. This can provide more comprehensive, scientific proof of the relationships among the forest, the tree groups, and the trees.

As another example, to study the performance of the New York City government as a "meso" subject in the fight against COVID-19, first, a bottom-to-middle approach is needed to analyze the perceptions of individual New Yorkers (micro) about the city government (meso). Second, a top-to-middle approach is necessary to discuss how the U.S. federal government and society as a whole (macro) evaluate the performance of the New York City government; and third, a middle-to-middle horizontal approach makes it possible to analyze how other large U.S. metropolitan areas evaluate New York City's performance. In addition, the top-to-bottom and bottom-to-top approaches can also be combined to verify the credibility and reliability of the three "middle-view" research conclusions. Furthermore, we can use the abductive method to explain the causes of the New York City government's insufficient, excessive, and propriety policies in the early, middle, and late stages of the pandemic, and to trace the consequences of the government's actions.

Therefore, exploring the combination of propriety economic concepts and research methods can overcome the limitations of a single method and help to complement the strengths and weaknesses to yield more comprehensive, accurate, scientific, and lasting research conclusions and results.

7.3 Propriety Perspectives on Well-known Curves in Economics[52]

The inherently subjective, dynamic, and relative essence of propriety philosophy poses a challenge when attempting to quantify it precisely. Nonetheless, this elusive concept can find expression through curves. Ever since the emergence of neoclassical economics in the late 19th century, numerous economists, whether consciously or unconsciously, have embarked on the task of representing the principles of propriety economics in a curvilinear fashion.

7.3.1 The Laffer Curve

The Laffer curve proposes a model well-suited for propriety economics.[53] In 1974, Arthur Laffer described the Laffer curve to characterize the relationship between tax rates and government revenue. It can be

Figure 7.1 The Laffer curve

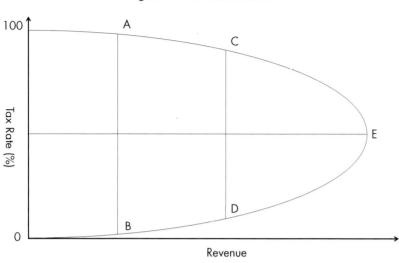

understood by the assumption of two extremes: one is an extreme excess, i.e., the government imposes a 100% tax rate to confiscate all laborers' incomes in the form of taxes so that no one wants to work and production terminates. As a result, the government's tax revenue may be zero, thus making the taxation scheme entirely counterproductive. At the other end of the spectrum, the government tax rate would be 0%, which would maximize the output of enterprises and the profits of businesses, but the government, military, and police, who depend on the tax revenue for their survival, could not exist, and the country would be in a state of anarchic warfare, with thieves on the loose, and the personal safety and stability of enterprises and business owners not secured.[54]

Therefore, the Laffer curve offers a favorable range of points C/D/E, with E as the optimal midpoint for determining tax rates (see Fig. 7.1). The conclusion is that the tax rate cannot be too low or too high and that the middle way or moderation is the best choice. Although Laffer intended to favor U.S. Republicans' tax reduction policy, the economic thought embodied in his curve seems to quantify Aristotle's and Smith's concept of propriety, with measurable boundaries of excess (100) and insufficiency (0).

Figure 7.2 The Phillips curve

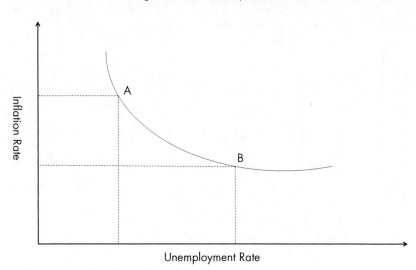

7.3.2 The Phillips Curve

In 1958, A. W. Phillips (1914–1975) introduced the Phillips curve, a renowned curve illustrating the fluctuating relationship between the rate of inflation and the rate of unemployment, which also exemplifies the principles of propriety economics.[55] It demonstrates that the lower the unemployment rate, the higher the inflation rate; conversely, the higher the unemployment rate, the lower the inflation rate. The policy effect of the Phillips curve is that the government can trade a higher unemployment rate for a lower inflation rate, or a higher inflation rate for a lower unemployment rate, but there is no way to get both perfectly. The optimal range is between A and B, signifying the propriety choice (see Fig. 7.2). Therefore, the Phillips curve is an effort to quantify and model the compromise and the middle path.

7.3.3 Marshall's Supply and Demand Curve

Alfred Marshall created the supply and demand curve in 1890, which indicates that the best intersection is called the equilibrium.[56]

Figure 7.3 Marshall's supply and demand curve

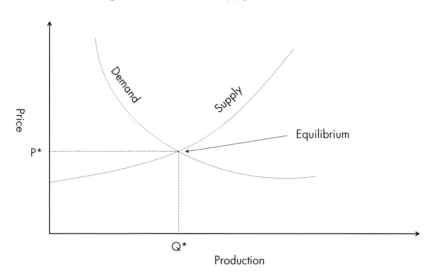

The equilibrium is the price of a commodity when the market demand curve and the market supply curve intersect. The horizontal coordinates in Figure 7.3 show the quantity of the commodity and the vertical coordinates represent the price of the commodity, with the lower line demonstrating the demand curve and the upper line signifying the supply curve. When the demand price is greater than the supply price, production increases; conversely, production decreases when the demand price is less than the supply price. If production (Q) and price (P) are in line, supply and demand are in equilibrium and the supply and demand curves intersect, indicating that the supply and demand relationship is in equilibrium, and equilibrium production and equilibrium price have emerged (see Fig. 7.3).

The idea of propriety, as expressed in Marshall's supply and demand curve, is that the market itself can constantly determine and find the equilibrium point of supply and demand and the equilibrium price.[57] Here, equilibrium aims to be measured, positioned, and modeled by an unbiased intersection and midpoint. Although the neoclassical school of economics does not admit it, the identification of this equilibrium can only be dynamic and evolutionary and requires constant adjustment of demand and supply according to the specific market situation and consumer population. The deviated market price and the equilibrium price tend to be consistent, leading them to finally approach the equilibrium point of supply and demand.[58]

When analyzing the three aforementioned curves—the Laffer curve, Phillips curve, and Marshall's supply and demand curve—it is imperative to pinpoint their optimal ranges within an equilibrium model. It is noteworthy that these optimal solutions often, in principle, resonate with propriety theory, despite their original application in financial contexts, especially the Laffer curve and the Phillips curve. The implications drawn from these three curves underscore their shared purpose and alignment with the principles of propriety philosophy, highlighting the paramount importance of balance and moderation.

However, it is worth acknowledging that the pursuit of optimal outcomes may occasionally lead us towards lofty ideals that are not always attainable in practice. Hence, propriety economics advocates for satisfaction as a measured, realistic objective for economic performance, recognizing that it strikes a harmonious balance, akin to the concept of the second best, between what is desired and what is feasible.

7.4 Diagrams in Propriety Economics

Motivated by the preceding three curves, the author aims to delineate certain diagrams and revised curves that embody the essence of propriety economics. It is worth noting that nonlinear stochastic processes like curves and diagrams, in contrast to linearity, encapsulate the dynamic nature of individuals and their evolving characteristics, evading a single, linear trajectory. This dynamic aspect harmonizes seamlessly with the triangle paradigm advocated by propriety economics.

Figure 7.4 Propriety relationship between government and the market

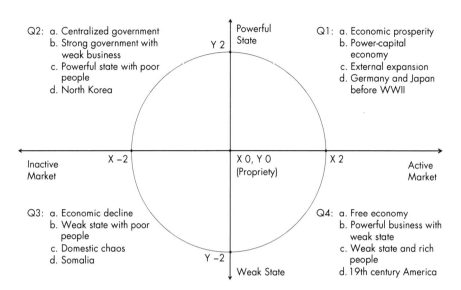

Q2: a. Centralized government
    b. Strong government with weak business
    c. Powerful state with poor people
    d. North Korea

Powerful State
Y 2

Q1: a. Economic prosperity
    b. Power-capital economy
    c. External expansion
    d. Germany and Japan before WWII

Inactive Market
X –2

X 0, Y 0
(Propriety)
X 2

Active Market

Q3: a. Economic decline
    b. Weak state with poor people
    c. Domestic chaos
    d. Somalia

Y –2
Weak State

Q4: a. Free economy
    b. Powerful business with weak state
    c. Weak state and rich people
    d. 19th century America

7.4.1 Propriety Diagrams of Government-Market Relationships[59]

In keeping with the eternal dilemma of economics—the relationship between government and the market—the author has tried to establish a vertical and horizontal relationship in a graph with four quadrants by taking propriety as the center of the circle (X 0, Y 0). While considering the active market and the inactive market as the horizontal axis (X), strong government and weak government are proposed as the vertical axis (Y). In this way, five locations emerge: the first is the central focus of propriety (X 0, Y 0), and the other four variables are shown by X 2, X –2, Y 2, and Y –2, each representing an optimization point on the boundary between the roles of the government and the market (see Fig. 7.4).

The ultimate index of propriety is X 0, Y 0 at the center of the circle, but paradoxically, extreme appropriateness can be a kind of inappropriateness. Therefore, the more reasonable standard of appropriateness is not X 0, Y 0 but a certain area encompassed by the circular boundary, that is, from X −2 to X 2 and Y −2 to Y 2. In this range, government power and market efficiency should be considered appropriate. Conversely, if any of the quadrants exceeds 2 or −2, it can be considered not moderate enough, or possibly too much. Excess and inadequacy are the targets that both the propriety government and propriety market need to correct together.

Meanwhile, according to the four quadrants in Figure 7.4, we can roughly judge the reality of different political and economic conditions. In quadrant 1 (Q1), the area outside the circle illustrates a society characterized by a pronounced fusion of a robust government and a dynamic market, with the three characteristics of economic prosperity, strong political power,[60] and aggressive external expansion, as seen in Germany[61] and Japan[62] before World War II. There is a logical connection between these three characteristics. Due to the active market and economic development, coupled with a strong government, political power and economic capital are highly integrated, leading to a high level of nationalism, hostile military engagement, and external expansion. These are the most negative consequences of excessive government power and excessive market expansion.

The part outside the circle in quadrant 2 (Q2) represents a mixture of strong government and inactive market, generally characterized by a centralized government, powerful regime and weak business, and strong state and poor people. Countries such as North Korea today fall broadly into this category. The extreme development of this combination of excessively strong government and an overly weak market economy may lead to economic collapse and threaten the stability of the regime, stimulating internal and external dynamics of change, and eventually forcing the government to cede some of its power.[63] In addition, the area outside the circle in quadrant 3 (Q3) indicates that the mixture of weak government and inactive markets may lead to economic decline, weakness, social unrest, and poverty, as in the case of Somalia in Africa today.[64]

Figure 7.5 A high degree of integration between government and market

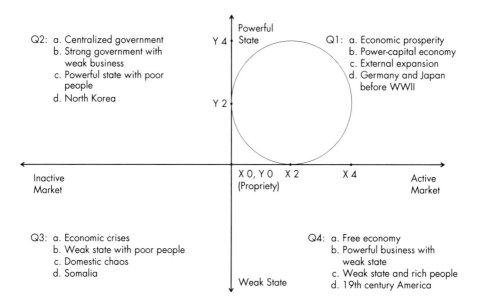

Q2: a. Centralized government
    b. Strong government with
      weak business
    c. Powerful state with poor
      people
    d. North Korea

Q1: a. Economic prosperity
    b. Power-capital economy
    c. External expansion
    d. Germany and Japan
      before WWII

Inactive Market

Active Market

Q3: a. Economic crises
    b. Weak state with poor people
    c. Domestic chaos
    d. Somalia

Q4: a. Free economy
    b. Powerful business with
      weak state
    c. Weak state and rich people
    d. 19th century America

Finally, the part outside the circle in quadrant 4 (Q4) shows the simultaneous emergence of an active market and a weak government, which is characterized by a laissez-faire economy, strong business, and powerless government, with a weak state and rich people. The 19th century United States, where laissez-faire was promoted, would have fallen into this category.[65]

It must be pointed out that the range of the moderate circle is constantly shifting according to the characteristics of the changing economic conditions, which can indicate the propriety index. If the intervals from X 2 to X –2 and Y 2 to Y –2 are the optimal range of the propriety index, then once the circle is moved to the upper right, the boundary of the circle no longer contains the center of the appropriateness circle, X 0, Y 0, and the entire circle appears only in quadrant 1. This denotes that the minimum propriety indexes appear—X 2 to X 4 and Y 2 to Y 4 (see Fig. 7.5)—leading to the

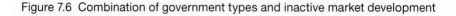

Figure 7.6 Combination of government types and inactive market development

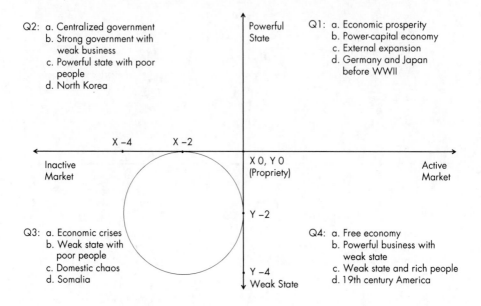

Q2: a. Centralized government
    b. Strong government with weak business
    c. Powerful state with poor people
    d. North Korea

Powerful State

Q1: a. Economic prosperity
    b. Power-capital economy
    c. External expansion
    d. Germany and Japan before WWII

X −4   X −2

Inactive Market

X 0, Y 0 (Propriety)

Active Market

Y −2

Q3: a. Economic crises
    b. Weak state with poor people
    c. Domestic chaos
    d. Somalia

Q4: a. Free economy
    b. Powerful business with weak state
    c. Weak state and rich people
    d. 19th century America

Y −4
Weak State

extremes of active government and efficient markets. The extreme, direct consequences of these conditions were evident in the Second World War.

With the accumulation of human experience, the improved knowledge of regulations, the growth of rational intelligence, and the increase of intervention tools, the moderate circle should become smaller and smaller, and the range of tension between government and market also trends smaller with the reduction of distance, slowly approaching the propriety focus (X 0, Y 0). But an extreme moderate state that stays in place for a long time only happens occasionally or is difficult to sustain. For example, if a person's normal blood glucose standard is 100 as the optimal point, the normal range is 90–110, but with improvements in people's experience, ability, and means, it is feasible to reduce the normal range to 95–105, and it is also possible to reach 100 occasionally. But it is impossible to remain at 100 for a long time. This extreme moderation cannot be sustained, nor is it necessary.

Figure 7.7 Combination of excessive market and propriety government power

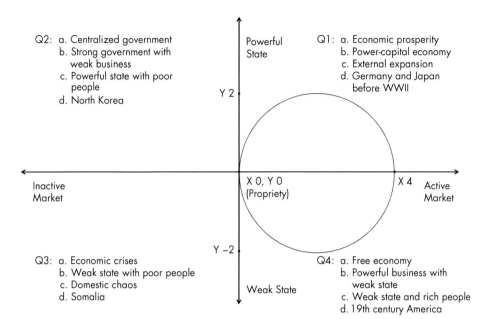

Q2: a. Centralized government
    b. Strong government with
       weak business
    c. Powerful state with poor
       people
    d. North Korea

Powerful State

Q1: a. Economic prosperity
    b. Power-capital economy
    c. External expansion
    d. Germany and Japan
       before WWII

Inactive Market

Active Market

X 0, Y 0 (Propriety)

Q3: a. Economic crises
    b. Weak state with poor people
    c. Domestic chaos
    d. Somalia

Weak State

Q4: a. Free economy
    b. Powerful business with
       weak state
    c. Weak state and rich people
    d. 19th century America

Conversely, if the circle moves to the lower left and does not intersect with X 0, Y 0, it only covers quadrant 3 and does not intersect with the other three quadrants at all (Fig. 7.6), resulting in the minimum propriety index of X –2 to X –4 and Y –2 to Y –4. Consequently, this may cause economic failure and government collapse at the same time, increasing poverty and weakness, and possibly leading to foreign invasion or civil war, as in the case of certain African countries.

Both Figure 7.5 and Figure 7.6 show extreme situations, which, in reality, mean the emergence of uncontrollable conditions. The general approach to social control is to intervene externally when the critical point, such as the Great Depression of 1929, the financial crisis of 2008, or the COVID-19 pandemic, is near because the endogenous dynamics and capacity are not sufficient. The purpose of external intervention is to bypass the critical area or node or to pass the critical area quickly so as to shorten the effect of crisis expansion in time and space.

Therefore, the principle of the propriety diagram is twofold: one is to position X 0, Y 0 always within the boundary of the circle; the other is that the more quadrants included within the boundary of the circle, the better. For example, Figure 7.4 covers four quadrants, a standard moderation; Figures 7.5 and 7.6 include only one quadrant, a low moderation; and the circle in Figure 7.7 covers two quadrants, a medium moderation, with a moderate index of X 0 to X 4 and Y 2 to Y –2.

7.4.2 Applications of the Propriety Economics Diagrams and Curves

Other than using propriety economics diagrams to explain the relationship between government power and market activity, the diagrams can also be applied to many other economic dilemmas. First, propriety economics diagrams can be used to analyze the relationship between the profitability of businesspeople and the rate of their charitable contributions, which can be expressed as a generosity index. The American Society for Public Administration has applied the generosity index to evaluate corporate social responsibility since the 1980s.[66] Quadrant 1 can be exemplified by Bill Gates, indicating a high corporate profit margin as well as a high generosity index and a large contribution to the public good.[67] Quadrant 2 can be signified by Oskar Schindler (1908–1974), a German businessman during World War II, whose business was hardly profitable but was willing to pay the price to save and protect Jews who were persecuted by the Nazis.[68] Quadrant 3 can be illustrated by the many businesses on the verge of bankruptcy which therefore cannot afford to donate. The last category (quadrant 4) includes a group of miserly, wealthy businesses with high corporate profits but a low generosity index (see Fig. 7.8). Therefore, most of the changes in similar relationships between business and society can be expressed and identified by propriety economics diagrams.

Correspondingly, the circle in this diagram can be constantly changing. The more quadrants covered and the closer to the X 0, Y 0 center

Figure 7.8 Relationship between profitability and generosity index

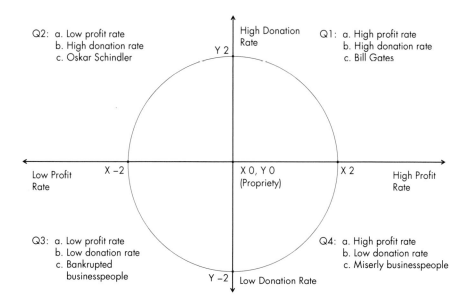

point, the higher the index of propriety, and the more balanced the relationship is between earning and giving. If there is a deviation from the propriety index, entrepreneurs need to constantly adjust their profitability and generosity index. An excessively high donation rate may result in reduced profits or even the closure of the business, while the combination of a high profit margin with a low donation rate can harm the company's reputation. Therefore, only through the invisible left hand and a visible right hand, constantly adjusting the deviation and bringing it closer to the point of propriety, will a business ensure a triple win at the personal, corporate, and social levels.[69]

It is important to point out that, although Confucius thought that excess is the same as insufficiency, reality shows that people are more prone to excess than inadequacy, and in an objective sense, the harm caused by excess is sometimes greater than that of insufficiency. For example, if the proper amount of self-affirmation is X 0, then the moderate boundary should be positioned at X -1 to X 3 instead of

Figure 7.9 Weighted plot of self-affirmation

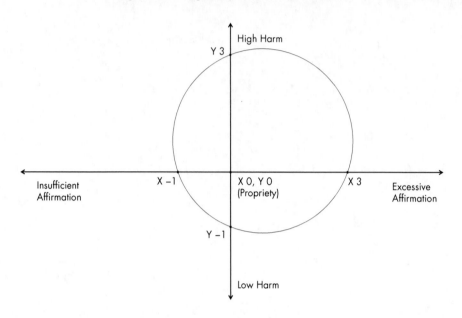

X –2 to X 2, because it needs to be negatively weighted and appropriately shifted for excessive self-affirmation, such as pride, exaggeration, overstatement, etc. After all, the drawbacks of excessive arrogance are generally greater than those of excessive humbleness. At the same time, the harm coefficient of the Y axis should be changed to Y 3 to Y –1 instead of Y 2 to Y –2 (see Fig. 7.9). Of course, it is also possible to negatively weigh insufficiency, especially when COVID-19 first emerged in 2020, when most countries took insufficient measures and missed the golden period to fight the pandemic, resulting in the deaths of a large number of innocent people. Therefore, in times of great disasters, excessive pandemic prevention policies should be preferred to inadequate ones.[70]

The use of the propriety economics diagrams, furthermore, can help to understand the equity and growth dilemma.[71] For example, when studying the dilemma of equity and efficiency in China's urbanization process, the introduction of a third variable, equality of rights,

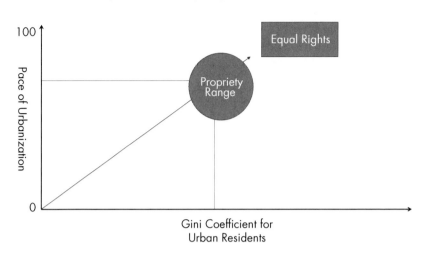

Figure 7.10 Ternary diagram of urbanization

may shape a curve that makes appropriate trade-offs between the Gini coefficient (polarization) of urban residents (A), the speed of urbanization (B), and equality of rights (C) to deepen understanding and solve the dilemma. Policymakers may shift their priorities to test the results. The first option is to prioritize the speed of urbanization (B) and equality of rights (C), but decide to temporarily sacrifice or ignore the problem of urban poverty (A). As a result, urban policy should be reformed by constructing a fair system, eliminating the restrictions of the household registration system in China, and implementing the same rights to education, housing, work, and insurance for migrant workers and urban workers. The problem of polarization will surely be solved in time. In the end, the three elements of A, B, and C will develop together. Option two is where the problems of poverty (A) and equal rights (C) are given priority; then the pace of urbanization (B) should be slowed, more small towns should be built between urban and rural areas, and more new villages should be developed. The last option is to put the issue of equal rights (C) on hold, which means that household registration reform will be suspended, and changes to education, housing, employment, and insurance policies for migrant workers will be delayed. However, it is necessary to implement equal

Figure 7.11 Propriety diagram of urbanization speed and equity (1)

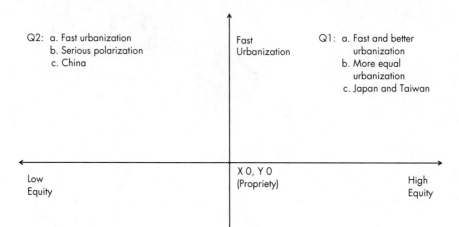

pay for equal work for rural and urban workers and a graduated income tax policy in favor of migrant workers (A) while speeding up the pace of urbanization (B).[72]

Once the three objectives A, B, and C have been evaluated through compromise and exchange, an intersection is reached, which is the moderate interval shown in Figure 7.10.

Similarly, we can also apply the aforementioned propriety diagrams to balance the dilemma between the speed of urbanization and the equity of urban wealth. According to current research, countries in quadrant 1, where urbanization is fast and equity is high, include Japan; mainland China seems to belong to quadrant 2, where urbanization is fast but the polarization between rich and poor is extreme. Some African and Latin American countries can be included in quadrant 3, where urbanization is slow and the rich-poor divide is wide; quite a few developed

Figure 7.12 Propriety diagram of urbanization speed and equity (2)

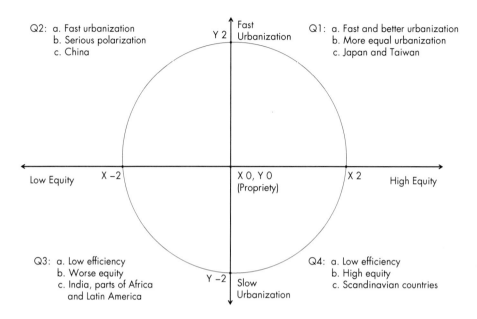

Q2: a. Fast urbanization
    b. Serious polarization
    c. China

Y 2   Fast Urbanization

Q1: a. Fast and better urbanization
    b. More equal urbanization
    c. Japan and Taiwan

Low Equity   X –2

X 0, Y 0 (Propriety)   X 2   High Equity

Q3: a. Low efficiency
    b. Worse equity
    c. India, parts of Africa
      and Latin America

Y –2   Slow Urbanization

Q4: a. Low efficiency
    b. High equity
    c. Scandinavian countries

countries, in particular some Scandinavian ones, fit in quadrant 4, where inefficiency and equity are high.[73] The countries that appear in these four quadrants may not be models of propriety urbanization (see Fig. 7.11).

Once a circle is added to Figure 7.11, the interval within the circle represents the balance between the appropriate rate of urbanization and the appropriate equity (see Fig. 7.12).

Considering the COVID-19 pandemic and related economic challenges in 2020, we can also revise the Laffer curve and Marshall's supply and demand curve to provide some clear, appropriate explanations for these two dilemmas. According to the Laffer curve, if the intensity of pandemic prevention is so high that all people are under prolonged lockdown, then the economy will collapse, accompanied by massive starvation. In contrast, if the economy is opened too fast and no pandemic prevention

Figure 7.13 Implications of the Laffer curve during a pandemic

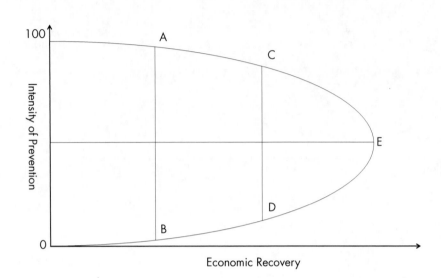

measures are taken, then everyone may succumb to disease. However, if the intensity of pandemic prevention is relaxed to point A, the economy will recover to point B. If the intensity of pandemic control continues to reduce to C, the economy may recuperate to D. The best moderate point is E, which signifies the middle point where pandemic control and economic recovery can reach a relative balance, that is, the most propriety. However, a more appropriate, realistic propriety option is to be in the range of C, D, and E (see Fig. 7.13).

It is also desirable to apply Marshall's supply and demand curve to the balance between pandemic preparedness and economic recovery. The downward curve here means that the strength of the pandemic is decreasing, while the upward curve means that the economy is recovering. Once the two intersect, it means that the pandemic prevention methods and the economy have reached a more balanced state (see Fig. 7.14).

Hence, the quest for propriety embodies an ongoing process of refinement, shaped by continual experimentation and learning from

Figure 7.14 Implications of Marshall's supply
and demand curve during a pandemic

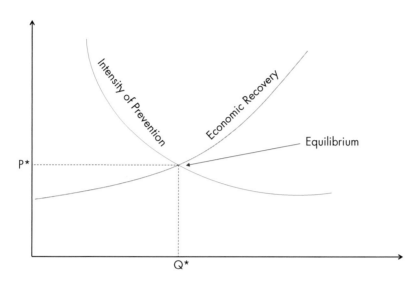

errors. The swift resumption of economic activities across the various U.S. states after the first wave of the pandemic served as a real-time experiment. In the event of a resurgence of pandemic-related challenges, swift course correction is imperative. The pivotal lesson lies in assimilating insights from these missteps and avoiding their repetition in perpetuity.

Furthermore, the propriety diagrams prove to be a valuable tool for dissecting the paradoxical themes often encountered in cultural economics. These include the interplay between integrity indexes and corporate efficiency, corporate social responsibility and its impact on efficiency, the correlation between corporate reputation and productivity, the relationship between happiness and monetary measures, as well as matters pertaining to moral and market regulation. Moreover, the versatility of the propriety diagram extends beyond the realm of economics into domains such as psychology, finance, political science, and history. In this regard, the applicability of propriety economics diagrams proves extensive.

In summary, the research methodology inherent to propriety economic thought fosters a synthesis, amalgamation, and harmonious integration of diverse methods. This approach contributes to the advancement and refinement of economic studies, facilitating a more comprehensive, profound, and lucid exploration of the subject matter.

Chapter 8

Government Policy Principles in Propriety Economics

There is a clear and substantial correlation between the development and implementation of economic policies within the domain of propriety economics research. Crafting effective propriety economic policies requires urgent consideration of three critical issues: the persistent challenge of inflation and deflation, the widening gap between the affluent and the disadvantaged, and the ongoing debate regarding government regulation versus market autonomy.

While neoclassical economics seems to be too optimistic in considering the economy as maintaining a static equilibrium state, propriety economics proposes reasonable, realistic expectations with an aim to regulate the collaborations among government policies, capital investment, and people's economic behavior. The essence of propriety economics is that economic policy must be active, moral, and benign. Most importantly, different from divine, fatalistic, and mysterious notions such as an invisible hand, propriety economics trusts that all self-interested, greedy, and harmful behaviors will not inevitably lead to a win-win situation for all of society, sooner or later. This is also where propriety economics differs from neoclassical economics which assumes that equilibrium is an existential reality, in which no one has an incentive to deviate from the perfect mode of behavior to the extent that speculation, exploitation, and free riding will not occur. In case of temporary deviation from equilibrium, the situation will soon be corrected and counterbalanced by an opposite force.[1] Therefore, the basic assumptions of neoclassical economics regarding equilibrium determine the purpose of economic research and policy, which neither study the causes and consequences of the exploitation of various systems nor consider the failure and exploitation of systems as the central problem of economic research.[2]

In contrast, propriety economics asserts that moderation is merely a potential future improvement—a goal toward which society collectively strives, an ideal to pursue, and an attainable yet relatively challenging outcome to reach. Every segment of society must remain cautious of inappropriate economic behaviors, anticipate a spectrum of potential scenarios involving underperformance and overperformance, and devise and implement viable solutions to address economic bubbles and collapses. In doing so, propriety economics offers crucial tools and solutions to cultivate a balanced, healthy economy for the future.

Furthermore, propriety economics embodies a form of idealistic realism that seamlessly blends ideals and realities, metaphysics and science, imagination and experimentation, sensibility and rationality, value-based rationality and instrumental rationality, as well as solutions and strategies. It facilitates the establishment of a dynamic feedback structure, continuous openness, and ongoing correction of biases and partialities, essentially weaving the economy into a "web of incentives." This system continually triggers corrective measures to address deficiencies and curb excesses, thereby resulting in new choices, strategies, and energies. Ultimately, it steers the entire economic system towards continuous positive transformation.[3] In fact, the concept of moderation can also furnish a web of incentives and a series of goals for our lives.

In this context, Ronald Coase underscores that the path to discovering the ideal world, such as a propriety economy, involves a more pragmatic approach. It entails an examination of the actual circumstances, identifying and analyzing the various real-world challenges encountered in unregulated economies, and subsequently designing moderate policies while forecasting their effectiveness in rectifying existing misguided measures. Only through this method can policy conclusions become pertinent and facilitate practical, successful, and sustainable economic decision-making.[4] In light of these considerations, the author proposes several guiding principles for crafting and executing propriety economic policies, drawing inspiration from the aforementioned concepts of propriety philosophy, the triad theory, the triangle paradigm, and propriety diagrams.

8.1 The Propriety Principle for Policymakers

To formulate and implement propriety economic policies, the first and foremost condition is that decision-makers should have the virtue and wisdom that enable them to embrace the principles of propriety and make every effort to cultivate and maintain a mindset conducive to moderation. In other words, to have moderate policies, we must have leaders and policymakers capable of envisioning and formulating such policies. Actually, the spirit of moderation focuses on temperance and balance in both nature and society, and the relationship between heaven and man is mainly expressed in unity and integration. To achieve the highest levels of virtue, sincerity, benevolence, and truth, we need to strike a proper balance between human spirituality and nature. This harmonious coexistence of mind, virtue, humanity, and nature requires a high degree of coupling of knowledge and action, inner saintliness and outer kingliness, and inner cultivation and outer practice.[5]

Xu Shen of the Han dynasty (202 BCE to 220) also believed that one of the key principles of moderation is practice.[6] In other words, moderation (*zhong yong*) needs to combine the philosophy of the middle (*zhong*) with the policy of practice (*yong*). Confucius once praised the virtue of the middle by saying, "execute its two ends and use its middle for the people,"[7] which is the policy of the middle way.[8] In particular, decision-makers need to be neutral, moderate, and appropriate instead of stubbornly sticking to only one option.[9] If moderation is a kind of mentality or knowledge, then policymaking is a way of putting such knowledge into practice. As one can imagine, the latter is more difficult than the former.[10]

8.1.1 The Virtue of Impartiality

A moderate economic policymaker needs to be virtuous, have an impartial mind, and turn the pursuit of moderation into a lifestyle habit, moral practice, and belief. Only in this way can this leader design and implement economic policies that establish, maintain, and develop moderation, and make moderation a basic criterion and an important guide for managing economic problems.

Chinese and Western theories of leadership also promote the virtues of balance and moderation that policymakers should possess. One scholar emphasizes that leaders at the highest level have a balanced mindset, i.e., a balance of personal humbleness and professional will.[11] Edgar Schein also mentions the important complementary, balancing role of being humble in a Western cultural environment that advocates positivity, exuberance, and self-confidence. In Schein's view, humble leadership is a higher level of leadership than that based on transactional relationships because it is a model that builds a more personal, trusting, and open culture, resulting in a more "personal intragroup" and tighter intergroup relationships.[12]

This philosophy of balance is similar to the Chinese concept of "inner sage and outer king" or "inner diplomacy and outer assertiveness," which not only emphasizes the balance of one's heart and body but also promotes the Confucian concept of balancing the two ends of the spectrum. For example, legalism in ancient China advocates strict adherence to laws, rules, and authority, placing emphasis on rigidity, merit, strength, and power as guiding principles for governing society. Daoism, on the other hand, advocates a more flexible approach, emphasizing qualities like softness, inaction, modesty, and tolerance as the preferred values. In contrast, Confucianism is a balance between the two, pursuing ideals, advocating morality, and aspiring to the middle ground. It is desirable to cultivate both the internality and externality of human nature by first refining the inner self and reaching the state of the "inner sage" before assuming the external leadership quality that is worthy of a king. As Jim Collins emphasizes, the inner mind must be cultivated to be humble, tolerant, and gentle, but external professional behavior needs to be decisive, responsible, and accountable. The decision-maker is the one who strives to balance the dualities of good and evil in people, to inspire good deeds while guarding against, preventing, and punishing evil deeds.

According to the *Analects,* Zi Lu, one of Confucius' best students, emphasizes that the best action and direction are the moderate, middle way.[13] Mencius criticized two kinds of leaders. One is those who are idealistic and radical, but whose actions are not as good as their words and whose theories are out of touch with reality. The other is indolent leaders who are not high-minded and lack ambition or a sense of mission regarding state affairs, but who nonetheless embody personal integrity and cleanliness without performing any significant, innovative work.[14] Moderate leaders, on the other hand, would demonstrate the positive elements of these two types of leadership but not the negatives. They are rooted in reality while in pursuit of the ideal and a long-term vision.[15]

The internal and external virtues, the combination of rigidity and flexibility, the unity of vision and reality, as well as the leadership ability to coordinate offense and defense, in accordance with the beliefs of Confucianism, Buddhism, and Daoism, create the prerequisites for designing and implementing a moderate, balanced economic policy. A decision-maker who does not know about moderation and the middle way but only knows how to go off the beaten path and divide the community and country is in no position to make an optimal policy. Moreover, the stronger the ability of radical leaders, the greater the damage to the economy, and the more likely the emergence of totalitarianism.

The character of the decision-maker plays a key role in determining the appropriateness of the policy. An institutional and cultural system can be rendered powerless by the shortcomings of human nature. After all, one of the main forces to implement the propriety system and enhance the appropriate culture is the human character.

Applying these human virtues to propriety economic policy is desirable to maintain a basic balance between supply and demand, unemployment and inflation, and fiscal and monetary policy in an effort to promote economic development in a long-term, sustainable manner. This kind of supply and demand balance should not only become the ideal state to be pursued but also transform from a rare into a normal occurrence through strenuous human efforts. Conversely, the supply-demand imbalance caused by inflation or deflation should become abnormal. To put it another way, moderation, balance, and harmony should be relatively long-term and natural, while excess, imbalance, and conflict should be rendered relatively short-term and accidental.

For example, since the first economic crisis in the United States in 1819, the length of each crisis caused by the imbalance between supply and demand has become longer and longer, and the regulatory ability of economic policies has become more and more effective, making extremely serious economic crises abnormal.[16] In the United States during the 19th century, there were four major economic crises (1819, 1837, 1857, and 1873), and the last one lasted for 23 years until 1896. In the 20th century, there were six major crises (1901, 1907, 1920, 1929, the 1970s, and 1987). Except for the Great Depression of 1929 and the oil crisis and stagflation in the 1970s, which lasted for almost a decade, the others were relatively short in duration. In the 21st century, there have been three major crises (2000, 2008, and 2020), but most of them were followed by a quick recovery.[17] The crisis in 2020 was caused mainly by the COVID-19 pandemic instead of economic factors, and stocks rose by 7.3% on the Dow, 16.3% on the S&P 500, and 43.6% on the NASDAQ for the entire year of 2020, despite four meltdowns.

After the stagflation crisis in the 1970s, American economists put forward concepts from monetarism, rational expectations theory, and public choice theory in time to overcome the negative consequences of U.S. economic policy. In a shift away from Keynesianism, these modern economic efforts have adjusted government-led policies towards market-led ones, mitigating the hazards of stagflation and promoting a propriety economic policy for sustainable development. This is why the theory of alienation under capitalism promoted by Marxism and the ideas about monopolistic, decaying imperialism advanced by Leninism did not materialize, as capitalism certainly did not come to a point of extinction in the 19th or 20th century. Rather, the way that the economy developed conformed to Schumpeter's theory of "creative destruction," for it showed an ability to constantly innovate, correct errors, modify deviations, find balance, and move toward moderation. As a result, the capitalist system destroyed old technologies, structures, and mechanisms, prompting capitalism to constantly redeem and rebirth itself, swinging from the left and right poles to the middle without depleting energy in this continual sway. Instead, it has been a constant process of replenishing, renewing, and perfecting. It is not difficult to imagine that if crises in the capitalist economy had become more and more frequent and serious, the predictions of Marx and Lenin may have already come true in the 20th century. The reality is that the Western capitalist economy has been engaged in continuous self-adjustment and self-strengthening in the gradual process of finding its point of propriety, considerable resilience, and flexibility. All of this has been achieved through the collective effort of policymakers and the public in their pursuit of propriety in the economic arena.

8.1.2 Responsiveness to Public Opinion

Economic policymakers need to enhance their ability to respond to public opinion in a prompt fashion. Generally speaking, most people are in favor of propriety, moderation, and harmony. Thus, policymakers must not be detached from the majority opinion of the population at a given time in a given place in order to find, judge, and choose unbiased economic policies.

For example, in the face of the COVID-19 pandemic, most countries were slow to respond and missed the most appropriate window for prevention and control. This is because the majority of the population could not accept extreme policies that restricted personal freedom, locked down cities, and shut down the economy. After all, the power of public opinion generated by the majority of the public is endogenous, with strong resistance to changing the status quo and opposing the sacrifice of individual interests, while a sudden pandemic and the government are exogenous. In such an unexpected situation, it is difficult for policymakers to act against people's will and opinions. Sometimes, this act of complying with public opinion is also related to the legitimacy and stability of the government, and there is a danger that the regime may be in crisis if it blatantly disregards public opinion.[18]

Likewise, policymakers need to be able to listen to public opinion and be brave and savvy at rectifying unpopular policies. For example, the policies of concession at the beginning of most Chinese dynasties— imposing light taxes and giving the peasantry room for recuperation— were responses to public discontent over the demise of the previous dynasty. They also reflected the desire of the majority of the people for peace and stability after widespread rebellion. Superficially, the relaxed policy may have appeared inadequate, but it was fundamentally a response to the previous dynasty's land seizures and oppressive taxation, which had triggered peasant uprisings.[19] Therefore, the standard of propriety depends on comparison, similar to the theory of comparative advantage in international trade espoused by David Ricardo (1772–1823). In Ricardo's view, the government devises import and export trade policies that adhere to the principle of competitive advantage while also considering protection against harm from specific economic conditions.[20]

8.1.3 Courage to Reject Public Opinion

Policymakers also need to have the courage, will, and determination to disregard some inappropriate public opinions because the truth is often in the hands of a few. It may seem contradictory to conventional wisdom, but the ability to reject public opinion is indicative of outstanding leadership that practices true moderation by finding a balance between two extremes. A bold, knowledgeable policymaker needs to take a moderate view of public opinion in a particular time and space with a judicious mind. It is a mistaken assumption that implementing a policy supported by the majority of the public must be moderate and correct.

According to the theory of public choice, the majority votes do not reflect the preference of each voter. A small number of voters may sometimes trade or even buy votes in order to pass their preferred motions, which may result in the passage of inappropriate motions in favor of the minority. In addition, this can lead to voter apathy because of the high costs and low benefits of elections, so the participation rate in U.S. presidential elections rarely exceeds 60%, and a simple majority vote does not necessarily reflect true public opinion.[21] In particular, according to Gustave Le Bon's (1841–1931) book, *The Crowd*, group behavior tends to lose its rationality and moderation because groups can be anxious, gullible, unintelligent, habitually violent, and morally inferior.[22]

Policymakers hence should not trust public opinion completely, as this may lead to irrational policymaking and unsuitable policy directions. For example, most people are in favor of less taxation, so many politicians cave to such views for the sake of receiving more votes. However, to protect social welfare spending, policymakers often rely on Keynesian theory, either printing more money or borrowing more to expand government spending.[23] The long-term impact of leaving debts to future generations is not the priority of short-sighted elected officials. In this way, most democratic governments are sometimes bound by their constituents to cut taxes, borrow money, and print more money. Propriety policy choices demand policymakers who are willing to make sacrifices, exchanges, and compromises. With a similar principle of compromise in mind, the Laffer curve strives to strike a balanced middle ground between government revenue and the burden on the public. On the other hand, the Phillips curve suggests accepting a degree of reduced employment to achieve a modest decline in inflation or permitting some inflation to sustain a moderate level of employment.

Therefore, not only does it take courage to reject misguided public opinions but it also requires insight and skill to do things right with a focus on procedures and details. Otherwise, the right thing will likely be done wrong.

8.1.4 The Boldness to Overcorrect

Policymakers sometimes need to stand firm in their support of "excessive" behavior, to push boundaries and embrace the beliefs and determination to accomplish what is deemed impossible.[24] On the surface, impartiality and the status quo exemplify propriety economic policy. In this way, propriety economic policy may become an excuse to reject innovation and oppose change. Many studies show that most people who support moderate policies are middle-of-the-road voters who are accustomed to living in peace and content to follow the mainstream. Decision-makers who can achieve great things often need the ability, courage, and charisma to lead the public in a new direction and respond to change. Consequently, their corresponding economic policies are generally quite strong and intense instead of moderate.

Based on historical experiences, a time of peace generally calls for moderate policy and leaders, while difficult times, such as war years, demand exceptional, excessive, and powerful leaders who may provide effective solutions when tackling crises, such as the New Deal in the United States during the Great Depression. Although moderation has a positive moral orientation, once it is practiced for a long time, it may lead to a lack of momentum and vitality for progress. Therefore, a timely impetus in the situation of excessive moderation, prolonged balance, and unchanging expectations may be necessary for social change and economic innovation in order to create the conditions for the next round of propriety and stability. For example, the excessive economic policies in Chinese history in response to rapid social change, such as Shang Yang's reforms in the Qin dynasty (221–207 BCE), Wang Anshi's reforms in the Song dynasty (960–1279), and Zhang Juzheng's reforms in the Ming dynasty (1368–1644), usually were condemned by their contemporaries but later were praised by historians. From a historical perspective, these talented, ruthless figures may have been both brutes and heroes.[25]

This is also related to the Arrow impossibility theorem, which states that sometimes only a dictator can make rational and decisive decisions. Pairwise majority voting is often not the best way to choose a country's leaders because the sum of individual wills is not equal to the best collective will. Thus, a centralized leader may be the one whose personal preference is equal to the preference of the whole society, indicating that the mechanism of social choice is likely to be controlled by one person yielding optimal results for everyone.[26]

In conclusion, in the face of the human and societal requirements for propriety policies, political power, intellectual elites, economic capital, and the general public need to exercise self-discipline, self-control, and self-awareness—all of which are key to the success and effectiveness of propriety economic policies.

8.2 Principles for Evaluating Propriety Economic Policies

A propriety economic policy requires decision-makers with moderate behaviors and qualities, as well as principles for the reasonable evaluation of moderate policies, discussion of dealing with economic imbalance, design of programs to prevent excessive self-interest, and development of criteria for identifying propriety economic performance.

8.2.1 Essential Assessments

The assessment of propriety economic policy should adhere to propriety philosophy. If it is believed that propriety economic operation is likely to be the norm, then people will have tolerant, positive expectations of economic policies in a given time and place, even though they may be overly liberal or conservative. They will accept that extreme policies are not only temporary but also create conditions for the next step of corrective, moderate policies.

For example, the inaction and slowness of some countries at the beginning of the COVID-19 pandemic in 2020 should be considered insufficient or extremely insufficient; and after the first wave of the pandemic, some regions faced a resurgence of disease and implemented extreme measures to lock down cities. However, the value of such oscillating policies should not be denied because the worthwhile experiences and lessons learned from such under- or over-doing are precisely the inspiration for the next round of propriety policies to be introduced. This is similar to the Glorious Revolution in Britain (1688) which was in fact a middle choice after the radical English Civil War (1642–1651) and the conservative Restoration (1660–1688), reflecting a typical pendulum effect. In the end, England retained its king while granting power to Parliament via a constitutional monarchy. As a result, England seemed more stable than the French republic that emerged in the next century.[27] Therefore, we cannot underestimate economic policies that were not adequate or excessive, as they may provide a reason for the next round of moderate policies and a motivation to correct mistakes. In other words, they have objective, potential, and long-term positive effects. Needless to say, propriety policies themselves require checks and balances from both internal and external forces.

For this reason, downplaying the value judgment of propriety is required. Once a concept has been elevated to faith or doctrine, it can be taken to extremes. The excessive promotion of propriety as an ideology and faith itself is absolutely inappropriate. When moderation is promoted to the extreme, it becomes a new kind of inappropriateness. Perhaps moderation should be seen as both a spiritual state or aspiring virtue, as advocated by scholars of the Axial Age, and should be achievable for the common people, as encouraged by the 12th century Song scholars and Adam Smith in the 18th century. Only with the right degree of both spirituality and practicality can we correctly approach the true meaning of propriety.[28]

8.2.2 Policy Essentials

Faced with widespread economic imbalances, such as injustice and inequality, there is a need to address policy essentials, which should be acceptable to the majority of the population. In response to the problem of unfair starting points as well as outcomes, an appropriate policy is to promote equal opportunity. Doing so involves understanding very complex historical factors and procedural justice issues because socioeconomic inequality is deeply ingrained in traditional, historical circumstances. A radical or conservative way of solving this inequality may inspire a violent revolution against the rich. Therefore, the middle, moderate choice is to strengthen the mechanism of equal opportunity when everyone has already started, but not yet reached, the endpoint through various moderate tax policies (such as progressive income tax, real estate tax, etc.) to exercise an equalizing effect. These policies can also help developing areas, disadvantaged groups, and lagging industries get an "unfair" share through the policy of redistribution.

When considering poverty, the correct, appropriate policy should address the issue of the poverty of rights. The root cause of poverty is not the apparent lack of money or skill, but the lack of fair, just rights. With rights, we can train and improve skills; with skills, it is possible to get the opportunity to work; with job opportunities, it is conceivable to get out of poverty permanently and continuously. By the same token, even if one has the financial resources, ability, and perseverance to work without the opportunity to work, everything comes to zero. Therefore, the essence of propriety economic policy is not to provide an extreme socialist policy that targets the rich to help the poor, nor an extreme capitalist policy that gives advantages to the rich. Instead, a propriety economic system can effectively protect the disadvantaged, discourage rent-seeking, and combat opportunism, so that equal opportunity and economic efficiency can be appropriately compatible and coupled.

Once more, it is essential to remember that the core principle of a market economy is not charity but efficiency, with the primary goal of profit maximization. Acts of philanthropy by capitalists serve as a supplementary component alongside the initial market-based distribution and subsequent government tax policies. Therefore, the market economy, private capitalists, and social philanthropists cannot take the main role in solving the problem of inequality of opportunity.[29]

Of course, the free market economy can help maintain fair competition, but it is difficult to resolve the problem of fair allocation of resources. Therefore, government nudging is essential, but this nudging cannot be simply attributed to the government's actions because an active government without supervision can easily become a corrupt, evil, and unlimited government. Therefore, in dealing with the problem of social injustice the government must ask questions about the moral sentiments and ethical principles of an "active" government. The opposite of an active government is a passive government or one that does not do much, not a government that acts recklessly. In both ancient and modern times, most people would rather accept a government's laissez-faire policy, as they are less worried about the government's inactions than its recklessness. The lesson of history is that once given the opportunity, governments tend to act irresponsibly, to say the least. Mainstream Western political science, therefore, emphasizes the importance of limited government, advocating for the containment of government power within institutional and legal boundaries.

It is important to note that Adam Smith neither coined the term "night-watchman state" nor argued that the function of government is merely that of a watchman against fire and burglary. In fact, the term "night-watchman state" (German: *Nachtwächterstaat*) was first introduced by the German socialist Ferdinand Lassalle (1825–1864) in 1862, with the aim of positioning the function of government and the state as merely to prevent robbery and theft,[30] similar to the anarchist view. Smith, however, positioned the function of government far beyond the role of a night watchman, for Smith believed that government must assume the important responsibilities of defense,[31] justice,[32] and public works,[33] performing as a good government.

In this regard, propriety philosophy can promote the concept of good government, as opposed to evil, chaotic government. A good government includes three aspects. First, it is a government of good behavior, which means that government officials should behave well and eliminate corruption. Second, it is a government of kind policies which can promote social development and public welfare. Third, it implies a government characterized by benevolence, emphasizing that it should refrain from behaving in a harmful manner, as seen in the British enclosure movement. In this historical context, wealthy landowners were permitted to reclaim land that had previously been collectively shared among common people, ultimately leading to the ruthless eviction of farmers and detrimental consequences.[34] At the same time, propriety philosophy also helps to promote a good government, including good and virtuous actions, preventing injustice, emphasizing the fairness of government actions, and stressing the government's ability to govern effectively.

Finally, in the face of social injustice, it is highly essential to consider the trade-offs of propriety philosophy because the process of finding appropriate economic policies involves compromise and change. For example, while fighting the COVID-19 pandemic, policymakers needed to weigh the conflicts between economic development and pandemic control, the quality of medical care for the rich and the basic survival needs of the poor, biological needs and social needs, and biological virus and social ills, such as anti-Asian crime and sentiments in the West. Ultimately, there is the need to find a fulcrum in order to balance opposing factors, rather than treating them as mutually independent and isolated. In this regard, Kenneth Arrow proposes principles of compromise and exchange on how to balance the dilemmas of growth and equity.[35]

Real-world policies have introduced many effective trade-offs for these complex dilemmas. For example, in dealing with the problem of air pollution caused by vehicles, we should not enforce an excessive policy of prohibiting people from using their cars, nor should we let the problem remain unsolved. A more reasonable policy is to encourage multiple people (at least two or more) to carpool and set up special carpool lanes for faster travel. It is also possible to impose substantial taxes and increase the cost of parking for those who use private cars to enter the city, but at the same time provide convenience and incentives for those who use urban public transportation. Similar measures are typical of propriety balancing policies.

8.2.3 Basic Implementation

There are numerous ways to prevent economic excesses or insufficiency through designing and implementing propriety economic measures. Due to limited space in this monograph, the author will discuss only a few issues related to the economic behavior of exploitation.

According to complexity economics, there are two major meanings of exploitation in economics. One is the use of something to obtain a benefit; the second is the selfish or unfair manipulation of a person or situation for personal gain. Here, in Arthur's view, "gaming" has a more harmful meaning: it means that economic agents manipulate a system to achieve their own goals, which often betrays the trust of others and hurts them.[36] Therefore, any perfect rule or system can hardly avoid being exploited or "gamed." In 2005, Janet Napolitano, the former governor of Arizona, addressed the issue of illegal immigration at the U.S.-Mexico border. In an attempt to illustrate the resourcefulness of illegal immigrants, she humorously summarized their mindset as follows: if the government builds a border wall 15 feet high, the immigrants would find a way to construct a 16-feet-high ladder.[37] This example profoundly demonstrates human nature, which is a battle between cat and mouse. It also reveals that exploitation is at the root of human nature; not only does it persist in human beings, but it is also difficult to detect, stop, and eradicate.

W. Brian Arthur lists various causes and manifestations of exploitative behavior. The first one is the use of asymmetric information. For example, many promoters of financial derivative products are well aware of the drawbacks of their products, but investors or customers are oblivious to them. Keywords are deliberately written in small font to avoid possible legal liability and to prevent consumers from understanding crucial information. Furthermore, "tailoring behavior" allows economic agents to actively engage in manipulating standards that require evaluation, assessment, and regulation while effectively meeting legal and regulatory criteria. Economic entities may take strategic action to customize their actions, products, or services in a way that aligns with the specific standards, regulations, or requirements in place. This adaptation aims to ensure compliance while still achieving their objectives and minimizing any potential obstacles or challenges related to legal and regulatory evaluations. These encompass a wide array of aspects, such as educational qualifications, environmental standards, funding criteria, accounting regulations, human rights prerequisites, product quality, tax reporting, officials' performance, governance effectiveness, and more. The objective is to navigate these requirements swiftly, seamlessly, and cost-effectively. In the case of governance, two laws have been developed to describe such exploitative behavior. One is Campbell's law, stipulating that the more frequently a large number of quantitative indicators are used as regulatory standards, the more likely they are to lead to corruption and distort the social process of regulation. Another is Goodhart's law, specifying that any observable statistical regularity used for excessive control purposes is bound to fail.[38] The key warning of these two laws is that any performance criteria will be maximized or overused, thus losing the true meaning and purpose of the original assessment.[39] In a hierarchical governance system, when the top authority insists on implementing a particular policy, the intermediate or lower levels often introduce additional layers of evaluation. This transforms what should be a balanced evaluation process into an excessively complex, tightly controlled, and potentially corrupt procedure, making effective oversight nearly impossible.

Taking partial control of a system is another common form of exploitation. This refers to small groups of privileged people controlling some important resources for their own interests, similar to a hacker's appropriation of data resources in computer systems. This parallels the actions and outcomes of certain managers in Chinese state-owned enterprises who deceptively acquired state-owned assets through fraudulent means.[40]

Furthermore, exploitation occurs when individuals utilize system elements in ways not intended by policy designers. This includes activities such as manipulating reviewers' ratings and designing rules as loopholes within the system. This may lead to a rule serving as a conduit for breaking the law, enabling money to flow quietly, freely, and legally.[41] Many instances of common illegal tax evasions under the guise of legal tax avoidance fall within this type of exploitation.

In this regard, policymakers need to formulate a propriety policy to prevent exploitation, but it cannot be done only once because once the dynamic, open process of implementation begins, exploitation will continue to occur. Policymakers and regulators need to continuously follow up and improve appropriately, and correct and rectify in a timely manner. During the COVID-19 pandemic, certain individuals actively decided against returning to work, perceiving that the incentives offered by specific U.S. policies, such as welfare and unemployment benefits, outweighed the rewards of reentering the workforce. At the same time, instances of potential misuse of government loans intended for small businesses raised suspicions of fraudulent claims. As of August 23, 2023, the U.S. Department of Justice reported the outcomes of a synchronized nationwide enforcement initiative aimed at combating COVID-19 fraud. This effort encompassed 718 enforcement actions, leading to federal criminal charges against 371 defendants involved in offenses tied to over $836 million in alleged COVID-19 fraud.[42]

The design of a propriety policy hence requires both the anticipation of possible excesses and inadequacy, as well as preparation of a plan to correct the deflections and return to moderation in the event of a pandemic rebound. It is vital to prevent speculation and exploitation by politicians, businesses, and the public in this process. Exploitation is not only the prerogative of capital and power but also the general public, and in the latter it is more difficult to identify and effectively prevent it promptly because they represent votes. Meanwhile, policymakers are required to "foresee or even warn of it in advance."[43]

Thus, Arthur proposes a "failure mode analysis" to foresee and warn of exploitation, a system for evaluating policy that requires several major steps. The first step is to grasp the experience, lessons, and information of past failures, which is also a kind of path dependence. The second is to microscopically examine the details that led to the collapse of the structure because, as the saying goes, the devil is in the details. The collapse of a dam can be caused by a swarm of ants that have eroded its foundation. Similarly, many exploitative behaviors come from individuals, whose behaviors must be predicted and forewarned. An additional step is to find places of high stress in the system, which often provide strong incentives for subjects to overstep their bounds and induce them to engage in self-interested exploitation, such as frequent tax evasion. The decision-makers then need to design a module based on their past experience and inject it into the system to track the exploiters' behavior and stop their actions.[44]

Therefore, propriety economics can employ "failure mode analysis" and stress-test intricate economic models to anticipate which incentives will lead to diminished, amplified, or suitable behaviors, compelling participants to opt for appropriateness when faced with these three alternatives. For example, in designing a mechanism to prevent corruption, a strong, realistic, and immediate punishment mechanism should be included as a deterrent for officials. They would also be discouraged from participating in corrupt activities due to attractive compensation that makes additional funds unnecessary, as well as because of honorable rewards and moral recognition.

Countries around the world have made significant progress in the design and implementation of various security systems since World War II, including security for aviation, nuclear facilities, buildings, food, medicine, the internet, etc., except for financial security and economic safety. One of the major reasons for this is the excessive trust that economists have in the idea of an invisible hand, believing that the omnipotent market will be able to lead the disorderly, dysfunctional, and unethical market economy to a balanced, appropriate conclusion sooner or later. But the more important reason is the lack of a propriety economic mechanism to find "possible failure modes"[45] and get the "meta-conditions right"[46] before the implementation of propriety economic policies.

Along with preventing and punishing exploitation, there should also be effective ways of dealing with other common problems, including opportunistic, irrational, and short-term free-riding, that are denounced as the conduct of "small-minded men" by Confucius and as vices deplored by Aristotle. These behaviors are characterized by excessive greed, excessive self-interest, and excessive harm to others.

8.2.4 Quantitative Criteria

Although quantitative indicators of propriety economics are difficult to identify, it is conceivable to provide a rough boundary and reference for propriety economies and policies based on a few popular criteria and historical records. According to the concept of the Goldilocks economy mentioned in Chapter 1, the criteria for great moderation in economic growth should be the positive performance of five major economic indicators, including the gross domestic product (GDP), industrial output, unemployment rate, wages, and prices.[47] These five indicators will specify whether economic growth is entering a "golden" period, meaning that the economy is neither too hot nor too cold and neither over-inflated nor under-employed. As the most desirable phase in the constantly fluctuating economic cycle, this is somewhat similar to the conditions in the United States in the 1990s and from 2017–2019, Japan from 1985–1990, and China from 2003–2007, most of which demonstrated a "golden" combination of high growth and low inflation.

At the same time, a propriety economy requires a realistic, reasonable, and normal rate of growth, mainly in five other areas: full employment, industrial coordination, stable operation, significant profits, and maximum welfare. Interestingly, this has a direct intersection with one of the criteria for great moderation in the Goldilocks economy: the unemployment rate. Notably, full employment is a measure of whether economic growth helps absorb idle resources, and it is closely related to production factors such as capital, labor, and technology management. The employment rate is in a sense an important sign of the economic growth rate. If investment grows and effective demand rises, the demand for labor by enterprises will increase accordingly. Thus, the employment rate will rise and the economy will grow. But this growth must be moderate and sustainable. If the effective demand is insufficient, the production capacity is limited, and the economic growth rate is too low, the unemployment rate will increase. On the contrary, if the economic growth rate is too high and exceeds the limit of production potential, it will lead to demand expansion and economic stagnation, which in turn will limit employment and lead to a nominal increase in employment and the economic growth rate.[48]

For this reason, Paul Samuelson believes that a 5% unemployment rate should be a nodal point for economic development because it is the standard for full employment. That is to say, once the unemployment rate drops from above 5% to below 5%, the market will enter an orderly and organic state, and the government should withdraw administrative intervention and encourage the market to spontaneously exert its role in resource allocation.[49] Therefore, the indicator of full employment in a propriety economy should also be around a 5% unemployment rate. If the unemployment rate is above 5%, the economy may be too cold and government intervention in fiscal and financial policies may be necessary, as in the case of the United States during the COVID-19 pandemic. Once the unemployment rate is below 3%, the risk of inflation may appear, indicating that the economy may be overheated and labor costs may increase, so the government needs to step in again and introduce economic policies to prevent inflation. Based on similar principles of full employment, the general experience of the historical development of the U.S. economy also requires that inflation be kept between approximately 2–5% in order to be considered moderate.

By the same token, the Gini coefficient, which measures income distribution, should be kept between 0.3 and 0.4; interest rates should be between 2% and 5%; the fiscal deficit should be retained within 3% of GDP; and the most appropriate annual GDP growth rate seems to be between 2% and 3%. It is interesting to note that many of the major economic growth indicators recognized by most countries are generally in the range of 2–5%.[50]

Certainly, all propriety economic indicators exert mutual influence and must undergo systematic analysis and comparison to ascertain the degree of moderation in economic development. An appropriate, balanced economic growth rate should embody the harmonization of needs and capabilities; the equilibrium between production and livelihoods; the synchronization of speed, proportion, and efficiency; and the synthesis of short-term and long-term considerations. This synthesis aims to foster a virtuous cycle of sustainable and effective growth.

Furthermore, by closely examining various quantitative indicators and conducting a comprehensive analysis of diverse factors, policymakers can make informed decisions regarding government intervention policies. These decisions revolve around three fundamental questions: firstly, the necessity of policy introduction; secondly, the suitable domains and types of policies to be introduced; and thirdly, the optimal strength and duration for the implementation of such policies. Propriety economics seeks to establish a framework for economic growth with well-defined boundaries. These boundaries are determined by the inherent elasticity or tension within economic factors, such as the degree of division of labor, which, in turn, determines the elasticity of scale and productivity. Upon reaching the optimal elasticity limit, an equilibrium point is attained.

In summary, formulating and implementing a propriety economic policy requires policymakers to embody moderate virtues, habits, and the determination to make principled decisions. This involves a comprehensive set of principles for evaluating moderate policies, encompassing evaluation criteria, essential policy components, foundational measures, and quantifiable benchmarks. These principles aim to provide tangible, verifiable tools for the effective application of propriety economic concepts.

Chapter 9

Macro Case Studies
of Propriety Economics

After delving into philosophical thought, conducting a comprehensive literature review, exploring core theories and fundamental methods, and establishing policy principles within the framework of propriety economics, it is essential to conduct an examination of specific macroeconomic situations. In this context, the author applies the principles of propriety economics to elucidate the dynamics of the American macro economy.[1] Additionally, a brief discussion on institutional changes during China's economic reforms in the 1980s and 1990s is included.

As explained in the subsequent sections, one can discern the presence of certain principles of propriety economics, including evolution, equilibrium, and sharing, within the economic landscapes of both the United States and China.

9.1 Evolutionary Rationality and the Colonial American Economy (1607–1776)

If the colonial American economy is understood in a static, dichotomous way, it is easy to conclude that manipulation by the British hindered its growth. For example, the Williams school argues that the colonial economy ensured the development of British mercantilist industry by providing an unlimited source for the original accumulation of British capital which ultimately stifled the economic development of British North America, focusing on the 13 American colonies.[2] This zero-sum paradigm is not in line with the triad theory of propriety economics, nor does it explain the historical fact that the economy grew at a rapid pace and the living standards of the majority of free people increased rapidly during the colonial period. Particularly in the two decades following the American Revolution, the U.S. economy experienced rapid growth. However, the economic progress of the 19th century would have lacked a solid foundation without the prosperity that the colonial economy had built over the course of 150 years. The economic development of British North America aligns with certain principles of propriety economics, notably rationality and evolutionary development. These principles act as guiding forces that both shape and are shaped by the socioeconomic context. Scholars can only be motivated to be more rational, objective, and comprehensive by practicing evolutionary rationality.

9.1.1 Colonial Economy

The most essential driving force of the colonial economy, which began in 1607 when the British settled in Jamestown, Virginia, came from the colonial trade in North America. The basic feature of colonial trade was the export of raw materials and the import of manufacture. The traditional view is that this was a typical exploitative trade economy, with the value of goods imported from Britain increasing by an average of 50% per person per year in the colonies during the period from 1720–1770.[3] Although industrial imports accounted for about 90% of total imports during the colonial period,[4] this high percentage does not prove that the economy was exploited by the British. For example, after achieving independence, industrial goods accounted for 79.4% of total imports to the U.S. from Britain in 1820, decreasing to 56.5% in 1890 due to heavy U.S. industrialization and rising as high as 77.3% by the 1960s.[5] We certainly cannot conclude that the U.S. economy in the 1960s was more backward than it was in 1890. The interdependence and interconnectedness of trade markets cannot be understood simply in terms of a dichotomy of control by one side and domination by the other. In fact, colonial trade, characterized by the import of large quantities of industrial goods, made various contributions to the rise of the colonial economy.

First of all, for a society with a predominantly agricultural economy, high-quality, low-priced imported manufacture could satisfy the needs of the consuming public and stimulate the purchasing power of the population. According to Adam Smith, British mercantilist export policy did not seriously harm the North American colonies because land was cheap and labor costs were expensive, so industrial goods imported from Britain were usually cheaper and better than domestic products.[6]

The importation of industrial goods and various finished products, in addition, promoted the advance of colonial markets. The continuous growth of imports in the North American colonies testified to the existence and development of a vast market. There was a market that required imports, and there was a demand for them to be continuously expanded to improve quality of life.[7] For example, the population in the North American colonies was accustomed to using poor-quality raw brown sugar. Thanks to the availability of imported products, most of the population began to consume refined sugar before the Revolution,[8] and the level of consumer goods was enhanced.

Meanwhile, imported products helped nurture the growth of import substitution industrialization in the colonies. To satisfy the colonial population's need for refined white sugar, a domestic sugar industry developed, and by 1770, the colonies were able to produce 2.3 million pounds of refined sugar, supplying 75% of the colonial population's needs.[9] By 1770, all types of British imports could neither fully monopolize the market in the colonies nor fully meet the needs of the colonial population, leaving a shortfall of 320,000 pounds of goods.[10] The existence and widening of this gap between American demands and British supply provided the foundation for American industries.

The colonial export trade also grew rapidly between 1700 and 1770, evidenced by the annual growth rate of British imports from the North American colonies which was about twice as high as that of total imports to Britain during the same period.[11] Moreover, the export trade facilitated the diversification of colonial agriculture, which in turn led to diversified demands of international markets and an escalation in the prices of colonial agricultural products, thus benefitting colonial farmers. More importantly, a strong export trade attracted British investment, injecting an average of £50,000 per year into the colonial economy.[12]

Consequently, import and export trade stimulated economic and trade interdependence between the two regions. The striking consistency in the number, magnitude, and periodicity of economic crises between the two regions from 1638 to 1777[13] indicates the emergence of a common market and the formation of an economic community.

The interdependence of the colonies with the British economy is also evidenced by the fact that the American economy declined sharply after the outbreak of the American Revolution. For example, the total value of annual exports per capita in the United States fell by 25% compared to the pre-Revolutionary period of 1768–1772.[14] During the Revolution from 1777–1783, the U.S. trade deficit rose to total $100 million.[15] In particular, this caused the U.S. gross national product to plummet, falling a disastrous 46% from 1775–1790; in comparison, during the Great Depression of 1929–1933, the darkest period in U.S. economic history, the gross national product fell by only 48%.[16]

This shows that the British and American economies had established a symbiotic interaction with a reciprocal effect rather than a zero-sum relationship. In using propriety economics to analyze the North American colonial economy, it is conceivable to derive a third perspective of the Anglo-American economic community, in which there is no clear winner or loser; rather, it was a win-win situation. This third viewpoint shows the effective function of the mutual constraints and interactions between Britain and the territories that would become the United States. Thus, shifting one's perspective is vital to interpreting economic development given the same research data and methods.

9.1.2 Colonial Industry

Although the 13 American colonies were still agrarian societies with more than 90% of the population involved in and over 90% of the colonial output coming from agriculture, the growth of colonial industry should not be underestimated. Otherwise, the development of the American industrial revolution in the early 19th century would have been a nonstarter. This is evidenced by the concepts of historical evolution in propriety economics and path dependence in new institutional economics.

Industry in the 13 American colonies was oriented toward promoting trade and production via sales, which gradually supported the expansion of export-oriented industry and developed the domestic market to meet the consumption requirements of the colonial population. Obviously, the increase of colonial trade and the growth of domestic and foreign markets directly induced the emergence of colonial industries.[17]

It is evident that there was a significant improvement in three industries at that time. For instance, the average annual output of the shipbuilding industry from 1763 to 1775 reached 40,000 tons, worth £300,000 at that time.[18] New England alone accounted for nearly 2,000 merchant ships, employing 33,000 seamen.[19] On the eve of the American Revolution, the total length of timber exported from the colonies reached 40 million feet, amounting to 15,000 tons of wood.[20] The growth of the lumber industry subsidized the colonial construction, furniture, and shipbuilding industries.[21] In addition, the colonial ironworks industry was able to produce 27,600 tons of iron in 1770, of which 8,000 tons were exported, accounting for 15% of the world's total production and exceeding the iron production of Great Britain.[22]

9.1.3 Standard of Living

There has been a common perception in historical studies that colonial people must have suffered from dire circumstances for a conceivably long time. However, it has been demonstrated that the living standards of free people in the American colonies not only improved but were also comparable to those in Britain.

The first indicator to consult is the birth rate, which often represents the living conditions, opportunities for development, and social stability in agricultural societies. Throughout the 18th century, for every 1,000 people in the American colonies, an average of 45–50 babies were born, while only 35–40 were born to the British population during the same period.[23] There were many reasons for the high birth rate, one of which was explained by Benjamin Franklin: marriage and family were common in the colonies.[24] This also shows that the later colonial population decided to remain in America for generations in contrast with the earlier colonists who just wanted to make their fortune and then return to England. Moreover, the ability to start a family and have children reveals that the population was financially well-off and stable. The colonies possessed fertile, inexpensive land that was not only self-sustaining but also capable of providing sustenance for the entire family. Early marriage was common in colonial America, which helped a woman make the most of her childbearing years and raise more children throughout her life. The average age of marriage for women in the American colonies was 20–23 years old, compared to 25 years old in Europe. Thus, in the American colonies, each family had an average of 6–7 children, while the average Europeans only had about 4–5 children per family during the same period.[25]

The mortality rate is the second reference for understanding living standards. The harsh environment and poor living conditions led to an alarming mortality rate in the early colonial period. The first successful American colony (Jamestown, Virginia) had a mortality rate of 60% in 1607, 45% in 1608 and 1609, and still over 50% by 1610.[26] However, the average mortality rate of the population throughout the colonial period was 2–2.5% compared to 2.5–3.5% in England during the same period.[27] The low mortality rate was due in large part to improved living conditions; the prices of necessities such as housing, land, food, fuel, and clothing were relatively more affordable in the colonies than in European societies, resulting in colonial women and children being generally healthier than their European counterparts. More importantly, the sparsely populated American colonies were less susceptible to widespread epidemics which reduced the mortality rate. Once past childhood, the average colonial male could live up to 60 years, similar to the life expectancy of American males in the mid-20th century.[28]

As the third indicator, the number of immigrants represented the attractive prosperity of colonial society. During the entire colonial period, the population of the American colonies grew by more than 42 times, while the British empire reproduced by only 50% during the same period.[29] The average annual growth rate of the colonial population was 3% from 1670 to 1770, while in the other British colonies it was 2.6%. The number of immigrants and the size of the growth directly reflected the positive economic situation. The main motivation for most people to immigrate to North America was the pursuit of a better life, freedom, and opportunities. The pursuit of both spiritual (religious freedom) and material (economic prosperity) aims by immigrants from Europe helped the 13 American colonies to become affluent. Consequently, it also enabled the colonies to develop a culture and spirit of freedom, which led to a spiritual civilization. As a result, the national character of the United States is neither too utilitarian nor too idealistic and has always hovered between economic capital and religious spirituality, which has, in turn, contributed to the propriety development of American society.[30]

The fourth indicator, the gross national income, is another important reference for analyzing the standard of living. For instance, per capita income increased by 0.6% per year throughout the colonial period.[31] The average annual income per free person in the colonies in 1774 was US$804, while 95 countries in the world had an annual per capita income of less than US$500 in 1973.[32] At the same time, the annual growth rate of per capita income in the North American colonies was 0.1% higher compared to that in Britain (0.6% vs. 0.5%).[33] By 1774,

Britain ranked first in the world, France second, the Netherlands third in terms of annual income per capita, and the American colonies ranked fourth.[34]

The amount of property owned per capita is the fifth critical indicator of people's living standards. By 1774, the free population of the colonies owned £76 in all types of property per capita.[35] This did not include the number of stock shares in England which amounted to £6.75 million, an average of £2.7 per person, compared to £3.5 in England in 1775,[36] thus showing the wealth of the so-called oppressed, exploited colonists.

The last indicator is the degree of socioeconomic disparity. If wealth is concentrated in the hands of a very small number of people, it does not necessarily indicate the general improvement of the living standards of the whole society. The proportion of the total national wealth controlled by the richest 1% of British residents was 15% in 1688, higher than that of the American colonies during the same period.[37] It is also useful to perform a comparison concerning the gap between the rich and the poor during the colonial period and after independence. In 1774, the Gini coefficient of the American colonies (including free and non-free residents) was 0.73, which dropped to 0.66 if slaves and indentured servants were excluded. But in 1860, the Gini coefficient rose to 0.83 (excluding slaves). The inequality between the rich and the poor in the American colonies was mainly manifested in two areas. One is the South, where slave owners were obviously much better off than the slaves they owned. The second is urban areas where, for instance, 10% of the rich in Philadelphia controlled 70% of all wealth in the period from 1766–1775.[38] In fact, the economic dynamics of the American Revolution can only be understood if one fully recognizes the wealth of the colonial population before the American Revolution. The American Revolution was not caused by widespread poverty but was the result of wealth which stimulated the expectations of freedom and independence from Great Britain.

However, it must be noted that according to colonial law (slave code) at the time, slaves were possessions who were counted as "property" instead of "people," and were not only excluded from the population base but were included in the number of properties. Thus, it can be seen that statistics is not only a science of numbers, but is conditioned by politics, law, and ideology.

The economic expansion and cultural pluralism of the American colonies eventually inspired their desire for political independence and democratic freedom. Economic marketization generally helps promote political democratization, but the British Kings were unwilling to tolerate colonial independence, freedom, and democracy. Therefore, the analysis of an economic case cannot be limited to isolation and stasis; only through rational analysis of historical evolution and value-free observation can we discover the historical value of the American colonial economy and the original impetus for its economic rise.

9.2 Balancing the Dilemmas of Early Industrialization

If the study of the American colonial economy requires the evolutionary perspective promoted by propriety economics, the study of early American industrialization warrants a propriety perspective in balancing the ensuing dilemmas. The United States started the process of economic advancement and early industrialization in the first half of the 19th century, but this brought both positive and negative socioeconomic effects. One was economic growth and the other was social instability, forcing American communities to find a balance between development and stability through socioeconomic reforms as a collective response.

9.2.1 Economic Factors

The economic factors in early American industrialization consisted mainly of the technological revolution, the transportation revolution, and the factory system revolution. The technological revolution was the fundamental driving force of American industrialization, representing the American spirit of innovation. In general, Americans can be seen as more aggressive, innovative, and open-minded than the British. The rate of fixed asset renewal in American factories was quite astonishing. For instance, a textile mill in Rhode Island, built in 1813, replaced all of its machinery within 15 years.[39] At the same time, the spirit of innovation in the United States can be observed in the development of the telegraph industry. In 1844, the United States constructed the first experimental telegraph line, and in just nine years, 23,000 miles of telegraph lines existed across the country. By 1861, telegraph lines had successfully connected the East and West coasts.[40]

Along with the technological revolution, the transportation revolution constituted another driving force of early American industrialization. The American transportation industry went through three major eras in just 50 years: roads,[41] canals,[42] and railroads.[43] While roads flourished for only 40 years (1790–1830) and canals for 35 years (1825–1860), railroads succeeded for 125 years (1825–1950) until 1950, when highways became dominant. This shows that roads and canals denote the transition from an agrarian to an industrial economy, while locomotives represent the backbone of an industrial society.

Meanwhile, the revolution of the American factory system partially transformed the traditional character of American society. Originating in Lynn, Massachusetts in the 1760s, the early American factory system had roots in shoemaking rather than the textile industry; the latter was more common in European countries. Directly connected to the traditional hand-loom textile industry, shoe manufacturing was a springboard for the transition from an agricultural to an industrial society. Moreover, a Connecticut gun factory used a production line for the first time in 1799.[44] Accordingly, the emergence of the factory system created modern workers instead of guild apprentices and capitalists instead of guild owners. Meanwhile, a paper contract replaced the old master-servant relationship, and the modern factory substituted the old family economy which had a double effect on the freedom of the population (not including slaves). First, people began to be free from the bondage of land. The use of machines lowered the requirements for skilled labor and the threshold for entry into the workforce, giving people the self-determination to choose their jobs. Second, although the factory system allowed for more freedom, freedom did not mean equality. Inequality inevitably constrained access to more freedom and affected its sustainability. Workers on the assembly line had little capacity to exercise their individual will or freedom.

The factory system has a dual impact not only on freedom but also on human independence. Machine production makes it necessary for all departments to work closely together and to be interdependent so that workers in each department are connected as a whole, and independent individuality and initiative become insignificant.[45] This principle of interchangeability of parts means that the individual role of each department is not the most important for the operation of the whole factory. It does not even matter if a worker goes on strike, or if this worker dies of old age. This indicates that the development of the factory system shaped the interdependence and independence of human relationships in an industrial society.[46]

9.2.2 The Dual Legacy

Early industrialization in the United States left two major legacies: mutually coexistent freedom and unrest. Industrialization brought human liberation and freedom, but freedom also generated instability that created great uncertainty for the further expansion and maintenance of freedom. In response, the American public held divergent views, with one group valuing freedom while the other prioritized stability.

Clearly, many Americans affirmed the positive results of industrialization and embraced freedom and democracy, believing that industrialization brings new opportunities, including those to get rich, acquire land, secure employment, and immigrate. However, when everyone has opportunities, it also means that anyone may lose them, and hope is often punctuated with disappointment and despair. As Charles Dickens said in *A Tale of Two Cities*, "it was the best of times, it was the worst of times."[47] Most of those opportunities were accompanied by violence, disaster, and even death. The American public's pessimistic, negative reactions to early industrialization in the first half of the 19th century stemmed mainly from numerous crises. For instance, there were periodic economic crises, starting in 1819 and subsequently in 1837 and 1857.[48] In addition, severe polarization between rich and poor occurred.[49] The Westward expansion movement posed a threat to law and order in American society, leading to the establishment of a "first-come, first-claim" principle. While engaging in ongoing combat against Native Americans, many Americans became lawless and violent.[50] In addition, secularization was evident. For instance, by the year 1820, the adherents of the eight major churches in the United States numbered only 8,845.[51] The tendency toward secularization further exacerbated materialism, providing conditions for all kinds of moral indiscretions and social instability. For example, alcoholism proliferated, posing a threat to social order and stability because individuals under the influence of alcohol were unable to control their behaviors rationally and responsibly.[52] As a means of releasing stress and dealing with the tensions and social alienations wrought by an industrializing society, alcoholism became an expression of freedom and individualism.[53] Coinciding with the influx of Irish immigrants in the first half of the 19th century who favored wine and beer, the demand for alcohol stimulated supply, leading to falling prices of alcoholic drinks and even wider consumption.[54] In addition, the average time spent in school in 1800 was 14 days.[55] Ignorance bred irrationality and their combination made it easier for the illiterate to accept violence and anarchy. Finally, mental illness became much more serious. Originally, it was considered an "aristocratic disease" mainly caused by emotional disputes and personal financial crises. So wealthy patients were often watched over by their families without causing any social problems during the colonial period. However, a large number of ordinary people had contracted this "disease of civilization" by the early 19th century, with no resources for medical treatment or care provided by family. As a result, many mentally ill people were living on the streets and engaged in various intentional and unintentional criminal activities, thus threatening social stability.[56]

How to confront and solve the aforementioned crises brought about by industrialization was a test of the ability of American society to strike a balance. At that time, dealing with both the freedom and turmoil brought by early industrialization forced the American people to accept coexistent, dualistic realities: freedom often came with instability; opportunities could generate crises; the pursuit of wealth was usually accompanied by human greed and moral degradation. These dilemmas deliver several major revelations and reflections on American society.

First of all, the evolution of civilization tends to have two pairs of positive and negative cause-and-effect relationships. Industrialization and liberalization form a positive symbiotic connection, that is, industrialization releases people's desire for freedom, while a free society provides a catalyst and guarantee for the start and development of industrialization. Meanwhile, freedom and unrest have a negative causal relationship, i.e., excessive freedom leads to social unrest, and social turbulence limits individual freedom. Freedom is not free. However, since social discontent is part of historical development, one cannot hope to avoid it, but can only strive to reduce and control it. Ironically, the most effective way to completely quell social turmoil is to return to the era of pre-industrial society rejecting all modernization.[57] At the same time, the negative manifestations of industrial civilization are universal, including economic crises, utilitarianism, unemployment, homelessness, speculation, polarization, etc. Therefore, since these negative phenomena are inevitable in a developed society, economic industrialization and social liberalization must not be discarded because of social unrest.

Additionally, the author believes that individual freedom and social stability are the dual needs of human nature, and it is the responsibility of society to harmonize the two to the greatest extent possible. The innate human need for freedom and order is like a pair of "invisible hands" instead of an invisible hand, adjusting the equilibrium of society all the time through both the left hand and right hand. Excessive freedom will destroy order and eventually freedom will be lost, so people and society will be forced to limit the extent of freedom and change its direction. Similarly, extreme emphasis on order will inevitably lead to tyranny, which will curtail freedom and force oppressed people to resort to any means to destroy excessive order or dictatorship. A case in point was the American Revolution, which eventually introduced a freer system of government. This pendulum-like social evolution shows that no society can exist in an environment of perfect order and absolute freedom for a long time. The duality of human nature and the resulting dichotomy of social forces eventually constrain society to two extremes at the macro level. This is the fundamental reason why early industrial American society, though punctuated with crises, was nonetheless resilient and capable of surviving them.

Moreover, the dual legacy of industrialization is an integrated unity. Freedom creates individual space and engenders opportunities, but its accompanying anxiety or even turbulence can be highly discomforting and unsettling. Therefore, advantages and disadvantages are relative and can be mutually reinforcing, and more importantly, they can be mutually transformative. The second best is the maximum convention, and bounded rationality and optimal choice require us to sacrifice a certain amount of personal freedom for relative social stability. Similarly, tolerating a certain amount of social unrest can ensure relative personal freedom. This is the fundamental philosophy of the middle way promoted by propriety economics. In reality, freedom and turbulence have both played essential roles in shaping the evolution of American industrialization. They act as interconnected variables, serving as both driving forces and sources of resistance, collectively shaping the character of American industrialization.[58]

9.2.3 Propriety Efforts at Socioeconomic Reforms

In the wake of the negative effects of industrialization, insightful individuals and community leaders in American society pushed for socioeconomic reforms during the first half of the 19th century, the essence of which was a balancing act that juxtaposed individualism with social order and reconciled individual liberty with social responsibility. Based on this concept, the socioeconomic reforms in the first half of the 19th century established two major moderate principles and goals. The first was to maximize individual freedom by reducing traditional institutions and centralized concepts that hindered free will, free spirit, and free behavior. The second purpose was to moderately re-establish social order and enhance individuals' sense of social responsibility. People have the right to embrace freedom, but they must abide by the law.

The various social reforms in the United States have included religious institutional reform, the women's rights movement, the abolitionist movement, education reform, the temperance movement, and asylum system reform. This section will focus only on the reform of the American asylum system, which was directly related to the socioeconomic transformation.

Poverty, vagrancy, and mental illness plagued early American industrial society. The two polar opposite solutions to these problems were either aggressive coercion or a passive laissez-faire approach. However, mainstream America chose neither heavy-handed regulation nor resigned acquiescence, opting instead for a middle-of-the-road, moderate socioeconomic reform movement following the principles of propriety economics.

To begin with, social assistance organizations were transformed and relief functions were improved. Given the fact that a large number of the mentally ill population were put in jail, social reformers pushed hard for the establishment of almshouses, orphanages, and mental hospitals from 1820 onward. Fueled by grassroots community initiatives, 28 out of the 33 states in the nation had established public facilities for the mentally ill by 1860. This achievement showcased the collaborative and propriety endeavors of both non-governmental organizations (NGOs) and governmental bodies.[59]

In addition, asylum system reform focused on restructuring the philosophy and administration of poverty alleviation. The reformers believed that changing morality was more important than saving lives, and that passive incarceration and relief were not sufficient to improve morality. Thus, they proposed moral education and strict discipline in the newly built asylums. As a result, a large number of volunteers went to these institutions to preach, heal, and pray together. The rule of law and the rule of morality were both implemented.[60]

One of the American characteristics of the reform was the non-involvement of the government in establishing and improving the asylum system. This inevitably had two consequences. One was to positively promote social reform not as a political movement, much less an executive order, but as a bottom-up grassroots community movement. Another was that it led to severely underfunded, understaffed institutions, making it difficult to sustain relief efforts and to ensure the quantity and quality of relief facilities and services. Regrettably, asylum system reforms faced significant setbacks in the early 1850s, resulting in overcrowding in relief agencies and facilities. This overcrowding, in turn, inadvertently exacerbated issues related to criminal behavior. Many old and sick people died in almshouses due to a lack of medical care. The poor quality of the administrators, who often resorted to terrible, harsh methods against patients, led to an ironic contrast between the original intention of transforming people's souls and the inhumane violence in practice. Thus, it was not until President Roosevelt's New Deal in the 1930s that the United States created a social insurance system to protect the poor and sick. Hence, the standard of propriety requires ongoing adjustment, and excessive moderation itself can be seen as a departure from propriety. In fact, the American experience has provided inspiration for people to embrace more balanced approaches in the future. Solutions for similar social problems should first be initiated by the community and society at the grassroots level followed by substantial government assistance, and the legal system should protect the asylum system so as to both solve urgent issues in the short term and carry out fundamental reform in the long run.[61]

It must be pointed out that the implementation of moderate socioeconomic reforms in American society at that time had many positive effects. At the outset, the reforms balanced the dual values of individualism and social order. This grassroots movement successfully connected the intermediary points of order and freedom, responsibility and rights, and law and morality. Merely following the minimum requirements of the law is too little for most people, but observing the highest levels of morality is too demanding. Within these two lines, there is a need to promote a middle line of rational economic men, as advocated by the classical economic school, that is, self-interest without harming others, subjective motivation for oneself, but an objective outcome for others. Adam Smith believed that if self-interest does not cause harm to others, it is not evil, though certainly not good. Between good and evil, there is a third moderate choice.

Furthermore, socioeconomic reforms are more effective, more sustainable, and more conducive to improving the social structure and thereby saving social costs and reducing social risks if these reforms are examined via the triangular paradigm of political and economic reforms. Due to its apolitical, non-confrontational, and non-violent nature, socioeconomic reform is less burdensome on society. While passionate individuals often propel social reforms, they tend to be less violent and more radical than revolutionary. Consequently, it is more feasible to mobilize a larger number of people to engage in social reforms.

In addition, socioeconomic reforms served the function of awakening awareness of human rights, pushing the United States toward modernization. From a logical standpoint, industrialization liberates humanity from nature, yet emancipation from natural constraints does not equate to attaining spiritual freedom, nor does it imply release from social obligations. There remains a need for a second liberation, one that liberates individuals from both natural and societal limitations.

Finally, socioeconomic reforms could enhance the power of the middle class, which, as a product of early industrialization, had the money, leisure, ability, and intention to promote socioeconomic reforms. Mainly composed of scholars, scientists, educators, lawyers, doctors (in other words, professional men and women, etc.), the middle class owned property so they wanted stability; they were educated and desired freedom. They did not align with the working class or proletariat, who might lean towards a violent revolution, nor did they resemble the conservative and conformist upper vested interest groups. The middle class, on the other hand, sought to achieve reform alongside stability and vice versa. As a result, the middle class played a vital role in maintaining a delicate balance between the opposing desires for both freedom and order.[62]

9.3 The Moderate Evolution of Government Regulation of the Economy (1783-1920)

The role of the U.S. government in the economy has gradually increased since the American Revolution. Such a moderate evolution ensured the relative stability of American society, the continuous prosperity of the economy, and the limited power of the government. The government's efforts are in line with the balanced, evolutionary, limited, and shared implications of propriety economics.

The U.S. government's regulations and economic interventions have resulted in a quintessential American political economy. The various entities that intervene in the economy are constantly changing, including state governments, the judiciary, the legislature, and the executive branch. U.S. government intervention in the economy from 1783 to 1920 can be roughly divided into three major stages. The first one was dominated by states' power, jointly promoted by the judicial branch (1783–1860). The second one was endorsed by the federal legislative branch (1860–1900). The last one was led by the strong federal executive branch (1900–1920).

9.3.1 States' Rights and Judicial Power

British mercantilism, which was mainly characterized by direct government intervention in the economy, began to withdraw from the historical stage after American independence. Subsequently, the laissez-faire principle of the classical economic school was gradually introduced into the United States. However, government support for the colonial economy had a long-term impact, so a nudge was needed to transition to a laissez-faire economy. It is essential to note that before the American Civil War, the role of the U.S. government was not that of a negative economic regulator, but a positive economic promoter. The main economic function of the U.S. government at that time was to help the economy embark on de-governmentization and laissez-faire, which could not be achieved without government intervention. Therefore, early American industrial capital welcomed government regulation of the market.[63]

Given the federal government's laissez-faire approach, state governments and the judiciary (the U.S. Supreme Court) played the leading role in promoting economic growth before the American Civil War. Therefore, the dual effects of the dependent colonial economy and liberal politics profoundly influenced the American laissez-faire economy and provided historical background for the relative expansion of state governments and judicial power, as well as the relative shrinkage of federal power.[64] Initially, the economic functions of American state governments primarily manifested in transportation construction. Since the U.S. Constitution did not explicitly define the federal government's ability to intervene in transportation construction on a national scale, except for military and postal purposes, President James Madison vetoed a bill regarding the federal government's involvement in interstate transportation in 1817.[65] Although the Era of Good Feelings included the establishment of the Second Bank of the United States and the implementation of a protective tariff, national transportation was dead in the water. However, the weakening of federal power allowed the states to step in and support the construction of roads, canals, and railroads. New York built the famous Erie Canal, and 55% of the investment in the Southern Railway came from the states.[66] Moreover, states gave away public land for free, and starting in 1781, state governments provided 46.6 million acres of land to railroad companies.[67] The second area that state governments got involved in was both industry and agriculture, where light industrial enterprises mostly received tax exemptions and free land from state governments. Moreover, a large number of preferential loans were provided to support agriculture, and government subsidies were heavily implemented in Maine.[68] The third area was the financial sector. Localism and states' rights, led by the seventh President Andrew Jackson, succeeded in destroying the Second Bank of the United States in 1836, which gave rise to state and local banks on a large scale. Moreover, state governments were directly involved in the capital turnover and personnel appointments of state banks. State governments provided at least 50% of the capital for the state banks and handled the appointment of the chairmen and half of the managers of the banks.[69]

Along with state government involvement, the role of the U.S. judiciary in the economy was also very robust. The U.S. judiciary stimulated economic development by overhauling traditional contract law, which was characterized by fairness in the 18th century but was gradually replaced in the 19th century by the doctrine of *caveat emptor*. This asserts that the buyer is responsible for assessing the quality of the seller's goods during a transaction. If a problem is found afterward, the court will not accept any appeal from the buyer who has suffered a loss. This new law protected the interests of emerging capitalists to the detriment of customers, especially in the futures market, as the buyer cannot go check all the goods in person and can only blame bad luck if a product is later found to be substandard. In reality, this new contract law secured the seller's freedom to make money unethically, allowing for fraud and reducing the legal risks and costs for investors. Accordingly, it gave early capitalists a legal right to reduce their responsibility for production and operation.[70]

Property law in the United States also began to serve as another tool to protect the emerging capitalist economy. For instance, property law in the 18th century, like contract law, was designed to protect equity. In contrast, the equitable focus of property law began to be replaced by the concept of the government's eminent domain over property in the 19th century. This new property law enabled the government to take over personal property in the interest of public facilities, transportation, and various industrial developments. At the same time, it granted the government the legal means to support one party in developing a private industry at the expense of certain legal rights held by another party.[71]

Two major cases in American history help to understand the changes in property law. For example, a New York chemical company planned to build a factory in a residential area in 1803. When residents sued the plant for infringing upon their property rights, the chemical company emphasized that the proposed factory fell within its property rights. As a result, the court ruled in favor of the chemical plant.[72] This case became famous because, for the first time, property was divided into two types: dynamic property and static property. Business property represented dynamic property while residential housing was considered static property, so business naturally had priority.[73] This delivered a strong message that laws often prioritized economic development over environmental protection in the early stages of economic growth. However, a similar case occurred in 1936 with the opposite result, as environmental protection became a priority.

The second example was the famous Charles River Bridge case in 1837, which reflected another perspective on the nature of the new property laws to protect capital. The case involved a dispute between two Massachusetts companies about building a bridge over the Charles River. Charles River Bridge Company (Party A), demonstrating a traditionally privileged interest, had already built a bridge over the Charles River, and in order to monopolize it, Party A objected to Warren Bridge of Boston (Party B) building a new bridge over the river. Consequently, the Chief Justice of the Supreme Court, Roger Taney, ruled in favor of Party B based on the reason that Party A's monopoly had to be broken and its privilege had to be curbed.[74] This is typical of the early industrialization period when the law was used to combat old privileges, support new capital, and provide a basis for the creation of new privileges.

Another economic effect of the justice system involved transformations in the dynamics between judges and juries. The lay jury was the supreme arbiter, often overriding the judge during the colonial period. However, the judge increasingly gained authority in the courtroom during the 19th century. This helped judges use legal means to protect economic development more comfortably and freely. Furthermore, legal instrumentalism, highlighting the practical consequences of legal decisions, and legal formalism, emphasizing the text of the law and the application of fixed rules, also advocated for the separation of law and politics. This approach promoted judicial independence from executive power and contributed to the professionalization of the legal system with dominant judges.[75] In this regard, John Marshall, Chief Justice of the Supreme Court from 1801 to 1835, made various momentous contributions. He presided over a series of cases that established a widely accepted judicial norm: only the Supreme Court had the power to comment on and overturn bills passed by Congress and to arbitrate in interstate disputes. This notion of requiring the authority of the law and the judiciary became widespread in American society after 1850. The law was seen as a symbol of objectivity, neutrality, independence, and justice. As a result, the law became a science and a sophisticated discipline that created the basis for the judiciary's arbitrary power to protect and promote economic development.[76]

9.3.2 Legislative Branch Involvement in Economic Regulation

State and local governments began to grapple with a predicament where they had limited authority in light of the rapidly growing economy from 1860 to 1900. Given that industrialization and urbanization were interregional in nature, and the interstate economy and the national market developed rapidly, local governments were powerless to intervene in the national economy.

At the same time, influential emerging business elites had taken charge of local government operations. These local governments found themselves compelled to either collude with or acquiesce to the strategies and wrongdoings of these newly privileged classes, rendering them ineffective in their ability to intervene, let alone halt these activities. Local government officials generally lacked capability and competence in dealing with professional economic and legal issues, so they were incapable of assuming substantial responsibility for analysis and decision-making.[77]

Therefore, the changing social economy made it necessary for the U.S. Congress to intervene in economic operations. The shifting political environment also provided the opportunity for congressional intervention because, after the outbreak of the Civil War in 1861, the southern congressmen who advocated states' rights withdrew from Congress and the Republican-dominated U.S. Congress was presented with a golden opportunity to regulate the economy. The Republican Party, which adhered to federalism, advocated strengthening the power of the federal government and allowing government intervention in the economy. Additionally, in the post-Civil War period until 1900, the Republican Party was dominant in the Senate and the White House (except for two terms).[78]

Thus, the U.S. Congress made some modest efforts in various areas during and after the Civil War, designed to promote positive economic development and correct negative phenomena in the process of economic expansion. Of course, it also left many significant legacies that provided new opportunities for the transformation and improvement of American society.

The Homestead Act of 1862 was a notable example of congressional intervention in the area of land legislation. The Act stipulated that every American adult (with some conditions) could acquire 160 acres of western land for a registration fee of $10. Subsequently, Congress enacted more than 10 consecutive laws in an attempt to correct the shortcomings of the Homestead Act, and Congress sold 72 million acres of land between 1860 and 1900.[79] However, by the end of the 19th century, the Homestead Act was unable to prevent land speculation, stop land monopolies, or ensure that the majority of small farmers received an autonomous piece of land. Only 25.1% of public land was sold to small farmers by Congress from 1871 to 1974, and a large number of small farmers' land was continuously annexed and confiscated.[80] Congress passed the landmark General Revision Act (sometimes known as the Land Revision Act) of 1891, which stopped cash sales and public auctions of public lands, encouraged the creation of state-owned forest reserves on public lands, and restricted the further privatization of public lands.[81] Congressional efforts began to change the approach to U.S. public lands from liberalized sales and gifts to state-owned lands under government control.

The second area was banking and financial policy in which the Republican-controlled Congress strongly supported federal banks and intervened in the financial sector. Given the huge government expenditure and deficit before and after the Civil War, the deficit crisis called for the rebirth of a unified national bank.[82] Congress thus passed the National Bank Act in 1863 to rebuild the national bank, imposing punitive taxes on bank bills issued by state banks from 1866, in an attempt to gradually control and monopolize the issuance of national bank bills. Congress also began to force individuals to exchange their paper money for hard currency in 1873, opposing currency devaluation. Meanwhile, Congress enacted the Gold Standard Act in 1900, which established a strong currency,[83] with the positive effect of reducing the debt to 3.7% of the gross national income.[84]

The third congressional effort to regulate the economy was tax and tariff policies. Given that taxes had increased greatly since the Civil War, the Republican Party, which represented the rich, gradually reduced taxes to stimulate investment after the end of the war. Personal income tax was abolished in 1872, and later, under the pressure of the labor and farmer movements, an almost negligible income tax of 2% was imposed on individuals with an annual income of more than $4,000 in 1894.[85] Furthermore, the U.S. Congress implemented robust, stringent tariff policies. The average tariff was as high as 47% by the end of the Civil War, more than double that in 1857, making it the highest tariff period in U.S. history.[86] In fact, the high tariff policy of Congress at that time was a major positive impetus to the healthy growth of the national economy. However, as industrialization in the United States matured after the 1870s, there were many calls to open markets, dump products, and reduce tariffs. Thus, Congress passed the Wilson-Gorman Tariff Act in 1894, which made wool duty-free. Meanwhile, it reduced tariffs by an average of 40–50% for coal, steel rails, tinplate, pottery, and iron ore, bringing the average tariff from 47% in 1865[87] to 21% in 1894. As the country's economic influence fluctuated, Congress held the capacity to efficiently regulate the economy. Moreover, newly emerging political powers worked in complement to the government's policy of expanding railroad infrastructure.

In addition to tax and tariff regulations, Congress openly, fully, and legally promoted railroad construction at the onset of the Civil War. For example, Congress passed the Pacific Railroad Act in 1862, which gave several major railroad companies a total of 170 million acres of free land before 1872.[88] Congress legislated the creation of two nationwide railroad corporations, Union Pacific and Central Pacific in 1862, which directly contributed to the completion of the first east-west railroad across the United States in 1869.[89] But as the large corporates encroached more on the interests of workers and farmers, Senator John Sherman of Ohio introduced the Antitrust Act in 1890, which stipulated that any organizations restricting trade would be subject to a $5,000 fine and one year in prison.[90]

Over time, Congress found it increasingly challenging to address monopolies due to the United States' deep-rooted tradition of liberalism. Any interference with business giants was perceived as a breach of freedom. Additionally, Congress faced inefficiencies in enforcing some legislation. Most significantly, during that period, the Supreme Court was at odds with Congress, as it made attempts to shield monopolies from regulation. For example, from 1887–1905, 16 cases concerning railroad violations of the Interstate Commerce Act reached the high court, and 15 of them resulted in acquittals for the railroad companies.[91] The Antitrust Act also intentionally defined the terms "trust" and "restraint of trade" in an unclear manner, i.e., confusing monopoly with restraint, resulting in the government sanctioning only 18 trusts between 1890 and 1904.[92] Hence, the substantial expansion of monopolies within the U.S. economy prompted the need for a more assertive federal government and resolute presidents.

9.3.3 Federal Executive Power and Economic Intervention

The history of the U.S. federal government as an enemy of large firms began with President Grover Cleveland (1885–1889, 1893–1897), a Democrat, and reached its peak in 1921, when Woodrow Wilson (1913–1921) completed his second term. The key figures who played a significant role in economic intervention on behalf of the U.S. federal government were Republican President Theodore Roosevelt (1901–1909) and Democratic President Wilson. Their actions exemplified that, irrespective of party affiliations, presidential policy was aligned against monopolies at the beginning of the 20th century. Roosevelt and Wilson, after 16 years of effort, constituted a remarkable chapter in the American Progressive movement. The author believes that the most important aspect of Roosevelt's and Wilson's policies is social justice, which promoted reforms around three major themes: fairness, sharing, and caring.

As a prominent advocate prior to becoming president, Roosevelt was a staunch supporter of the Progressive movement and actively implemented its comprehensive policies once he took office. The Progressive movement, rooted in the core principle of social justice, initially served a relatively moderate purpose. Parties and groups of all kinds shared a common characteristic, namely, they all supported the ideas of social justice, regardless of whether they were liberal or conservative. Their different political and social motives notwithstanding, they all competed to use social justice as a banner for political change in late 19th- and early 20th-century America. The Constitution of the United States, written in 1787, explicitly defined the purpose of a perfect nation as "to establish justice," thus imprinting the word "justice" with intrinsic historical value and legitimacy.[93] Both the Republican Roosevelt and the Democratic Wilson held onto the banner of social justice, and the more radical People's Party platform of social justice[94] was partially accepted.[95] The two major parties, the Republican and the Democratic Parties, promoted social justice with the direct motivation of winning votes because most Americans were eagerly calling for change in a social environment where monopolies were prevalent, politics was corrupt, rich and poor were divided, and materialism was rampant. The practical need for gaining votes aside, promoting the cause of social justice actually had the political utility of killing not just two but three birds with one stone.

One of these was to please both sides of the political spectrum, thus satisfying the demands of workers and farmers against powerful groups, while also fulfilling the desire of the wealthy to defend their fundamental interests and mitigating their fears of changes to the capitalist system. The second was to reduce advantaged groups' wariness of a violent revolution and social unrest, convincing them to take the initiative to participate in political change while urging the under-represented classes to eschew aggressive resistance and join peaceful, rational elections. As a result, the presidents' efforts might transform radical forces outside the system into a driving force for progressive changes within the system. Moreover, progressive efforts were able to combat monopolistic consortia on the right, corrupt forces in the government, and authoritarian tendencies in national politics, while at the same time suppressing radical forces on the left, preventing the spread of socialist movements, and disrupting organized violence and unruly activities.[96]

Furthermore, the Progressive movement embodied the principle of fairness. This principle aims to emphasize fair economic competition and fair political participation through institutional arrangements. For example, under Roosevelt's leadership, the Department of Commerce and Labor was established in 1903, and Wilson set up the Federal Trade Commission in 1914.[97] These government agencies were launched to investigate, prosecute, and dissolve monopolistic organizations. Roosevelt also strengthened the function of the Department of Justice, bypassing the Supreme Court and allowing the Department of Justice to work closely with the President and act as a substitute for some judicial duties,[98] which may have set a bad precedent. Since then, the U.S. judiciary has no longer been fully independent because prosecutors are not elected while the courts have always been independent, although Supreme Court judges are appointed. These two U.S. presidents also signed a series of anti-trust legislation to reinforce existing anti-trust laws, limit the uncontrolled growth of monopolies, and intervene in the monopolistic prices of railroad companies. For example, the Pure Food and Drug Act and the Federal Meat Inspection Act were enacted in 1906, prohibiting the sale of counterfeit drugs and rotten food, and a total of 43 monopolies were prosecuted during Roosevelt's two terms of office.[99] Another effort was to set up new democratic measures, such as the promotion of nationwide initiatives, referendum, recall, and women's suffrage, aimed at eliminating election fraud, encouraging popular participation, and returning politics to the people. Consequently, these efforts succeeded in the ratification of the 17th and 19th constitutional amendments, which explicitly provided that voters in each state had the right to directly elect U.S. senators and that all women had the right to vote in elections.[100] Therefore, the principle of fairness refers mainly to the equality of the starting point of competition and the fairness of the opportunity to compete. Directly related to this is the fairness and impartiality of the law, which is a source of security for many people.

Along with the principle of fairness, the Progressive movement also implemented the principle of sharing, which emphasizes justice of results and compensation for unfair results. In particular, it requires the establishment of laws and systems for wealth sharing, secondary distribution of income, and institutional compensation for disadvantaged groups to ensure the continuity and fairness of society. For example, regarding income tax, inheritance tax, social welfare, health insurance, and housing policies, the rich and the poor should not be treated equally. Instead, the poor should be able to share partial profits of economic growth and wealth revenue legally, reasonably, and peacefully. While traditional Jeffersonian liberalism focuses only on openness and equality of opportunity, social justice highlights equality of outcome and skewed opportunity to build an equal-wealth society. For example, in terms of tax law, President Wilson enacted the Revenue Act of 1913, which imposed a 7% income tax on individuals earning more than $500,000 per year, and which later became the 16th Amendment to the U.S. Constitution.[101] This marked a historic victory for the U.S. legal system, as it established a federal policy for the second distribution of income and institutionalized the graduated income tax. Another was the creation of national parks, where Presidents Roosevelt and Wilson took steps to protect and conserve natural resources. Roosevelt preserved nearly 200 million acres of public land and established national parks, including Yellowstone National Park, not allowing monopolized capital to interfere.[102] There is also the control of public lands by the government, as a result of which one-third of the land in the United States is still publicly owned, and the federal government owns 700 million acres of land, including 96% of the land in Alaska and 86% of the land in Nevada.[103] In this sense, the U.S. is not a typical capitalist system or a privatized country, but rather has a relatively moderate private land system.

The principle of sharing is not a substitute for the principle of caring, which is mainly manifested in caring for disadvantaged groups in society. It represents a form of social justice that utilizes moral and religious influence to encourage lawmakers to establish a legal framework for income distribution and social welfare that embody the concept of "unfair care." President Roosevelt invited Booker T. Washington, a famous African-American leader, to the White House for dinner at the risk of racial conflict on October 16, 1901. Roosevelt summoned labor union leaders and business representatives to the White House for the first time and mediated with them during a strike in October 1902. In the end, both sides gave in and reached a historic "Square Deal."[104] His approach to caring for disadvantaged social groups and a series of other administrative measures helped the U.S. government to gradually become more fair, neutral, and moderate in dealing with social frictions between the rich and the poor, labor and management, and racial confrontations. At the same time, President Wilson was involved in three epochal caring efforts: one prohibited child labor in interstate industrial and commercial enterprises; another required interstate railroad workers to work no more than eight hours a day; and the third provided labor protection and pensions to federal government and agency employees in the event of workplace accidents.[105] These two presidents also supported the development of trade unions, so the number of American trade union members increased more than 2.5 times to 3,061,000 during the Progressive movement (1900–1917).[106]

It is important to note that absolute fairness is not in line with the principles of propriety economics, as it is actually unfair to disadvantaged groups, because the rich and the poor, the strong and the weak have different starting points and results in the competition of life. To address disparities among the rich and the poor, various races, and genders, the Johnson administration implemented affirmative action in 1965 as part of a deliberate effort to promote a more equitable social policy.

9.3.4 Effects of Government Intervention in the Economy

After the Progressive movement, the effects of U.S. executive and judicial branch intervention in the economy were more positive than negative. State governments prior to the 1870s facilitated the destruction of traditional privileges and assisted emerging business leaders to become rich and powerful. However, the new elite, protected by new policies, began to reject free competition once they had established their economic power. These new powerful elites, once dominant, began to discard free competition and established new monopolies which were much greater in intensity and breadth than the old ones.

The joint intervention of federal legislative and executive power in monopolies further guided the direction of economic development after 1870. If the government's role in the economy before 1870 was that of a protector, it evolved into that of a navigator afterwards. In fact, the privileged groups of the United States went through three stages. First, the privileges created by mercantilism during the colonial period; second, the laissez-faire economy advocated by liberal capitalism after independence, which carried out a comprehensive attack on privileges. Finally, when the liberal economy developed into an economy controlled by monopolies, privileges again proliferated, so the federal government took strong action.

The government's intervention in the economy at the end of the 19th century and the beginning of the 20th century actually eased the capitalist economic crisis, avoided violent revolts, and prompted society to take a moderate, propriety path of benign reforms and democracy. Russia embarked on a path to communism in 1917 through violent revolution, and Germany gradually marched on to fascism. In contrast, the United States chose a moderate middle path: modernization through government intervention in curbing monopolies, rather than destroying them, prompted a smooth transition for the whole society. Therefore, negative economic phenomena, such as monopolies, should not be driven into extinction.

Finally, U.S. intervention policy has introduced many laws, abstemiously balancing the dilemma of efficiency and equity, and establishing an open system that promotes the exchange, integration, and combination of capitalist and socialist principles. For example, the U.S. public land system, national park system, graduated income tax system, and workers' compensation, followed by the social insurance system and welfare system of the New Deal in the 1930s, led to the hybridization of two systems. The major values, systems, and ideas of capitalism and socialism are not mutually antagonistic and exclusively class-based but can be complementary and mutually beneficial instrumentalities. Instrumental rationality is neither virtuous nor vile; it is only concerned with efficiency. Therefore, in the face of two systems, it is vital to pursue more shared values rather than universal values.[107]

9.4 Evolution of the War on Poverty (1933–2000)

Using propriety economics to analyze the path of the war on poverty in the United States since President Franklin D. Roosevelt's New Deal can provide many useful insights.[108] Anti-poverty policies in the U.S. since the 1930s have broadly undergone a rational evolution in four major stages from addressing material poverty to poverty of capability, poverty of rights, and poverty of motivation.

9.4.1 Material Poverty

The goal of poverty alleviation in the United States was to confront material poverty during the New Deal era. As the starting point of the modern American welfare state, the Social Security Act was enacted in 1935, which included a two-track relief policy. One was social insurance, i.e., a portion of the income tax revenue of employers and hired workers was allocated into a retirement fund, unemployment fund, disability fund, and medical benefits. The second was public assistance, i.e., government financial support for those who could not work, such as minors, the poor elderly, and the disabled. Meanwhile, facing an unemployment rate of more than 25%, the United States established the Works Progress Administration in 1935, which was funded by the government up to a total of $11 billion from 1933 to 1943, providing 8 million jobs in the field of public works. Additionally, Roosevelt's New Deal established a minimum wage of 25 cents per hour in 1938. Compared with the early American poor laws, the greatest contribution of Roosevelt's New Deal was the shift of anti-poverty resources from local to state and federal governments. Other achievements were to eliminate the traditional laissez-faire policy on urban poverty, modify the target of relief from all poor people to poor families, and grant relief on a family rather than an individual basis. More importantly, these efforts changed the source of funds for relief payments from traditional property taxes to income taxes for employers and employees, and finally shifted traditional in-kind and cash relief to check payments.[109]

Consequently, Roosevelt's New Deal provided significant assistance to the poor, with spending on social welfare in the United States jumping from 3.9% ($3.9 billion) of the nation's GNP to 9.2% ($8.8 billion) from 1929 to 1940. However, the New Deal was fraught with injustices and inequalities, including discrimination against women and the poor in the workplace, the preservation of the existing economic order, and the protection of vested interests. There are still debates as to whether the New Deal's anti-poverty policies were truly "new."[110]

9.4.2 Poverty of Capability

The second stage of anti-poverty efforts in the United States began in 1961 by tackling mass poverty of capability. By the 1960s, due to rapid economic growth, the United States had been divided into "two nations": one for the rich and the other for the poor.[111] During the two years of President John F. Kennedy's administration (1961–1963), the focus of the fight against poverty shifted to the empowerment of the poor, that is, federal government policies evolved from material and monetary support to the provision of services and skills, hoping to move from passive "blood transfusion" to active "blood production" for the poor. The main symbol of this historic modification was the Public Welfare Amendments enacted in 1962 which covered several areas. The first was service, which aimed to help each poor family improve its ability to become independent and self-sufficient. The second was prevention, designed to support helpless people and provide services while the poverty crisis was rampant. The third was incentive, which aimed to encourage beneficiaries of relief to gradually become less dependent on government subsidies. The last one was training, providing sufficient educational opportunities and options to enable the poor to become self-reliant.[112]

At the same time, to complement the development of poor people's capabilities, U.S. poverty alleviation policy began to move from centralization to decentralization by mobilizing local governments, especially the community, to deliver services and training.[113] Private organizations, such as the Ford Foundation, funded the famous Mobilization for Youth program, which aimed to encourage local non-professional youth to become volunteer instructors. This intended to support the poor to solve problems and improve their skills and knowledge to deal with poverty, thereby reducing the cost of training social workers.[114] In particular, the Kennedy administration approved the Area Redevelopment Act and the Manpower Development and Training Act in 1961 and 1962, respectively, to offer vocational training to the poor and disadvantaged and to promote access to education.

9.4.3 Poverty of Rights

The third phase of poverty mitigation was activated in 1964 with the priority of fighting the poverty of rights. African-American people had made major contributions towards the fight against poverty through the emergence of a fruitful civil rights movement in the 1950s and '60s. President Lyndon B. Johnson (1963–1969) announced the concept of a "war on poverty" on January 8, 1964.[115] In response, Johnson continued to increase funding for poverty relief, and federal funding for social welfare from 1965 to 1969 jumped from 11% of GNP ($77.1 billion) to 15.2% of GNP ($145 billion).[116] The Johnson administration also launched many historic welfare and anti-poverty programs, including the well-known health benefits programs (Medicare and Medicaid), the food stamp program (the Food Stamp Act), and many training programs directed at empowering the poor, such as the Job Corps and the Work Incentive Program, among others.

But more importantly, President Johnson began to focus on the poverty of opportunity, of which the most indicative act was the Economic Opportunity Act of 1964, an attempt to maximize access to relief and welfare programs for the poor, especially African Americans who were victims of racial discrimination. In tandem with this, the U.S. Congress under President Johnson enacted three celebrated pieces of legislation, Civil Rights Acts in 1964 and 1968 and the Voting Rights Act of 1965, respectively, which promoted the equality and universality of civil rights.

Therefore, if we compare Roosevelt's New Deal with Johnson's Great Society, we can easily find that Roosevelt's New Deal objectified many poor people, and it treated the fight against poverty as part of reforming the whole economic system. The New Deal helped the poor using material means. As a result, the New Deal made it difficult to treat each poor person with respect. Johnson's policies, however, placed more focus on the individual rights of the poor, especially the rights of African Americans. They thus treated the poor humanely as a disfranchised group of people, and strongly elevated the prospects for the poor to participate in and enjoy the economic security of the United States. In short, Johnson promoted a people-centered rather than a goods-centered anti-poverty policy, which was not only far-reaching but also effective. For example, the number of people living in poverty in the United States fell sharply from 40 million to 23 million in 1960 compared to 1973.[117]

9.4.4 Poverty of Motivation

The fourth phase of poverty relief in the United States was initiated in the 1970s and focused on fighting the lack of motivation among the poor. In light of increasing welfare spending, American society developed a "welfare state" somewhat similar to that in European societies. Some scholars debated that the fundamental cause of poverty in the United States was not a lack of money, ability, or rights, but a lack of motivation and incentive. They believed that some poor people had lost their motivation and willingness to find work due to substantial welfare benefits, and the disintegration of some poor American families directly contributed to growing poverty. Some directly blamed the inertia of the poor, arguing that many people had been dependent on welfare and benefits for a long time and refused to work, and that this dependence would lead to the end of the capitalist tradition in the long run.[118]

In line with the policy of the Republican Party, Presidents Richard Nixon (1969–1974) and Gerald Ford (1974–1977) increasingly focused on promoting business investment and reducing income taxes to encourage the rich to invest in industry and increase employment. These efforts developed the strategy of investing in poverty alleviation by providing employment instead of actively using monetary resources to ease poverty. In particular, they advocated reducing the federal government's involvement in poverty alleviation and mobilizing the power of state and local governments to actively address poverty-related problems. President Ford launched a $4.5 billion stimulus package, of which $2.5 billion was earmarked in 1975 to help state and local governments hire unemployed workers and give low-wage workers the earned income tax credit. This was actually an additional bonus for workers, encouraging the poor to forgo free assistance, seek employment, and become self-supporting. The federal government, hence, gave out $1.25 billion in income tax incentives in 1975, which jumped to $11.914 billion by 1993. But such measures to tackle the poor's lack of incentive to escape poverty often had high thresholds, and many single-parent families were ineligible for the money.[119] President Jimmy Carter (1977–1981), a Democrat, still seemed to continue the Republican practice of focusing on the lack of incentive for people to get out of poverty. However, his efforts evolved from creating jobs in public works to those in public services[120] because the poor who had not been employed for a long time were happier to work in the relatively easy service industry rather than in more physically demanding, skill-oriented public works.

More importantly, the Ronald Reagan administration (1981–1989) implemented aggressive conservative policies to address the poor's lack of motivation. Reagan first effected the deepest tax cuts in U.S. history to stimulate investment and increase employment. A surprising $280 billion in tax cuts and a 25% reduction in personal income tax rates were effected in just three years. However, welfare spending and poverty programs for the poor fell victim to the lack of interest to address poverty, as the Reagan administration drastically reduced government welfare and relief spending. Consequently, 408,000 families with minor children lost their eligibility for government assistance and 299,000 families had their welfare benefits cut, by which the federal and state governments saved $1.1 billion in one year in 1983.[121] From 1978 under Carter to 1987 under Reagan, federal welfare spending increased by 2.9% in absolute terms ($116.2 billion to $119.6 billion) but decreased by 22.5% on a per capita basis ($4,744 to $3,675).[122]

Reagan's New Federalism introduced various reforms in the fight against poverty in the United States. To force the poor to find jobs, Regan was in favor of "workfare," or even "learnfare," as the prerequisite for receiving welfare. He also reduced or eliminated existing welfare programs as much as possible while requiring state and local governments to bear more of the burden of poverty relief.[123] In privatizing some programs related to relief and welfare, the Reagan administration encouraged job training programs, welfare service programs, and job investment programs to be transferred from the government to the private sector.[124] Under the Reagan administration, for example, the U.S. Congress passed a historic bill, the Family Support Act in 1988, which required young parents with a child over the age of three to join mandatory vocational training and basic education, or their child would not receive government assistance. However, few people participated in this program because young single mothers had to stay at home to take care of their children. Consequently, this hindered their ability to receive education, which affected their willingness and availability to receive training. Truthfully, the intent of the Reagan administration was not to end poverty but to end dependency.[125]

Subsequent Presidents George H. W. Bush (1989–1993) and Bill Clinton (1993–2001) mostly continued Reagan's policy of ending the overdependence of the poor. Although Bush and Clinton belonged to different parties, they both encouraged the correction of welfare issues. Clinton, in particular, was more interested in reinforcing the government's administrative supervision function and mechanism by forcing poor people on welfare to enter the job market. Both Bush and Clinton believed that poverty was simply a harmful economic phenomenon that was not difficult to solve, whereas dependence was an unhealthy cultural behavior that must be dealt with strictly, quickly, and seriously, and the personal responsibility of the poor must be strengthened through the dual efforts of administrative coercion and economic incentives.[126] Inadequate motivation and incentives resulted from a combination of individual misconduct and government negligence. Therefore, poverty alleviation policies were designed to ultimately change the welfare culture by revitalizing the traditional American beliefs in free competition and survival of the fittest.

What is striking and deserving of contemplation is the emergence of a detrimental historical cycle within the context of anti-poverty endeavors and policies in the United States during the 1990s. As a result of overly conservative anti-poverty policies since the Reagan era, the United States eventually saw a large number of newly poor people and a widespread return to poverty.[127] The U.S. poverty rate remained below 10% from 1969 to 1979, then surpassed 10% again in 1984 during the Reagan era, reaching 11.6%, and has been above 10% ever since.[128] By the end of 2001, the U.S. poverty rate was 11.7%, with 32.9 million people living in poverty.[129] In 1983, during the heyday of "Reaganomics," there was a positive correlation between the U.S. economic boom and the number of people living in poverty, both of which reached record highs since 1965, with the number of people living in poverty exceeding 35 million in 1983.[130] In particular, poverty rates across the board rose in the post-Reagan era, with the white poverty rate increasing from 8.3% to 8.8% between 1989 and 1990 (and as high as 9.9% in 2001);[131] the African-American poverty rate growing from 30.7% to 31.9%; and the Hispanic poverty rate rising from 26.2% to 28.1%.[132] Moreover, between 1988 and 1991, as many as 1.9 million people under the age of 18 were added to the poor population,[133] and by the end of 2001, the child poverty rate was 16.3%, much higher than the poverty rate of 11.7% for the total population.[134]

Thus, there is a renewed demand in American society for the government to focus on material poverty, and the material relief of the Roosevelt New Deal has become a social priority again. This has seemingly given way to significant feelings of frustration and helplessness. The war on poverty appears to have regressed to the initial stages of a vicious cycle.

9.4.5 Reflections on Poverty Alleviation Strategies

The ongoing but cyclical journey of anti-poverty initiatives in the United States, spanning from the 1930s to the beginning of this century, has yielded both valuable experiences and cautionary lessons. To begin with, effective anti-poverty endeavors necessitate a dialectical, dynamic, and harmonized approach that addresses the four dimensions of poverty alleviation, encompassing material, capability, rights, and motivational aspects. The four major historical stages the United States has traversed during its anti-poverty efforts exhibit a certain logical development, inherent rationality, and universal applicability. Despite the differences in national conditions, the occurrence and development of poverty have considerable intrinsic laws that cannot be easily traversed. For example, when there is starvation everywhere, the priority of the government is of course material relief; but when the poorest people can obtain basic food and necessities, the government should support them in developing the ability to help themselves. However, having the ability is not the same as having the opportunity, so the government should establish a fair, just institutional mechanism to safeguard the rights of the poor. Once excessive welfare becomes mainstream and poor people's dependence on relief becomes a set way of life or cultural behavior, the government needs to help the poor feel increased motivation to change the status quo, induce them to enter the job market, and reduce their inertia. Thus, it is clear that the evolution of the four major stages is closely related to the level of economic development and the political and cultural environment at the time. The lesson learned in the United States is that shifting the priorities of poverty alleviation policies without a systematic vision at different stages eventually leads to an increasing number of poor people.

Poverty control policies should be intelligently crafted to address the unique needs of both impoverished individuals seeking prosperity and affluent individuals seeking social harmony, with the goal of achieving a mutually beneficial outcome for all. On the one hand, to reduce social conflicts and prevent the poor from protesting, the state must redistribute existing economic and social resources; on the other hand, all forms of redistribution, no matter how small in scale and magnitude, are bound to cause conflicts.[135] In order to reduce poverty, policymakers have to redistribute resources because this is the fundamental way to avoid social instability or even violence. Since redistribution is designed to help the disadvantaged, anti-poverty policies can only and must be more favorable to the poor, thus threatening the prosperity of other interest groups.[136]

Significantly, the win-win principle of economics can facilitate the identification of common interests for both social polarities within the framework of social justice. The U.S. experience demonstrates that, in most cases, the affluent are not inclined to voluntarily share their wealth with the less fortunate; such redistribution typically occurs when they are confronted with actual labor strikes, farmer movements, and civil unrest. In such cases, they are compelled to adhere to progressive income taxes and substantial estate taxes imposed by the government. The rich hence need to cooperate with the government before a violent rebellion of the poor occurs. In the secondary distribution of wealth, it is necessary to follow caring and sharing principles in asking the rich to pay more taxes in exchange for social stability and a better investment environment. It is also feasible for the rich to engage in volunteer efforts and donations as part of a third distribution of wealth. In this regard, the rich and the poor need to find an intersection where the poor's desire for wealth and the rich's desire for peace converge. The wealthy, in particular, should draw lessons from the experiences of other nations and avoid exerting excessive pressure on the less fortunate. They should refrain from amassing wealth excessively and greedily, recognizing that the rich and the poor share a common fate. Above all, they should realize that one of the primary advantages of affluent individuals investing in poverty alleviation is the reduction of crime rates and social unrest.[137]

In fact, the lessons from the United States tell the world that economic poverty itself is not the worst-case scenario; rather inequality in the process and opportunities for the poor to escape poverty are more troubling. Therefore, society and the government need to apply the gas pedal to the mechanism of poverty eradication for the poor, especially in generating a social force conducive to sensible economic equity rather than expanding social estrangement. If the norm of party politics is that different parties take turns to govern, then the norm of the social economy should also be that both the rich and the poor might fluctuate in their socioeconomic standing and this should be the common ground between democratic politics and the market economy. Fostering an environment where social mobility is not only possible but likely serves as a strong motivator for individuals of lower socioeconomic status to strive even harder. Meanwhile, the possibility of the rich losing their wealth can reinforce their crisis consciousness as well as the societal aspiration for fair competition. Enacting policies and processes that make it possible for either upward or downward social mobility helps to mitigate class tensions and conflicts and stave off social unrest.[138]

Furthermore, it is sensible to appropriately respond to the dilemma between the people-oriented and material-oriented approaches to poverty relief by focusing on the former, as poverty reduction is not only implemented for the sake of economic development and wealth accumulation. It should not be perceived as a purely profitable investment, and the concept of developmental poverty alleviation should not be overemphasized. Specifically, the success of poverty relief cannot be solely assessed by the quantity of material investment and financial resources allocated. Only when people become the major players can poverty be eased and positive social change and development result.[139] At the same time, it must be acknowledged that the market cannot eliminate poverty because the market is dehumanizing and generally unwilling to enter the arena of public welfare.

Therefore, in fighting poverty, countries around the world need not only material poverty alleviation but more importantly, humanitarian consideration and emotional investment. The social rights and basic well-being of the people must be the highest priority of any government. In accordance with the International Covenant on Economic, Social and Cultural Rights, adopted by the United Nations in 1966, the state is obligated to take measures to provide the maximum available resources to accelerate the realization of citizens' rights.[140] In this way, once human priority is recognized, the people not only have nothing to fear from the government but should be able to justly demand that their public servants fulfill their obligations. The social and humanitarian benefits of poverty alleviation without care and concern will only be partly effective because the disadvantaged, who are full of grievances and anger, will still be discontented with the government and society because more material relief and benefits do not necessarily succeed in preempting social unrest. On the contrary, if the government's material investment is limited, but the process of poverty alleviation is humane and caring, the effect is inevitably positive. In other words, the cultural function of emotional investment over material investment should not be overlooked. In Eastern societies, which highly value benevolence and social decorum, it is still important to underscore cultural values and traditions. Thus, fostering collaboration between government and the private sector to combat poverty, providing robust support for the creation of private foundations, advancing social philanthropy, and enabling financial institutions to engage in microfinance programs for the less fortunate encapsulate the essence of humanizing poverty alleviation. This aligns with the sharing principle advocated by propriety economics.

Finally, the dilemma between fair opportunity and "unfair" caring and sharing should be properly handled based on the concept of affirmative action in the United States. This prominent anti-discrimination policy was designed to compel federal departments, federally funded educational institutions, and businesses that have commercial contracts with the federal government to meet certain requirements of recruiting, hiring, and promoting certain percentages of women and minorities, with deadlines imposed on the violators to rectify their behavior.

Failure to meet the deadlines would result in the offending entities losing their government funding or contract at a given time. The federal government also established the Equal Employment Opportunity Commission and the Office of Federal Compliance Programs as the enforcement units for anti-discrimination actions. This groundbreaking policy has contributed significantly to the advancement of gender and racial equality in American society, especially for those who are disadvantaged economically, as their opportunities for work, schooling, and advancement have greatly improved, helping them to accelerate their progress out of poverty.[141]

The basic idea of affirmative action is not only to create an equal society for all, but more importantly, to create a mechanism for "unfair" caring and sharing.[142] In order to make things right, the government must provide "unfair" care and "unjust" sharing to those groups that have been disadvantaged for years; otherwise, they will never be able to catch up with vested interests. Similar administrative interventions to maintain social justice, protect civil rights, and eliminate various kinds of discrimination are not only the natural responsibilities of the government but are also applauded by the public and the international community. More importantly, affirmative action does not violate the basic principles of a free market economy because the government, as a funding entity, has the right to impose conditions on beneficiaries regarding social welfare and civil rights. In particular, affirmative action, with its low economic costs and high social benefits, is critical in promoting poverty relief. These endeavors not only contribute to the enhancement of social justice, civil rights, and the government's reputation but also serve to curb the influence of powerful capital and combat social injustice. They pave the way for a rational, humane reconfiguration of the majority of people's interests for the future.[143]

In addition to the aforementioned historically significant American socioeconomic cases related to propriety economics, there are actually more cases in the United States that are closely linked to propriety economics at the macroeconomic and microeconomic levels in contemporary society. For example, in the dilemma between economic development and environmental protection, where the goal is to promote economic growth and increase energy supply through means such as oil production while simultaneously protecting the environment and mitigating the devastating impact of climate change, some ideas and methods from propriety economics need to be applied. These concepts can help explore how to moderately develop clean energy sources, limit oil extraction, and vigorously promote alternatives such as electric vehicles as a balanced, moderate approach.

Similarly, in the era after the COVID-19 pandemic, considering propriety economic theory in determining employees' working arrangements can be advantageous. Exploring a potential hybrid working model that strikes a balance between the freedom of remote work and the more conventional on-site work, while retaining employees without compromising work performance, aligns with the tenets of propriety economics.

Likewise, when addressing the issue of drug legalization, seeking a compromise between the extreme positions of absolute, indiscriminate, zero tolerance on one end and permissiveness, tolerance, and the proliferation of drugs on the other involves a gradual, differentiated approach. This includes moderately relaxing restrictions on substances like marijuana, which are less toxic and have relatively lower risk of addiction, as a middle-ground compromise.

9.5 The Moderate Path of China's Economic Reform (1978-2002)

In a sense, China's economic development from 1978 to 2002 has also followed a relatively moderate path. Whether something is considered moderate or not depends on a particular time, place, and economic subject, and the comparison of different objects within a system. Therefore, the definition of moderate, propriety characteristics is distinctly relative, historical, and dynamic.

9.5.1 The Moderate Choice of Economic System

If one places China's economy after reform within the bipolar system of the former Soviet Union's planned economy and the Western market economy, then China's path after 1978 is a moderate compromise since it is a hybrid system of planned and market economies.

China's planned economic system, which endured from 1949 to 1978, did not automatically collapse after 1978, nor did it entirely embrace the free market economy. As a result, China's economic system underwent a gradual transformation in the 1980s, giving rise to the so-called socialist market economy with Chinese characteristics.

In 1992, China's economic system faced another critical crossroads, influenced by the dissolution of the former Soviet Union and the 1989 Tiananmen incident. China had to make a pivotal choice once more, considering two alternatives: one involved a return to a planned economy, reinforcing the state-owned structure, and halting reform; the other entailed following the Russian-style "shock therapy" and rapidly transitioning to a Western market economy. The former option would have faced resistance from those who had benefited from the previous 15 years of reform, while the latter risked generating severe societal upheaval, potentially erasing the gains of reform. Intriguingly and wisely, China opted for a third path, continuing its reform and open-door policies after 1992.

In this way, China's economic system, through blending and taking the middle way, has developed its own distinct characteristics. The unique pairs of politics and economy, state and civil society, power and capital, and planning and the market are difficult to distinguish from each other. According to Deng Xiaoping who was the initiator of China's reform, crossing the river by feeling for stones was a necessary strategy to ensure the stability of China's institutional transition.[144] These experimental "stones" provided the option to move forward and the room for a possible retreat. In other words, the "stones," by allowing those who found them to choose the lesser of two evils and the middle of two opposite ends, helped China in its transition to avoid extreme freedom and violent turmoil. This approach not only respects heritage but also responds to times of change; it not only retains the historical privilege of political power but also takes into consideration the profit impulse of economic capital. Meanwhile, it creates a relatively free "birdcage" for contained economic development, and it also promotes the private sector. More importantly, this strategy encourages a few people to get rich first, setting the path for others who are willing and able to follow.

The reform of China's economic system is like the invention of a "square-shaped wheel," which seems to be an impossible miracle, but in fact has adapted to the rugged trails of Chinese society. If China had started off by imitating the Western market economic model using a perfectly round wheel, this wheel, lacking friction, would probably have moved too fast and overturned on the treacherous terrain. But given that China has a "square-shaped wheel" full of angles, it keeps grinding along the winding mountain roads, and gradually the square wheel wears away into other shapes and finally becomes a rough yet relatively round wheel adapted to the Chinese political, cultural, and social landscape.[145]

9.5.2 Case Studies on Economic Institutional Arrangements

Over the past 45 years, reforms at all levels of China's economy have designed, crafted, and operated various types of "square-shaped wheels," attesting to the peculiarity of China's conditions. For example, the household responsibility system of the 1980s was neither an instance of the private ownership of land found in the West nor the public ownership of land that is inherent in socialism. Rather, it constituted incomplete changes to land use and contract rights without eroding the collective ownership of land. According to classical economics theory and Western practice, this type of land reform is peculiar because without stable ownership, there can be no rational, long-term behavior of investing in and protecting land. In theory, land property rights must be clear, and responsibilities and rights must be distinct, but under the constraints of the historical legacy of collective land ownership in China, the post-1978 land system has taken a middle path between the people's commune and private land. Although the economic and social costs of this "square-shaped wheel" are extremely high, it fits into the logic of the evolving Chinese economy. The development of rural China from 1978 to the mid-1990s shows that these land reforms, which do not conform to Western norms, are not only feasible but effective.[146]

Furthermore, the property rights reform of township and village enterprises (TVEs) in China is also a propriety institutional transformation. The TVE, which was developed in the 1990s, was neither a purely private enterprise in that it was derived from the people's commune period and had considerable traces of a collectivist operation, nor was it a truly public or state-owned enterprise because it was a self-financing, autonomous, and independent economic entity. TVEs were neither a pure shareholding system nor a collective cooperative system in the people's commune style, but a hybrid yet neutral shareholding cooperative system that introduced Western shares into the traditional Chinese peasant cooperative model. This joint-stock cooperative system was a major invention by Chinese peasants, aiming at gradually diluting government intervention and control over enterprises, and clarifying property rights and equality between the government, enterprises, and workers. As a result, it achieved the multiple purposes of raising funds, improving efficiency, and stimulating the production motivation of local leaders and workers.[147]

The reform of state-owned enterprises (SOEs) in China also followed the "square-shaped wheel" model. Faced with the business crisis of SOEs, China's reform direction was neither a capitalist shareholding system nor a socialist cooperative system, but a peculiar shareholding cooperative system. The property rights of the Western shareholding system are clear but rigid, while the Chinese shareholding system was vague but flexible, with a large number of "strange shares" such as government shares, power-capital shares, shares based on special connections to the enterprises, and collective shares. The Western personnel system and decision-making apparatus in an enterprise are democratically decided by the board of directors, but inefficient, while the decision-making process in Chinese SOEs is centralized but fast and effective. The West advocates capital control over labor, emphasizing one share, one vote and more shares, more votes, while China has to consider labor influencing capital, and was used to one person, one vote during the Mao era from 1949 to 1976. Similarly, the West is accustomed to managing enterprises under the rule of law, while China is more willing to resolve disputes through the rule of man and human efforts, an approach that eases the tension between labor and management when dealing with the serious challenge of labor layoffs to public order and corporate governance.[148] Finally, China has implemented the reform of enterprise property rights under the rule of factory managers and introduced foreign and private capital as third parties. Accordingly, the new system has broken the long-established symmetrical, stable structure of state-owned enterprises and brought vitality and dynamism. This phenomenon has also been proven by the "catfish effect": a small catfish introduced from outside can activate other inert fish, leading to competition, vitality, and optimization of the overall living environment.[149] Therefore, in a bipolar confrontation, the optimal choice is not necessarily one for conservative stabilization, but one for innovation and a new non-homogeneous arrangement. Moreover, the choice itself is a test of propriety, the degree of its tension, the strength of its elasticity, and the rise and fall of its transformation, all of which are advantages of having multiple options.

Moreover, China's approach to urbanization followed a unique, balanced path in the 1980s. One notable aspect of China's urbanization strategy is its emphasis on the development of townships other than large cities. China faced the challenge of neither tying farmers to the land nor overwhelming its cities with a massive influx of rural residents. To address this, China has established a network of townships situated between urban and rural areas to gradually shift the location of farmers. This approach facilitates the modernization and poverty alleviation of rural residents while preventing the emergence of extensive slums and overcrowding in major cities. To ensure a smooth transition into urbanization, China has opted for a gradual increase in the urbanization rate while addressing urban poverty systematically and incrementally.[150] In essence, during the 1980s and 1990s, China pursued a strategy that prioritized townization over rapid urbanization, although many small cities like Shenzhen were successfully developed into larger urban centers.[151]

Therefore, the Chinese economy, which represents the third option, can hardly return to a planned economy because the "chicken" has already been made into an irreversible "chicken soup." At the same time, China's economy is not fully consistent with the Western market economy; rather, it is a relatively independent, sustainable economic form rooted in China's unique political culture, social practices, and popular psychology. China's economic system, therefore, may not be a stop-gap solution, but rather a propriety arrangement that can last for a long time.

The case studies in this chapter and the policy principles in Chapter 8 both explore a major dilemma: how to effectively achieve a propriety economy. The study of propriety economics needs to further consider specific cases, not only the macroeconomic ones as articulated in this chapter but also microeconomic and meso-economic cases. Furthermore, it should be supported not only by cases from individual countries but also by comparisons among countries.

Chapter 10

Conclusion

The concluding chapter of this book endeavors to summarize the historical evolution of Western economic thought, delineate the distinctive contributions made by propriety economics to economic philosophy, and underscore the defining features that position propriety economics between the spectrums of neoclassicism and modern economics. Furthermore, it delves into potential avenues for the future of economics, along with an analysis of the prospective roles that propriety economics may assume in shaping the economics of tomorrow.

Reflecting upon the interdisciplinary journey of propriety philosophy and propriety economics over the past two millennia, the author recognizes that both Eastern and Western sages in the Axial Age introduced the notion of moral philosophy centered around moderation and propriety. Consequently, Western economists have articulated research methodologies and principles for propriety economics. This interplay finds resonance in certain theoretical underpinnings from the realms of social sciences and natural sciences, offering interdisciplinary convergence for the triad theory underpinning propriety economic thought. Additionally, within Western economics, certain curves provide a promising avenue for exploring a distinctive research approach to propriety economics. Ultimately, propriety economics formulates principles, regulations, and benchmarks for shaping and executing propriety economic policies, all grounded in case studies drawn from the economic development experiences of both the United States and China.

10.1 Perspectives on the History of Western Economic Thought

Examining propriety economics within the framework of a broader history of Western economic thought helps to reveal its uniqueness and directions for the future development of economics. The different historical phases of Western economic thought reflect the different philosophical concepts and understandings of different scholars. This author prefers to use a four-stage theory—the beginning, development, turn, and convergence—to understand and review the evolving history of Western economic thought over 2,500 years.

The terms beginning, development, turn, and convergence are taken from Deji Fan's *Poetic Style* (*Shige*) published during the Yuan dynasty (1271–1368) in China: "There are four ways to compose a poem: the beginning should be straight; the development connects the preceding and following contexts; the turn heralds change; and the convergence points toward the conclusion and summary."[1] This literary interpretation of the four stages is a linear description from beginning to end.

However, the author believes that the beginning, development, turn, and convergence can be interpreted as a continuous cycle of thought and philosophy: the beginning is the initiation which is the base. While development is the elaboration which is the inheritance of the past and legacy for the future, the turn indicates the change of thought, including the forward, reverse, and inverse. More importantly, convergence does not mean the end, but the combination, synthesis, integration, and even the return to the beginning. Together the four stages demonstrate the effect of the dialectic evolution that leads to a new beginning. As Pu Pang points out, movement is carried out on a circumference or realized in a circular shape. If the movement is in a straight line and proceeds in a forward motion, there is no return. Even if the movement is reversed, it follows a backward trajectory and there is no possibility of repetition. It must be a circular motion, and progress will appear as a back-and-forth movement.[2]

This kind of philosophical reflection on the beginning, development, turn, and convergence can serve as a reference for understanding the history of Western economic thought in the past 2,500 years. As the starting point, many scholars tend to use Adam Smith's *The Wealth of Nations* published in 1776 because Smith is the originator of economic theory in the true sense. However, this author prefers to trace economic thought back to the ancient Greek period, and religious texts such as the Old Testament of the Bible also contain economic ideas that should not be ignored. Given that the theme of this book is economic thought, it is inappropriate to discuss the essence of Western economic thought without revisiting the classics and original philosophies since ancient Greece.

10.1.1 The Beginning: Pre-Classical Economics (5th Century BCE to 1776)

Broadly speaking, the first stage in the history of Western economic thought is the pre-classical period of economics from the 5th century BCE to 1776. Although *Oeconomicus* written by Xenophon (c. 430–355 BCE) was considered in ancient Greece as a study of household management, it can still be recognized as the first Western economic work because it makes a preliminary effort to study human economic thought. Borrowing from the dialogue between Socrates and others, Xenophon not only introduces the word "economy" (Οἰκονομικός) but also elaborates on the relationship between agriculture and industry, the meaning of human happiness, the ways and means to possess and increase wealth, the dynamics of human resources for economic development, and the role of money.[3] Subsequently, Plato, Aristotle, and other sages made foundational contributions to economic philosophy.

Xenophon, Plato, and Aristotle all lived in the Axial Age, while Confucius and Siddhartha Gautama (the Buddha) emerged in the East during this period. The academic community has often been faced with a major puzzle: Why did the Axial Age witness a significant, widespread enrichment of human spiritual resources and a sudden emergence of philosophers? The development of thought in the Axial Age was not the result of any divine intervention but was mainly due to the fact that human civilization had been in progress for about 2,000 years by then and human desires far exceeded economic supplies. As a result, the expansion of human greed led to polarization, social turbulence, and constant warfare, such as the Peloponnesian War that began in Athens and the Spring and Autumn and Warring States periods in China. In this regard, the sages keenly saw this critical weakness of human beings and shifted their philosophical thinking from the universe and nature to the existence of people and society.[4]

The sages of the Axial Age knew that they were only scholars and could not directly contribute to productivity, technology, and material supply. However, they were able to promote morality and self-cultivation through intellectual enlightenment and religious education, preaching frugality, integrity, abstinence, moderation, and propriety for the purpose of elevating moral virtue, loyalty, filial piety, and justice. Once human greed is controlled and reduced, demand is decreased and supply is increased relatively. This can help to bring society and the economy to a propriety balance and provide a recipe for social harmony and peace. Therefore, the sages of the Axial Age were not economists, but they were thinkers who were much more visionary than economists.

In the pre-classical period, the 12th–14th century scholastic schools largely inherited the ancient Greek tradition, which led to medieval economics mostly based in theology and philosophy shaped by two major principles. One of these involves religious ethics, governed by theological principles that reflect certain economic ideals such as abstinence, altruism, and frugality. Another pertains to natural law, lending a semblance of rationality to morality. Mercantilism and agrarianism after the 14th century also made significant contributions to economic thought. Economic thought in the pre-classical period, thus, can be summarized into three major themes: the dominance of religion, morality, and government. Together, they established the initial foundation of Western economic thought.[5]

10.1.2 The Development: Classical and Neoclassical Economics (1776–1936)

If the pre-classical period represents the beginning, the classical and neoclassical period from 1776 to 1936 denotes development, characterized by both inheritance and advancement. Most scholars divide the classical and neoclassical periods into two major phases, but this author believes that, although the two periods differed in terms of methods, theories, tools, and policies, their main ideas were similar because they share the three main tenets of economics: freedom, market, and rational self-interest.

The main figures of the classical school include Adam Smith, David Ricardo (1772–1823), Thomas Malthus (1766–1834), Jeremy Bentham (1748–1832), and Jean-Baptiste Say (1767–1832). For neoclassicism after 1870, it is important to recognize the marginal schools founded by William Jevons (1835–1882), Carl Menger (1840–1921), and Léon Walras (1834–1910), especially the Cambridge school and the general equilibrium theory developed by Alfred Marshall (1842–1924). They continued to insist on market-driven, laissez-faire ideas, but with more scientific essentials and mathematical overtones.

10.1.3 The Turn: The Keynesian School of Economics (1936 to the 1970s)

The third stage in the history of Western economic thought began when Keynes published *The General Theory of Employment, Interest, and Money* in 1936, establishing Keynesian economics. In light of the worldwide economic depression of the 1930s, Keynesianism, which advocated government intervention and emphasized market failure, was born. In a philosophical sense, it was a repetition of some ideas of the pre-classical or mercantilist doctrine. Keynes challenged the classical and neoclassical theories of market equilibrium and put forward the view of market disequilibrium, noting that the lack of demand in capitalism is innate and inevitable, so socioeconomic stability must be maintained through the government's monetary and fiscal policies. He also presented new insights into the areas of employment, income, prices, and money. Keynes is therefore referred to as the father of modern macroeconomics, and the theories derived from his work are simply known as macroeconomics.

It must be pointed out that, while Keynesianism has clear principles with few elements of propriety and balance, during the global economic crisis, when some countries in Europe and the United States faced the two extreme choices of German fascism or Soviet communism, Keynesianism offered a third approach. This involved advocating government intervention, stimulating aggregate demand, and promoting full employment to alleviate social and class conflicts. The New Deal in the United States adopted many Keynesian economic policies, which succeeded in ending the Great Depression and maintaining capitalism. In this sense, Keynesianism and the American policies at the time constituted moderate efforts and a compromise. Therefore, although Keynesianism represents a "turn" in the history of economic thought, it is not a "sharp turn" or a "reverse turn," but a stable, integrated, and innovative turn.

10.1.4 The Convergence: The Modern School of Economics (the 1970s to 2023)

The Western economy experienced a stagflation crisis and Keynesianism gradually faded after the 1970s. The mainstream thinking of economists reversed again, led by monetarism, rational expectations, and the public choice school, which strongly opposed Keynesianism and revived classical and neoclassical free-market thinking with opposition to government intervention as its main mission. Meanwhile, modern Western economics has also begun to integrate and revive some pre-classical ideas.

For example, new institutional economics began to challenge and revise mathematical economics by focusing on evolutionary economic history and soft institutional change. In 2015, Paul Romer published a paper challenging his mentor, Robert Lucas, and highlighted the overuse of mathematics in economics today.[6] Behavioral economics, cultural economics, and complexity economics began to reduce the emphasis on mathematics, steering economics away from the trend of excessive mathematical rigor, models, and universalism. They commenced underscoring propriety development, relative values, moral economy, and religious norms. As a result, three major features emerged: counteracting Keynes, advocating bounded rationality, and stressing propriety synthesis.

The evolution of Western economic thought unfolds across four key stages: beginning (pre-classical), development (classical and neoclassical), turn (Keynesianism), and convergence (modern economics). Although this trend of convergence has not yet entered the mainstream, the gradual construction of propriety economic thought has effectively reinforced the dynamics of such convergence and synthesis. This kind of succession is not a linear development, but a discursive cycle that has many philosophical implications in economic thought.

In short, over the past 2,500 years, the oscillations between conservative and liberal economic thought have completed exactly two major cycles: the overlap between Keynesianism and pre-classical economics (e.g., mercantilism); and the intersection of modern economics with liberal classical and neoclassical economics. But given this pendulum shift in thinking and a more complex economic environment in the 21st century, it is the right time to highlight propriety theory and the idea of the middle way. For this reason, the ideas, theories, and methods presented by new institutional economics, behavioral economics, cultural economics, and complexity economics that have emerged in the post-war period in the West deserve much wider attention.

10.2 Distinct Viewpoints of Propriety Economics

In the cluster of modern Western economics that emerged after the 1970s, propriety economics reinforces the fourth stage of Western economic thought toward combination, convergence, and synergism, maintaining a distinction from the pre-classical, classical, neoclassical, and Keynesian schools, and even differing from modern economics. Propriety economics has its unique status and contributions, which are different from other modern economic schools of thought. According to the principles of propriety economics, the basic characteristics of one school of economic thought can be found more clearly only through the comparison of three variables or schools of thought. For this reason, the author will contrast propriety economics with the main theories of neoclassical economics and complexity economics in a simple, clear analysis to highlight its uniqueness.

10.2.1 Certainty and Uncertainty

The neoclassical approach to uncertainty in economics is not considered a central issue because its basic principle underlines certainty and promotes order, rationality, and perfection. This idea was mainly influenced by the 18th century Enlightenment, which believed that chaos and disorder were only superficial phenomena and that there was an "invisible hand" that seemed to play a divine role in maintaining order and harmony. The application of this philosophical concept has led to the use of simple mathematical equations to explain the complexity of economic theories. As a result, neoclassical scholars have simplified ever-changing economic phenomena and developed them as universally applicable axioms. These axioms have a strong exclusivity, making economics a closed system that cannot accept other ideas.[7]

In contrast, complexity economics recognizes the concept of Knightian uncertainty outlined by Frank Knight (1885–1972), who considers risk as uncertainty that can be pre-calculated and anticipated in advance, while uncertainty itself is a risk that cannot be calculated or evaluated in advance. Risk and uncertainty are simultaneously interrelated and independent of each other.[8] The new understanding of uncertainty by W. Brian Arthur, one of the pioneers of complexity economics, is that the economic subject is not only unaware of how the economic object will react, but also unaware of how economic subjects will react to others' responses. It gives rise to uncertainty within uncertainty, so to speak, double or multiple uncertainties, and poses a greater challenge to human economic behavior and countermeasures. For example, in 2020, China, as an economic entity, not only had to respond to the COVID-19 pandemic as an object but also consider how the United States, as an economic entity, reacted to China's pandemic prevention. There are nearly 200 countries/territories in the world, so it is difficult to count the number of uncertain economic entities that China needs to face, and hence, the degree of uncertainty increases dramatically.

Propriety economics generally agrees with Knightian uncertainty and considers that uncertainty is closely related to the view of complexity. Given that there are too many uncertainties, in reality, it is challenging to search for the right margin of appropriateness and impartiality. Knightian uncertainty requires each economic subject to know and understand the problem correctly and precisely, which makes it essential for economic research to be closely related to cognitive and behavioral economics.[9]

In the face of uncertainty and the focus on short-term behavior, it becomes increasingly important to implement appropriate policies that can counteract volatile decision-making. Economic entities, especially in times of uncertainty, require level-headed policymakers and restrained behavior to create rational, stable, and long-term results. This approach is crucial for the development of relatively stable and appropriate economic policies.

10.2.2 Equilibrium and Disequilibrium

On the issue of equilibrium and disequilibrium, neoclassical economics promotes general equilibrium. Samuelson argued in 1983 that "unstable equilibrium," if it exists at all, must be only a temporary, non-persistent state. He asked, when have you ever seen an "egg standing on its end?"[10] In a discussion with Schumpeter in 1909, Léon Walras expressed a similar view that the nature of life is negative and therefore the theory of the "stationary process" constitutes, in effect, the whole of theoretical economics.[11] The concept that extinction contributes to stability bears some resemblance to the Chinese Daoist principle of "*wu wei*" and the constancy of order. Therefore, neoclassical economists insist that equilibrium is the natural state of economic operations.

Complexity economics offers a robust critique of equilibrium, contending that it extends the purview of economics beyond equilibrium to disequilibrium scenarios.[12] As a result, complexity economics shares a close connection with disequilibrium macroeconomics. It stresses that the economy is always in a state of change, so the disequilibrium state is the natural state of the economy; to put it another way, this state comes from within the economy rather than from any external influences. Its arguments criticize the equilibrium theory as "too pure and too brittle," resulting in neoclassical economics living in an ordered, static, knowable, and perfect Platonic world.[13] However, it is essential to acknowledge that an idealized, overly rationalized world is neither realistic nor natural. In this context, complexity economics asserts that mainstream economics should embrace disequilibrium, capturing the vitality, dynamics, nature, and reality of the social economy.

Noticeably, there are differences between propriety economics and complexity economics, but they are complementary. First of all, disequilibrium can also be understood from the perspective of equilibrium. The essence of disequilibrium is technological progress, which makes the system and technology constantly "self-creating," "self-producing," and "autopoietic."[14] However, once technology and the system are successfully renewed and transformed, equilibrium will emerge. Whether creation is longer than destruction or equilibrium is longer than disequilibrium depends on the specific topics analyzed. Similarly, the length of time between moderation and inappropriate states (including insufficiency and excess) should be determined by reference to the specific time, place, and people. For example, the emergence of an economic crisis indicates an imbalance between supply and demand, negative feedback, diminishing returns, and nonlinearity, but history shows that the frequency and duration of economic crises in the U.S. since the 1980s are apparently shortening compared to those of previous crises.[15]

Propriety economics recognizes the fact that disequilibrium is a frequent occurrence because human economic behavior often appears to be inappropriate, either deficient or extreme, while moderation and equilibrium are both ideal states. In reality, the probability of achieving a perfect balance between supply and demand, such as a Goldilocks economy, is extraordinarily small. But the difference is that complexity economics completely rejects the ideal of equilibrium or a moderate state, believing that, even if some equilibrium occurred by chance, it was meaningless. Propriety economics notes that moderation as an ideal is difficult to achieve, but that does not mean the ideal can be abandoned. The essential distinction is between optimism and pessimism in economic philosophy. Complexity economics adopts a pessimistic view, suggesting that the ideal should be abandoned or even rejected if it proves difficult to attain. In contrast, propriety economics emphasizes the importance of diligent efforts and perseverance in confronting challenging realities.[16]

The debate between pessimism and optimism is similar to the different philosophies expressed in the U.S. Constitution and the Declaration of Independence. The U.S. Constitution is full of pessimism about human nature and the conscious virtue of officials, so it hopes to confine the power of government within an institutional framework by establishing separation of powers. In contrast, the Declaration of Independence is packed with optimism about human nature and expresses the belief that everyone has the right to pursue equality, freedom, and happiness.[17]

Furthermore, as discussed in Chapter 8 of this book, the increasing intellectual development, technological progress, and the proliferation of policy tools have given rise to more frequent occurrences of unconventional moderate economic phenomena. The frequency of the economic bubble bursting and economic system collapsing, thus, has become less and less. Even if there is a major crisis, such as the financial crisis of 2008 and during the COVID-19 pandemic, it can be contained within a certain period. Human efforts prevented the world economy from deteriorating for a prolonged amount of time, as in the Great Depression of 1929 and the Great Stagflation of the 1970s.

Further, propriety economics suggests that equilibrium and disequilibrium and static and dynamic problems are directly related. The emphasis on the static nature of economics and the disregard for dynamic time is a major basis of neoclassical thought. For example, Joan Robinson argues that the concept of equilibrium is untenable and all traditional economics needs to "be thought out afresh" if economists recognize that the economy exists in time, that history is moving in a direction from an irreversible past to an unpredictable future.[18] The neoclassical school, hence, must adhere to economic equilibrium as the bottom line because only in equilibrium will an outcome always continue and time and evolution be meaningless. Economics is in fact a "noun-based" rather than a "verb-based science."[19] Complexity economics and other modern schools of economics assume that the economic operation must be dynamic, historical, and evolutionary. In particular, time will determine the structure, function, institutions, technology, past experience, and lessons twisted by the path of dependence, which is significant for today's and tomorrow's economic correction and improvement.

In this regard, propriety economics maintains that economic research and economic operations cannot be diametrically opposed to static and dynamic concepts, just as history has to be inherited (static) and developed (dynamic), and the normal state of economic operation is dynamic and static, seemingly dynamic and static, or half dynamic and half static. Moreover, static and dynamic economic operations are mutually causal and interdependent, just like sunrise and sunset— today's static (sunset) is for tomorrow's dynamic (sunrise); without yesterday's static, how can we talk about today's dynamic? This fundamental awareness should become common sense for economists.

Economics should be both a noun and a verb, and sometimes an adjective that serves as an embellishment for other topics, such as economic philosophy, which aims to study the economic factors that influence the subject of philosophy.

In fact, propriety economics highlights not only the temporal but also the spatial aspects of economics. Vertical time is important, but spatiality should not be ignored. Even at the same point in time, the economic phenomena in different locations are obviously different. Economic progress is not simply time-relevant but is also conditioned by different spaces and locations. Needless to say, different countries have very different economic structures and functions. The economic theory that can guide area A may not be fully applicable to areas B and C. The notion that an economic theory can be applied universally is increasingly challenged.

10.2.3 Increasing and Diminishing Returns

A major cornerstone of neoclassicism is the theory of marginal utility, which advocates diminishing returns, where the marginal utility obtained after a certain level of input is exceeded decreases continuously. In contrast, Arthur, a leading figure in complexity economics, proposed the theory of increasing returns in the 1980s, which conflicted with the neoclassical theory of diminishing returns and price equilibrium, and was a serious challenge to Marshall's concept of static equilibrium. It is well known that this theory of increasing returns has been widely accepted in the theory of allocation, international trade theory, evolutionary theory of technological change, economic geography, and studies of impoverishment and ethnic segregation.[20] This theory argues that in an unbalanced economy, the economic system will experience negative feedback and increasing returns. So, on the surface, complexity economics promotes incremental gains and negative feedback, but it also underlines the need for negative and positive feedback to interact and activate the economic system.

This kind of interaction between two elements generates a new third element of energy, which is what the triad theory of propriety economics insists on. Propriety philosophy underscores the idea of relativity and is in search of the appropriate range through gradual trial and error at both ends of the spectrum of inadequacy and excess. In fact, propriety economics recognizes increasing returns, but there must be a limit to the returns; once the limit is passed, there will definitely be diminishing returns. For example, in the initial phases of some developing countries' economies, a shortage economy is the norm, and continuous investment can generally lead to increasing returns, such as in China during the 1980s. However, once the economic transformation starts, the shortage may begin to change into surplus, and if we continue to invest blindly and excessively without considering the differences in structure, region, and industry, there may be diminishing returns. Sometimes patience is required to manage diminishing returns. This does not mean that once there are diminishing returns, propriety becomes evident immediately because the economic revenue increase or decrease will take time to manifest. Therefore, carrying out rational, patient observation and comparison is desirable.

Propriety economics insists that diminishing and increasing returns occur frequently because they are a two-in-one system and that negative and positive feedback often interact with and superimpose each other. If a system has only negative feedback or diminishing returns, it will soon converge to equilibrium and the behavior will be static. However, if a system has only positive feedback, it will deviate from equilibrium and exhibit "explosive behavior." Only when both positive and negative feedback are present can the system exhibit moderate behavior. This new third element of energy generated through the interaction of positive and negative feedback is repeatedly stressed by the triad theory of propriety economics.

Moreover, propriety philosophy puts emphasis on relativity. For example, if a professor and a student are in the same teaching environment, the professor's income may not increase or decrease during the COVID-19 pandemic. However, online teaching saves on transportation and other costs, so the professor's income increases in relative terms. As for students or their parents, the tuition they pay remains the same or does not change much, while the quality of online teaching and the opportunity to enjoy campus life are greatly compromised. The longer social distancing is in place, the more diminishing returns may result for some students.

Thus, propriety economics underscores the evolutional, systemic, organic, and relative nature of economic development. Today's increasing returns may be the cause of tomorrow's diminishing returns, while yesterday's decreases are the impetus and cause of today's increments. The evaluation of diminishing or increasing returns needs to be value-neutral.

10.2.4 Triangular Research Perspective

On the question of how to use multiple perspectives to analyze economic behavior, the neoclassical school supports the general static monadic or binary approach, such as the binary elements of supply and demand that affect market prices. Complexity economics, on the other hand, challenges the monadic and binary perspectives when analyzing complex economic phenomena. It asserts that a monadic, binary, or even triangular viewpoint is insufficient. Instead, it advocates the utilization of computer systems for multiple observations and designs to better understand these complexities. In contrast, propriety economics insists on the ternary because the monad is too simple, binary is too antagonistic, and the plural or more than three perspectives is too complicated. In fact, the ternary is a good perspective for finding, weighing, and discovering moderation. However, the views of complexity economics on the issue of pluralism have various implications for the triad theory of propriety economic thought.

The first is to help propriety economics understand the appropriate boundaries of the role of government. When the market fails, such as in the financial crisis in 2008 and the COVID-19 pandemic, the government must do something to avoid both the Daoist style of "doing nothing" and the legalistic style of "doing something aggressively." The government could and should act as a liberal, paternalistic "nudging hand" and adopt policies that fall between the laissez-faire approach and aggressive intervention.

The second is to confront an economic collapse or market bubble with a rational mind. A collapse or bubble mean that the economy is too cold or too hot, or in a state of inflation or deflation. When faced with the surprising, continuous COVID-19 pandemic, we have to fend off irrationality and find ways to cope with the "new normal." However, with the ups and downs of the market, there is always a critical point to which the pendulum will eventually swing back, thus achieving a state of propriety.

Finally, concerning "vertical dependence" like path dependence and historical evolution, and "parallel dependence" such as combinatorial evolution and cooperation in economic development, complexity economics emphasizes the latter, rejecting and criticizing Darwinian historical evolution. In contrast, propriety economics hopes to find a third possibility between vertical dependence and parallel dependence, equilibrium and disequilibrium, linear and non-linear, and static and dynamic polar changes. Given that the complexity of economic phenomena determines the uncertainty of economic operations, making it difficult to obtain the best, optimal results, our behavior and expectations can only be moderate and propriety.

Based on the above-mentioned similarities and differences of economic concepts such as certainty and uncertainty, equilibrium and disequilibrium, increasing and diminishing returns, and the perspective of unity, duality, plurality, and trinity, we are prompted to reflect on whether future economics needs to return to Aristotle's virtue of propriety and Adam Smith's propriety sentiments. In addition, we should draw on the balance of classical economics, the equilibrium of neoclassical economics, the evolution of institutional economics, the bounded rationality of behavioral economics, the sharing of cultural economics, and the uncertainty of complexity economics to construct and improve the research framework and themes of propriety economics.[21]

10.2.5 Unique Research Methodology

Along with its uniqueness in articulating a different economic thought, propriety economics also has its own characteristics in terms of research methods. For one thing, propriety economics advocates a moderate combination of qualitative and quantitative methods, and a hybrid approach that combines both types of research is evolved and optimized. The order of this mixed method can be reversed as appropriate. One option is quantitative, qualitative, and quantitative. The second is qualitative, quantitative, and qualitative accordingly. Another choice is continuous quantitative followed by continuous qualitative. Furthermore, incorporating more rounds of quantitative and qualitative cycles into mixed methods research is desirable, if the results of the first round of qualitative/quantitative/qualitative research are not yet complete or precise enough to understand the object of study.

Moreover, it is essential to integrate different approaches, including physiological inquiries and computer experiments. Most of the three different experimental methods employed by Tania Singer, Edward Glaeser, Paul Zak, Robert Axelrod, and W. Brian Arthur, as mentioned in Chapter 6 of this book, do not use mathematical measures. Propriety economics is in favor of inclusive research methods and the selection of the most effective combination according to different research objects. Simple research methods should not be easily dismissed as they may become a valuable stepping stone and a building block for the evolution of the combination. Besides, unidirectional and unidimensional experimental methods are not sufficient, and the combination of multiple experimental methods is compulsory to discover the complementary, interactive effects among them.

In addition, an organic combination of inductive, deductive, and abductive research methods should be implemented. Neoclassical economics and complexity economics are focused on the debate about whether inductive or deductive methods are better. In contrast, propriety economics believes that research methods are just a set of tools whose only difference is their degree of effectiveness, depending on the research objects and topics that they serve. The triad theory of propriety economic thought should inspire scholars to go beyond the two ends of the spectrum and seek a third approach, such as the abductive method. Benefitting from a unique retrospective, creative, trial-and-error, and random nature in tracing the causes of various economic phenomena that have already occurred, the abductive method especially provides conditions for the evolutionary combination of the three research methods.

The author appreciates a story in which Arthur describes his research on complexity economics: A physicist once asked: Why must economists study equilibrium? What would happen to economics without equilibrium? Then Arthur asked, what if there was no gravity?[22] In contrast, the author's question is: What about economics without "hypotheses?" This is the charm of thought experiments and intellectual imagination.

10.3 Reflections on Future Economics

By reviewing the history of Western economic thought over the past 2,500 years and summarizing the characteristics of propriety economic thought, we can examine the past and ponder the possible directions of future economics.

10.3.1 Possibility of Returning to the Beginning

In light of the extreme uncertainty, instability, anxiety, and restlessness of the new era, the future of economic research needs to return to the origins of Western economic thought. Doing so requires striving for propriety, the middle way, stability, and major tenets of preclassicalism. Although rationality and science are the essence of mainstream economics, the spiritual order, propriety philosophy, and religious sentiment pursued by pre-classical economics have not died out. On the contrary, they should be given new value befitting the new era and be further explored and developed.

First of all, economics is inseparable from the subjective preferences of human beings. Many impossibility theorems and numerous paradoxes in modern economics aim to resolve the contradictions between the scientific nature of economics and the subjective nature of economic behavior. As long as economics still insists on studying the subjective preferences of people, it cannot avoid their beliefs and consciousness, which in turn formulate their preferences. Frugal and extravagant consumer groups display different consumption behaviors and market effects. As the tensions among different religions and civilizations around the world increase and expand, these differences will become more obvious, sharper, and difficult to reconcile. In addition, there is no single set of preferences in any economic entity, but there may be competing preferences, including physical vs. spiritual, conscious vs. unconscious, good vs. evil, and fast vs. slow tendencies.

Consequently, the economics of preferences and beliefs cannot be separated from the irrational, semi-rational, bounded, or propriety rational side of human beings. Faith, to some extent, has a rational side, as well as a sensitive, spontaneous side. As long as rationality is conditioned by specific circumstances involving a particular time, place, and people, it is invariably intermingled with subjective emotions. The interaction between reason and situation is not only a physical reaction but also a biological one. Similarly, as long as rationality is inseparable from the historical context, rationality is individual, specific, and evolutionary without being able to achieve the desired level of universality and consistency. In this way, if the study of economics cannot be separated from subjective preferences and emotional choices, economics does not belong to the field of pure science.

David Hume has argued that "Reason is, and ought only to be the slave of the passions, and can never pretend to any other office than to serve and obey them."[23] The significance of Hume's thought is the recognition that human beings are basically emotional "animals." With the same product, the same customer, and the same salesperson, why do the results of the transaction often differ? The answer is because of the different methods, timing, and sequence of applying emotion and reason.

Friedrich Nietzsche (1844–1900) said in *The Birth of Tragedy* that there are two spiritual qualities in human beings: one is the Dionysian spirit and the other is the Apollonian spirit. The spirit of Dionysus represents sensual passion, which encompasses feelings, optimism, romance, and idealism. It may include strong religious feelings, transcending the limits of individual life. In contrast, the spirit of Apollo exemplifies rationality, observing moral laws, emphasizing self-knowledge, and pursuing personal freedom and social order under the rule of clarity and tranquility.[24] On the surface, adherence to the spirit of Apollo is a manifestation of rationality, but it is easier to know than to do. Forcing people to strictly follow the example of Apollo will lead to another kind of idealism and evolve into Dionysus, opposed by Apollo himself. In other words, the meeting of two opposites would end up returning to the original point. In the interplay between Apollo and Dionysus, it is advisable for the economic actor to establish a third "deity" within their heart: an impartial god of propriety capable of offering rational, ideal, and spiritual judgments and guidance.

Furthermore, it is impossible for economists to escape the fetters of moral norms. As early as 1215, the medieval master of pre-classical economics, Thomas de Chobham who published *Summa Confessorum*, proposed moral economics. In addition, although Smith was the originator of classical economics, he was also a professor of moral philosophy, and the work he valued most in his life was not *The Wealth of Nations* published in 1776, but his other lesser-known book *The Theory of Moral Sentiments*, published in 1759. However, the relationship between morality and economics has always been controversial, and one of the major difficulties is whether there is a value judgment in economic rationality. Moreover, moral economics finds it difficult to mathematically calculate all economic activities, so it is challenging to define as a pure science.

Since economics cannot avoid preference, faith, sensibility, and morality, it also cannot bypass religion. Marshall, the neoclassical master who insisted that economics is a science, went so far as to suggest that economics has two fundamental factors: economics itself and religion. He believed that these were the two axioms of social theory, so he wrote about the power of religion in the preface of his famous book.[25] Max Weber also trusted that the economy determines the preparatory point of institutional evolution, but culture and religion govern its direction. In his view, religion is not only a belief, but it also has a significant institutional effect, such as religious rituals and procedures designed to regulate the behavior of believers.[26] The famous *Robert's Rules of Order* were first used in an American church by the author Henry Robert (1837–1923).[27] Some famous scientists were also devout believers. Albert Einstein once said: "Science without religion is lame, religion without science is blind."[28] At the same time, a significant number of polling places for general elections in the United States are located in churches partially because they are not only highly organized, but also increase voters' trust in the fairness, equity, and openness of the election process. Most of the institutions and rules that have lasted throughout history have come from religion. In this regard, economics, whose mission is to study human behavior and institutions, should not and cannot ignore religion. Moreover, religions do not necessarily impede the progress of social civilization. For example, Europe, which was predominately Catholic in the Middle Ages, still gave rise to the Renaissance in the 14th century. It was also with great financial support of the Roman Catholic pope that Renaissance masters such as Michelangelo Buonarroti (1475–1564) and Leonardo da Vinci (1452–1519) succeeded in completing their legendary works.

The fact that religious economics or economics of religion and religious market studies are flourishing in the United States today may be evidence of the critical role of religion in economics. As long as human reason is bounded, religion has a chance to exist. The same is true of the relationship between science and religion. So long as science is not omnipotent, there is a need for religion; the reverse is true as well. In a materialistic society, is there a need for more restraint? Is it necessary to be more virtuous when confronted with irrational development? In an era of lost faith, is there a need for more spiritual capital?[29]

At the same time, it is crucial to foster a renaissance of human-centric thinking within economics. Beyond a focus on god-centeredness and material-centeredness, the future calls for a shift towards human-centeredness. While the fundamental purpose of economic research remains the study of the scarcity of human resources, it is worth noting that the scarcities of labor, capital, and resources vary across different eras. With the advent of artificial intelligence aiding in human resource management, and considering the evolving rationality, indifference, passion, and antagonism in human behavior, the scarcest resources in the economy of the future are likely to be humanity, sensibility, and virtue. Those who can address these scarce assets, encompassing human capital, social capital, and spiritual capital, will harbor the most profound economic insights, consequently taking the lead and exerting a significant influence on the future trajectory of economics.

It goes without saying that the chaos of the 2020 U.S. presidential election has led to a crisis of trust in the electoral system for many people. It can be argued that the electoral system designed by the country's founding fathers was well established and has withstood the rigors of nearly 250 years, including the American Civil War. However, the successful operation of this system depends on a basic shared understanding, including compliance with the rules, obedience to the law, reality, rationality, and peace. If these bottom lines are lost, even the most perfect system will fail, and even the most advanced culture will appear ineffective. After all, the main force in making and implementing systems is people, and the humanity, integrity, and virtue of these people directly determine the success or failure of all systems and cultures.

Therefore, while emphasizing institutional economics and cultural economics, economists need to revive the essence of humanist economics, advocating respect for morality, values, and life; protecting human happiness and dignity; and promoting the rights of and fairness towards disadvantaged groups and regions. Meanwhile, humanist economics is in favor of balancing the divine, material, and human, and promoting the harmonious development of economy and society, humanity and nature, and material and spiritual.[30] Propriety economics embodies the spiritual essence of humanity, humanism, and humaneness. Even though propriety is ideal, once the ideal is combined with human nature, it can enhance the "shallow goods" of the economy, which are characterized by techniques and calculations, and raise them to "deep goods," such as morality, integrity, and benevolence, giving economics a powerful spiritual life.

Moreover, the term "humanomics" was coined around 2010. As Deirdre Nansen McCloskey suggests, economics should be oriented toward enhancing the well-being of human lives and should enrich academic exploration by adopting the perspective of humanomics. This is because economic agents are not solely driven by the goal of maximizing their utility but are also influenced by other factors, including the persuasive power of language.[31]

In short, we need to return to the origins of economic thought; revisit politics, governance, and policies; and absorb the three concepts of faith, morality, and religion in pre-classical economic thought, so as to promote and innovate spirituality, propriety philosophy, and religious sentiment. In fact, while religion wishes to improve imperfect human nature, economics generally believes that human nature is self-interested and difficult to change, and that human behavior can only be improved and restrained by changing institutions. The author trusts that it is more effective to promote the virtues of humanity by limiting human greed through the integrated effect of endogenous religious beliefs and exogenous legal systems, both in terms of the rule of law and the rule of morality. Especially when a society is well-fed and well-off, it is more important for people to care about metaphysical philosophy and focus on the spiritual order, moral sentiment, and care for others. The consciousness, relativity, and morality of the economic subject's behavior, as revealed by pre-classical economics, are partially in line with propriety economics and may provide some inspiration for the future direction of economics.

10.3.2 Future Directions

In the appendix of his *Complexity and the Economy*, Arthur proposes "principles of future economics," defining classical and neoclassical economics as old economics and post-war modern economics or his complexity economics as new economics. This author adds a third category of economic thought to Arthur's list of old and new principles: propriety economics, which can also be called "future economics," in an effort to compare the three types of economic thought (Fig. 10.1).

Based on the above distinction, the author believes that future economics needs to complete the fourth stage in the history of Western economic thought, designed to promote the convergence of economic thought following its beginning, development, and turn. Modern economists have already started the process of integration beginning in the 1970s, but it has not yet been completed. Completing this process is one of the missions of propriety economics.

The first step in integration is the combination of research methods. Contemporary economic research methods are endless, but the main task of economists is not to create more, newer research methods, techniques, and tools, but to implement evolutionary, creative combinations of existing methods. Arthur and other complexity economists over the past 40 years have provided the conceptual of economic methods. However, after nearly half a century of effort, the trend of modern combinations of economic methods has not yet become dominant. The classical and neoclassical approaches continue to direct the mainstream because the perfect rationality and perfect equilibrium assumptions they promote increasingly transform the problem of resource allocation into a mathematical equation. Obviously, economic development cannot be solved by such simple, uniform mathematics.[32]

The research approach advocated by propriety economics and future economics, thus, is to embrace and combine all reasonable, effective research tools, not to be exclusive to mathematics or treat mathematics as a negative factor. Further, propriety economics also does not disrespect quantitative or discriminate against qualitative analyses and does not make deductive and inductive methods mutually exclusive. The rapid development of advanced technologies, such as digitization, spatialization, big data, machine learning, the metaverse, and artificial intelligence, provides great possibilities and opportunities for the integration and combination of economic methods and technologies. These new scientific techniques are likely to be creatively combined with traditional empirical research, mathematical modeling, computer simulation, physiology, biology, neuroscience, and so on, to yield an organic generation of various existing methods in a cloud or algorithm that is compatible. At the same time, spatially intelligent data analysis systems can be established to simplify front-end analysis and to dynamically update and synthesize information through machine learning. Moreover, we can also analyze the relationship between data through pattern recognition, selecting the propriety of time and space, and drawing on models of ecological chains. It is also possible to use AI to provide a more detailed, clear analysis of indicators and relationships based on information from various literature and web resources. Finally, we can choose the most appropriate, optimal, and effective methods according to the needs of each scholar's research topic. The emergence of artificial intelligence is not only a challenge to research methods in economics but also an opportunity to rejuvenate the amalgamation of methods in the future. Future research methods

Figure 10.1 Comparison of three major economic philosophies and research methods

Old Economics	New Economics	Future Economics (Propriety Economics)
Diminishing returns	Increasing returns	Intertwined diminishing and increasing returns
Maximizing principles	Other principles	Principle of satisfaction maximization
Preferences given	Formation of preferences becomes central	Competitive, relative, and constantly changing preferences
Individual self-interest	Individual not necessarily selfish	Interactions between selfishness, self-interest, and altruism
Technology given	Technology initially fluid, then tends to set	Technology as a tool
Essentially deterministic, forecastable	Non-deterministic. Unforecastable due to fluctuations and strange attractors	Non-deterministic, but predictable
Based on 19th-century physics (equilibrium = stability, deterministic dynamics)	Based on biology (structure, patterns, self-organization, life cycles)	Based on history (evolution, dynamics, and triad theory)
Time is not considered at all	Time becomes central	Dynamic time and space are the core
Emphasis on quantities, prices, and equilibrium	Emphasis on structure, pattern, and function	Emphasis on faith, ideology, values, and morals
Language: 19th-century math and game theory and fixed point topology	Language more qualitative. Game theory recognized for its qualitative uses. Other qualitative mathematics useful	Emphasis on "soft" non-mathematical, moderate mix of qualitative and quantitative studies
Heavy use of indexes. People identical	Focus on individual life. People separate and different	Focus on meso groups and regions

No real dynamics in the sense that everything is at equilibrium	Economy is always on the edge of time. It rushes forward, structures constantly coalescing, decomposing, changing	Recognition of disequilibrium and disproportionality, but seeks equilibrium and propriety
Hypotheses testable. Assumes laws exist	Questions remain hard to answer. But assumptions clearly spelled out	Hypotheses are not sufficient and are unnecessary conditions
Sees subject as structurally simple	Sees subject as inherently complex	Moderate the research subject
Economics as soft physics	Economics as high complex science	Economics as economic philosophy and non-mathematical
Exchange- and resource-driven economy	Externalities, differences, ordering principles, compatibility, mindset, family, possible life cycle, and increasing returns drive institutions, society, and economy	Propriety rationality, development, exchange, and competition-driven economy

Source: Arthur, *Complexity and the Economy*[33]

in economics need to sync the static state of traditional economics and the temporal state of complexity economics into a system of space-time interaction. On the other hand, economic research should elevate traditional linear, flat, and one-dimensional thinking to a three-dimensional state and implement thought experiments.

The second attempt at integration is the synthesis of schools of thought. The future of economics requires not only a mixture of methods but also a fusion of concepts that have come before. Here, Samuelson, the first American Nobel laureate in economics, is a model of synthesis. He conceived of neoclassical synthesis, which attempts to integrate Marshall's microeconomics and Keynesian macroeconomics.

It was designed to promote a moderate compromise, hybridization, and synthesis between the relatively radical neoclassical economics and the relatively conservative Keynesian economics. It hoped to combine Keynes' government intervention with the free market approaches of neoclassical economics, and suggest the appropriate use of different policies at different times and places.[34]

For example, Samuelson states that when demand is low and unemployment is high, the government should intervene in the economy, aiming to stimulate aggregate demand and promote full employment. But after the economy reaches full employment, such as when the unemployment rate is around 5%, the market should be allowed to play more of a role in allocating resources. Neoclassical synthesis does not believe that laissez-faire can lead to full employment, but it has faith that full employment is possible through propriety government regulations and resource reallocation. Samuelson advocated a return to Marshall's neoclassical doctrine after World War II when full employment had occurred in the United States. Samuelson also argues that this propriety, balanced, and integrated theory should be accepted by 95% of economists with the exception of about 5% of far-left and far-right economists.[35] Therefore, future economics needs to reduce the "rigid sense of determinism" and gradually weaken "positivist thinking"; reduce mechanics, absolutism, and universality; but increase variability, relativity, and propriety.[36]

In fact, the comprehensive efforts of these schools of thought over the years are highly consistent with the essence of propriety economics and the direction of future economic development. Future economics calls for the integration of microscopic, macroscopic, and mesoscopic approaches to improve the effectiveness and accuracy of economic research. Meanwhile, relying on both government assistance and market leadership, future economics appeals to the combined efforts of government, market, enterprise, and community to facilitate the comprehensive capability of economic research. In addition, future economics requires logic, but it should not be the pure logic of the neoclassical school; it needs rationality, but it is impossible to achieve perfect, full rationality. Similarly, it wants social order, but not "pure order," and it is in favor of seeking general principles but cannot expect the universal acceptance of a large number of laws based on public rationality.[37] The essential principles are communication, compromise, and synthesis while pursuing propriety, including propriety logic, reason, order, law, and amalgamation.

The third endeavor for future economics is the integration of ideas. Given the increasingly antagonistic world, especially the unprecedented ideological disharmony, racial discord, and prejudice brought about by the COVID-19 pandemic, the world has become more hostile and fragmented.[38] The new ideology-driven confrontations are likely to resume in full swing. Therefore, future economic research may be guided by propriety philosophy and propriety economics to promote dialogue among scholars, advocating various economic ideas to advance complementarity and pursue the middle way. Reaching peace and harmony should be the priority before exploring the middle path between the left and right poles. Moving from harmony to unity, finally, is an objective to address the challenges of the new era.

The representative of the old school of institutional economics, John Commons, has set an example in his efforts to find harmony between economic thought and realpolitik. He advocated the conciliatory function of laws and courts and emphasized the peacemaking effect of collectives and organizations on individual disagreements. Insisting that rational communication is the basic criterion for resolving the confrontation between the government and the people, and the struggle between capital and labor, he suggested that institutions are the most effective vehicles for resolving conflicts and contradictions. Therefore, if the combination of methods is the first level of harmony, synthesis of schools is the second level of agreement, and integration of ideas is the highest level of coherence.

The economic history of the United States has successfully demonstrated the significance of the reconciliation of different parties, ideas, and classes. Given that President Theodore Roosevelt endorsed the Progressive movement and Franklin D. Roosevelt championed the New Deal, U.S. capitalist economic policy has integrated ideas from socialist economic policy. The U.S. government's efforts have seeped into all aspects of U.S. society, resulting in the fact that the dichotomy between liberal and conservative ideologies, government and market, capital and labor, has become increasingly weakened and blurred, although there has been a reversal of this trend in recent years.[39]

Hence, the evolution of economics demands more than just the amalgamation of methodologies and the fusion of various economic schools. It necessitates the harmonization of ideas within the backdrop of Western economics' 2,500-year history. Through this approach, we can actualize a more advanced phase of dialectical evolution, involving the reevaluation, abandonment, and transformation of concepts, which in turn presents an opening for a fresh cycle of development.

Before concluding this book, the author would like to emphasize three issues. The first is the definition of propriety economics. When this book was published by the City University of Hong Kong Press in Chinese in 2021, the title was *Conceptualizing Propriety in Economic Thought*.[40] Although it is ideal to have rigorous, sophisticated mathematical modeling to support an independent, mature economic school, propriety economics, given its subjective, evolutionary nature, cannot easily incorporate mathematical modeling. Therefore, when publishing this English version, I am ambitious enough to change the title to *Introduction to Propriety Economics*, pointing out that propriety economics is guided by the idea of propriety philosophy, triad theory, triangular thinking, propriety diagrams, and characterized by mixed methods. With this book, the author hopes to inspire more scholars to ponder propriety economics.

The second point is about the role of thought in economics. The top priority of propriety economics is to address the role of thought in economic research and economic development. It seems that technology is the first productive force in economic development, but technology can only turn 1 into N instead of changing 0 to 1, and it cannot make economic development sustainable. Therefore, innovation is the first productive force, aiming to increase and guarantee the ability to turn 0 into 1. However, innovation must be supported by a good system to stimulate and protect it. If there is no strict protection for intellectual property rights, then theft will be rampant, and innovation may even be counterproductive. As a result, innovators will be unwilling and unable to be creative. However, a good system also needs to be supported by a healthy culture that provides support for institutional innovation. Even if a legal system is in place to punish people who violate intellectual property regulations, what if the perpetrators do not believe in the rule of law but only in political power? If the general public which lacks awareness of intellectual property protection tolerates "copycat" behavior and believes that "theft of books is not considered theft,"[41] then technological innovations, however advanced they are, will be the victim of a harmful culture. Consequently, we need to continue to ask, if there is good technology, innovation, institutions, and culture, must there be high-speed, stable, and sustainable economic development? Not necessarily! The most important scarce resource for economic development now is virtue because human qualities determine technological inventions, scientific discovery, legal systems, and advanced culture. If there is no "market for ideas" as mentioned by Coase, how is it possible to establish sustainable markets of economy, technology, innovation, institution, and culture? Therefore, the author believes that in today's world, thought is the first productive force because it encompasses the four essentials of awakening, enlightenment, reasoning, and the Dao (see Chapter 1 of this book), followed by culture, system, innovation, and technology.

The final concern pertains to the transcendence of the propriety concept. While this book primarily delves into propriety economics, its applicability extends well beyond the realm of economics. For instance, Marshall's equilibrium price concept can inspire the expansion of the equilibrium principle to encompass institutional equilibrium and human equilibrium. In essence, the aim is to attain harmonious, comprehensive development of humanity through institutional arrangements, fostering motivation in others while yielding tangible benefits, thus achieving a well-balanced growth that combines self-interest and altruism. At the same time, the relative value theories endorsed by old institutional economics also offer potential pathways for the advancement of economics and other non-economic disciplines. These pathways encompass bounded rationality, market freedom, and government intervention. Furthermore, in the face of ideological disputes, both economics and non-economic disciplines must seek an alternative path that transcends the binary choices of freedom versus intervention, market versus government, and micro versus macro developments. Similarly, the concept of bounded rationality can also serve as a source of inspiration for non-economists to explore new possibilities. Is there potential for bounded markets, limited freedom, and the existence of "invisible hands" in reality, including a semi-visible hand that plays a substantial role in specific socioeconomic contexts? Moreover, given the challenge of achieving complete propriety, propriety economics embraces the notions of relative, limited, partial, and transient propriety, all of which may apply to various non-economic disciplines. It is fitting to emphasize gradual progress, where things come to fruition before reaching perfection, rather than aiming for immediate, complete results.

In summary, in an era marked by stark ideological divides and intense polarization, the triad theory, triangle paradigm, and balanced trajectory of propriety economics offer valuable tools for crafting and executing economic policies that prioritize equilibrium, evolution, and ethical conduct. The concept of propriety represents a multifaceted framework, simultaneously embodying the intuitive wisdom of the common people and presenting a formidable challenge in both rhetoric and practice. This inherent paradox underscores the historical puzzle of knowing what is right yet struggling to consistently embody it, illustrating the intricate, ever-shifting nature of propriety.

To bridge this gap, a concerted effort is required, encompassing education and cultural transformation for the broader populace and the strengthening of decision-makers' cognitive capacities and resolve. Nurturing the five productive forces of thought, culture, system, innovation, and technology becomes imperative, fostering the amalgamation of methodologies, the synthesis of diverse schools of thought, and the harmonization of ideas within future economics. Through these collective endeavors, the pursuit of propriety and the cultivation of a balanced path in human economic behavior can be advanced.

Notes

Preface

1 W. Brian Arthur, *Complexity and the Economy* (New York: Oxford University Press, 2015).

Chapter 1 Introduction

1 Alan Adams Jacobs, "Free Will and Predetermination," *Advaita Vision*, July 10, 2012, www.advaita.org.uk/discourses/teachers/freewill_jacobs.htm (accessed March 22, 2017).

2 Gail Fine, *The Possibility of Inquiry: Meno's Paradox from Socrates to Sextus* (Oxford: Oxford University Press, 2014). Meno raises a valid concern, contending that the pursuit of something unknown is a daunting task, as it is challenging to recognize when one has discovered it. In response, Socrates presents a fascinating and often-cited concept known as "Meno's paradox" or the "learner's paradox." He introduces the theory of knowledge as recollection, or anamnesis, as a means to address this conundrum.

3 Plato, *The Republic of Plato*, 2nd ed., Allan Bloom, trans. (New York: Basic Books, 1968), book VII, pp. 193–195.

4 Karl R. Popper, *The Myth of the Framework: In Defense of Science and Rationality* (London and New York: Routledge, 1994).

5 Noel Joseph Terence Montgomery Needham, *Li Yuese Zhongguo Kexue Jishu Shi* [*History of Science and Technology in China*] (Beijing: Science Press, 2006). The four great inventions of ancient China are the compass, gunpowder, movable-type printing, and papermaking.

6 Pu Pang, *Pang Pu Wenji – Disi Juan – Yifen Weisan* [*The Collected Works of Pang Pu – Volume IV – One for Three*] (Jinan: Shandong University Press, 2005), pp. 213, 215.

7 Pang, *Pang Pu Wenji,* p. 214.

8 Pang, *Pang Pu Wenji,* pp. 2, 14, 20.

9 Pang, *Pang Pu Wenji,* p. 214; Fuguan Xu, *Zhongguo Sixiangshi Lunji Xuebian* [*A Continuation of the Essays on the History of Chinese Thought*] (Shanghai: Shanghai Shudian Press, 2004); Fuguan Xu, *Xu Fuguan Quanji* [*Xu Fuguan Complete Collection*] (Beijing: Jiuzhou Press, 2014); Xing Han, "Xu Fuguan Xingerzhongxue Taiwei" ["Xu Fuguan's Exploration of the Metaphysical Middle School"], *Heilongjiang Shehui Kexue* [*Social Sciences of Heilongjiang*], 3 (2018), pp. 101–109.

10 Nathan Bennett and G. James Lemoine, "What VUCA Really Means for You," *Harvard Business Review* (January–February 2014), p. 27.

11 Arthur, *Complexity and the Economy*, p. 7.

12 Lawrence Rosenthal, *Empire of Resentment: Populism's Toxic Embrace of Nationalism* (New York: The New Press, 2020).

13 The German thinker Karl Jaspers (1883–1969) called the breakthrough in human culture that occurred in China, the West, and India around 500 BCE (between 800 and 200 BCE) the "Axial Age." Karl Jaspers, *The Origin and Goal of History* (New York: Routledge, 2010), p. 1.

14 Immanuel Kant, *The Critique of Practical Reason* (Cambridge: Cambridge University Press, 2015).

15 Arthur, *Complexity and the Economy*, p. ix.

16 Geoffrey M. Hodgson, *Economics and Evolution: Bringing Life Back into Economics* (Cambridge, UK and Ann Arbor, MI: Polity Press and University of Michigan Press, 1993).

17 Ulrich Witt, "What is Specific about Evolutionary Economics?", *Journal of Evolutionary Economics*, 18 (5) (2008), pp. 547–575; Ulrich Witt, *Evolutionary Economics* (London: Edward Elgar Publishing, Inc., 1993).

18 Celeste Kidd, Steven T. Piantadosi, and Richard N. Aslin, "The Goldilocks Effect: Human Infants Allocate Attention to Visual Sequences that Are Neither Too Simple nor Too Complex," *Plos One*, 7 (5) (2012).

19 Ben Bernanke, "The Great Moderation," *Federal Reserve History*, November 22, 2013, www.federalreservehistory.org/essays/great_moderation (accessed March 1, 2020).

20 Michael Hudson, "The Bubble Economy: From Asset-Price Inflation to Debt Deflation," *Counterpunch*, July 5, 2013.

21 Tomáš Sedláček, *Economics of Good and Evil: The Quest for Economic Meaning from Gilgamesh to Wall Street* (Oxford: Oxford University Press, 2011).

22 Detailed citations for these ideas will be included in chapters 3–5.

Chapter 2   The Origin and Definition of Propriety Philosophy

1 Handing Hong, *Quanshi Xue: Ta de Lishi he Dangdai Fazhan [Hermeneutics: Its History and Contemporary Development]* (Beijing: People's Publishing House, 2001), p. 205.

2 Chang Ji (King Wen of Zhou), *Zhou Yi [I Ching]* (Beijing: China Bookstore, 2016).

3 Anonymous, ed., *Shangshu – Pan Geng [The Books of Shang – Pan Geng]; Shangshu – Jiugao [The Books of Shang – Letters Patent for Wine]; Shangshu – Lu Xin [The Books of Shang – Lu Xin]; Shangshu – Hang Fan [The Books of Shang – Hong Fan]* (Prague: Arts & Crafts Publishing House, 2017).

4 Anonymous, ed., *Zhouli – Diguan – Dasitu [Rites of Zhou – Di Guan – Da Si Tu]; Zhouli – Chunguang – Dasile [Rites of Zhou – Chun Guan – Da Si Le]* (Beijing: Zhongzhou Ancient Books Publishing House, 2018).

5 Qiuming Zuo, *Zuo Zhuan [Zuo Tradition]* (Wuhan: Hubei Ci Shu Publishing House, 2017).

6 Zi Si, *Zhongyong Quanjie [Complete Interpretation of Moderation]* (Beijing: China Hua Qiao Publishing House, 2016).

7 *Lun Yu [The Analects – Yao Yao Yi]* (Changchun: Jilin Photography Press, 2004).

8 *Lun Yu [The Analects – Yan Yuan]*.

9 *Lun Yu [The Analects – Zi Lu]*.

10 *Lun Yu [The Analects – Xianjin]*.

11 Zi Si, *Zhongyong Quanjie*, Chapter 4.

12 *I Ching*.

13 Zhuangzi, *Zhuangzi [Zhuangzi – Dasheng]*, in *Zhongzi Jicheng [Collection of Scholars' Works, 3]* (Shanghai: Shanghai Bookstore, 1986), p. 117.

14 Mencius, *Mengzi [Mencius – Under Li Lou]* (Prague: Artesia Publishing House, 2017).

15 Pang, *Pang Pu Wenji*, p. 11.

16 Feizi Han, *Han Feizi [Han Feizi – Yang Quan]*, in *Zhuzi Jicheng 5* (Shanghai: Shanghai Bookstore, 1986), p. 30.

17 Guanzi, *Guanzi [Guanzi – Zuhe]*, in *Zhongzi Jicheng 5*, p. 62; *Guanzi – Baixin*, in *Zhuzi Jicheng 5*, p. 228.

18 Yi Cheng, *Zhouyi Chengsi Zhuang* [*Cheng's Biography of Zhou Yi*] (Beijing: China Book Bureau, 2016).

19 Xi Zhu, *Sishu Zhangju Jizhu* [*The Four Books, Chapters and Sentences – Zhong Yong Chapter and Sentences*] (Shanghai: Shanghai Ancient Books Publishing House, 2006), p. 23.

20 Xiaoqing Gan and Kezhen Yuan, "Cong Zhouxin Shidai de Zhonghe Sixiang dao Xiandai Wenming Duihua" ["From the Axial Age of Neutral Thought to the Dialogue of Modern Civilization"], *Hunan Shehui Kexue* [*Journal of Shenzhen University*], 3 (2017), p. 21.

21 Gan and Yuan, "Cong Zhouxin Shidai de Zhonghe Sixiang dao Xiandai Wenming Duihua," p. 21.

22 Yuechuan Wang, "Zhongxi Sixiang Shi Shang de Zhongyong Zhidao" ["Moderation in the History of Chinese and Western Thought"], *Hunan Shehui Kexue* [*Hunan Social Sciences*], 6 (2007), p. 39.

23 Pang, *Pang Pu Wenji*, p. 31.

24 Mencius, *Mengzi*.

25 Zi Si, *Zhongyong*, Chapter 6.

26 Fuzhi Wang, *Shuowen Guang Yi* [*The Broad Definition of the Chinese Language*], vol. 2, in *Chuanshan Quanshu* [*The Complete Book of Chuanshan*], vol. 9, (Changsha: Yuelu Shushe, 1996), p. 240.

27 Yuechuan Wang, "Zhongyong de Chaoyuexin Sixiang yu Pushixing Jiazhi" ["The Transcendental Thought and Universal Value of Moderate"], *Shehui Kexue Zhanxian* [*Social Science Battle Line*], 5 (2009), p. 139.

28 Sheng Dai, ed., *Liji – Zhongyong* [*The Book of Rites – Zhong Yong*] (Prague: Yea Publishing House, 2017).

29 *I Ching*.

30 *Lun Yu – Yongye*.

31 Zi Si, *Zhongyong*, Chapter 2.

32 Zi Si, *Zhongyong*, Chapter 2.

33 Isocrates, *Isocrates with an English Translation in Three Volumes* (Cambridge, MA: Harvard University Press, 1980).

34 Aristotle, *Nicomachean Ethics* (Kitchener, Ontario: Batoche Books, 1999), p. 21.

35 Aristotle, *Nicomachean Ethics*, pp. 26–27.

36 Aristotle, *Nicomachean Ethics*, p. 27.

37 English translation: "Therefore virtue is a kind of mean, since, as we have seen, it aims at what is intermediate." Aristotle, *Nicomachean Ethics*, p. 27.

38 English translation: "That moral virtue is a mean, then, and in what sense it is so, and that it is a mean between two vices, the one involving excess, the other deficiency, and that it is such because its character is to aim at what is intermediate in passions and in actions, has been sufficiently stated." Aristotle, *Nicomachean Ethics*, p. 32.

39 Adam Smith, *The Theory of Moral Sentiments* (Indianapolis: Liberty Fund, Inc., 1982), p. 294.

40 Aristotle, *Nicomachean Ethics*, p. 31.

41 Aristotle, *Nicomachean Ethics,* p. 69.

42 Aristotle, *Nicomachean Ethics*, pp. 70–71.

43 Wang, "Zhongyong de Chaoyuexing Sixiang yu Pushixing Jiazhi," p. 139.

44 Original words: "Our continual observations upon the conduct of others, insensibly lead us to form to ourselves certain general rules concerning what is fit and proper either to be done or to be avoided." Smith, *The Theory of Moral Sentiments*, p. 159.

45 Original words: "In the race for wealth, and honours, and preferment, he may run as hard as he can, and strain every nerve and every muscle, in order to outstrip all his competitors. But if he should justle, or throw down any of them, the indulgence of the spectators is entirely at an end. It is a violation of fair play, which they cannot admit of." Smith, *The Theory of Moral Sentiments*, p. 83.

46 English translation: "For in everything it is no easy task to find the middle." Aristotle, *Nicomachean Ethics*, p. 32.

47 English translation: "but to do this to the right person, to the right extent, at the right time, with the right motive, and in the right way, that is not for everyone, nor is it easy." Aristotle, *Nicomachean Ethics*, p. 32.

48 English translation: "We have next to discuss the one remaining division of moral rectitude. That is the one in which we find considerateness and self-control, which give, as it were, a sort of polish to life; it embraces also temperance, complete subjection of all the passions, and moderation in all things. Under this head is further included what, in Latin, may be called decorum (propriety); for in Greek it is called πρέπον. Such is its essential nature, that it is inseparable from moral goodness; for what is proper is morally right, and what is morally right is proper. The nature of the difference between morality and propriety can be more easily felt than expressed." Cicero, *De Officiis, Latin Text with an English Translation by Walter Miller* (Cambridge, MA: Harvard University Press, 1990), I:93.

49 Cicero, *De Officiis*, I:96.

50 Smith, *The Theory of Moral Sentiments*, p. 27.

51 Anonymous, *Erya Yizhu [Erya Translation and Commentary]* (Shanghai: Shanghai Ancient Books Publishing House, 2016).

52 Xi Zhu, *Sishu Zhangju Jizhu*, p. 23.

53 Xiang Chen, *Gu Ling Ji [Ancient Spirit Collection]* (Kunming: Yunnan Education Publishing House, 2007), vol. 12, p. 4304.

54 Fuguan Xu, *Zhongguo Renxin Lunshi [A History of Chinese Humanism]* (Shanghai: East China Normal University Press, 2005), p. 70.

55 Wang, "Zhongyong de Chaoyuexing sixiang yu Pushixing Jiazhi," p. 135.

56 Xianqian Wang, *Xunzi Jijie [Comprehensive Interpretation on Xunzi]* (Beijing: China Book Bureau, 1988), p. 94.

57 Yiming Tang, ed., *Yansi Jiaxun Jiedu [The Interpretation of the Yan Family Disciplines]* (Beijing: National Library Press, 2017).

58 Lu Xun, *Hua Gai Ji [Collection of Hua Gai – Correspondence]*, in *Lunxun Quanji [The Complete Works of Lu Xun]*, vol. 3 (Beijing: People's Literature Publishing House, 2005), p. 26.

59 English translation: propriety "being determined by a rational principle, and by that principle by which the man of practical wisdom would determine it." Aristotle, *Nicomachean Ethics*, p. 28.

60 English translation: "In entering upon any course of action, then, we must hold fast to three principles: first, that impulse shall obey reason; for there is no better way than this to secure the observance of duties; second, that we estimate carefully the importance of the object that we wish to accomplish, so that neither more nor less care and attention may be expended

upon it than the case requires; the third principle is that we be careful to observe moderation in all that is essential to the outward appearance and dignity of a gentleman ... Yet of these three principles, the one of prime importance is to keep impulse subservient to reason." Cicero, *De Officiis*, I:141.

61 Cicero, *De Officiis,* I:159.

62 Cicero, *De Officiis*, III:35.

63 Gaoyan Xiao, "Xisanluo yu Majiweili Lun Zhengzhi Daode" ["Cicero and Machiavelli on Political Morality"], *Zhengzhi Kexue Luncong* [*Political Science Series*], 16 (2012), p. 10.

64 David Hume, *A Treatise of Human Nature: Being an Attempt to Introduce the Experimental Method of Reasoning into Moral Subjects*, Book II (New York: Cover Publications, 2003), pp. 339–366.

65 Smith, *The Theory of Moral Sentiments*, p. 237.

66 Original words: "This disposition to admire, and almost to worship, the rich and the powerful, and to despise, or, at least, to neglect persons of poor and mean condition, though necessary both to establish and to maintain the distinction of ranks and the order of society, is at the same time, the great and most universal cause of the corruption of moral sentiments." Also, "To attain to this envied situation, the candidates for fortune too frequently abandon the paths of virtue; for unhappily, the road which leads to the one, and that which leads to the other, lie sometimes in very opposite directions." Smith, *The Theory of Moral Sentiments*, pp. 61, 64.

67 Pang, *Pang Pu Wenji*, p. 266.

68 Immanuel Kant, *Critique of Pure Reason* (New York: Barnes & Noble, 2004).

69 Leroy E. Loemker, ed., "Gottfried Wilhelm Leibniz. Philosophical Papers and Letters," *Philosophical Quarterly*, 8 (32) (1958), pp. 283–285.

70 Zuo, *Zuo Zhuan*.

71 *Lun Yu – Zilu*.

72 *Lun Yu – Weizheng*.

73 Wang, "Zhongxi Sixiangshi shang de Zhongyong Zhidao," p. 41.

74 Weidong Luo, *Qinggan, Zhixu, Meide: Yadang Simi de Lunlixue Shijie* [*Emotion, Order, Virtue: The Ethical World of Adam Smith*] (Beijing: Renmin University of China Press, 2006).

Chapter 3   Balance and Equilibrium in Classical and Neoclassical Economics

1 Cited from Arthur, *Complexity and the Economy*, p. 172.

2 D. D. Raphael, *The Impartial Spectator: Adam Smith's Moral Philosophy* (New York: Oxford University Press, 2007), p. 1.

3 Smith, *The Theory of Moral Sentiments*, p. 294.

4 Weidong Luo and Lu Liu, "Jiyu Yadang Simi Heyixing Lilun de Renlei Geti Xingwei Moxing" ["A Model of Human Individual Behavior based on Adam Smith's 'Propriety Theory'"], *Shehui Kexue Zhanxian* [*Social Science Front*], 7 (2016), p. 45.

5 Smith, *The Theory of Moral Sentiments*, pp. 223–224.

6 Smith, *The Theory of Moral Sentiments*, pp. 38–39.

7 Smith, *The Theory of Moral Sentiments*, pp. 294–300.

8 "The virtues of prudence, justice, and beneficence, may, upon different occasions, be recommended to us almost equally by two different principles; those of self-command are,

upon most occasions, principally and almost entirely recommended to us by one; by the sense of propriety, regard to the sentiments of the supposed impartial spectator." Smith, *The Theory of Moral Sentiments*, p. 262.

9 Tania Singer and Matthieu Richard, eds., *Caring Economics: Conversations on Altruism and Compassion, between Scientists, Economists, and the Dalai Lama* (New York: Picador, 2015).

10 Paul Zak, ed., "The Neuroeconomics of Distrust: Sex Differences in Behavior and Physiology," *American Economic Review Papers and Proceedings*, 95 (2005), pp. 360–364; Paul Zak, ed., *Moral Markets: The Critical Role of Values in the Economy* (Princeton, NJ: Princeton University Press, 2008); Paul Zak, "The Physiology of Moral Sentiments," *Journal of Economic Behavior & Organization*, 77 (1) (2011), pp. 53–65.

11 Syed Ahmad, "Adam Smith's Four Invisible Hands," *History of Political Economy*, 22 (1990), p. 142.

12 Adam Smith, *The Glasgow Edition of the Works and Correspondence of Adam Smith* (Oxford: Oxford University Press, 1980), vol. III, p. 49.

13 Smith, *The Theory of Moral Sentiments*, p. 466.

14 Adam Smith, *The Wealth of Nations* (New York: Shine Classics, 2014), pp. 242–243.

15 Zhaohui Hong, "'Yizhi Kanbujian Shou' de Bainian Wudu—Wenxian Huanyuan Yadang Simi de Yinyu" ["Demystifying an Enduring Fallacy: Adam Smith's 'Invisible Hand'"], *Naguo Xueshu [South China Quarterly]*, 1 (2021), pp. 4–15.

16 Jinzhong Lin, "Cong 'Kanbujian de Shou' dao 'Shichang Shenhua'" ["From 'Invisible Hand' to 'Market Myth'"], *Jingji Xuejia [The Economist]*, 7 (2021), p. 14.

17 Smith, *The Wealth of Nations*, p. 353.

18 Smith, *The Wealth of Nations*, p. 35.

19 Guoqiang Tian, *Gaoji Weiguan Jingjixue [Advanced Microeconomics]* (Beijing: Renmin University of China Press, 2020), pp. 11–12.

20 Smith, *The Wealth of Nations*, p. 20.

21 Smith, *The Wealth of Nations*, p. 31.

22 Luo and Liu, "Jiyu Yadang Simi Heyixing Lilun de Renlei Geti Xingwei Moxing," p. 41.

23 Luo and Liu, "Jiyu Yadang Simi Heyixing Lilun de Renlei Geti Xingwei Moxing," pp. 42–43.

24 Smith, *The Wealth of Nations*, p. 84.

25 Smith, *The Wealth of Nations*, pp. 85, 86, 261.

26 Smith, *The Wealth of Nations*, p. 652.

27 Smith, *The Wealth of Nations*, pp. 125–126, 135.

28 Smith, *The Wealth of Nations*, pp. 142–143.

29 Smith uses the example of exclusive apprenticeship to emphasize that the apprenticeship system impedes the free flow of labor; in contrast, in enterprises governed by corporate law, the free flow of stock is possible. Smith, *The Wealth of Nations*, pp. 191–192.

30 Smith, *The Wealth of Nations*, p. 154.

31 Smith, *The Wealth of Nations*, p. 419.

32 Smith, *The Wealth of Nations*, pp. 393, 621.

33 Smith, *The Wealth of Nations*, pp. 1195–1196.

34 Smith, *The Wealth of Nations*, pp. 501, 561–588, 617–653.

35 Smith, *The Wealth of Nations*, pp. 806–807.

36 Smith, *The Wealth of Nations*, pp. 827–828.

37 Smith, *The Wealth of Nations*, p. 1064.

38 Smith, *The Wealth of Nations*, p. 1105.

39 Smith, *The Wealth of Nations*, p. 712.

40 Smith, *The Wealth of Nations*, p. 230.

41 Smith, *The Wealth of Nations*, p. 75.

42 Smith, *The Wealth of Nations*, p. 50.

43 Smith, *The Wealth of Nations*, p. 164.

44 Smith, *The Wealth of Nations*, p. 445.

45 Raphael, *The Impartial Spectator*, p. 1.

46 Smith, *The Wealth of Nations*, p. 445.

47 Smith, *The Wealth of Nations*, p. 1090.

48 Smith, *The Wealth of Nations*, p. 822.

49 Smith, *The Theory of Moral Sentiments*, p. 315.

50 Smith, *The Theory of Moral Sentiments*, pp. 326–327.

51 Smith, *The Wealth of Nations*, p. 539.

52 Smith, *The Wealth of Nations*, pp. 517–518.

53 Yining Li, *Wenhua Jingjixue [Cultural Economics]* (Beijing: Shangwu Yinshuguan, 2018), pp. 153–154, 374, 377.

54 Maria Pia Paganelli, "In Medio Stat Virtus: An Alternative View of Usury in Adam Smith's Thinking," *History of Political Economy*, 35 (1) (2003), p. 46; Maria Pia Paganelli, "Adam Smith and Economic Development: Theory and Practice," *Journal of the History of Economic Thought*, 44 (1) (2022), pp. 95–104.

55 Luo and Liu, "Jiyu Yadang Simi Heyixing Lilun de Renlei Geti Xingwei Moxing," p. 45.

56 Alfred Marshall, *Principles of Economics: Unabridged Eighth Edition* (New York: Cosimo, Inc., 2009), pp. 281–291.

57 Marshall, *Principles of Economics,* pp. 302–315.

58 Marshall, *Principles of Economics,* pp. 411–417.

59 Arthur, *Complexity and the Economy*, p. 4.

60 Marshall, *Principles of Economics*, pp. 276–280.

61 Marshall, *Principles of Economics*, pp. 58–59.

62 Léon Walras, *Elements of Theoretical Economics: The Theory of Social Wealth* (Cambridge: Cambridge University Press, 2014).

63 Tian, *Gaoji Weiguan Jingjixue*, p. 8.

64 Smith, *The Wealth of Nations*, pp. 27–31.

65 Marshall, *Principles of Economics*, pp. 243–261, 602–623.

66 Ronald H. Coase, "The Nature of the Firm," *Economica*, 4 (16) (1937), p. 388.

67 Tian, *Gaoji Weiguan Jingjixue*, p. 3.

68 Roberto Marchionatti and Fiorenzo Mornati, eds., *Considerations on the Fundamental Principles of Pure Political Economy* (New York: Routledge, 2007), p. xi.

69 Arthur C. Pigou, *The Economics of Welfare* (London: Macmillan and Co., 1929), 3rd ed., p. ix.

70 Vilfredo Pareto, *The Mind and Society*, Arthur Livingston, ed. (New York: Harcourt, Brace & Company, 1935); Tian, *Gaoji Weiguan Jingjixue*, pp. 616, 621.

71 Tian, *Gaoji Weiguan Jingjixue*, p. 625.

72 Nicholas Kaldor, "Welfare Propositions of Economics and Interpersonal Comparisons of Utility," *The Economic Journal*, 49 (195) (1939), pp. 551–552.

73 Kaldor, "Welfare Propositions of Economics and Interpersonal Comparisons of Utility," pp. 551–552.

74 Tian, *Gaoji Weiguan Jingjixue*, pp. 629, 643.

75 Tian, *Gaoji Weiguan Jingjixue*, p. 539.

76 Tian, *Gaoji Weiguan Jingjixue*, p. 539.

77 Tian, *Gaoji Weiguan Jingjixue*, p. 537.

78 Herbert Simon, "Bounded Rationality in Social Science: Today and Tomorrow," *Mind & Society*, 1 (1) (2000), p. 26.

Chapter 4 The Neutrality of Institutional Economics and the Subjectivity of Behavioral Economics

1 Malcolm Rutherford, "Introduction to the Transaction Edition," in John Commons, *Institutional Economics: Its Place in Political Economy* (New Brunswick, NJ: Transaction Publishers, 2009), p. 4.

2 John Commons, "Institutional Economics," *American Economic Review*, 26 (1) (1936), p. 244.

3 Commons, "Institutional Economics," p. 248.

4 Commons, "Institutional Economics," p. 248.

5 Commons, "Institutional Economics," p. 246.

6 Commons, *Institutional Economics*, p. 712.

7 Commons, *Institutional Economics*, p. 1.

8 Commons, *Institutional Economics*, p. 70.

9 Commons, *Institutional Economics*, pp. 72–73.

10 Commons, *Institutional Economics*, p. 4.

11 Commons, *Institutional Economics*, pp. 59–68.

12 Commons, *Institutional Economics*, p. xii.

13 John Commons, *A Sociological View of Sovereignty* (New York: Augustus M. Kelley, 1967), p. 45.

14 Commons, *Institutional Economics*, p. 2.

15 Commons, *Institutional Economics*, p. 58.

16 Coase, "The Nature of the Firm," p. 389.

17 Commons, *Institutional Economics*, p. 8.

18 Coase, "The Nature of the Firm," pp. 390–391.

19 Douglass North, "Institutions and Economic Growth: An Historical Introduction," *World Development*, 17 (9) (1989), p. 1319.

20 Steven Cheung, "The Fable of the Bees: An Economic Investigation," *Journal of Law and Economics*, 16 (1) (1973), pp. 32–33.

21 Zhaofeng Xue, *Xue Zhaofeng Jingjixue Jiangyi [Xue Zhaofeng Lectures on Economics]* (Beijing: Zhongxin Chuban Jituan, 2018), pp. 78–83; see Richard Epstein, *Takings: Private Property and the Power of Eminent Domain* (Cambridge, MA: Harvard University Press, 1985).

22 Ronald H. Coase, "The Problem of Social Cost," *Journal of Law and Economics*, 3 (1960), p. 18.

23 Coase, "The Problem of Social Cost," p. 16.

24 Coase, "The Problem of Social Cost," p. 16.

25 Coase, "The Problem of Social Cost," p. 16.

26 Coase, "The Nature of the Firm," pp. 390–391.

27 Coase, "The Nature of the Firm," p. 389.

28 Paul Zak and Stephen Knack, "Trust and Growth," *The Economic Journal*, 111 (470) (2001), pp. 295–321.

29 Karen Middleton and Meheroo Jussawalla, eds., *The Economics of Communication: A Selected Bibliography with Abstracts* (New York: Pergamon Press, 1981), pp. xi–xvi, 1–7.

30 Thomas Schelling, *The Strategy of Conflict* (Cambridge, MA: Harvard University Press, 1960), p. 57.

31 Francis Fukuyama, *Xinren: Shehui Meide yu Chuangzhao Jingji Fanrong* [*Trust: The Social Virtues and the Creation of Prosperity*] (Guilin: Guangxi Normal University Press, 2016), pp. 251–275.

32 Haocai Luo, *Ruanfa de Lilun yu Shijian* [*The Theory and Practice of Soft Law*] (Beijing: Beijing University Press, 2010).

33 Yuhua Guo, "Daodu: Fushan de Huiyan" ["Introduction: Fukuyama's Wise Eyes: The Accumulation of Social Capital and the Power of the Self-Society"]; see Fukuyama, *Xinren*, p. iii.

34 Weiqi Jin, ed., *Qingguan Lu Jiashu* [*Clean Official Lu Jiashu*] (Hangzhou: Zhejiang Guji Publisher, 2020).

35 Longxin Li, "Cong Qiye dao Qiye Wenhua de Jingjixue Jieshi" ["Economic Explanation from Business to Corporate Culture"], *Shangye Yanjiu* [*Business Research*], 2 (2013), pp. 115–120.

36 David Lindenfeld, "The Myth of the Older Historical School of Economics," *Central European History*, 26 (4) (1993), pp. 405–416.

37 Zak, "The Physiology of Moral Sentiments," p. 62; Paul Zak, "The Neurobiology of Trust," *Scientific American*, 298 (6) (2008), pp. 88–95.

38 Coase, "The Problem of Social Cost," pp. 17–18.

39 Coase, "The Problem of Social Cost," p. 28.

40 Ronald H. Coase, "The Federal Communications Commission," *Journal of Law and Economics*, 2 (October) (1959), p. 18.

41 Coase, "The Problem of Social Cost," p. 18.

42 Commons, *Institutional Economics*, pp. 386–389.

43 Commons, *Institutional Economics*, pp. 144–149.

44 John Commons, *Legal Foundation of Capitalism* (New Brunswick, NJ: Transaction Publishers, 1995), p. 302.

45 Commons, *Legal Foundation of Capitalism*, p. 300.

46 Commons, *Institutional Economics*, p. 74.

47 Commons, *Institutional Economics*, p. 16.

48 Commons, *Institutional Economics*, p. 331.

49 Douglass North, "Economic Performance Through Time," *American Economic Review*, 84 (3) (1994), p. 365.

50 Douglass North, "Institutions and Economic Theory," *The American Economists*, 36 (1) (1992), p. 4.

51 Thorstein Veblen, "Why is Economics not an Evolutionary Science?", *The Quarterly Journal of Economics*, 12 (4) (1898), pp. 373–397.

52 North, "Institutions and Economic Theory," pp. 4–5.

53 Paul D. Bush, "The Theory of Institutional Change," *Journal of Economic Issues*, 21 (3) (1987), p. 1075.

54 Veblen, "Why is Economics not an Evolutionary Science?", pp. 373–397.

55 Commons, *Institutional Economics*, pp. 386–389.

56 Bush, "The Theory of Institutional Change," pp. 1079–1080.

57 Clarence Ayres, *Toward a Reasonable Society* (Austin: University of Texas Press, 1971), p. 241.

58 North, "Institutions and Economic Growth," p. 1321.

59 North, "Institutions and Economic Growth," pp. 1319–1321.

60 North, "Institutions and Economic Theory," p. 6.

61 Yngve Ramstad, "John R. Commons' Puzzling Inconsequentiality as an Economic Theorist," *Journal of Economic Issues*, 29 (4) (1995), pp. 991–1113.

62 Lin Zhang, *Xin Zhidu Zhuyi [New Institutionalism]* (Beijing: Economic Press, 2005), pp. 71–72.

63 Frank Hahn, "Next Hundred Years," *Economic Journal*, 101 (404) (1991), p. 47.

64 North, "Institutions and Economic Theory," p. 6; North, "Institutions and Economic Growth," pp. 1319–1332.

65 Bush, "The Theory of Institutional Change," p. 1076.

66 Bush, "The Theory of Institutional Change," pp. 1077–1078.

67 Leon Levy and Nassau W. Senior, *The Prophet of Modern Capitalism* (Boston: Bruce Humphries, 1943).

68 John Stuart Mill, *On Liberty* (London: John W. Parker and Son, West Strand, 1859).

69 Pareto, *The Mind and Society*.

70 Zhaohui Hong, "Wenxian Huaiyuan Yadang Simi de Shichang Zhenyi" ["Authenticating Adam Smith: Re-Examination and Reinterpretation of the Market Theory"], *Nanguo Xueshu [South China Quarterly]*, 1 (2022), p. 14.

71 Herbert Simon, "A Behavioral Model of Rational Choice," *The Quarterly Journal of Economics*, 69 (1) (1955), p. 99.

72 Richard Thaler, *Misbehaving: The Making of Behavioral Economics* (New York: W. W. Norton & Company, 2016), p. 3.

73 Thaler, *Misbehaving*, p. 4.

74 Thaler, *Misbehaving*, pp. 4–5.

75 Thorstein Veblen, *The Theory of the Leisure Class—An Economic Study of Institutions* (New York: Macmillan, 1899), p. 70.

76 Malcolm Rutherford, "The Old and the New Institutionalism: Can Bridges Be Built?", *Journal of Economic Issues*, 29 (1995), p. 449.

77 Thaler, *Misbehaving*, p. 8.

78 Herbert Simon, *Models of Bounded Rationality: Empirically Grounded Economic Reason* (Cambridge, MA: The MIT Press, 1997), vol. 3, pp. 267–274.

79 Denis Diderot, "Regrets on Parting with My Old Dressing Gown," translated by Kate Tunstall and Katie Scott, *Oxford Art Journal*, 29 (2) (August 2016), pp. 175–184.

80 Grant David McCracken, *The Long Interview—Qualitative Research Methods Series 13* (Newbury Park, CA: A Sage University Paper, 1988).

81 Juliet Schor, *The Overspent American: Why We Want What We Don't Need* (New York: Harper Perennial, 1999), pp. 143–168.

82 Simon, "A Behavioral Model of Rational Choice," p. 100.

83 Herbert Simon, "Theories of Bounded Rationality," in C. B. McGuire and Roy Radner, eds., *Decision and Organization: A Volume in Honor of Jacob Marschak* (Amsterdam: North-Holland Publishing Company, 1972), pp. 163–164.

84 Simon, "A Behavioral Model of Rational Choice," p. 114.

85 Simon, "A Behavioral Model of Rational Choice," p. 100.

86 Simon, "Theories of Bounded Rationality," p. 162.

87 Herbert Simon, "Rationality and Organizational Learning," *Organization Science*, 2 (1) (1991), p. 132.

88 Simon, "Bounded Rationality in Social Science: Today and Tomorrow," p. 25.

89 Sendhil Mullainathan and Richard Thaler, "Behavioral Economics," *National Bureau of Economic Research Working Paper Series 7948* (Washington, D.C.: National Bureau of Economic Research, 2000), p. 1.

90 Arthur, *Complexity and the Economy*, p. 31.

91 Simon, "Bounded Rationality in Social Science: Today and Tomorrow," p. 26.

92 Simon, "Bounded Rationality in Social Science: Today and Tomorrow," p. 29.

93 Richard Thaler and Cass R. Sunstein, *Nudge: Improving Decisions about Health, Wealth, and Happiness* (New York: Penguin Books, 2009), pp. 5–6.

94 Thaler and Sunstein, *Nudge*, p. 8.

95 Thaler and Sunstein, *Nudge*, p. 6.

96 Thaler and Sunstein, *Nudge*, pp. 231–238.

97 Thaler and Sunstein, *Nudge*, p. 13.

98 Thaler and Sunstein, *Nudge*, pp. 255–256.

99 Smith, *The Theory of Moral Sentiments*, p. 61.

100 Smith, *The Theory of Moral Sentiments*, p. 64.

101 Smith, *The Theory of Moral Sentiments*, p. 231.

102 Daniel Kahneman and Amos Tversky, "Prospect Theory: An Analysis of Decision under Risk," *Econometrica*, 47 (2) (1979), p. 263.

103 Kahneman and Tversky, "Prospect Theory: An Analysis of Decision under Risk," p. 269.

104 Kahneman and Tversky, "Prospect Theory: An Analysis of Decision under Risk," p. 269.

105 Kahneman and Tversky, "Prospect Theory: An Analysis of Decision under Risk," p. 280.

106 Kahneman and Tversky, "Prospect Theory: An Analysis of Decision under Risk," p. 288.

107 Mullainathan and Thaler, "Behavioral Economics," p. 6.

108 Mullainathan and Thaler, "Behavioral Economics," p. 5.

109 North, "Institutions and Economic Theory," p. 5.

110 Richard Thaler, "Mental Accounting and Consumer Choice," *Marketing Science*, 4 (3) (1985), pp. 199–200.

111 Mullainathan and Thaler, "Behavioral Economics," pp. 1–13.

112 Dingding Wang, *Xingwei Jingjixue Yaoyi [Essentials of Behavioral Economics]* (Shanghai: Shanghai People's Publishing House, 2015), pp. 147–228.

113 Thaler and Sunstein, *Nudge*, p. viii.

Chapter 5　Shared Values in Cultural Economics and the Definition of Propriety Economics

1　Ruth Towse, *A Textbook of Cultural Economics* (Cambridge: Cambridge University Press, 2019).

2　Marco Castellani, "Does Culture Matter for the Economic Performance of Countries? An Overview of the Literature," *The Society for Policy Modeling*, 41 (4) (2019), p. 703; Luigi Guiso, Paola Sapienza, and Luigi Zingales, "Does Culture Affect Economic Outcomes?", *Journal of Economic Perspectives*, 20 (2) (2006), p. 23; Jeanette D. Snowball, *Measuring the Value of Culture* (New York: Springer, 2008); Samuel Bowles, "Endogenous Preferences: The Cultural Consequences of Markets and Other Economic Institutions," *Journal of Economic Literature*, 36 (1) (1998), pp. 75–111.

3　Singer and Ricard, eds., *Caring Economics: Conversations on Altruism and Compassion, between Scientists, Economists, and the Dalai Lama.*

4　Zhaohui Hong, *Meizhong Shehui Yixiang Toushi* [*Critical Reflections on Social Issues in the United States and China*] (New York: Bouden House, 2021), p. 10.

5　Siew Kim Jean Lee and Kelvin Yu, "Corporate Culture and Organizational Performance," *Journal of Managerial Psychology*, 19 (4) (2004), pp. 340–359; Vijay Sathe, "Implications of Corporate Culture: A Manager's Guide to Action," *Organizational Dynamics*, 12 (2) (1983), pp. 5–23.

6　Fukuyama, *Xinren*, p. 16.

7　Fukuyama, *Xinren*, p. 12.

8　Fukuyama, *Xinren*, p. 15.

9　Fukuyama, *Xinren*, p. 269.

10　Fukuyama, *Xinren*, p. 219.

11　Zhiping Song, "Women de fenpei jizhi haishi you wenti" ["There is still an issue with our distribution mechanism"], *National Revitalization Think-tank*, November 21, 2019, www.xbzk.org/news/edp.asp?id=901 (accessed November 3, 2023).

12　Li, *Wenhua Jingjixue*, pp. 151–152.

13　Li, *Wenhua Jingjixue,* pp. 153–154.

14　Li, *Wenhua Jingjixue*, p. 74.

15　Guofan Zeng, *Zeng Guofan Jiashu Jiaxun* [*Zeng Guofan's Book of the Family*] (Tianjin: Tianjin Guji Shudian, 1991).

16　John Rawls, *A Theory of Justice* (Revised Edition) (Cambridge, MA: Harvard University Press, 1999), pp. 3–4.

17　*Lun Yu.*

18　John Hicks, *A Theory of Economic History* (Oxford: Oxford University Press, 1969), pp. 9–24.

19　Thomas de Chobham, *Summa Confessorum* (Paris: Béatrice Nauwelaerts, 1968), pp. xi–lxix.

20　Jennifer J. Griffin and John F. Mahon, "The Corporate Social Performance and Corporate Financial Performance Debate: Twenty-five years of Incomparable Research," *Business and Society*, 36 (5) (1997), pp. 5–6.

21　Li, *Wenhua Jingjixue*, p. 141.

22　Li, *Wenhua Jingjixue*, pp. 224–225.

23　Li, *Wenhua Jingjixue*, pp. 241–244.

24 Lawrence E. Harrison, "Why Culture Matters," in Lawrence E. Harrison and Samuel P. Huntington, eds., *Culture Matters: How Values Shape Human Progress* (New York: Basic Books, 2000), pp. xxiv–xxv; David Landes, "Culture Makes Almost All the Difference," in Harrison and Huntington, eds., *Culture Matters*, p. 2.

25 George Stigler and Gary Becker, "De Gustibus Non Est Disputandum," *American Economic Review*, 67 (2) (1977), pp. 76–90.

26 Armen A. Alchian, "Some Economics of Property Rights," *Politico*, 30 (4) (1965), p. 818.

27 Guinevere Nell, *The Driving Force of the Collective: Post-Austrian Theory in Response to Israel Kirzner* (New York: Palgrave Macmillan, 2017), pp. 23–42.

28 Mark Blaug, *The Methodology of Economics: Or, How Economists Explain* (Cambridge: Cambridge University Press, 1992), pp. 45–46.

29 Alan Kirman, "The Intrinsic Limits of Modern Economic Theory: The Emperor has No Clothes," *The Economic Journal*, 99 (395) (1989), pp. 126–139.

Chapter 6 Trichotomism and Propriety Economic Theory

1 Sang-hoon Jee, "A Critical Evaluation of Trichotomism: A Response to Biblical References for Trichotomism," *Catalyst*, 15 (1) (2017), pp. 55–57.

2 Millard Erickson, *Christian Theology* (Grand Rapids, MI: Baker Books, 1998), pp. 538–543.

3 Karl R. Popper, *Objective Knowledge: An Evolutionary Approach* (Oxford: Oxford University Press, 1972).

4 Pang, *Pang Pu Wenji*, p. 325.

5 Kant, *Critique of Pure Reason*, pp. 21–29.

6 Fuxiang Ye, *Sanyuan Zhexue Henxin Sixiang* [*The Core Ideas of Ternary Philosophy*], wenku. baidu.com/view/d473416ca45177232f60a25b.html (accessed May 1, 2020).

7 Laozi, *Daode Jing* [*Dao De Jing*] (Beijing: China Bookstore, 2019).

8 Liqiang Wang, *Sanyuanlun yu Sanyuan Yijing* [*The Three Sources Theory and the Three Sources of the I Ching*] (Nanjing: Southeast University Press, 2014), Part 1, Chapter 1.

9 Ye, *Sanyuan Zhexue yu Hexin Sixiang*.

10 Tao Xu, "Ni Xisheng de Sanyuanlun Sixiang Taijiu" ["An Exploration of Ni Xisheng's Triadic Thought"], *Zhongguo Shenxue Yanjiuyuan Qikan* [*Journal of the Chinese Theological Seminary*], 1 (2013), p. 40.

11 Robert Sternberg, *Beyond IQ: A Triarchic Theory of Human Intelligence* (New York: Cambridge University Press, 1985), pp. 1–40; Robert Sternberg, ed., *Handbook of Intelligence* (Cambridge: Cambridge University Press, 2000), pp. 3–15.

12 John Holland, *Yinzhixu—Shiyingxing Zaojiu Fuzaxing* [*Hidden Order: How Adaptation Builds Complexity*], Xiaomu Zhou and Hui Han, trans. (Shanghai: Shanghai Technological Education Press, 2019), p. 3.

13 Hanlin Ke, "Zhonghemei de Zhexue Dingwei" ["Philosophical Positioning of Neutral Beauty"], *Huanan Shifan Daxue Xuebao* [*Journal of South China Normal University*], 4 (1995), p. 71.

14 Robert Sternberg and Karin Sternberg, eds., *The New Psychology of Love* (2nd revised edition) (Cambridge: Cambridge University Press, 2018), pp. 280–299.

15 Zhaohui Hong, "Shidu Jingjixue Sixiang de Kuaxueke Yanhua" ["Interdisciplinary Evolution of Propriety Economic Thought"], *Nanguo Xueshu* [*South China Quarterly*], 3 (2020), pp. 404–405.

16 Philip W. Anderson, "More is Different," *Science*, 117 (4047) (1972), pp. 393–396.

17 Lewis Carroll, *A Survey of Symbolic Logic* (London: Forgotten Books, 2015), pp. 1–4; Jan Woleński, "Jan Łukasiewicz on the Liar Paradox, Logical Consequence, Truth, and Induction," *Modern Logic*, 4 (4) (October 1994), pp. 392–400.

18 Lotfi A. Zadeh, "Fuzzy Sets," *Information and Control*, 8 (3) (1965), pp. 338–339.

19 George Boole, *The Mathematical Analysis of Logic, Being an Essay towards a Calculus of Deductive Reasoning* (London: Macmillan, Barclay, & Macmillan, 1847).

20 Ying Ye, "Jianli zai Sanyuan Luoji Jichu Shang de Snayuan Kexue" ["Triadic Science Based on Triadic Logic"], *Zhejiang Daxue Xuebao [Journal of Zhejiang University]*, 3 (2000), p. 338.

21 Virginia Trimble, "Existence and Nature of Dark Matter in the Universe," *Annual Review of Astronomy and Astrophysics*, 25 (1) (1987), pp. 425–472.

22 Weijia Wang, *Anzhishi—Jiqi Renzhi Ruhe Dianfu Shanye he Shehui [Dark Knowledge—How Machine Cognition is Disrupting Business and Society]* (Beijing: Zhongxin Press, 2019).

23 Julong Deng, "Control Problems of Grey Systems," *Systems and Control Letters*, 5 (1982), pp. 288–294; "Introduction to Grey System Theory," *The Journal of Grey System*, 1 (1989), pp. 1–24.

24 Zhengfei Ren, "Guanli de Huidu" ["Shades of Gray in Management"], *Shanjie (Pinglun) [Business Review]*, 4 (2010), pp. 48–50.

25 Kurt Gödel, *Collected Works. I: Publications 1929–1936* (Oxford: Oxford University Press, 1986), pp. 1–36.

26 Kenneth Arrow, "A Difficulty in the Concept of Social Welfare," *Journal of Political Economy*, 58 (4) (1950), pp. 328–346.

27 Amartya Sen, "The Impossibility of a Paretian Liberal," *The Journal of Political Economy*, 78 (1) (1970), pp. 152–157.

28 Xuewen Wu, "Sanyuan Lilun Jichu he Yingyong Juli" ["Fundamentals and Applications of Ternary Theory"], *Zhongwai Yixue [Chinese and Foreign Medical Journal]*, 9 (2008), p. 41.

29 Patrick Lee and Robert P. George, *Body-Self Dualism in Contemporary Ethics and Politics* (Cambridge: Cambridge University Press, 2007).

30 Zhaohui Hong, "Zhongguan Shixue Daolun" ["Introduction to Meso-History"], *Guangming Daily—History*, January 8, 1988.

31 Allan A. Metcalf, *Predicting New Words: The Secrets of Their Success* (Boston: Houghton Mifflin Co., 2002), pp. 106–107.

32 Maurice Obstfeld, Jay C. Shambaugh, and Alan M. Taylor, "The Trilemma in History: Tradeoffs Among Exchange Rates, Monetary Policies, and Capital Mobility," *The Review of Economics and Statistics*, 87 (3) (2005), pp. 423–438.

33 Dani Rodrik, *The Globalization Paradox: Democracy and the Future of the World Economy* (New York: W. W. Norton & Company, 2011), pp. ix–xxii.

34 Peter A. Swenson, *Fair Shares: Unions, Pay, and Politics in Sweden and West Germany* (Ithaca, NY: Cornell University Press, 1989), pp. 1–10.

35 Editorial, "The Uneasy Triangle," *The Economist*, August 9, 1952.

36 John Maynard Keynes, *The General Theory of Employment, Interest and Money* (London: Macmillan, 1936), p. 267.

37 Steven Pinker, *The Blank Slate: The Modern Denial of Human Nature* (London: Penguin, 2002), pp. 1–4.

38 Arthur C. Clarke, *The Ghost from the Grand Banks* (London: Gollancz, 1990), p. 73.

39 Yoshihiro Hamakawa, "New Energy Option for 21st Century: Recent Progress in Solar Photovoltaic Energy Conversion," *Japan Society of Applied Physics International*, 5 (2002), pp. 30–35.

40 See David Hume, *Dialogues Concerning Natural Religion* (New York: Hackett Publishing Co., 1998). Others believe that this was proposed by ancient Greek skeptics. See Mark Joseph Larrimore, *The Problem of Evil: A Reader* (New York: Blackwell, 2001), p. xx.

41 Kenneth Arrow, "The Principle of Rationality in Collective Decisions," in Kenneth Arrow, ed., *Collected Papers of Kenneth J. Arrow: Social Choice and Justice* (Cambridge, MA: The Belknap Press of Harvard University Press, 1983), pp. 45–58. Tian also mentions the rationale that choosing two out of three is more optimal than choosing one out of two. See Tian, *Gaoji Weiguan Jingjixue*, p. 678.

42 John Gribbin, *In Search of Schrödinger's Cat: Quantum Physics and Reality* (New York: Random House Publishing Group, 2011), p. 234.

43 Aristotle, *Nicomachean Ethics*, pp. 24–25.

44 Zhaohui Hong, *The Price of China's Economic Development: Power, Capital, and the Poverty of Rights* (Lexington: The University Press of Kentucky, 2015), pp. 36–37.

45 Aurora Cuito and Cristina Montes, *Antoni Gaudi: Complete Works* (Madrid: H. Kliczkowski-Only Book, 2002).

46 Hong, *The Price of China's Economic Development*, pp. 2–10.

47 Pang, *Pang Pu Wenji*, p. 110.

48 Pang, *Pang Pu Wenji*, p. 326.

49 Holland, *Yinzhixu*, p. 2.

50 Tian, *Gaoji Weiguan Jingjixue*, p. 21.

51 Zhaohui Hong, *Shehui Jingji Bianqian de Zhuti [The Themes of Social Economic Transition: Reinterpretation on the Process of American Modernization]* (Hangzhou: Hangzhou University Press, 1994), p. 9.

52 United Nations, Department of Economic and Social Affairs, Population Division, *World Urbanization Prospects: The 2018 Revision* (ST/ESA/SER.A/420) (New York: United Nations, 2019), pp. 55–80.

53 Yuan Xu, *Cong Gongyehua dao Chengshihua [From Industrialization to Urbanization]* (Beijing: Zhongxin Press, 2019), chapter 7.

54 Leonid Hurwicz and Stanley Reiter, *Designing Economic Mechanisms* (New York: Cambridge University Press, 2008), p. 2; Leonid Hurwicz, "The Design of Mechanisms for Resource Allocation," *The American Economic Review: Papers and Proceedings of the Eighty-fifth Annual Meeting of the American Economic Association*, 63 (2) (1973), pp. 1–30.

55 Tian, *Gaoji Weiguan Jingjixue*, p. 830.

56 Werner Sombart, *War and Capitalism* (New Stratford, NH: Ayer Company, 1975).

57 Joseph Schumpeter, *Capitalism, Socialism and Democracy* (New York: Routledge, 2006), pp. 81–86.

58 David R. Henderson, ed., "Joseph Schumpeter," *The Concise Encyclopedia of Economics, Library of Economics and Liberty*, 2000, www.econlib.org/library/Enc/bios/Schumpeter.html (accessed March 1, 2020).

59 Tian, *Gaoji Weiguan Jingjixue*, p. 161.

60 Arthur, *Complexity and the Economy*, pp. 6–7.

Chapter 7 Research Methodology of Propriety Economics

1 Arthur, *Complexity and the Economy*, p. xvii.

2 Original words: "New technologies are constructed—put together—from technologies that already exist; these in turn offer themselves as building-block components for the creation of yet further new technologies. In this way technology (the collection of devices and methods available to society) builds itself out of itself. I call this mechanism of evolution by the creation of novel combinations and selection of those that work well combinatorial evolution." Arthur, *Complexity and the Economy*, p. 119.

3 Barney G. Glaser and Anselm Strauss, *The Discovery of Grounded Theory: Strategies for Qualitative Research* (New York: Routledge, 2017), pp. 15–18.

4 Glaser and Strauss, *The Discovery of Grounded Theory*, p. 18.

5 Castellani, "Does Culture Matter for the Economic Performance of Countries? An Overview of the Literature," p. 703.

6 Glaser and Strauss, *The Discovery of Grounded Theory*, pp. 185–222.

7 Glaser and Strauss, *The Discovery of Grounded Theory*, pp. 185–222.

8 Laure Sharp and Joy Frechtling, "Overview of the Design Process for Mixed Method Evaluation," in Laure Sharp and Joy Frechtling, eds., *User-Friendly Handbook for Mixed Method Evaluations,* 1997, www.nsf.gov/pubs/1997/nsf97153/start.htm (accessed July 1, 2019).

9 Judith A. Holton and Isabelle Walsh, *Classic Grounded Theory: Applications with Qualitative & Quantitative Data* (Los Angeles: SAGE, 2017), pp. 272–281.

10 Holton and Walsh, *Classic Grounded Theory*, pp. 180–181.

11 Holton and Walsh, *Classic Grounded Theory*, p. 92.

12 Holton and Walsh, *Classic Grounded Theory*, p. 62.

13 Hong, "Wenxian Huaiyuan Yadang Simi de Shichang Zhenyi," pp. 6–11.

14 Zhaohui Hong and Jianfeng Jin, "Spatial Study of Mosques: Xinjiang and Ningxia as Case Studies," *Review of Religion and Chinese Society*, 3 (2) (2016), pp. 223–260; Zhaohui Hong and Jianfeng Jin, "The Digital and Spatial Study of Catholic Market in Urban China," in Xiaobing Li and Xiansheng Tian, eds., *Urban Cry: Power vs. People in Chinese Cities* (New York: Lexington Books, 2016), pp. 121–134.

15 Zhaohui Hong, Jiamin Yan, and Lu Cao, "Spatial and Statistical Perspectives on the Protestant Church Shortage in China: Case Studies in Hangzhou, Zhengzhou, Hefei and Fuzhou Cities," *Journal of Third World Studies*, 31 (1) (2014), pp. 81–99.

16 Rachel Crosona and Simon Gächterb, "The Science of Experimental Economics," *Journal of Economic Behavior & Organization*, 73 (1) (2010), pp. 122–131.

17 Tania Singer, "Introduction," in Singer and Richard, eds., *Caring Economics: Conversations on Altruism and Compassion, between Scientists, Economists, and the Dalai Lama.*

18 Edward Glaeser, David Laibson, Jose Scheinkman, and Christine Soutter, "Measuring Trust," *Quarterly Journal of Economics*, 115 (3) (2000), pp. 811–846.

19 The Royal Swedish Academy of Sciences, "Press Release: The Prize in Economic Sciences 2019," October 14, 2019, www.nobelprize.org/prizes/economic-sciences/2019/press-release/ (accessed November 30, 2019).

20 Beth Daley, "Economics Nobel 2019: Why Banerjee, Duflo and Kremer won," *The Conversation*, October 14, 2019, theconversation.com/economics-nobel-2019-why-banerjee-duflo-and-kremer-won-125276 (accessed November 6, 2023).

21 Robert Axelrod and W. D. Hamilton, "The Evolution of Cooperation," *Science*, 211 (4489) (1981), pp. 1390–1396; Zhaohui Hong, "Shui Nongdiu le Meiguo—Zhongmei Guanxi Jiju Ehua Xinjie" ["Who Lost America?—A New Interpretation of the Rapid Deterioration of U.S.-China Relations"], *Dangdai Zhongguo Pinglun [Contemporary China Review Quarterly]*, 2 (2020), p. 74.

22 Arthur, *Complexity and the Economy*, pp. ix–x.

23 Arthur, *Complexity and the Economy*, p. 120; W. Brian Arthur and Wolfgang Polak, "The Evolution of Technology within a Simple Computer Model," *Complexity*, 11 (5) (2006), pp. 23–31.

24 Zak, "The Physiology of Moral Sentiments," p. 63.

25 Zak, "The Physiology of Moral Sentiments," p. 54.

26 Zak, "The Physiology of Moral Sentiments," p. 58.

27 Dingding Wang, "Lijie Yongxian Zhixu" ["Understanding the Order of Emergence"], in W. Brian Arthur, *Fuza Jingjixue [Complexity and the Economy]* (Hangzhou: Zhejiang People's Press, 2018), pp. vi–vii.

28 Scott Schneberger, Hugh Watson, and Carol Pollard, "The Efficacy of 'Little t' Theories," *IEEE Proceedings of the 40th Hawaii International Conference on System Sciences*, (2007), p. 1.

29 Zhaohui Hong and Yi Sun, "The Butterfly Effect and the Making of 'Ping-Pong Diplomacy'," *Journal of Contemporary China*, 9 (25) (2000), pp. 429–430.

30 Wang, *Lijie Yongxian Zhixu*, pp. v–vi.

31 Arthur, *Complexity and the Economy*, p. xiv.

32 Cuncheng Liu and Hanpo Hou, *Chengshi de Jueqi—Chengshi Xitongxue yu Zhongguo Chengshihua [The Rise of the City—Urban Systematics and Urbanization in China]* (Beijing: Zhongyang Wenxian Chubanshe, 2012), pp. 120–121.

33 Karma Ura, Sabina Alkire, Tshoki Zangmo, and Karma Wangdi, *A Short Guide to Gross National Happiness Index* (Thimphu, Bhutan: The Centre for Bhutan Studies, 2012), pp. 4–12; Gang Li, Bin Wang, and Shuihui Liu, "Guomin Xingfu Zhishu Cesuan Fangfa Yanjiu" ["Research on the Measurement Method of National Happiness Index"], *Dongbei Daxue Xuebao [Journal of Northeastern University]*, 17 (2015), pp. 376–383.

34 Daniel Kahneman, Alan B. Krueger, David A. Schkade, Norbert Schwarz, and Arthur A. Stone, "A Survey Method for Characterizing Daily Life Experience: The Day Reconstruction Method," *Science*, 306 (5702) (2004), p. 1777.

35 Arthur, *Complexity and the Economy*, p. 4.

36 Arthur, *Complexity and the Economy*, pp. 5–6.

37 W. Brian Arthur, "Complexity and the Economy," *Science*, 284 (107) (1999), p. 108.

38 Arthur, *Complexity and the Economy*, p. 6.

39 Joseph Schumpeter, *The Theory of Economic Development* (London: Oxford University Press, 1961). Cited from Arthur, *Complexity and the Economy*, p. 6.

40 Arthur, *Complexity and the Economy*, p. 21.

41 Charles Peirce, *Reasoning and the Logic of Things* (Cambridge, MA: Harvard University Press, 1992), pp. 105–242.

42 Herbert Simon, *Models of Discovery* (Dordrecht: Reidel, 1977), p. 286.

43 Ramzi Mabsout, "Abduction and Economics: The Contributions of Charles Peirce and Herbert Simon," *Journal of Economic Methodology*, 22 (4), p. 491.

44 Norwood Hanson, *Patterns of Discovery* (Cambridge: Cambridge University Press, 1958), pp. 70–92.

45 Mabsout, "Abduction and Economics," pp. 491–492.

46 Robert Fogel and Stanley Engerman, *Time on the Cross—The Economics of American Negro Slavery* (New York: W. W. Norton & Company, 1974), pp. 191–257; Robert Fogel, *Without Consent or Contract: The Rise and Fall of American Slavery* (New York: W. W. Norton & Company, 1989), pp. 60–80.

47 Mabsout, "Abduction and Economics," pp. 491–516.

48 Elliott Sober, *Core Questions in Philosophy: A Text with Readings* (6th ed.) (Boston: Pearson Education, 2013), p. 28.

49 Judea Pearl and Dana Mackenzie, *The Book of Why: The New Science of Cause and Effect* (New York: Basic Books, 2018), pp. 349–370.

50 Arthur, *Complexity and the Economy*, p. 166.

51 Arthur, *Complexity and the Economy*, p. 181.

52 Zhaohui Hong, "Shidu Jingjixue Sixiang de Kuaixueke Yanhua" ["The Interdisciplinary Evolution of Propriety Economic Thought"], *Nanguo Xueshu* [*South China Quarterly*], 3 (2020), pp. 407–408.

53 Jude Wanniski, "Taxes, Revenues, & the 'Laffer Curve'," *The Public Interest*, 50 (1978), p. 4.

54 Arthur Laffer, Stephen Moore, and Peter Tanous, *The End of Prosperity: How Higher Taxes Will Doom the Economy—If We Let It Happen* (New York: Threshold Editions, 2008), pp. 29–42.

55 A. W. Phillips, "The Relation between Unemployment and the Rate of Change of Money Wage Rates in the United Kingdom, 1861–1957," *Economica*, 25 (100) (1958), pp. 283–299.

56 Marshall, *Principles of Economics*, p. 202.

57 Hong, "Shidu Jingjixue Sixiang de Kuaixueke Yanhua," p. 408.

58 Marshall, *Principles of Economics*, p. 202.

59 Hong, "Shidu Jingjixue Sixiang de Kuaixueke Yanhua," pp. 408–410.

60 Hong, *The Price of China's Economic Development*, pp. 2–10.

61 Benjamin Hett, *The Death of Democracy: Hitler's Rise to Power and the Downfall of the Weimar Republic* (New York: Henry Holt and Company, 2018), pp. 208–236.

62 Edwin Reischauer, *Japan: The Story of a Nation* (New York: Alfred A. Knopf, 1989).

63 Scott Snyder and Kyung-Ae Park, "North Korea in Transition: Evolution or Revolution?", in Scott Snyder and Kyung-Ae Park, eds., *North Korea in Transition: Politics, Economy, and Society* (New York: Rowman & Littlefield Publishers, Inc., 2019), pp. 275–294.

64 Peter Little, *Somalia: Economy without State* (Bloomington: Indiana University Press, 2003), pp. 1–20.

65 Jonathan Hughes and Louis Cain, *American Economic History* (New York: Pearson Education, Inc., 2011), pp. 163–183, 362–383.

66 Griffin and Mahon, "The Corporate Social Performance and Corporate Financial Performance Debate," pp. 5–31.

67 Robert Heller, *Bill Gates* (London: Dorling Kindersley, 2001).

68 Yosefa Loshitzky, ed., *Schindler's Holocaust: Critical Perspective on Schindler's List* (Bloomington: Indiana University Press, 1997), pp. 1–17.

69 Hong, "Shidu Jingjixue Sixiang de Kuaixueke Yanhua," p. 410.

70 Hong, "Shidu Jingjixue Sixiang de Kuaixueke Yanhua," p. 410.

71 Kenneth Arrow, "The Trade-off between Growth and Equity," in Kenneth Arrow, ed., *Collected Papers of Kenneth J. Arrow: Social Choice and Justice* (Cambridge, MA: The Belknap Press of Harvard University Press, 1983), pp. 190–200.

72 Hong, *Meizhong Shehui Yixiang Toushi*, p. 46.

73 Sirio Cividino, Rares Halbac-Cotoara-Zamfir, and Luca Salvati, "Revisiting the 'City Life Cycle': Global Urbanization and Implications for Regional Development," *Sustainability*, 12 (1151) (2020), pp. 1–18.

Chapter 8 Government Policy Principles in Propriety Economics

1 Arthur, *Complexity and the Economy*, p. 24.

2 Arthur, *Complexity and the Economy*, p. 104.

3 Arthur, *Complexity and the Economy*, p. 24.

4 Coase, "The Problem of Social Cost," p. 43.

5 Wang, "Zhongyong de Chaoyuexing Sixiang yu Pushixing Jiazhi," p. 146.

6 Shen Xu, *Shuowen Jiezi* [*Interpretation of Literature and Characters*] (Hangzhou: Zhejiang Ancient Books Publishing House, 2016).

7 Zi Si, *Zhongyong Quanjie.*

8 *Lun Yu.*

9 Pang, *Pang Pu Wenji,* p. 106.

10 Wang, "Zhongxi Sixiang Shi Shang de Zhongyong Zhidao," p. 39.

11 Jim Collins, *From Good to Great: Why Some Companies Make the Leap…and Others Don't* (New York: Harper Business, 2001), pp. 17–40.

12 Edgar Schein and Peter Schein, *Humble Leadership: The Power of Relationships, Openness, and Trust* (Oakland, CA: Berrett-Koehler Publishers, Inc., 2018), p. x.

13 *Lun Yu.*

14 Mencius, *Mengzi.*

15 Jing Li, "Cong Zhong, Yong dao Zhong Yong" ["From the Middle and Ordinary to Moderation"], *Kongzi Yanjiu* [*Confucius Studies*], 5 (2007), p. 46.

16 Hong, *Shehui Jingji Bianqian de Zhuti*, p. 100.

17 John Kenneth Galbraith, *A Short History of Financial Euphoria* (New York: Penguin Books, 1990); Quentin Skrabec, Jr., *The 100 Most Important American Financial Crises: An Encyclopedia of the Lowest Points in American Economic History* (New York: Greenwood, 2014).

18 Henry Rothstein, David Demeritt, Regine Paul, and Li Wang, "True to Type? How Governance Traditions Shaped Responses to Covid-19 in China, Germany, UK, and USA," in Patrick Brown and Jens Zinn, eds., *Covid-19 and the Sociology of Risk and Uncertainty— Studies of Social Phenomena and Social Theory Across 6 Continents* (New York: Palgrave Macmillan, 2022), pp. 115–143.

19 Qidong Zheng, "Shilun Qing Zhengfu Zhenya Taiping Tianguo hou de Rangbu Zhengce" ["A Discussion of the Qing Government's Concessions after the Suppression of the Taiping Rebellion"], *Study on Qing History*, 3 (2008), pp. 59–69.

20 David Ricardo, *On the Principles of Political Economy and Taxation* (Kitchener, Ontario: Batoche Books, 2001), pp. 85–103.

21 Nicolaus Tideman, *Collective Decision and Voting: The Potential for Public Choice* (Burlington, VT: Ashgate Publishing Company, 2006).

22 Gustave Le Bon, *The Crowd: A Study of the Popular Mind* (New York: The Macmillan Company, 1897).

23 Keynes, *The General Theory of Employment, Interest, and Money*, pp. 1–30.

24 *Lun Yu.*

25 Zhaohui Hong, "Shidu Jingjixue Sixiang de Kuaxueke Yanhua" ["The Interdisciplinary Evolution of Propriety Economic Thought"], *Nanguo Xueshu [South China Quarterly]*, 3 (2020), pp. 411–412; Xiangcan Zhong, "Zhongguo Gudai Neng Chansheng Shichang Jizhi Ma?" ["Can Market Mechanisms Emerge in Ancient China: A Discussion with Mr. Sheng Hong"], *Taishuo yu Zhengmin [Exploration and Debate]*, 2 (2004), pp. 19–20.

26 Arrow, "A Difficulty in the Concept of Social Welfare," pp. 328–346.

27 Gary De Krey, *Restoration and Revolution in Britain: A Political History of the Era of Charles II and the Glorious Revolution* (New York: Palgrave Macmillan, 2007).

28 Hong, "Shidu Jingjixue Sixiang de Kuaxueke Yanhua," p. 412.

29 Tian, *Gaoji Weiguan Jingjixue*, p. 677.

30 Marian Sawer, *The Ethical State? Social Liberalism in Australia* (Melbourne: Melbourne University Press, 2003), p. 87; also see Liankui Gao, *Fan Wudao: Yige Jingji Xuejia de Xingwu [Countering Misinformation: Awakening of an Economist]* (Beijing: Oriental Press, 2014).

31 Smith, *The Wealth of Nations*, p. 922.

32 Smith, *The Wealth of Nations*, p. 946.

33 Smith, *The Wealth of Nations*, pp. 963–976.

34 Christopher Dyer, "Conflict in the Landscape: The Enclosure Movement in England, 1220–1349," *Landscape History*, 28 (1) (2006), pp. 21–33.

35 Arrow, "The Trade-off between Growth and Equity," pp. 190–200.

36 Arthur, *Complexity and the Economy*, p. 105.

37 Arthur, *Complexity and the Economy,* pp. 103–104.

38 Justin Zobel, "When Measurement Misleads: The Limits of Batch Assessment of Retrieval Systems," *ACM SIGIR Forum*, 56 (1) (2022), pp. 1–20; Alec Chrystal and Paul Mizen, "Goodhart's Law: Its Origins, Meaning and Implications for Monetary Policy," working paper, cyberlibris.typepad.com/blog/files/ Goodharts_Law.pdf, 2001 (accessed March 1, 2020).

39 Arthur, *Complexity and the Economy*, p. 108.

40 Hong, *The Price of China's Economic Development*, pp. 40–42.

41 Arthur, *Complexity and the Economy*, p. 109.

42 U.S. Department of Justice, "Justice Department Announces Results of Nationwide COVID-19 Fraud Enforcement Action," *Office of Public Affairs, USDJ website*, August 23, 2023, www.justice.gov/opa/pr/justice-department-announces-results-nationwide-covid-19-fraud-enforcement-action (accessed January 4, 2024).

43 Arthur, *Complexity and the Economy*, p. 105.

44 Arthur, *Complexity and the Economy*, p. 110.

45 Arthur, *Complexity and the Economy*, p. 117.

46 David Colander and Roland Kupers, *Laissez-Faire Activism: The Complexity Frame for Policy* (Princeton, NJ: Princeton University Press, 2014). Cited from Arthur, *Complexity and the Economy*, p. 24.

47 Bernanke, "The Great Moderation."

48 Buttonwood, *The Economist*, "Economic Optimism Drives Stockmarket Highs," October 17, 2017.

49 Paul Samuelson, *Economics: An Introductory Analysis*, 19th ed. (New York: McGraw-Hill Book Co., 2009), p. 212.

50 The U.S. Federal Reserve's official website provides information on current and historical interest rates; the Bureau of Economic Analysis (BEA), part of the U.S. Department of Commerce, offers comprehensive data on GDP and related economic indicators; information on income inequality, such as Gini coefficient data, can be found on the U.S. Census Bureau's website; data related to the fiscal deficit and government finances is available on the U.S. Treasury's website; sources like Bloomberg, Reuters, *The Wall Street Journal*, and others often provide up-to-date information and analysis on these economic indicators; institutions like the World Bank, International Monetary Fund (IMF), and various universities and think tanks may also publish data and reports on these topics.

Chapter 9　Macro Case Studies of Propriety Economics

1 See Hong, *Shehui Jingji Bianqian de Zhuti.*

2 Eric Williams, *From Columbus to Castro: The History of the Caribbean 1492–1969* (London: Vintage Books, A Division of Random House, 1970), p. 48.

3 U.S. Bureau of the Census, *Historical Statistics of the United States, from Colonial Times to 1970* (Washington, D.C.: U.S. Government Printing Office, 1975), vol. 2, pp. 879–880.

4 John McCusker and Russell Menard, *The Economy of British America, 1607–1789* (Chapel Hill: North Carolina University Press, 1985), p. 285.

5 U.S. Bureau of the Census, *Historical Statistics of the United States*, pp. 889–890.

6 Smith, *The Wealth of Nations,* p. 582.

7 Albert Hirschman, *The Strategy of Economic Development* (New Haven, CT: Yale University Press, 1958), p. 121.

8 McCusker and Menard, *The Economy of British America, 1607–1789*, pp. 293, 281.

9 John McCusker and Barbara Petchenik, "Economic Activity," in John McCusker and Lester Cappon, eds., *Atlas of Early American History* (Princeton, NJ: Princeton University Press, 1976), pp. 26–27, 103–104.

10 McCusker and Menard, *The Economy of British America, 1607–1789*, p. 281.

11 Jacob Price, "Colonial Trade and British Economic Development, 1660–1775," *The International Journal of Law and Science*, 14 (1978), p. 109.

12 Gary Walton and James Shepherd, *The Economic Rise of Early America* (Cambridge: Cambridge University Press, 1979), p. 111.

13 McCusker and Menard, *The Economy of British America, 1607–1789*, pp. 62–63.

14 U.S. Bureau of the Census, *Historical Statistics of the United States*, p. 13.

15 Curtis Nettels, *The Emergence of a National Economy, 1775–1815* (New York: M. E. Sharpe, 1962), pp. 20–21.

16 McCusker and Menard, *The Economy of British America, 1607–1789*, pp. 373–374.

17 Hong, *Shehui Jingji Bianqian de Zhuti*, pp. 31–32.

18 Jacob Price, "A Note on the Value of Colonial Exports of Shipping," *Journal of Economic History*, 36 (1976), p. 722.

19 Jerome Reich, *Colonial America* (Englewood Cliffs, NJ: Pearson Education, Inc., 1989), pp. 85–86.

20 Reich, *Colonial America*, p. 165.

21 Brooke Hindle, ed., *America's Wooden Age: Aspects of Its Early Technology* (New York: Sleepy Hollow Restorations, 1975).

22 Reich, *Colonial America*, p. 70.

23 Walton and Shepherd, *The Economic Rise of Early America*, pp. 53–54.

24 Benjamin Franklin, *The Papers of Benjamin Franklin*, Leonard Labaree, ed. (New Haven, CT: Yale University Press, 1959), vol. 4, pp. 227–228.

25 Walton and Shepherd, *The Economic Rise of Early America*, pp. 53–54.

26 McCusker and Menard, *The Economy of British America, 1607–1789*, p. 118.

27 Walton and Shepherd, *The Economic Rise of Early America*, p. 54.

28 Gary Walton, "Colonial Economy," in Glenn Porter, ed., *Encyclopedia of American Economic History* (New York: Simon & Schuster Trade, 1980), vol. 1, p. 48.

29 U.S. Bureau of the Census, *Historical Statistics of the United States*, vol. 2, p. 1168.

30 Hong, *Shehui Jingji Bianqian de Zhuti*, pp. 47–48.

31 Thomas Berry, *Revised Annual Estimates of American Gross National Product: Preliminary Annual Estimates of Four Major Components of Demand, 1789–1889* (Richmond, VA: Bostwick Press, 1978), pp. 6–7

32 World Bank, *World Bank Atlas* (Washington, D.C.: World Bank Group, 1975), p. 8.

33 Phyllis Deane and William Cole, *British Economic Growth* (Cambridge: Cambridge University Press, 1967), p. 80.

34 Walton, "Colonial Economy," p. 48.

35 Walton, "Colonial Economy," p. 48.

36 McCusker and Menard, *The Economy of British America, 1607–1789*, p. 338.

37 Alice Jones, *Wealth of a Nation to Be: The American Colonies on the Eve of the Revolution* (New York: Columbia University Press, 1980), p. 265.

38 Jones, *Wealth of a Nation to Be*, p. 260.

39 H. J. Habakkuk, *American and British Technology in the Nineteenth Century* (Cambridge: Cambridge University Press, 1962), pp. 56–57.

40 Mary Norton, *A People and A Nation: A History of the United States* (Boston: Cengage Learning, 1990), vol. 1, pp. 248–249.

41 Peter McClelland, "Transportation," in Glenn Potter, ed., *Encyclopedia of American Economic History*, vol. 1, p. 310.

42 McClelland, "Transportation," pp. 310–311.

43 McClelland, "Transportation," pp. 314–326.

44 Habakkuk, *American and British Technology in the Nineteenth Century*, pp. 104–105.

45 Daniel Boorstin, *The Americans, The National Experience* (New York: Vintage Books, 1965), p. 34.

46 Hong, *Shehui Jingji Bianqian de Zhuti*, pp. 95–96.

47 Charles Dickens, *A Tale of Two Cities* (London: Penguin Books, 2000), p. 5.

48 Geoffrey Moore, "Business Cycles, Panics, and Depressions," in Glenn Potter, ed., *Encyclopedia of American Economic History*, vol. 1, pp. 151–156.

49 Edward Pessen, "Social Mobility," in Glenn Potter, ed., *Encyclopedia of American Economic History*, vol. 2, pp. 1127–1128.

50 Bootstin, *The Americans, The National Experience*, p. 78.

51 James Henretta, *America's History* (New York: Worth Publishers, 1993), vol. 1, p. 314.

52 John Cary, *The Social Fabric: American Life from 1607 to the Civil War* (Boston: Little, Brown and Co., 1989), vol. 1, p. 195.

53 Richard Current, *American History* (New York: Knopf, 1983), vol. 1, p. 360.

54 Current, *American History*, vol. 1, pp. 333–334.

55 Albert Fishlow, "The Common School Revival: Fact or Fancy?", in Henry Rosovsky, ed., *Industrialization in Two Systems* (New York: Wiley, 1966), pp. 63–65.

56 John Cary, *The Social Fabric* (Boston: Little, Brown & Co., 1989), vol. 1, p. 195.

57 Hong, *Shehui Jingji Bianqian de Zhuti*, pp. 105–107.

58 Hong, *Shehui Jingji Bianqian de Zhuti*, pp. 105–106.

59 Current, *American History*, p. 363.

60 David Rothman, *The Discovery of the Asylum, Social Order and Disorder in the New Republic* (New Haven, CT: Yale University, 1971), p. xix.

61 Hong, *Shehui Jingji Bianqian de Zhuti*, p. 123.

62 Hong, *Shehui Jingji Bianqian de Zhuti*, pp. 136–138.

63 Gerald Nash, "States and Local Governments," in Glenn Potter, ed., *Encyclopedia of American Economic History*, vol. 2, p. 515.

64 Hong, *Shehui Jingji Bianqian de Zhuti*, p. 245.

65 Current, *American History*, vol. 1, p. 241.

66 Nash, "States and Local Governments," p. 515.

67 U.S. Bureau of Land Management, *Public Land Statistics* (Washington, D.C.: The Bureau of Land Management's National Operations Center, 1974), p. 6, table 3.

68 Douglass North, *Growth and Welfare in the American Past: A New Economic History* (subsequent edition) (Englewood Cliffs, NJ: Prentice-Hall, Inc., 1982), p. 92.

69 Edward Kirkland, *A History of American Economic Life* (New York: Appleton-Century-Crofts, 1969), pp. 206–207.

70 Lawrence Friedman, *A History of American Law* (New York: Touchstone, 1973), p. 233.

71 Harry Scheiber, "Law and Political Institutions," in Glenn Potter, ed., *Encyclopedia of American Economic History*, vol. 2, p. 499.

72 Scheiber, "Law and Political Institutions," pp. 487–488.

73 James Hurst, *Law and the Conditions of Freedom in the Nineteenth Century United States* (Madison: The University of Wisconsin Press, 1956), p. 283.

74 Current, *American History*, vol. 1, p. 300.

75 Morton Horwitz, *The Transformation of American Law, 1780–1860: The Crises of Legal Orthodoxy* (Cambridge, MA: Harvard University Press, 1979), p. 28.

76 Scheiber, "Law and Political Institutions," p. 497.

77 Nash, "States and Local Governments," p. 517.

78 Hong, *Shehui Jingji Bianqian de Zhuti*, p. 252.

79 Allan Bogue, "Land Policies and Sales," in Glenn Potter, ed., *Encyclopedia of American Economic History*, vol. 2, p. 594.

80 U.S. Bureau of Land Management, *Public Land Statistics*, p. 6.

81 Paul Gates, "The Homestead Law in an Incongruous Land System," *American Historical Review*, 41 (1936), p. 681.

82 Kirkland, *A History of American Economic Life*, pp. 347, 350.

83 Paul Trescott, "Central Banking," in Glenn Potter, ed., *Encyclopedia of American Economic History*, vol. 2, p. 743.

84 Kirkland, *A History of American Economic Life*, p. 350.

85 Sidney Ratner, "Taxation," in Glenn Potter, ed., *Encyclopedia of American Economic History*, vol. 1, pp. 455–456.

86 Norton, *A People and A Nation: A History of the United States*, vol. 1, pp. 412–413.

87 J. J. Pincus, "Tariffs," in Glenn Potter, ed., *Encyclopedia of American Economic History*, vol. 1, pp. 440, 445.

88 Paul Boyer, *The Enduring Vision* (Boston: Wadsworth, 1993), vol. 2, p. 564.

89 Current, *American History*, vol. 1, p. 422.

90 Boyer, *The Enduring Vision*, vol. 2, p. 596.

91 Boyer, *The Enduring Vision*, vol. 2, p. 591.

92 Boyer, *The Enduring Vision*, vol. 2, p. 598.

93 See "Preamble," Constitution of the United States of America and Amendments. See Boyer, *The Enduring Vision*, vol. 2, p. A-9.

94 Ralph Henry Gabriel, *The Course of American Democratic Thought* (New York: Ronald Press Co., 1956), p. 205.

95 George Mowry, *The Progressive Era, 1900–20: The Reform Persuasion* (Washington, D.C.: American Historical Association, 1972), p. 5.

96 Zhaohui Hong, *Zhongguo Teshu Lun [The China Uniqueness—Dilemmas and Directions of China's Development]* (New York: Cozy House Publisher, 2004), p. 22.

97 Ratner, "Taxation," p. 456.

98 Boyer, *The Enduring Vision*, vol. 2, p. 748.

99 Boyer, *The Enduring Vision*, vol. 2, pp. 749, 756.

100 Hong, *Zhongguo Teshu Lun*, p. 23.

101 Ratner, "Taxation," p. 456.

102 Boyer, *The Enduring Vision*, vol. 2, pp. 750–752.

103 Bogue, "Land Policies and Sales," p. 588.

104 Boyer, *The Enduring Vision*, vol. 2, p. 747.

105 Boyer, *The Enduring Vision*, vol. 2, pp. 756–757.

106 U.S. Bureau of the Census, *Historical Statistics of the United States, from Colonial Period to 1957* (Washington, D.C.: U.S. Government Printing Office, 1960), p. 67.

107 Hong, *Shehui Jingji Bianqian de Zhuti*, pp. 264–267.

108 This section is mainly derived from the author's monograph: Zhaohui Hong, *Zhongguo Teshu Lun*, pp. 67–74.

109 Edward D. Berkowitz, *America's Welfare State: From Roosevelt to Reagan* (Baltimore, MD: The Johns Hopkins University Press, 1991), p. 5.

110 Neil Gilbert, *Capitalism and the Welfare State* (New Haven, CT: Yale University Press, 1983).

111 Michael Harrington, *The Other America: Poverty in the United States* (New York: Penguin Books, 1968), p. 167.

112 E. W. Kelley, *Policy and Politics in the United States: The Limits of Localism* (Philadelphia: Temple University Press, 1987), p. 240.

113 Lillian B. Rubin, "Maximum Feasible Participation: The Origins, Implications, and Present Status," *The Annals of the American Academy of Political and Social Science*, 385 (September 1969), p. 20.

114 Rubin, "Maximum Feasible Participation," p. 20.

115 Robert J. Lampman, *Ends and Means of Reducing Income Poverty* (Chicago: Markham, 1971), p. 7.

116 Gilbert, *Capitalism and the Welfare State*, p. 142.

117 Joel A. Devine and James D. Wright, *The Greatest of Evils: Urban Poverty and the American Underclass* (New York: Aldine De Gruyter, 1993), pp. 27–28.

118 Lawrence M. Mead, "Social Programs and Social Obligations," *The Public Interest*, 69 (3) (Fall 1982), pp. 17–32.

119 Harrell R. Rodgers, Jr., *Poor Women, Poor Family: The Economic Plight of America's Female-Headed Households* (Armonk, NY: M. E. Sharpe, 1990).

120 James Jennings, *Understanding the Nature of Poverty in Urban America* (Westport, CT: Praeger, 1994), pp. 40–41.

121 David Stoesz, "Poor Policy: The Legacy of the Kerner Commission for Social Welfare," *North Carolina Law Review*, 71 (5) (1993), p. 1680.

122 Jennings, *Understanding the Nature of Poverty in Urban America*, p. 116, table 13.

123 Rodgers, *Poor Women, Poor Family*, p. 120.

124 Jennings, *Understanding the Nature of Poverty in Urban America*, p. 36.

125 Laurie Udesky, "Welfare Reform and Its Victims," *The Nation*, September 24, 1990.

126 Michael Abramowitz, "Doledrums," *The New Republic*, 206 (March 30, 1992), pp. 16–18.

127 K. Sue Jewell, *Survival of the Black Family: The Institutional Impact of U.S. Social Policy* (Westport, CT: Praeger, 1988), p. 57.

128 U.S. Bureau of the Census, *Current Population Reports: Poverty in the United States: 1990*, Series, P-60, No. 175 (Washington, D.C.: U.S. Government Printing Office, 1991), table 16.

129 U.S. Bureau of the Census, *Current Population Reports: Poverty in the United States: 2002*, Series, P 60-219 (Washington, D.C.: U.S. Government Printing Office, 2002), p. 7.

130 Devine and Wright, *The Greatest of Evils*, p. 28.

131 U.S. Bureau of the Census, *Current Population Reports: Poverty in the United States: 2002*, p. 11.

132 U.S. Bureau of the Census, *Current Population Reports: Poverty in the United States: 1990*, table A.

133 Corbett, "Child Poverty and Welfare Reform: Progress or Paralyses?", p. 4.

134 U.S. Bureau of the Census, *Current Population Reports: Poverty in the United States: 2002*, p. 7.

135 Ezell Eyen, "Jianshao Pinkun de Zhengzhi" ["The Politics of Poverty Reduction"], *Journal of International Social Sciences*, 17 (2000), p. 44.

136 Eyen, "Jianshao Pinkun de Zhengzhi," p. 44.

137 Hong, *The Price of China's Economic Development*, pp. 100–101.

138 Xiaoguang Kang, "Weilan 3–5 Nian Zhongguo Dalu Zhengzhi Wendingxing Fenxi" ["Analysis of Political Stability in Mainland China in the Next 3–5 Years"], *Strategy and Management*, 2 (2002), p. 11.

139 George Clare, "Xiaochu Pinkun yu Shehui Zhenghe" ["Poverty Eradication and Social Integration: The British Position"], *Journal of International Social Sciences*, 4 (2000), p. 49.

140 Office of High Commissioner in United Nations Human Rights, *International Covenant on Economic, Social and Cultural Rights*, 1966, www.ohchr.org/en/instruments-mechanisms/instruments/international-covenant-economic-social-and-cultural-rights (accessed November 7, 2023).

141 Christopher Edley, Jr., *Not All Black and White: Affirmative Action, Race, and American Values* (New York: Hill and Wang, 1996).

142 Zhaohui Hong, "Shehui Gongzheng yu Zhongguo de Zhengzhi Gaige" ["Social Justice and Political Reform in China"], *Contemporary China Studies*, 1 (1999), pp. 13–33.

143 Hong, *Shehui Jingji Zhuanxing de Zhuti*, pp. 74–80.

144 Zhenfeng Han, "The Origin and Development of the Reform Method of 'Crossing the River by Feeling for Stones'," *Guangming Daily*, April 9, 2014, column 14.

145 Hong, *The Price of China's Economic Development*, pp. 193–199.

146 Zhaohui Hong, "Comparative Studies on Land Reform Advancement between Mainland China and Taiwan," *Asian Profile*, 25 (2), pp. 1–23.

147 Zhaohui Hong, "Zhongguo Xiangzhen Qiye Chanquan Gaige yu Zhongyang" ["Property Rights Reform of Chinese Township Enterprises and the Interaction of Central-Local Power"], *Contemporary China Study*, 2 (1995), pp. 23–41; Zhaohui Hong, "Gufen Hezuozhi Gaige yu Zhongguo Dalu Xiangzhen Jiti Qiye" ["Shareholding Cooperative Reform and Collective Enterprises in Mainland China's Townships"], *Mainland China Studies*, 4 (1996), pp. 6–17.

148 Zhaohui Hong, "Reform of Township-Village Enterprises and Local-Central Relations in China—A Case Study of Zhejiang Province," *Asian Thought & Society: An International Review*, 23 (September–December 1998), pp. 198–211; Zhaohui Hong and Hong Liang, "Cultural Dimensions of China's Corporate Government Reform," *Asian Thought and Society*, 25 (75), pp. 304–321.

149 Bingxin Hu, *Breaking Grounds—The Journal of a Top Chinese Woman Manager in Retail*, Chengchi Wang, trans. (Paramus, NJ: Homa & Sekey Books, 2004); Shumin Zhu, Hua Yang, and Hailin Wang, "Nianyu Xiaoying yu Xiandan Tushuguan Renli Ziyuan Guanli" ["Catfish Effect and Human Resource Management in Modern Libraries"], *Journal of Hunan Industry University*, 10 (2004), pp. 89–90.

150 Zhaohui Hong, "Lun Zhongguo Nongmingong de Shehui Quanli Pinkun" ["On the Poverty of Social Rights for Migrant Workers in China"], *Contemporary China Studies*, 4 (2007), pp. 56–76.

151 Cheng He Guan and Peter Rowe, "The Concept of Urban Intensity and China's Townization Policy: Cases from Zhejiang Province," *Cities*, 55 (2016), p. 22.

Chapter 10   Conclusion

1 Deji Fan, *Shige* [*Poetic Style*]. See "Meiri Toutiao" ["Daily Headlines"], February 25, 2017, kknews.cc/culture/oygn82m.html (accessed March 1, 2020).

2 Pang, *Pang Pu Wenji*, pp. 109–110.

3 Xenophon, *Oeconomicus* (Oxford: Oxford University Press, 1995).

4 Zhaohui Hong, *Zuoyou Zhijian Liangji Zhishan: Shidu Jingjixue Daolun* [*Conceptualizing Propriety in Economic Thought*] (Hong Kong: City University of Hong Kong Press, 2021), p. 183.

5 Hong, *Zuoyou Zhijian Liangji Zhishan,* pp. 183–184.

6 Paul Romer, "Mathiness in the Theory of Economic Growth," *American Economic Review*, 105 (5) (2015), pp. 89–93.

7 Arthur, *Complexity and the Economy*, p. xx.

8 Frank Knight, *Risk, Uncertainty, and Profit—Economic Theory of Uncertainty in Business Enterprises, and Its Connection to Profit and Prosperity in Society* (New York: Adansonia Press, 2018), pp. 7–33, 347–376.

9 W. Brian Arthur, "Bulanen Fangtanlu" ["Interviews with Brian Arthur"] in Arthur, *Fuza Jingjixue*, p. xvi.

10 Paul Samuelson, *Foundations of Economic Analysis* (Cambridge, MA: Harvard University Press, 1983). Cited from Arthur, *Complexity and the Economy*, pp. 4–5.

11 William Tabb, *Reconstructing Political Economy* (New York: Routledge, 1999). Cited from Arthur, *Complexity and the Economy*, p. 5, footnote 5.

12 Arthur, "Bulanen Fantailu," p. xviii.

13 Arthur, *Complexity and the Economy*, p. 4.

14 Arthur, *Complexity and the Economy*, p. 20.

15 Hong, *Zuoyou Zhijian Liangji Zhishang*, p. 189.

16 Zhaohui Hong, "Shidu Jingjixue Sixiang de Kuaxueke Yanhua" ["Interdisciplinary Evolution of Propriety Economic Thought"], *Nanguo Xueshu [South China Quarterly]*, 3 (2020), pp. 412–413.

17 Hong, *Zuoyou Zhijian Liangji Zhishang*, p. 183.

18 Joan Robinson, "Time in Economic Theory," *Kyklos*, 33 (2) (1980), pp. 219–229. See Arthur, *Complexity and the Economy*, p. 23.

19 Arthur, *Complexity and the Economy*, p. 23.

20 W. Brian Arthur, *Increasing Returns and Path Dependence in the Economy* (Ann Arbor: University of Michigan Press, 1994); Elhanan Helpman and Paul Krugman, *Market Structure and Foreign Trade* (Cambridge, MA: MIT Press, 1985); W. Brian Arthur, "Competing Technologies, Increasing Returns, and Lock-in by Historical Events," *The Economic Journal*, 99 (394) (1989), pp. 116–131.

21 Hong, *Zuoyou Zhijian Liangji Zhishang*, pp. 193–194.

22 Arthur, *Complexity and the Economy*, p. xii.

23 David Hume, *A Treatise of Human Nature*, p. 453.

24 Friedrich Nietzsche, *Beiju de Daisheng [The Birth of Tragedy]* (Shanghai: Sanlian Shudian, 1986), pp. 6, 15. Cited from Tonglu Li, "Zhouzuoren: Zhongguo Xiandai Jiegou Piping de Xianqu" ["Zhouzuoren: Pioneers of Modern Chinese Deconstruction Criticism"], in Ying Wang, ed., *Wenxue Lilun Qianyan (3) [Frontiers in Literary Theory (3rd Series)]* (Beijing: Beijing University Press, 2006), pp. 276–277.

25 Marshall, *Principles of Economics*, pp. 1–11.

26 Max Weber, *General Economic History* (New York: Cosimo, Inc., 2007), p. 271.

27 Abraham Pais, *Subtle is the Lord: The Science and the Life of Albert Einstein* (Oxford: Oxford University Press, 2005), p. vi; Max Jammer, *Einstein and Religion: Physics and Theology* (Princeton, NJ: Princeton University Press, 2011), p. 94.

28 Friedrich Hayek, *The Road to Serfdom* (Chicago: The University of Chicago Press, 2011), pp. 47–56.

29 Samuel Rima, *Spiritual Capital: A Moral Core for Social and Economic Justice* (London and New York: Routledge, 2013), pp. 109–130.

30 Mark Lutz, *Economics for the Common Good: Two Centuries of Economic Thought in the Humanist Tradition* (London and New York: Routledge, 1999), pp. 15–18; Howard Bowen, "Toward a Humanist Economics," *Nebraska Journal of Economics and Business*, 11 (4) (1972), pp. 9–24.

31 Deirdre Nansen McCloskey, *Bettering Humanomics—A New, and Old, Approach to Economic Science* (Chicago: The University of Chicago Press, 2021), pp. 3–8.

32 Arthur, *Complexity and the Economy*, pp. 22–23.

33 The contents of the two columns on the left and in the middle are compiled from Arthur, *Complexity and the Economy*, pp. 189–191.

34 Samuelson, *Economics*.

35 Samuelson, *Economics,* p. 212.

36 Arthur, *Complexity and the Economy*, p. 172.

37 Arthur, *Complexity and the Economy*, pp. xx–xxi.

38 Dorothea Hilhorst and Rodrigo Mena, "When Covid-19 Meets Conflict: Politics of the Pandemic Response in Fragile and Conflict—Affected States," *Disasters*, 45 (1) (2021), pp. S174–S194.

39 Thomas Piketty, *Capital in the Twenty-First Century* (Cambridge, MA: The Belknap Press of Harvard University Press, 2014); Thomas Piketty, *Capital and Ideology* (Cambridge, MA: The Belknap Press of Harvard University Press, 2020).

40 Hong, *Zuoyou Zhijian Liangji Zhishan*.

41 Lu Xun, "Kong Yiji" ["Kong Yiji"], *New Youth Magazine*, 6 (4) (1919), p. 15.

References

Abramowitz, Michael. (1992). "Doledrums," *The New Republic*, 206 (March 30):16–18.

Ahmad, Syed. (1990). "Adam Smith's Four Invisible Hands," *History of Political Economy*, 22:142–150.

Alchian, Armen A. (1965). "Some Economics of Property Rights," *Politico*, 30 (4):818–840.

Anderson, Philip W. (1972). "More is Different," *Science*, 177 (4047):393–396.

Anonymous. (2016). *Erya Yizhu* [*Erya Translation and Commentary*]. Shanghai: Shanghai Ancient Books Publishing House.

Anonymous, ed. (2017). *Shangshu* [*The Books of Shang*]. Prague: Arts & Crafts Publishing House.

Anonymous, ed. (2018). *Zhouli* [*Rites of Zhou*]. Beijing: Zhongzhou Ancient Books Publishing House.

Aristotle. (1999). *Nicomachean Ethics*. Kitchener, Ontario: Batoche Books.

Arrow, Kenneth. (1950). "A Difficulty in the Concept of Social Welfare," *Journal of Political Economy*, 58 (4):328–346.

Arrow, Kenneth. (1983). "The Principle of Rationality in Collective Decisions," in Kenneth Arrow, ed., *Collected Papers of Kenneth J. Arrow: Social Choice and Justice*, pp. 45–58. Cambridge, MA: The Belknap Press of Harvard University Press.

Arrow, Kenneth. (1983). "The Trade-off between Growth and Equity," in Kenneth Arrow, ed., *Collected Papers of Kenneth J. Arrow: Social Choice and Justice*, pp. 190–200. Cambridge, MA: The Belknap Press of Harvard University Press.

Arthur, W. Brian. (1989). "Competing Technologies, Increasing Returns, and Lock-in by Historical Events," *The Economic Journal*, 99 (394):116–131.

Arthur, W. Brian. (1994). *Increasing Returns and Path Dependence in the Economy*. Ann Arbor: University of Michigan Press.

Arthur, W. Brian. (1999). "Complexity and the Economy," *Science*, 284 (107):108–110.

Arthur, W. Brian. (2015). *Complexity and the Economy*. New York: Oxford University Press.

Arthur, W. Brian. (2018). "Bulanen Fangtanlu" ["Interviews with Brian Arthur"] in W. Brian Arthur, *Fuza Jingjixue* [*Complexity and the Economy*], pp. i–xvi. Hangzhou: Zhejiang People's Press.

Arthur, W. Brian and Wolfgang Polak. (2006). "The Evolution of Technology within a Simple Computer Model," *Complexity*, 11 (5):23–31.

Axelrod, Robert and W. D. Hamilton. (1981). "The Evolution of Cooperation," *Science*, 211 (4489):1390–1396.

Ayres, Clarence. (1971). *Toward a Reasonable Society*. Austin: University of Texas Press.

Bennett, Nathan and G. James Lemoine. (2014). "What VUCA Really Means for You," *Harvard Business Review*, (January–February):27–40.

Berkowitz, Edward D. (1991). *America's Welfare State: From Roosevelt to Reagan*. Baltimore, MD: The Johns Hopkins University Press.

Bernanke, Ben. (2013). "The Great Moderation," *Federal Reserve History*, November 22. www.federalreservehistory.org/essays/great_moderation.

Berry, Thomas. (1978). *Revised Annual Estimates of American Gross National Product: Preliminary Annual Estimates of Four Major Components of Demand, 1789–1889*. Richmond, VA: Bostwick Press.

Blaug, Mark. (1992). *The Methodology of Economics: Or, How Economists Explain*. Cambridge: Cambridge University Press.

Boole, George. (1847). *The Mathematical Analysis of Logic, Being an Essay towards a Calculus of Deductive Reasoning*. London: Macmillan, Barclay, & Macmillan.

Boorstin, Daniel. (1965). *The Americans, The National Experience*. New York: Vintage Books.

Bowen, Howard. (1972). "Toward a Humanist Economics," *Nebraska Journal of Economics and Business*, 11 (4):9–24.

Bowles, Samuel. (1998). "Endogenous Preferences: The Cultural Consequences of Markets and Other Economic Institutions," *Journal of Economic Literature,* 36 (1):75–111.

Boyer, Paul. (1993). *The Enduring Vision*. Vol. 2. Boston: Wadsworth.

Bush, Paul D. (1987). "The Theory of Institutional Change," *Journal of Economic Issues*, 21 (3):1075–1090.

Buttonwood, *The Economist*. (2017). "Economic Optimism Drives Stockmarket Highs," October 17.

Carroll, Lewis. (2015). *A Survey of Symbolic Logic*. London: Forgotten Books.

Cary, John. (1989). *The Social Fabric: American Life from 1607 to the Civil War*. Boston: Little, Brown & Co.

Castellani, Marco. (2019). "Does Culture Matter for the Economic Performance of Countries? An Overview of the Literature," *The Society for Policy Modeling*, 41 (4):703–717.

Chen, Xiang. (2007). *Gu Ling Ji [Ancient Spirit Collection]*, vol. 12, in Zhonghua Dadian Gongzuo Weiyuanhui [Chinese Canon Working Committee], ed., *Zhonghua Dadian [The Chinese Canon]*. Kunming: Yunnan Education Publishing House.

Cheng, Yi. (2016). *Zhouyi Chengsi Zhuang [Cheng's Biography of Zhou Yi]*. Beijing: China Book Bureau.

Cheung, Steven. (1973). "The Fable of the Bees: An Economic Investigation," *Journal of Law and Economics*, 16 (1):11–33.

Chrystal, Alec and Paul Mizen. (2001). "Goodhart's Law: Its Origins, Meaning and Implications for Monetary Policy," working paper, November 15–16. cyberlibris.typepad.com/blog/files/Goodharts_Law.pdf.

Cicero. (1990). *De Officiis, Latin Text with an English Translation by Walter Miller*. Cambridge, MA: Harvard University Press.

Cividino, Sirio, Rares Halbac-Cotoara-Zamfir, and Luca Salvati. (2020). "Revisiting the 'City Life Cycle': Global Urbanization and Implications for Regional Development," *Sustainability*, 12 (1151):1–18.

Clare, George. (2000). "Xiaochu Pinkun yu Shehui Zhenghe" ["Poverty Eradication and Social Integration: The British Position"], *Journal of International Social Sciences*, 4:49–55.

Clarke, Arthur C. (1990). *The Ghost from the Grand Banks*. London: Gollancz.

Coase, Ronald H. (1937). "The Nature of the Firm," *Economica*, 4 (16):386–405.

Coase, Ronald H. (1959). "The Federal Communications Commission," *Journal of Law and Economics*, 2 (October):1–40.

Coase, Ronald H. (1960). "The Problem of Social Cost," *Journal of Law and Economics*, 3 (October):1–44.

Colander, David and Roland Kupers. (2014). *Laissez-Faire Activism: The Complexity Frame for Policy*. Princeton, NJ: Princeton University Press.

Collins, Jim. (2001). *From Good to Great: Why Some Companies Make the Leap…and Others Don't.* New York: Harper Business.

Commons, John. (1936). "Institutional Economics," *American Economic Review,* 26 (1):237–249.

Commons, John. (1967). *A Sociological View of Sovereignty.* New York: Augustus M. Kelley.

Commons, John. (1995). *Legal Foundation of Capitalism.* New Brunswick, NJ: Transaction Publishers.

Crosona, Rachel and Simon Gächterb. (2010). "The Science of Experimental Economics," *Journal of Economic Behavior & Organization,* 73 (1):122–131.

Cuito, Aurora and Cristina Montes. (2002). *Antoni Gaudi: Complete Works.* Madrid: H. Kliczkowski-Only Book.

Current, Richard. (1983). *American History.* Vol. 1. New York: Knopf.

Dai, Sheng, ed. (2017). *Liji – Zhongyong [Rites of Passage – Zhong Yong].* Prague: Yea Publishing House.

Daley, Beth. (2023). "Economics Nobel 2019: Why Banerjee, Duflo and Kremer won," *The Conversation,* October 14, 2019. theconversation.com/economics-nobel-2019-why-banerjee-duflo-and-kremer-won-125276.

de Chobham, Thomas. (1968). *Summa Confessorum.* Paris: Béatrice Nauwelaerts.

De Krey, Gary. (2007). *Restoration and Revolution in Britain: A Political History of the Era of Charles II and the Glorious Revolution.* New York: Palgrave Macmillan.

Deane, Phyllis and William Cole. (1967). *British Economic Growth.* Cambridge: Cambridge University Press.

Deng, Julong. (1982). "Control Problems of Grey Systems," *Systems and Control Letters,* 5:288–294.

Deng, Julong. (1989). "Introduction to Grey System Theory," *The Journal of Grey System,* 1:1–24.

Devine, Joel A. and James D. Wright. (1993). *The Greatest of Evils: Urban Poverty and the American Underclass.* New York: Aldine De Gruyter.

Dickens, Charles. (2000). *A Tale of Two Cities.* London: Penguin Books.

Diderot, Denis. (2016). "Regrets on Parting with My Old Dressing Gown," translated by Kate Tunstall and Katie Scott. *Oxford Art Journal,* 29 (2):175–184.

Dyer, Christopher. (2006). "Conflict in the Landscape: The Enclosure Movement in England, 1220–1349," *Landscape History*, 28 (1):21–33.

Editorial. (1952). "The Uneasy Triangle," *The Economist*, August 9.

Edley, Christopher, Jr. (1996). *Not All Black and White: Affirmative Action, Race, and American Values*. New York: Hill and Wang.

Epstein, Richard. (1985). *Takings: Private Property and the Power of Eminent Domain*. Cambridge, MA: Harvard University Press.

Erickson, Millard. (1998). *Christian Theology*. Grand Rapids, MI: Baker Books.

Eyen, Ezell. (2000). "Jianshao Pinkun de Zhengzhi" ["The Politics of Poverty Reduction"], *Journal of International Social Sciences*, 17:40–48.

Fan, Deji. (2017). *Shige [Poetic Style]*. "Meiri Toutiao" ["Daily Headlines"]. kknews.cc/culture/oygn82m.html.

Fine, Gail. (2014). *The Possibility of Inquiry: Meno's Paradox from Socrates to Sextus*. Oxford: Oxford University Press.

Fishlow, Albert. (1966). "The Common School Revival: Fact or Fancy?", in Henry Rosovsky, ed., *Industrialization in Two Systems*. New York: Wiley.

Fogel, Robert. (1989). *Without Consent or Contract: The Rise and Fall of American Slavery*. New York: W. W. Norton & Company.

Fogel, Robert and Stanley Engerman. (1974). *Time on the Cross—The Economics of American Negro Slavery*. New York: W. W. Norton & Company.

Franklin, Benjamin. (1959). *The Papers of Benjamin Franklin*, Leonard Labaree, ed. Vol. 4. New Haven, CT: Yale University Press.

Friedman, Lawrence. (1973). *A History of American Law*. New York: Touchstone.

Fukuyama, Francis. (2016). *Xinren: Shehui Meide yu Chuangzhao Jingji Fanrong [Trust: The Social Virtues and the Creation of Prosperity]*. Guilin: Guangxi Normal University Press.

Gabriel, Ralph Henry. (1956). *The Course of American Democratic Thought*. New York: Ronald Press Co.

Galbraith, John Kenneth. (1990). *A Short History of Financial Euphoria*. New York: Penguin Books.

Gan, Xiaoqing and Kezhen Yuan. (2017). "Cong Zhouxin Shidai de Zhonghe Sixiang dao Xiandai Wenming Duihua" ["From the Axial

Age of Neutral Thought to the Dialogue of Modern Civilization"], *Hunan Shehui Kexue [Journal of Shenzhen University]*, 3:21–25.

Gao, Liankui. (2014). *Fan Wudao: Yige Jingji Xuejia de Xingwu [Countering Misinformation: Awakening of an Economist]*. Beijing: Oriental Press.

Gates, Paul. (1936). "The Homestead Law in an Incongruous Land System," *American Historical Review*, 41:652–681.

Gilbert, Neil. (1983). *Capitalism and the Welfare State*. New Haven, CT: Yale University Press.

Glaeser, Edward, David Laibson, Jose Scheinkman, and Christine Soutter. (2000). "Measuring Trust," *Quarterly Journal of Economics*, 115 (3):811–846.

Glaser, Barney G. and Anselm Strauss. (2017). *The Discovery of Grounded Theory: Strategies for Qualitative Research*. New York: Routledge.

Gödel, Kurt. (1986). *Collected Works. I: Publications 1929–1936*. Oxford: Oxford University Press.

Gribbin, John. (2011). *In Search of Schrödinger's Cat: Quantum Physics and Reality*. New York: Random House Publishing Group.

Griffin, Jennifer J. and John F. Mahon. (1997). "The Corporate Social Performance and Corporate Financial Performance Debate: Twenty-five Years of Incomparable Research," *Business and Society*, 36 (5):5–31.

Guan, Cheng He and Peter Rowe. (2016). "The Concept of Urban Intensity and China's Townization Policy: Cases from Zhejiang Province," *Cities*, 55:22–41.

Guan, Zi. (1986). *Guan Zi [Guanzi – Zuhe]*, in *Zhongzi Jicheng 5*. Shanghai: Shanghai Bookstore.

Guiso, Luigi, Paola Sapienza, and Luigi Zingales. (2006). "Does Culture Affect Economic Outcomes?", *Journal of Economic Perspectives*, 20 (2):23–48.

Guo, Yuhua. (2019). "Daodu: Fushan de Huiyan" ["Introduction: Fukuyama's Wise Eyes: The Accumulation of Social Capital and the Power of the Self-Society"], in Francis Fukuyama, *Xinren: Shehui Meide yu Chuangzhao Jingji Fanrong [Trust: The Social Virtues and the Creation of Prosperity]*, pp. i–xiii. Guilin: Guangxi Normal University Press.

Habakkuk, H. J. (1962). *American and British Technology in the Nineteenth Century*. Cambridge: Cambridge University Press.

Hahn, Frank. (1991). "Next Hundred Years," *Economic Journal*, 101 (404):47–50.

Hamakawa, Yoshihiro. (2002). "New Energy Option for 21st Century: Recent Progress in Solar Photovoltaic Energy Conversion," *Japan Society of Applied Physics International*, 5:993–998.

Han, Feizi. (1986). *Han Feizi* [*Han Feizi – Yang Quan*], in *Zhuzi Jicheng 5*. Shanghai: Shanghai Bookstore.

Han, Xing. (2018). "Xu Fuguan Xingerzhongxue Taiwei" ["Xu Fuguan's Exploration of the Metaphysical Middle School"], *Heilongjiang Shehui Kexue* [*Social Sciences of Heilongjiang*], 3:101–109.

Han, Zhenfeng. (2014). "The Origin and Development of the Reform Method of 'Crossing the River by Feeling for Stones'," *Guangming Daily*, April 9, Column 14.

Hanson, Norwood. (1958). *Patterns of Discovery*. Cambridge: Cambridge University Press.

Harrington, Michael. (1968). *The Other America: Poverty in the United States*. New York: Penguin Books.

Harrison, Lawrence E. (2000). "Why Culture Matters," in Lawrence E. Harrison and Samuel P. Huntington, eds., *Culture Matters: How Values Shape Human Progress*, pp. xvii–xxxiv. New York: Basic Books.

Hayek, Friedrich. (2011). *The Road to Serfdom*. Chicago: The University of Chicago Press.

Heller, Robert. (2001). *Bill Gates*. London: Dorling Kindersley.

Helpman, Elhanan and Paul Krugman. (1985). *Market Structure and Foreign Trade*. Cambridge, MA: MIT Press.

Henderson, David R., ed. (2000). "Joseph Schumpeter," *The Concise Encyclopedia of Economics, Library of Economics and Liberty*. www.econlib.org/library/Enc/bios/Schumpeter.html.

Henretta, James. (1993). *America's History*. New York: Worth Publishers.

Hett, Benjamin. (2018). *The Death of Democracy: Hitler's Rise to Power and the Downfall of the Weimar Republic*. New York: Henry Holt and Company.

Hicks, John. (1969). *A Theory of Economic History*. Oxford: Oxford University Press.

Hilhorst, Dorothea and Rodrigo Mena. (2021). "When Covid-19 Meets Conflict: Politics of the Pandemic Response in Fragile and Conflict—Affected States," *Disasters*, 45:S174–S194.

Hindle, Brooke, ed. (1975). *America's Wooden Age: Aspects of Its Early Technology*. New York: Sleepy Hollow Restorations.

Hirschman, Albert. (1958). *The Strategy of Economic Development*. New Haven, CT: Yale University Press.

Hodgson, Geoffrey M. (1993). *Economics and Evolution: Bringing Life Back into Economics*. Cambridge, UK and Ann Arbor, MI: Polity Press and University of Michigan Press.

Holland, John. (2019). *Yinzhixu—Shiyingxing Zaojiu Fuzaxing* [*Hidden Order: How Adaptation Builds Complexity*]. Xiaomu Zhou and Hui Han, trans. Shanghai: Shanghai Technological Education Press.

Holton, Judith A. and Isabelle Walsh. (2017). *Classic Grounded Theory: Applications with Qualitative & Quantitative Data*. Los Angeles: SAGE.

Hong, Handing. (2001). *Quanshi Xue: Ta de Lishi he Dangdai Fazhan* [*Hermeneutics: Its History and Contemporary Development*]. Beijing: People's Publishing House.

Hong, Zhaohui. (1988). "Zhongguan Shixue Daolun" ["Introduction to Meso-History"], *Guangming Daily—History*, January 8.

Hong, Zhaohui. (1994). *Shehui Jingji Bianqian de Zhuti* [*The Themes of Social Economic Transition: Reinterpretation on the Process of American Modernization*]. Hangzhou: Hangzhou University Press.

Hong, Zhaohui. (1995). "Zhongguo Xiangzhen Qiye Chanquan Gaige yu Zhongyang" ["Property Rights Reform of Chinese Township Enterprises and the Interaction of Central-Local Power"], *Contemporary China Study*, 2:23–41.

Hong, Zhaohui. (1996). "Comparative Studies on Land Reform Advancement between Mainland China and Taiwan," *Asian Profile*, 24 (4):1–23.

Hong, Zhaohui. (1996). "Gufen Hezuozhi Gaige yu Zhongguo Dalu Xiangzhen Jiti Qiye" ["Shareholding Cooperative Reform and Collective Enterprises in Mainland China's Townships"], *Mainland China Studies*, 4:6–17.

Hong, Zhaohui. (1998). "Reform of Township-Village Enterprises and Local-Central Relations in China—A Case Study of Zhejiang Province," *Asian Thought & Society: An International Review*, 23 (September–December):198–211.

Hong, Zhaohui. (1999). "Shehui Gongzheng yu Zhongguo de Zhengzhi Gaige" ["Social Justice and Political Reform in China"], *Contemporary China Studies*, 1:13–33.

Hong, Zhaohui. (2004). *Zhongguo Teshu Lun [The China Uniqueness—Dilemmas and Directions of China's Development]*. New York: Cozy House Publisher.

Hong, Zhaohui. (2007). "Lun Zhongguo Nongmingong de Shehui Quanli Pinkun" ["On the Poverty of Social Rights for Migrant Workers in China"], *Contemporary China Studies*, 4:56–76.

Hong, Zhaohui. (2015). *The Price of China's Economic Development: Power, Capital, and the Poverty of Rights*. Lexington: The University Press of Kentucky.

Hong, Zhaohui. (2020). "Shidu Jingjixue Sixiang de Kuaxueke Yanhua" ["Interdisciplinary Evolution of Propriety Economic Thought"], *Nanguo Xueshu [South China Quarterly]*, 3:397–413.

Hong, Zhaohui. (2020). "Shui Nongdiu le Meiguo—Zhongmei Guanxi Jiju Ehua Xinjie" ["Who Lost America?—A New Interpretation of the Rapid Deterioration of U.S.-China Relations"], *Dangdai Zhongguo Pinglun [Contemporary China Review Quarterly]*, 2:70–81.

Hong, Zhaohui. (2021). *Meizhong Shehui Yixiang Toushi [Critical Reflections on Social Issues in the United States and China]*. New York: Bouden House.

Hong, Zhaohui. (2021). "'Yizhi Kanbujian Shou' de Bainian Wudu—Wenxian Huanyuan Yadang Simi de Yinyu" ["Demystifying an Enduring Fallacy: Adam Smith's 'Invisible Hand'"], *Naguo Xueshu [South China Quarterly]*, 1:4–15.

Hong, Zhaohui. (2021). *Zuoyou Zhijian Liangji Zhishang: Shidu Jingjixue Daolun [Conceptualizing Propriety in Economic Thought]*. Hong Kong: City University of Hong Kong Press.

Hong, Zhaohui. (2022). "Wenxian Huaiyuan Yadang Simi de Shichang Zhenyi" ["Authenticating Adam Smith: Re-Examination and Reinterpretation of the Market Theory"], *Nanguo Xueshu [South China Quarterly]*, 1:4–16.

Hong, Zhaohui and Jianfeng Jin. (2016). "The Digital and Spatial Study of Catholic Market in Urban China," in Xiaobing Li and Xiansheng Tian, eds., *Urban Cry: Power vs. People in Chinese Cities*, pp. 121–134. New York: Lexington Books.

Hong, Zhaohui and Jianfeng Jin. (2016). "Spatial Study of Mosques: Xinjiang and Ningxia as Case Studies," *Review of Religion and Chinese Society*, 3 (2):223–260.

Hong, Zhaohui and Hong Liang. (2000). "Cultural Dimensions of China's Corporate Government Reform," *Asian Thought and Society*, 25 (75):304–321.

Hong, Zhaohui and Yi Sun. (1999). "The Butterfly Effect and the Making of 'Ping-Pong Diplomacy'," *Journal of Contemporary China*, 9 (25):429–448.

Hong, Zhaohui, Jiamin Yan, and Lu Cao. (2014). "Spatial and Statistical Perspectives on the Protestant Church Shortage in China: Case Studies in Hangzhou, Zhengzhou, Hefei and Fuzhou Cities," *Journal of Third World Studies*, 31 (1):81–99.

Horwitz, Morton. (1979). *The Transformation of American Law, 1780–1860: The Crises of Legal Orthodoxy*. Cambridge, MA: Harvard University Press.

Hu, Bingxin. (2004). *Breaking Grounds—The Journal of a Top Chinese Woman Manager in Retail*, Chengchi Wang, trans. Paramus, NJ: Homa & Sekey Books.

Hudson, Michael. (2013). "The Bubble Economy: From Asset-Price Inflation to Debt Deflation," *Counterpunch*, July 5.

Hughes, Jonathan and Louis Cain. (2011). *American Economic History*. New York: Pearson Education, Inc.

Hume, David. (1998). *Dialogues Concerning Natural Religion*. New York: Hackett Publishing Co.

Hume, David. (2003). *A Treatise of Human Nature: Being an Attempt to Introduce the Experimental Method of Reasoning into Moral Subjects*. New York: Cover Publications.

Hurst, James. (1956). *Law and the Conditions of Freedom in the Nineteenth Century United States*. Madison: The University of Wisconsin Press.

Hurwicz, Leonid. (1973). "The Design of Mechanisms for Resource Allocation," *The American Economic Review: Papers and Proceedings of the Eighty-fifth Annual Meeting of the American Economic Association*, 63 (2):1–30.

Hurwicz, Leonid and Stanley Reiter. (2008). *Designing Economic Mechanisms*. New York: Cambridge University Press.

Isocrates. (1980). *Isocrates with an English Translation in Three Volumes*. Cambridge, MA: Harvard University Press.

Jacobs, Alan Adams. (2012). "Free Will and Predetermination," *Advaita Vision*, July 10. www.advaita.org.uk/discourses/teachers/freewill_jacobs.htm.

Jammer, Max. (2011). *Einstein and Religion: Physics and Theology.* Princeton, NJ: Princeton University Press.

Jaspers, Karl. (2010). *The Origin and Goal of History.* New York: Routledge.

Jee, Sang-hoon. (2017). "A Critical Evaluation of Trichotomism: A Response to Biblical References for Trichotomism," *Catalyst,* 15 (1):55–57.

Jennings, James. (1994). *Understanding the Nature of Poverty in Urban America.* Westport, CT: Praeger.

Jewell, K. Sue. (1988). *Survival of the Black Family: The Institutional Impact of U.S. Social Policy.* Westport, CT: Praeger.

Ji, Chang (King Wen of Zhou). (2016). *Zhou Yi* [*I Ching*]. Beijing: China Bookstore.

Jin, Weiqi, ed. (2020). *Qingguan Lu Jiashu* [*Clean Official Lu Jiashu*]. Hangzhou: Zhejiang Guji Publisher.

Jones, Alice. (1980). *Wealth of a Nation to Be: The American Colonies on the Eve of the Revolution.* New York: Columbia University Press.

Kahneman, Daniel and Amos Tversky. (1979). "Prospect Theory: An Analysis of Decision under Risk," *Econometrica,* 47 (2):263–292.

Kahneman, Daniel, Alan B. Krueger, David A. Schkade, Norbert Schwarz, and Arthur A. Stone. (2004). "A Survey Method for Characterizing Daily Life Experience: The Day Reconstruction Method," *Science,* 306 (5702):1776–1780.

Kaldor, Nicholas. (1939). "Welfare Propositions of Economics and Interpersonal Comparisons of Utility," *The Economic Journal,* 49 (195):549–552.

Kang, Xiaoguang. (2002). "Weilan 3–5 Nian Zhongguo Dalu Zhengzhi Wendingxing Fenxi" ["Analysis of Political Stability in Mainland China in the Next 3–5 Years"], *Strategy and Management,* 2:1–15.

Kant, Immanuel. (2004). *Critique of Pure Reason.* New York: Barnes & Noble.

Kant, Immanuel. (2015). *The Critique of Practical Reason.* Cambridge: Cambridge University Press.

Ke, Hanlin. (1995). "Zhonghemei de Zhexue Dingwei" ["Philosophical Positioning of Neutral Beauty"], *Huanan Shifan Daxue Xuebao* [*Journal of South China Normal University*], 4:71–78.

Kelley, E. W. (1987). *Policy and Politics in the United States: The Limits of Localism.* Philadelphia: Temple University Press.

Keynes, John Maynard. (1936). *The General Theory of Employment, Interest and Money*. London: Macmillan.

Kidd, Celeste, Steven T. Piantadosi, and Richard N. Aslin. (2012). "The Goldilocks Effect: Human Infants Allocate Attention to Visual Sequences That Are Neither Too Simple nor Too Complex," *Plos One*, 7 (5).

Kirkland, Edward. (1969). *A History of American Economic Life*. New York: Appleton-Century-Crofts.

Kirman, Alan. (1989). "The Intrinsic Limits of Modern Economic Theory: The Emperor has No Clothes," *The Economic Journal*, 99 (395):126–139.

Knight, Frank. (2018). *Risk, Uncertainty, and Profit—Economic Theory of Uncertainty in Business Enterprises, and Its Connection to Profit and Prosperity in Society*. New York: Adansonia Press.

Laffer, Arthur, Stephen Moore, and Peter Tanous. (2008). *The End of Prosperity: How Higher Taxes Will Doom the Economy—If We Let It Happen*. New York: Threshold Editions.

Lampman, Robert J. (1971). *Ends and Means of Reducing Income Poverty*. Chicago: Markham.

Landes, David. (2000). "Culture Makes Almost All the Difference," in Lawrence E. Harrison and Samuel P. Huntington, eds., *Culture Matters: How Values Shape Human Progress*, pp. 2–13. New York: Basic Books.

Laozi. (2019). *Daode Jing [Dao De Jing]*. Beijing: China Bookstore.

Larrimore, Mark Joseph. (2001). *The Problem of Evil: A Reader*. New York: Blackwell.

Le Bon, Gustave. (1897). *The Crowd: A Study of the Popular Mind*. New York: The Macmillan Company.

Lee, Patrick and Robert P. George. (2008). *Body-Self Dualism in Contemporary Ethics and Politics*. Cambridge: Cambridge University Press.

Lee, Siew Kim Jean and Kelvin Yu. (2004). "Corporate Culture and Organizational Performance," *Journal of Managerial Psychology*, 19 (4):340–359.

Levy, Leon and Nassau W. Senior. (1943). *The Prophet of Modern Capitalism*. Boston: Bruce Humphries.

Li, Gang, Bin Wang, and Shuihui Liu. (2015). "Guomin Xingfu Zhishu Cesuan Fangfa Yanjiu" ["Research on the Measurement Method of National Happiness Index"], *Dongbei Daxue Xuebao* [*Journal of Northeastern University*], 17:376–383.

Li, Jing. (2007). "Cong Zhong, Yong dao Zhong Yong" ["From the Middle and Ordinary to Moderation"], *Kongzi Yanjiu* [*Confucius Studies*], 5:46–50.

Li, Longxin. (2013). "Cong Qiye dao Qiye Wenhua de Jingjixue Jieshi" ["Economic Explanation from Business to Corporate Culture"], *Shangye Yanjiu* [*Business Research*], 2:115–120.

Li, Tonglu. (2006). "Zhouzuoren: Zhongguo Xiandai Jiegou Piping de Xianqu" ["Zhouzuoren: Pioneers of Modern Chinese Deconstruction Criticism"], in Ying Wang, ed., *Wenxue Lilun Qianyan* (3) [*Frontiers in Literary Theory (3rd Series)*], pp. 276–277. Beijing: Beijing University Press.

Li, Yining. (2018). *Wenhua Jingjixue* [*Cultural Economics*]. Beijing: Shangwu Yinshuguan.

Lin, Jinzhong. (2021). "Cong 'Kanbujian de Shou' dao 'Shichang Shenhua'" ["From 'Invisible Hand' to 'Market Myth'"], *Jingji Xuejia* [*The Economist*], 7:10–14.

Lindenfeld, David. (1993). "The Myth of the Older Historical School of Economics," *Central European History*, 26 (4):405–416.

Little, Peter. (2003). *Somalia: Economy without State*. Bloomington: Indiana University Press.

Liu, Cuncheng and Hanpo Hou. (2012). *Chengshi de Jueqi—Chengshi Xitongxue yu Zhongguo Chengshihua* [*The Rise of the City—Urban Systematics and Urbanization in China*]. Beijing: Zhongyang Wenxian Chubanshe.

Loemker, Leroy, ed. (1958). "Gottfried Wilhelm Leibniz. Philosophical Papers and Letters," *Philosophical Quarterly*, 8 (32):283–285.

Loshitzky, Yosefa, ed. (1997). *Schindler's Holocaust: Critical Perspective on Schindler's List*. Bloomington: Indiana University Press.

Lu, Xun. (1919). "Kong Yiji" ["Kong Yiji"], *New Youth Magazine*, 6 (4):15–17.

Lu, Xun. (2005). *Hua Gai Ji* [*Collection of Hua Gai – Correspondence*], in *Lunxun Quanji* [*The Complete Works of Lu Xun*], vol. 3. Beijing: People's Literature Publishing House.

Lun Yu [*The Analects*]. (2004). Changchun: Jilin Photography Press.

Luo, Haocai. (2010). *Ruanfa de Lilun yu Shijian* [*The Theory and Practice of Soft Law*]. Beijing: Beijing University Press.

Luo, Weidong. (2006). *Qinggan, Zhixu, Meide: Yadang Simi de Lunlixue Shijie [Emotion, Order, Virtue: The Ethical World of Adam Smith]*. Beijing: Renmin University of China Press.

Luo, Weidong and Lu Liu. (2016). "Jiyu Yadang Simi Heyixing Lilun de Renlei Geti Xingwei Moxing" ["A Model of Human Individual Behavior based on Adam Smith's 'Propriety Theory'"], *Shehui Kexue Zhanxian [Social Science Front]*, 7:38–45.

Lutz, Mark. (1999). *Economics for the Common Good: Two Centuries of Economic Thought in the Humanist Tradition*. London and New York: Routledge.

Mabsout, Ramzi. (2015). "Abduction and Economics: The Contributions of Charles Peirce and Herbert Simon," *Journal of Economic Methodology*, 22 (4):491–516.

Marshall, Alfred. (2009). *Principles of Economics: Unabridged Eighth Edition*. New York: Cosimo, Inc.

McCloskey, Deirdre Nansen. (2021). *Bettering Humanomics—A New, and Old, Approach to Economic Science*. Chicago: The University of Chicago Press.

McCracken, Grant David. (1988). *The Long Interview—Qualitative Research Methods Series 13*. Newbury Park, CA: A Sage University Paper.

McCusker, John and Russell Menard. (1985). *The Economy of British America, 1607–1789*. Chapel Hill: North Carolina University Press.

McCusker, John and Barbara Petchenik. (1976). "Economic Activity," in John McCusker and Lester Cappon, eds., *Atlas of Early American History*. Princeton, NJ: Princeton University Press.

Mead, Lawrence M. (1982). "Social Programs and Social Obligations," *The Public Interest*, 69 (3):17–32.

Mencius. (2017). *Mengzi [Mencius]*. Prague: Artesia Publishing House.

Metcalf, Allan A. (2002). *Predicting New Words: The Secrets of Their Success*. Boston: Houghton Mifflin Co.

Middleton, Karen and Meheroo Jussawalla, eds. (1981). *The Economics of Communication: A Selected Bibliography with Abstracts*. New York: Pergamon Press.

Mill, John Stuart. (1859). *On Liberty*. London: John W. Parker and Son, West Strand.

Mowry, George. (1972). *The Progressive Era, 1900–20: The Reform Persuasion*. Washington, D.C.: American Historical Association.

Mullainathan, Sendhil and Richard Thaler. (2000). "Behavioral Economics," *National Bureau of Economic Research Working Paper Series 7948*. Washington, D.C.: National Bureau of Economic Research.

Needham, Noel Joseph Terence Montgomery. (2006). *Li Yuese Zhongguo Kexue Jishu Shi [History of Science and Technology in China]*. Beijing: Science Press.

Nell, Guinevere. (2017). *The Driving Force of the Collective: Post-Austrian Theory in Response to Israel Kirzner*. New York: Palgrave Macmillan.

Nettels, Curtis. (1962). *The Emergence of a National Economy, 1775–1815*. New York: M. E. Sharpe.

Nietzsche, Friedrich. (1986). *Beiju de Daisheng [The Birth of Tragedy]*. Shanghai: Sanlian Shudian.

North, Douglass. (1982). *Growth and Welfare in the American Past: A New Economic History*. Subsequent edition. Englewood Cliffs, NJ: Prentice-Hall, Inc.

North, Douglass. (1989). "Institutions and Economic Growth: An Historical Introduction," *World Development*, 17 (9):1319–1332.

North, Douglass. (1992). "Institutions and Economic Theory," *The American Economists*, 36 (1):3–6.

North, Douglass. (1994). "Economic Performance Through Time," *American Economic Review*, 84 (3):359–368.

Norton, Mary. (1990). *A People and A Nation: A History of the United States*. Vol. 1. Boston: Cengage Learning.

Obstfeld, Maurice, Jay C. Shambaugh, and Alan M. Taylor. (2005). "The Trilemma in History: Tradeoffs Among Exchange Rates, Monetary Policies, and Capital Mobility," *The Review of Economics and Statistics*, 87 (3):423–438.

Office of High Commissioner in United Nations Human Rights. (1966). *International Covenant on Economic, Social and Cultural Rights*. www.ohchr.org/en/instruments-mechanisms/instruments/international-covenant-economic-social-and-cultural-rights.

Paganelli, Maria Pia. (2003). "In Medio Stat Virtus: An Alternative View of Usury in Adam Smith's Thinking," *History of Political Economy*, 35 (1):21–48.

Paganelli, Maria Pia. (2022). "Adam Smith and Economic Development: Theory and Practice," *Journal of the History of Economic Thought*, 44 (1):95–104.

Pais, Abraham. (2005). *Subtle is the Lord: The Science and the Life of Albert Einstein.* Oxford: Oxford University Press.

Pang, Pu. (2005). *Pang Pu Wenji – Disi Juan – Yifen Weisan [The Collected Works of Pang Pu – Volume IV – One for Three].* Jinan: Shandong University Press.

Pareto, Vilfredo. (1935). *The Mind and Society,* Arthur Livingston, ed. New York: Harcourt, Brace & Company.

Pearl, Judea and Dana Mackenzie. (2018). *The Book of Why: The New Science of Cause and Effect.* New York: Basic Books.

Peirce, Charles. (1992). *Reasoning and the Logic of Things.* Cambridge, MA: Harvard University Press.

Phillips, A. W. (1958). "The Relation between Unemployment and the Rate of Change of Money Wage Rates in the United Kingdom, 1861–1957," *Economica,* 25 (100):283–299.

Pigou, Arthur C. (1929). *The Economics of Welfare.* London: Macmillan and Co.

Piketty, Thomas. (2014). *Capital in the Twenty-First Century.* Cambridge, MA: The Belknap Press of Harvard University Press.

Piketty, Thomas. (2020). *Capital and Ideology.* Cambridge, MA: The Belknap Press of Harvard University Press.

Pinker, Steven. (2002). *The Blank Slate: The Modern Denial of Human Nature.* London: Penguin.

Plato. (1968). *The Republic of Plato.* 2nd ed. Allan Bloom, trans. New York: Basic Books.

Popper, Karl. (1972). *Objective Knowledge: An Evolutionary Approach.* Oxford: Oxford University Press.

Popper, Karl. (1994). *The Myth of the Framework: In Defense of Science and Rationality.* London and New York: Routledge.

Porter, Glenn, ed. (1980). *Encyclopedia of American Economic History.* Vol. 1 and Vol. 2. New York: Simon & Schuster Trade.

Price, Jacob. (1976). "A Note on the Value of Colonial Exports of Shipping," *Journal of Economic History,* 36:704–724.

Price, Jacob. (1978). "Colonial Trade and British Economic Development, 1660–1775," *The International Journal of Law and Science,* 14:106–126.

Ramstad, Yngve. (1995). "John R. Commons' Puzzling Inconsequentiality as an Economic Theorist," *Journal of Economic Issues,* 29 (4):991–1012.

Raphael, D. D. (2007). *The Impartial Spectator: Adam Smith's Moral Philosophy*. New York: Oxford University Press.

Rawls, John. (1999). *A Theory of Justice*. Revised edition. Cambridge, MA: Harvard University Press.

Reich, Jerome. (1989). *Colonial America*. Englewood Cliffs, NJ: Pearson Education, Inc.

Reischauer, Edwin. (1989). *Japan: The Story of a Nation*. New York: Alfred A. Knopf.

Ren, Zhengfei. (2010). "Guanli de Huidu" ["Shades of Gray in Management"], *Shanjie (Pinglun)* [*Business Review*], 4:48–50.

Ricardo, David. (2001). *On the Principles of Political Economy and Taxation*. Kitchener, Ontario: Batoche Books.

Rima, Samuel. (2013). *Spiritual Capital: A Moral Core for Social and Economic Justice*. London and New York: Routledge.

Robinson, Joan. (1980). "Time in Economic Theory," *Kyklos*, 33 (2):219–229.

Rodgers, Harrell R., Jr. (1990). *Poor Women, Poor Family: The Economic Plight of America's Female-Headed Households*. Armonk, NY: M. E. Sharpe.

Rodrik, Dani. (2011). *The Globalization Paradox: Democracy and the Future of the World Economy*. New York: W. W. Norton & Company.

Romer, Paul. (2015). "Mathiness in the Theory of Economic Growth," *American Economic Review*, 105 (5):89–93.

Rosenthal, Lawrence. (2020). *Empire of Resentment: Populism's Toxic Embrace of Nationalism*. New York: The New Press.

Rothman, David. (1971). *The Discovery of the Asylum, Social Order and Disorder in the New Republic*. New Haven, CT: Yale University.

Rothstein, Henry, David Demeritt, Regine Paul, and Li Wang. (2022). "True to Type? How Governance Traditions Shaped Responses to Covid-19 in China, Germany, UK, and USA," in Patrick Brown and Jens Zinn, eds., *Covid-19 and the Sociology of Risk and Uncertainty— Studies of Social Phenomena and Social Theory Across 6 Continents*, pp. 115–143. New York: Palgrave Macmillan.

The Royal Swedish Academy of Sciences. (2019). "Press Release: The Prize in Economic Sciences 2019," October 14. www.nobelprize.org/prizes/economic-sciences/2019/press-release/.

Rubin, Lillian B. (1969). "Maximum Feasible Participation: The Origins, Implications, and Present Status," *The Annals of the American Academy of Political and Social Science*, 385:14–29.

Rutherford, Malcolm. (1995). "The Old and the New Institutionalism: Can Bridges Be Built?", *Journal of Economic Issues*, 29 (2):443–451.

Rutherford, Malcolm. (2009). "Introduction to the Transaction Edition," in John Commons, *Institutional Economics: Its Place in Political Economy*, pp. i–xxii. New Brunswick, NJ: Transaction Publishers.

Samuelson, Paul. (1983). *Foundations of Economic Analysis.* Cambridge, MA: Harvard University Press.

Samuelson, Paul. (2009). *Economics: An Introductory Analysis.* 19th ed. New York: McGraw-Hill Book Co.

Sathe, Vijay. (1983). "Implications of Corporate Culture: A Manager's Guide to Action," *Organizational Dynamics*, 12 (2):5–23.

Sawer, Marian. (2003). *The Ethical State? Social Liberalism in Australia.* Melbourne: Melbourne University Press.

Schein, Edgar and Peter Schein. (2018). *Humble Leadership: The Power of Relationships, Openness, and Trust.* Oakland, CA: Berrett-Koehler Publishers, Inc.

Schelling, Thomas. (1960). *The Strategy of Conflict.* Cambridge, MA: Harvard University Press.

Schneberger, Scott, Hugh Watson, and Carol Pollard. (2007). "The Efficacy of 'Little t' Theories," *IEEE Proceedings of the 40th Hawaii International Conference on System Sciences*, 1–10.

Schor, Juliet. (1999). *The Overspent American: Why We Want What We Don't Need.* New York: Harper Perennial.

Schumpeter, Joseph. (1961). *The Theory of Economic Development.* London: Oxford University Press.

Schumpeter, Joseph. (2006). *Capitalism, Socialism and Democracy.* New York: Routledge.

Sedláček, Tomáš. (2011). *Economics of Good and Evil: The Quest for Economic Meaning from Gilgamesh to Wall Street.* Oxford: Oxford University Press.

Sen, Amartya. (1970). "The Impossibility of a Paretian Liberal," *The Journal of Political Economy*, 78 (1):152 157.

Sharp, Laure and Joy Frechtling. (1997). "Overview of the Design Process for Mixed Method Evaluation," in Laure Sharp and Joy Frechtling, eds., *User-Friendly Handbook for Mixed Method Evaluations*. www.nsf. gov/pubs/1997/nsf97153/start.htm.

Simon, Herbert. (1955). "A Behavioral Model of Rational Choice," *The Quarterly Journal of Economics*, 69 (1):99–118.

Simon, Herbert. (1972). "Theories of Bounded Rationality," in C. B. McGuire and Roy Radner, eds., *Decision and Organization: A Volume in Honor of Jacob Marschak*, pp. 161–176. Amsterdam: North-Holland Publishing Company.

Simon, Herbert. (1977). *Models of Discovery*. Dordrecht: Reidel.

Simon, Herbert. (1991). "Rationality and Organizational Learning," *Organization Science*, 2 (1):125–145.

Simon, Herbert. (1997). *Models of Bounded Rationality: Empirically Grounded Economic Reason*. Cambridge, MA: The MIT Press.

Simon, Herbert. (2000). "Bounded Rationality in Social Science: Today and Tomorrow," *Mind & Society*, 1 (1):25–39.

Singer, Tania and Matthieu Ricard, eds. (2015). *Caring Economics: Conversations on Altruism and Compassion, between Scientists, Economists, and the Dalai Lama*. New York: Picador.

Skrabec, Quentin, Jr. (2014). *The 100 Most Important American Financial Crises: An Encyclopedia of the Lowest Points in American Economic History*. New York: Greenwood.

Smith, Adam. (1980). *The Glasgow Edition of the Works and Correspondence of Adam Smith*. Vol. III. Oxford: Oxford University Press.

Smith, Adam. (1982). *The Theory of Moral Sentiments*. Indianapolis: Liberty Fund, Inc.

Smith, Adam. (2014). *The Wealth of Nations*. New York: Shine Classics.

Snowball, Jeanette D. (2008). *Measuring the Value of Culture*. New York: Springer.

Snyder, Scott and Kyung-Ae Park. (2019). "North Korea in Transition: Evolution or Revolution?", in Scott Snyder and Kyung-Ae Park, eds., *North Korea in Transition: Politics, Economy, and Society*, pp. 275–294. New York: Rowman & Littlefield Publishers, Inc.

Sober, Elliott. (2013). *Core Questions in Philosophy: A Text with Readings*. 6th ed. Boston: Pearson Education.

Sombart, Werner. (1975). *War and Capitalism*. New Stratford, NH: Ayer Company.

Song, Zhiping. (2019). "Women de fenpei jizhi haishi you wenti" ["There is still an issue with our distribution mechanism"], *National Revitalization Think-tank*, November 21. www.xbzk.org/news/edp.asp?id=901.

Sternberg, Robert. (1985). *Beyond IQ: A Triarchic Theory of Human Intelligence*. New York: Cambridge University Press.

Sternberg, Robert, ed. (2000). *Handbook of Intelligence*. Cambridge: Cambridge University Press.

Sternberg, Robert and Karin Sternberg, eds. (2018). *The New Psychology of Love*. 2nd revised edition. Cambridge: Cambridge University Press.

Stigler, George and Gary Becker. (1977). "De Gustibus Non Est Disputandum," *American Economic Review*, 67 (2):76–90.

Stoesz, David. (1993). "Poor Policy: The Legacy of the Kerner Commission for Social Welfare," *North Carolina Law Review*, 71 (5):1675–1691.

Swenson, Peter A. (1989). *Fair Shares: Unions, Pay, and Politics in Sweden and West Germany*. Ithaca, NY: Cornell University Press.

Tabb, William. (1999). *Reconstructing Political Economy*. New York: Routledge.

Tang, Yiming, ed. (2017). *Yansi Jiaxun Jiedu* [*The Interpretation of the Yan Family Disciplines*]. Beijing: National Library Press.

Thaler, Richard. (1985). "Mental Accounting and Consumer Choice," *Marketing Science*, 4 (3):199–214.

Thaler, Richard. (2016). *Misbehaving: The Making of Behavioral Economics*. New York: W. W. Norton & Company.

Thaler, Richard and Cass R. Sunstein. (2009). *Nudge: Improving Decisions about Health, Wealth, and Happiness*. New York: Penguin Books.

Tian, Guoqiang. (2020). *Gaoji Weiguan Jingjixue* [*Advanced Microeconomics*]. Beijing: Renmin University of China Press.

Tideman, Nicolaus. (2006). *Collective Decision and Voting: The Potential for Public Choice*. Burlington, VT: Ashgate Publishing Company.

Towse, Ruth. (2019). *A Textbook of Cultural Economics*. Cambridge: Cambridge University Press.

Trimble, Virginia. (1987). "Existence and Nature of Dark Matter in the Universe," *Annual Review of Astronomy and Astrophysics*, 25 (1):425–472.

United Nations, Department of Economics and Social Affairs, Population Division. (2019). *World Urbanization Prospects: The 2018 Revision.* (ST/ESA/SER.A/420). New York: United Nations.

Ura, Karma, Sabina Alkire, Tshoki Zangmo, and Karma Wangdi. (2012). *A Short Guide to Gross National Happiness Index.* Thimphu, Bhutan: The Centre for Bhutan Studies.

U.S. Bureau of the Census. (1960). *Historical Statistics of the United States, from Colonial Period to 1957.* Washington, D.C.: U.S. Government Printing Office.

U.S. Bureau of the Census. (1975). *Historical Statistics of the United States, from Colonial Times to 1970.* Vol. 2. Washington, D.C.: U.S. Government Printing Office.

U.S. Bureau of the Census. (1991). *Current Population Reports, Poverty in the United States: 1990,* Series, P-60, No. 175. Washington, D.C.: U.S. Government Printing Office.

U.S. Bureau of the Census. (2002). *Current Population Reports, Poverty in the United States: 2002,* Series, P 60-219. Washington, D.C.: U.S. Government Printing Office.

U.S. Bureau of Land Management. (1974). *Public Land Statistics.* Washington, D.C.: The Bureau of Land Management's National Operations Center.

U.S. Department of Justice. (2023). "Justice Department Announces Results of Nationwide COVID-19 Fraud Enforcement Action," *Office of Public Affairs, USDJ website,* August 23. www.justice.gov/opa/pr/justice-department-announces-results-nationwide-covid-19-fraud-enforcement-action.

Veblen, Thorstein. (1898). "Why is Economics not an Evolutionary Science?", *The Quarterly Journal of Economics,* 12 (4):373–397.

Veblen, Thorstein. (1899). *The Theory of the Leisure Class—An Economic Study of Institutions.* New York: Macmillan.

Walras, Léon. (2014). *Elements of Theoretical Economics: The Theory of Social Wealth.* Cambridge: Cambridge University Press.

Walton, Gary and James Shepherd. (1979). *The Economic Rise of Early America.* Cambridge: Cambridge University Press.

Wang, Dingding. (2015). *Xingwei Jingjixue Yaoyi [Essentials of Behavioral Economics].* Shanghai: Shanghai People's Publishing House.

Wang, Dingding. (2018). "Lijie Yongxian Zhixu" ["Understanding the Order of Emergence"], in W. Brian Arthur, *Fuza Jingjixue [Complexity and the Economy]*. Hangzhou: Zhejiang People's Press.

Wang, Fuzhi. (1996). *Shuowen Guang Yi [The Broad Definition of the Chinese Language]*, vol. 2, in *Chuanshan Quanshu [The Complete Book of Chuanshan]*, vol. 9. Changsha: Yuelu Shushe.

Wang, Liqiang. (2014). *Sanyuanlun yu Sanyuan Yijing [The Three Sources Theory and the Three Sources of the Yi Jing]*, Part 1, Chapter 1. Nanjing: Southeast University Press.

Wang, Weijia. (2019). *Anzhishi—Jiqi Renzhi Ruhe Dianfu Shanye he Shehui [Dark Knowledge—How Machine Cognition is Disrupting Business and Society]*. Beijing: Zhongxin Press.

Wang, Xianqian. (1988). *Xunzi Jijie [Comprehensive Interpretation on Xunzi]*. Beijing: China Book Bureau.

Wang, Yuechuan. (2007). "Zhongxi Sixiang Shi shang de Zhongyong Zhidao" ["Modcration in the History of Chinese and Western Thought"], *Hunan Shehui Kexue [Hunan Social Sciences]*, 6:36–47.

Wang, Yuechuan. (2009). "Zhongyong de Chaoyuexin Sixiang yu Pushixing Jiazhi" ["The Transcendental Thought and Universal Value of Moderate"], *Shehui Kexue Zhanxian [Social Science Battle Line]*, 5:133–150.

Wanniski, Jude. (1978). "Taxes, Revenues & the 'Laffer Curve'," *The Public Interest*, 50:1–12.

Weber, Max. (2007). *General Economic History*. New York: Cosimo, Inc.

Williams, Eric. (1970). *From Columbus to Castro: The History of the Caribbean 1492–1969*. London: Vintage Books, A Division of Random House.

Witt, Ulrich. (1993). *Evolutionary Economics*. London: Edward Elgar Publishing, Inc.

Witt, Ulrich. (2008). "What is Specific about Evolutionary Economics?", *Journal of Evolutionary Economics*, 18 (5):547–575.

Woleński, Jan. (1994). "Jan Łukasiewicz on the Liar Paradox, Logical Consequence, Truth, and Induction," *Modern Logic*, 4 (4):392–400.

World Bank. (1975). *World Bank Atlas*. Washington, D.C.: World Bank Group.

Wu, Xuewen. (2008). "Sanyuan Lilun Jichu he Yingyong Juli" ["Fundamentals and Applications of Ternary Theory"], *Zhongwai Yixue [Chinese and Foreign Medical Journal]*, 9:41–45.

Xenophon. (1995). *Oeconomicus*. Oxford: Oxford University Press.

Xiao, Gaoyan. (2012). "Xisanluo yu Majiweili Lun Zhengzhi Daode" ["Cicero and Machiavelli on Political Morality"], *Zhengzhi Kexue Luncong [Political Science Series]*, 16:5–20.

Xu, Fuguan. (2004). *Zhongguo Sixiangshi Lunji Xuebian [A Continuation of the Essays on the History of Chinese Thought]*. Shanghai: Shanghai Shudian Press.

Xu, Fuguan. (2005). *Zhongguo Renxin Lunshi [A History of Chinese Humanism]*. Shanghai: East China Normal University Press.

Xu, Fuguan. (2014). *Xu Fuguan Quanji [Xu Fuguan Complete Collection]*. Beijing: Jiuzhou Press.

Xu, Shen. (2016). *Shuowen Jiezi [Interpretation of Literature and Characters]*. Hangzhou: Zhejiang Ancient Books Publishing House.

Xu, Tao. (2013). "Ni Xisheng de Sanyuanlun Sixiang Taijiu" ["An Exploration of Ni Xisheng's Triadic Thought"], *Zhongguo Shenxue Yanjiuyuan Qikan [Journal of the Chinese Theological Seminary]*, 1:30–40.

Xu, Yuan. (2019). *Cong Gongyehua dao Chengshihua [From Industrialization to Urbanization]*. Beijing: Zhongxin Press.

Xue, Zhaofeng. (2018). *Xue Zhaofeng Jingjixue Jiangyi [Xue Zhaofeng Lectures on Economics]*. Beijing: Zhongxin Chuban Jituan.

Ye, Fuxiang. (2010). *Sanyuan Zhexue Henxin Sixiang [The Core Ideas of Ternary Philosophy]*. wenku.baidu.com/view/d473416ca45177232f60a25b.html.

Ye, Ying. (2000). "Jianli zai Sanyuan Luoji Jichu Shang de Snayuan Kexue" ["Triadic Science Based on Triadic Logic"], *Zhejiang Daxue Xuebao [Journal of Zhejiang University]*, 3:330–338.

Zadeh, Lotfi A. (1965). "Fuzzy Sets," *Information and Control*, 8 (3):338–353.

Zak, Paul, ed. (2005). "The Neuroeconomics of Distrust: Sex Differences in Behavior and Physiology," *American Economic Review Papers and Proceedings*, 95:360–364.

Zak, Paul. (2008). "The Neurobiology of Trust," *Scientific American*, 298 (6):88–92.

Zak, Paul, ed. (2008). *Moral Markets: The Critical Role of Values in the Economy*. Princeton, NJ: Princeton University Press.

Zak, Paul. (2011). "The Physiology of Moral Sentiments," *Journal of Economic Behavior & Organization*, 77 (1):53–65.

Zak, Paul and Stephen Knack. (2001). "Trust and Growth," *The Economic Journal*, 111 (470):295–321.

Zeng, Guofan. (1991). *Zeng Guofan Jiashu Jiaxun [Zeng Guofan's Book of the Family]*. Tianjin: Tianjin Guji Shudian [Tianjin Antiquarian Bookstore].

Zhang, Lin. (2005). *Xin Zhidu Zhuyi [New Institutionalism]*. Beijing: Economic Press.

Zheng, Qidong. (2008). "Shilun Qing Zhengfu Zhenya Taiping Tianguo hou de Rangbu Zhengce" ["A Discussion of the Qing Government's Concessions after the Suppression of the Taiping Rebellion"], *Study on Qing History*, 3:59–69.

Zhong, Xiangcan. (2004). "Zhongguo Gudai Neng Chansheng Shichang Jizhi Ma?" ["Can Market Mechanisms Emerge in Ancient China: A Discussion with Mr. Sheng Hong"], *Taishuo yu Zhengmin [Exploration and Debate]*, 2:19–20.

Zhu, Shumin, Hua Yang, and Hailin Wang. (2004). "Nianyu Xiaoying yu Xiandan Tushuguan Renli Ziyuan Guanli" ["Catfish Effect and Human Resource Management in Modern Libraries"], *Journal of Hunan Industry University*, 10:89–90.

Zhu, Xi. (2006). *Sishu Zhangju Jizhu [The Four Books, Chapters and Sentences – Zhong Yong Chapter and Sentences]*. Shanghai: Shanghai Ancient Books Publishing House.

Zhuangzi. (1986). *Zhuangzi [Zhuangzi – Dasheng]*, in *Zhongzi Jicheng [Collection of Scholars' Works, 3]*. Shanghai: Shanghai Bookstore.

Zi, Si. (2016). *Zhongyong Quanjie [Complete Interpretation of Moderation]*. Beijing: China Hua Qiao Publishing House.

Zobel, Justin. (2022). "When Measurement Misleads: The Limits of Batch Assessment of Retrieval Systems," *ACM SIGIR Forum*, 56 (1):1–20.

Zuo, Qiuming. (2017). *Zuo Zhuan* [Zuo Tradition]. Wuhan: Hubei Ci Shu Publishing House.

Index